DANGEROUS MUSE

BY NANCY SCHOENBERGER

NONFICTION

A Talent for Genius: The Life and Times of Oscar Levant
(with Sam Kashner)
Hollywood Kryptonite: The Bulldog, the Lady,
and the Death of Superman
(with Sam Kashner)

POETRY

The Taxidermist's Daughter
Girl on a White Porch
Long Like a River

DANGEROUS MUSE

·The Life of Lady Caroline Blackwood·

NANCY SCHOENBERGER

DA CAPO PRESS

A Member of the Perseus Books Group

Frontispiece: Caroline Blackwood by Walker Evans. Copyright © 1999 Walker Evans Archive, The Metropolitan Museum of Art.

Cataloging-in-Publication data for this book is available from the Library of Congress.

First Da Capo Press edition 2002
Reprinted by arrangement with the Doubleday Broadway Publishing Group, a division of Random House, Inc.
ISBN 0-306-81187-1

Published by Da Capo Press
A Member of the Perseus Books Group
http://www.dacapopress.com

Da Capo Press books are available at special discounts for bulk purchases in the U.S. by corporations, institutions, and other organizations. For more information, please contact the Special Markets Department at the Perseus Books Group, 11 Cambridge Center, Cambridge, MA 02142, or call (800) 255-1514 or (617) 252-5298, or e-mail j.mccrary@perseusbooks.com.

1 2 3 4 5 6 7 8 9—06 05 04 03 02

· Copyrights
and Permissions ·

Excerpts from Walker Evans's letter to James and Tania Stern, reprinted by permission of the Walker Evans Archive, The Metropolitan Museum of Art.

Excerpts from Israel Citkowitz's letters to Aaron Copland, courtesy Elena Citkowitz and the Aaron Copland Archive, Library of Congress.

For Sam, as always—

Beauty is only the promise of happiness.

—STENDHAL

· *Acknowledgments* ·

Among the many I want to thank for their cooperation and inspiration, Steven M. L. Aronson looms large. His remarkable interview with Caroline Blackwood, published in *Town & Country* in 1993, first planted the seed for this book, and further conversations with Steven illuminated Caroline Blackwood's sometimes maddening complexities. I already knew something about Blackwood from having worked on *A Mania for Phrases*, the "Voices and Visions" documentary film for PBS about Blackwood's third husband, the poet Robert Lowell, and from Ian Hamilton's impressive *Robert Lowell: A Biography*. So when the writer Shana Alexander called me one afternoon in 1995 and mentioned that Blackwood, who lived near her on the east end of Long Island, was looking around for a biographer and asked whether I would consider it, I was immediately intrigued. The idea had already taken root—I had long meditated on the sometimes treacherous task women undertake in making themselves into writers—but here was a possible chance to work with the writer herself. I had envisioned a kind of "life with comments," and the one conversation I had with Blackwood over the phone seemed to promise just such a venture. "Come see me in Sag Harbor," she said in her smoky, deep-throated voice. She also asked me to send her a copy of *A Mania for Phrases*; she had resisted watching it for a long time, as the film contained archival footage of Lowell reading his poems, still painful for her to watch.

But the day I arrived on Long Island to meet with Caroline, she went into the hospital—and died two weeks later. We never met face to face.

And yet I decided to continue. I met with her middle daughter, Evgenia Citkowitz, and Evgenia's husband, the actor Julian Sands, in their home just above Sunset Boulevard in Los Angeles (in a restored villa that had once belonged to Busby Berkeley). Evgenia showed me her father's piano, while Julian, who loves the culinary arts, offered to scramble some eggs. We ended up feasting on oil-cured olives culled from an ancient olive tree Sands had replanted in their walled garden. Heartened by this early meeting, I hoped to have the cooperation of the Blackwood family, but with the exception of Caroline's sister, Lady Perdita Blackwood—who was a biographer's dream and a woman of exceptional honesty and generosity—the subject's grown children eventually shied from the venture. I had begun the book, I felt, with cooperation, but soon found myself writing an "opposed biography." Ivana Lowell, Caroline's youngest daughter, who had assumed the name of her stepfather Robert Lowell, once said about her family, "There were a lot of unspoken things and a lot of closed doors."[1] Once I got to know Caroline better, I understood why.

First, there was the issue of Blackwood's alcoholism, which her family, like most, did not want to make public—or relive—in any form. But even more than that, Caroline's personality was so over-

---

[1] Melissa Ceria, "Poetic License," *W*, October 1999, p. 100.

powering that she seemed to have left, after her death, a residue of spirit. I began to feel haunted by her. An aura of danger surrounded Caroline, a fact that struck home when I was involved in a car accident after returning to Virginia from my meeting with Evgenia and Julian Sands. "I'll bet you were thinking about my mother when you hit that car," Evgenia said afterward. And of course I was. I was becoming obsessed with her, as all biographers become obsessed with their subjects. "Mummy would have loved that," Evgenia told me. Later, in London, I met with a close friend of Caroline's, who warned me that Caroline had considered her mother "a witch," and that Caroline herself had certain witchlike qualities. The following day I made a surprise call on Lady Maureen Dufferin, Caroline's mother (it's amazing what biographers will do), at her home in Knightsbridge. A scrap of paper had blown onto her front steps at 4 Hans Crescent. I bent over and picked it up. It was a page from a notepad upon which someone had scrawled, "Just remember I am a witch."

There were other occasions when I felt haunted by Caroline, as so many others have been. I look upon this book as an exorcism as well as a biography. That said, let me acknowledge the many who helped, beginning with several of Caroline's friends who offered anonymous interviews. You know who you are, and I thank you. Others who helped make this book possible and who have my gratitude are Ellen Adler, Gillon Aitken, Lola Armstrong, Don Bachardy, the late Bruce Bernard, Frank Bidart, Lady Perdita Blackwood, Michael Bloch, Simon Blow, Robert Boyers, Dr. Paul Brass, John Byrne, Blair and Joanna Clark, John Craxton, Robert Dash, David Diamond, Lady "Lindy" Dufferin, the late Lady Maureen Dufferin, Cornelia Foss, Jonathan Fryer, the late Ian Hamilton, Xandra Hardie, Andrew Harvey, Nicholas Haslam, Gloria Jones, Lorraine Karafel, Charles Krewson, Jeremy Lewis, Christopher Mason, Peter Mayer, Paul Mariani, Suzanne McNear, Karl Miller, Ivan Moffat, Anne Moynihan, Stanley Moss, Howard Pollack, Jonathan Raban, Suzanne Raitt, Belinda Rathbone, John Richardson, Christopher Ricks, Ned Rorem, Leonard Rosenman, the late Alan Ross, the late Lorna Sage, Simonette Strachey, Sara Payne Stuart, Pat

Sweeney, Eleanor Ross Taylor, Joan Wyndham, and Sir George Weidenfeld. Lord Gowrie, who declined to grant me an interview about Caroline, whom he had loved as a friend, nonetheless gave me invaluable advice: "Look to the published record—Lowell's poems, her own books. Everything you need to know about her is there."

To this list let me add Jeffrey Rosenheim, Mary Doherty, and Doug Eklund at the Metropolitan Museum of Art; Philip R. Jensen and Charis Ryder for their valuable research assistance; the Harry R. Ransom Humanities Research Center in Austin, Texas; the Hulton Getty Archive and the National Portrait Gallery in London; the research librarians Don Welch and Bettina Manzo at Swem Library, the College of William and Mary; and the remarkable Bob Ludemann at the Merrick Public Library on Long Island. My gratitude also goes to David Laskin, who shared insights and photographs, and to Tom Heacox and Henry Hart, who read early versions of the manuscript.

To my genius agents, Joy Harris and Leslie Daniels, who found me the best editor in New York, the legendary Nan Talese—my thanks. Kudos to Nan's unfailingly cheerful—and careful—assistant editor, Lorna Owen, and to the unimpeachable copy editor, Frances "Pixie" Apt. In London, my editor Rebecca Wilson and her able assistant Catherine Hill at Wiedenfeld and Nicolson deserve my gratitude, as does Laura Morris, formerly of the literary agency Abner Stein—and my husband, Sam Kashner, whose help, advice, forbearance, wit, and generosity of spirit kept me going.

· Contents ·

DANGEROUS MUSE

PROLOGUE

The three Blackwood children had very different last memories of their father. Caroline Blackwood was born in 1931 at Clandeboye, the Dufferins' grand family estate in Northern Ireland, in the prewar years of the Protestant ascendancy. Her father, the fourth Marquess of Dufferin and Ava, was killed in the last year of the Second World War. Sheridan, Caroline's younger brother, who would become the fifth marquess on his father's death, was only seven when Lord Dufferin was killed by an enemy's bullet in Burma. "I have only one memory of him," Sheridan wrote in 1985. "He was back on leave from India and I remember staring at him in the bath covered with mosquito bites."[1]

Perdita, Caroline's younger sister, was ten at the time of her father's death. "I didn't see him much growing up," she recalled. "I do remember being given a box of chocolates, probably from an American soldier. I was absolutely looking forward to eating them, but for some reason I left them in the library, the big room everyone used at Clandeboye, where you'd come in and leave your Wellies. And he came in and he ate the whole thing. It was my first indication of what grown-ups could do! He loved sweets."2

Caroline, three years older than Perdita, wrote later that her father always seemed like a missing person, someone known mostly through photographs. But she did have one memory of being a little girl and accompanying her father on a pheasant shoot, on the vast, interlocking fields of green that made up the enchanted Clandeboye estate. It may have been on one of those days when low bands of mist shrouded the grounds, an Irish mist that gave rise to stories of a ghost, a woman in white who haunted the man-made lake.3 Caroline was asked to fetch and carry the dead birds. What had started out as a grown-up pleasure of inclusion and sportsmanship—time spent with her father—turned cruel. The bloodied pheasants smeared her hands and her clothes and her face; the plump birds, which had seemed so beautiful in flight, with their bright plumes and whirring calls, were damaged things, still warm, but matted and lifeless. She tried to wash their blood from her hands in the cold waters of the lake. It was the last memory she would ever have of being with her father.

Caroline would grow up and become a writer. She would also marry three brilliant men: the painter Lucian Freud, the composer Israel Citkowitz, and the poet Robert Lowell. Freud painted a number of stunning portraits of his young wife, notably "Girl in Bed," which was bought by Lord Glenconner almost the moment the paint had dried. Cyril Connolly, who was also for a time infatuated with Caroline, had tried to buy the painting, but settled for another portrait of her, "Girl Reading." Lowell later purchased "Girl in Bed" from Glenconner; it was the only memento he brought with him from the wreckage of his seven-year attachment to Caroline.

The striking portrait was painted during a brief transitional phase, when Lucian, still in his twenties, was leaving the dreamlike, expressionistic style of his teacher Cedric Morris and moving toward the cold exactitude of realism. He captured Caroline on the cusp of womanhood; one wonders whether the intensely staring creature, her hair the color of wheat, is indeed a girl or a woman. At twenty-one, she is both. The most striking feature in the painting is Caroline's large, luminous eyes. In a poem, Lowell described the portrait's "huge eyes and dawn-gaze . . ."[4] Lucian painted it in 1952; he had left his wife and child and had run off to Paris with Caroline. He captured her intense stare, which seems to look back unflinchingly on some hidden childhood sorrow. Or horror. Lowell also wrote: "The painter, your first husband, made girls stare."[5] But Caroline didn't learn her unflinching gaze from Lucian Freud; she had always had it, and her willingness to stare into the face of blackness would always be with her, expressed again and again in her many darkly comic works of fiction and nonfiction.

But who really was the girl-woman in the portrait? Lowell asked, "One wondered who would see and date you next / and grapple for the danger of your hand."[6] Because the men she loved were artists and writers, Caroline has been called a muse and has been compared with women like Alma Mahler Werfel, Maud Gonne, and Nora Joyce.

One can argue, however, that Caroline Blackwood was both a muse and an anti-muse. Lucian Freud's paintings of Caroline Blackwood are among the most tender and lyrical portraits he's ever executed. Caroline herself felt that Lucian's portraits of women turned cruel and corpse-like after she left him—true executions. But Caroline's second husband, Israel Citkowitz, seemed to have traded in the creative life of a composer to become a caretaker for Caroline and their daughters. His old friends were shocked to see Israel—once a protégé of Aaron Copland's and his circle of new American composers—doing laundry and fussing over the children, his artistic life abandoned. Robert Lowell won his second Pulitzer Prize for *The Dolphin*, dedicated to Caroline and clearly inspired by her. In poem after poem, Lowell apotheosized Caroline as a dolphin figure who inspires and guides his craft. As their marriage disintegrated, however, Lowell's dolphin is transformed into a treacherous Siren who lures travelers and dines on the bones of her lovers. After Lowell's death, Caroline entered into a love affair with a young classics scholar, translator, and poet named Andrew Harvey. They traveled together and lived in London for a year, and when that relationship ended, Harvey wrote a book of poems dedicated to Caroline in which she appears as Lydia, a taunting, terrifying initiator into wisdom, who forces the poet into creative depths by tricking and humiliating him. "Caroline was the angel of creation *and* destruction," Harvey would later say. "She would initiate you into her own darkness, and that's what made her a muse figure. It was her destiny to play that role."[7]

In 1996 the dance critic Arlene Croce wrote, "Muses are not wanted anymore." She argued that muses "are born, not made," which is one reason that they're disappearing from Western culture.[8] Furthermore, she observed, a muse may or may not possess talent, but she usually possesses beauty and, always, mystery. Caroline did indeed possess beauty and mystery. Many have testified to Caroline's heart-stopping beauty as a young woman—her "Alice-in-Wonderland straight gold hair, / fair-featured, curve and bone from hair to socks," as Lowell wrote in "Mermaid 2."[9] The mystery was there, too; Caroline was known for her silences. She could be maddeningly shy, her tongue loosened only by alcohol. And she sprang from the insular world of the Protestant ascendancy in Northern Ireland, the product of a long line of colonial administrators on her father's side and the Guinnesses on her mother's. To have been born a Guinness was mystery enough, a clannish family made legendary by great wealth and by whispers of a generational curse. By the time Lowell knew Caroline, her father's world of vast country estates and crumbling Georgian mansions—a world condemned by its colonial aspirations—was already passing into memory.

Croce also pointed out that though the tradition usually demands virginity, there is a subtradition that "honors promiscuity"; the woman of deep experience can also be mysterious and compelling, and as gratifying as the "pure young girl."[10] Caroline was that pure young girl for Lucian Freud. For Lowell, perhaps, part of her mystery was her history of fascinating men—Freud and Citkowitz. For Andrew Harvey, who was twenty years younger than Caroline, and gay, her passionate sexuality was part of her glamour. What Freud, Lowell, and Harvey all succeeded in doing was to vividly embody various aspects of Caroline in their works of art, giving her posthumous life. Croce may well have been thinking of Caroline when she wrote, "Whenever a gifted male artist has embraced his Muse he has in fact made a woman appear in the art . . . It is not the man speaking through the woman; it is the woman speaking through the man."[11]

The idea of "the Muse Incarnate" declined in the second half of the past century as women's roles changed. It is contrary to modern feminism because it rests on the idea of being chosen, rather than being the one to choose: "Muses are passive, therefore passé."[12] The curious thing is that Caroline would have agreed with the last statement; she rejected the idea of being a muse. She was not really a feminist either; she had her generation's mistrust of "women's lib." As an Anglo-Irish aristocrat—and a wealthy Guinness—she could do pretty much as she pleased. But she preferred to be the creator, not the inspirer, using her gothic imagination and her wicked wit to satirize the class she had been born into, and to expose a universe she perceived as infused with malevolent bad luck, like a fine silk shot through with rot.

If Caroline hated being defined as a muse, who, then, was she? Part of the enigma of Caroline Blackwood is that she is described differently by the various people who knew her. There are those who perceived her as capable of cruelty and drunken negligence. Others—particularly her women friends—saw her as generous, courageous, loving, and loyal. Several of Lowell's cronies thought her destructive and victimizing; others saw her as a lost soul, victimized by men who loved her only for her wealth or her title.

But all agreed on Caroline's gifts as a writer and her capacity for hard work. In fact, work became a kind of salvation for her. Despite a lifetime of Job-like afflictions—a neglected childhood, alcoholism, depression, illness, coping with Lowell's mania, the early deaths of a daughter and of her beloved brother—Caroline developed into an original and disciplined writer. Caroline's lost father, who died young, wrote, in his last letter to her and her siblings, "Above all, all of you, work hard all your lives."[13] Caroline took that advice to heart; she wrote nine books of fiction and nonfiction, and collaborated on a cookbook, before her death at the age of sixty-four.

In work and in life, Caroline hadn't quite made up her mind if the world was a godless place or one ruled by a malicious intelligence. Of the many paths to wisdom, Caroline chose the downward path. Or perhaps it chose her. The writer Jonathan Raban knew that about her when he eulogized Caroline, whom he had known when he was a young writer and critic renting a basement flat in her London house (while Lowell raged on the top floor and Citkowitz jangled his caretaker's keys in the middle flat).

> She violated every nursery maxim. She never failed to look on the dark side, or to search for the cloud in every silver lining. Intense apprehension—in both senses—was a guiding principle, and the phrase "the worst" was a favorite in her conversation. "It's the worst," she'd say with relish; "really the worst . . ."—a sure prelude to the unfolding of a new black comedy.
>
> More than any optimist I've ever known—far more—Caroline the pessimist made the world a happier place to be in because she could make mocking music of its terrors. She was brilliance in the dark, laughter in the silence.[14]

Part of this ability to "make mocking music" of the world's terrors was Caroline's gift for language, not just in her writing but in her conversation. And her conversation was always the more valuable because she never completely lost her deep silences. She would always need the libation of alcohol to guide her from a nearly mute state to those places where language flowed. Her silences, remembered Raban,

> *were* voids—*depthless, black, abrupt. And her talk was a suspension bridge, spanning the emptiness: each new sentence a girder, boldly swung out into perilous space. Caroline talking was devastatingly fluent, scandalous, and funny; on a roll, she'd scorch the air with words . . . an evening with friends would yield a full-length gothic novel.*

Caroline's wit, more so in her conversation than in her writing, was redemptive. It was her crowing over chaos; her black humor was like the phoenix rising from the ashes—she could win hilarity from darkness. She could find the one detail in the disaster that would make you laugh, and that was courage-giving. Caroline talked—and wrote—in order to face down misfortune. "All sorrows can be born," a sage once said—and I think Caroline would have agreed—"if they can be made into a story."[15]

· *One* ·

THE HOUSE OF
BLACKWOOD

How was he to tell her that her eyes would never again close—that in the
nights they would stare forever into the darkness . . .[1]

Scoptophilia: the morbid need to gaze.[2]

The first thing people recall about Caroline Blackwood is her enormous eyes. The composer Ned Rorem described them as blue as a peacock egg. The editor and poet Alan Ross thought they were green. Lucian Freud painted them blue-gray and staring. Always careless about her appearance—and many claimed she was one of the great beauties of her day—Caroline seemed to take pride only in the striking appearance of her eyes. In middle age, when drink and ill health had coarsened her features, she heavily outlined her eyes in black.

Like the jaded housewife in Caroline's short story "Please Baby Don't Cry," who undergoes cosmetic eye surgery and, as a result, can no longer close her eyes, Caroline was known for her gaze. Her unflinching stare was a need to observe, to see and to know, a willingness to look on all aspects of life, especially the seamy sides others turn from. In part it was a search for knowledge; in part it was a disdain for sentimentality. In part it was her rebellion against the self-satisfied social realm she was born to: she would be the one to look on life's ugliness and make the dreaded remark. To *see* was for Caroline an act of courage.

Caroline looked at the world around her and found it wanting. Born to wealth and privilege, on July 16, 1931, in Northern Ireland, she had been granted an impossible mixture of good and bad luck. She had beauty, talent, intelligence, wit, and courage. But her mother seemed incapable of loving her, and her father—who might have loved her—died when she was thirteen. Lord and Lady Dufferin—Basil "Ava" Blackwood and Maureen Guinness Blackwood—were alcoholics, although Maureen found a way to stop drinking in middle age. Alcohol probably ruined Lord Dufferin's political career. Caroline and her younger sister and brother were raised in a grand country house near Belfast by careless and sadistic nannies, were indifferently educated, and were launched into the world by a woman who seemed to care only for Society, practical jokes, and flattery. It's surprising that Caroline, with no training and little education, became a serious writer. But having been born in the waning years of Protestant rule in Northern Ireland, she witnessed the excesses, the boredom, and the siege mentality of that world; she had tales to tell. She would begin with social satire and end with the macabre.

She began by directing her gaze toward her ancestors and the great house and lands that had been snatched from the Irish and given to her Scots forebears by James I. She could be very dismissive, and funny, about her lineage and the privileges and horrors of growing up in a Georgian mansion in the declining years of the ascendancy. As a fiction writer, Caroline can be compared with Elizabeth Bowen and with Molly Keane, who wrote under the name M. J. Farrell, with some important differences. In her biography of Elizabeth Bowen, Victoria Glendinning wrote that when Bowen died, in 1973, *the Anglo-Irish literary tradition died with her. When she was growing up, all Ireland was still part of Great Britain. She lived between Ireland and England all her life. Since the twenty-six counties of the Republic of Ireland became a separate nation, the Anglo-Irish have lost their peculiar position and their cultural identity. There is no Anglo-Irish writer of Elizabeth Bowen's generation of the same stature, and hers was the last generation in which Anglo-Ireland, in its strict sense, existed.[3]*

In story after story, Bowen evoked the world of the Irish country house, usually tinged with a sense of nostalgia. Houses were forever being lost, mothers died, children were disinherited, sons gambled away the family fortune, furniture was auctioned off, and the great Georgian houses were sold and sometimes torn down, as was Elizabeth's own Bowen Court. While Anglo-Irish aristocrats played bridge and danced at their cotillions, British patrols moved uneasily among Irish tenants, searching for guns hidden under beds. What Bowen knew "was an Eden in the seconds after the apple has been eaten, when Evil was known, immanent and unavoidable, but while there was still awareness of what Innocence had been."[4]

Molly Keane was born five years after Elizabeth Bowen. Though probably aware of how untenable was the Protestant ascendancy in Northern Ireland, she celebrated that world and accepted its pleasures as well as its discomforts and moral quandaries. Like Bowen, Keane was well aware that the Protestant ruling class had to shut Catholic Ireland out at night by barring the great hall door. Nonetheless, Keane lovingly described many Anglo-Irish customs from her childhood that seem now, at the beginning of a new century, to be stifling or quaint or just inconvenient; Keane evoked them with a rosy glow. Although daughters living at home were not educated for any employment or profession, family life held many pleasures:

One was sure of a horse and two or three days' hunting in the week. . . . With a full staff of servants, there was nothing in the way

*of housework to be done. A girl with a talent for music or painting
had leisure to practise her art.[5]*

Indeed, an ascendancy family was a little universe unto itself. When
it ran smoothly—when parents had their children's best interests at
heart and there was enough money to keep the mountain of unpaid
bills at a manageable altitude—there were many deep pleasures inherent in that life. Even the unmarried "home girls" had a place in
society, and were often inherited, along with the manor house, where
they would lend their talents to gardening, if they wished, or ruin
their eyesight by mending tapestries. Whoever inherited the house
had to take care of them. Game was plentiful; without refrigeration,
"everything from spring lamb to green peas was eaten in its season."[6]
Morning prayers were said daily, and there was plenty to do if you
were the sporting type—and if you were born into the Anglo-Irish,
you were expected to be. Grouse and snipe shooting, fox hunting as
often as possible, horseback riding and show jumping were *de rigueur*.
In fact, horses, hunting, and racing were the only accepted topics of
conversation; literary types were considered "creeps," according to
Molly Keane.[7] The eldest son always inherited; younger sons had to
make do by joining the army, navy, or diplomatic services and living
on their pensions. It was better never to marry than to marry beneath
your class. This was the world Caroline was born to.

The drawback to this cozy, insular world was that, as Desmond
Guinness—one of Caroline's cousins—wrote in his book on Irish castles, the Anglo-Irish ruling class had to be on the alert, as if they were
living in a foreign country: "Irish in England and English in Ireland."

*The Protestant landlords had loyalties to England that were not
shared by their tenants . . . In Ireland, the two were separated by
barriers of race, religion, and in some districts language . . . the
castle stronghold survived far longer [in Ireland] than was necessary in England.[8]*

Long after Caroline left Northern Ireland to live in London and New York, her mother and sister-in-law would sometimes have to place a log across the road to Clandeboye to protect themselves during the Troubles. Caroline thought it a rather mad idea that such a maneuver could be helpful in keeping out the IRA.

Caroline was born twenty-seven years after Molly Keane. The world Keane relished in her novels—the lighting of the bedroom fire at eight o'clock, "when tea was brought to the bedside, the china invariably patterned with tiny violets"[9]—Caroline would describe as soul-numbing boredom. Prosperous Anglo-Irish women couldn't even "enjoy their money," according to Caroline. She described an era of isolation, perpetual rain, lack of petrol, a short hunting season, and long, dark nights. "In wartime," she wrote, "their isolation became hellish . . . The young men were all away, and there was neither point, nor petrol, for them to make [social] calls."[10]

She was even grimmer when considering the effect of the Troubles on Anglo-Irish ladies, who recalled a time when landlords couldn't walk around their estates without armed guards. Caroline grew up in the memory of a time when "the murder of a landlord was considered a hallowed act, and the Irish children played games of 'Kill the Landlord.' "[11]

Caroline's friend Lady Gowrie—now Xandra Hardie, since her divorce from the Irish earl Greysteil Gowrie—shared Caroline's Anglo-Irish background and her harsh judgment of that world:

Our lot had a great run. They really did. Caroline came from the end of that tribe. Mostly we were completely useless and worthless. It was a totally work-free life our tribe lived before the war. We did nothing worthwhile. We contributed to some charities, and a few people collected paintings . . . P. G. Wodehouse presented the genial, playful attitude towards all that, but if you look past it, you see it was ghastly—it really was.[12]

One of the pleasures of Caroline's autobiographical second novel, *Great Granny Webster,* is her vivid description of the decaying house at Clandeboye under her unfortunate grandfather Frederick's reign. Calling the Georgian house "Dunmartin Hall," Caroline wrote about her childhood memories of growing up there. "Dunmartin Hall had always had an aura of impermanence. The house had both the melancholy and the magic of something inherently doomed by the height of its own ancient colonial aspirations. It was like a grey and decaying palace fortress."[13] Stinging nettles had taken over the driveway, and weeds invaded the tennis court. The roses grew wild from lack of attention; only the hydrangeas, needing no special care, flourished. The tenant farmers, who seemed to exist on bacon fat and potatoes, produced nothing from the barren soil and could not pay their rent. The swimming pool rotted. The viceroy's vast library mildewed. The roof leaked incessantly, so jam jars and pots and pans were scattered around the house and emptied on a daily basis. Soggy string, meant to direct the leaks into their respective pots and pans, hung from damp ceilings. The English butler and footmen hired by Caroline's grandfather Frederick ("Dunmartin") sloshed around the mansion in Wellingtons, disdainfully drinking their way through their employer's wine cellar, while Dunmartin sold off fields to pay their salaries. A trio of slovenly Irish sisters, hired as cooks, proved disastrous, transforming the game pheasant into deep brown objects swimming in lard. The kitchen was sticky, unscrubbed, bedecked with the corpses of mice smashed in mousetraps on the unswept stone floor, among the potato peelings and sharp bones of pheasants. The house was so cold that one had to wear an overcoat just to traverse the halls; the plumbing was inadequate, so a hot bath was a rarity. The stables were empty, the chickens laid no eggs, the orchards failed to produce apples. The once beautiful imported trees had to be cut down for firewood; more and more acres were sold off to pay inherited and mounting debts.

Nonetheless, Caroline would always have a particular love for great houses and for Georgian architecture, though she came to question the tradition-bound, Anglo-Irish life that, in her experience, went with it. Caroline, unlike Molly Keane and Elizabeth Bowen, saw only the ghastliness of the world she had been born to. She considered the Irish house a curse as well as a blessing, but she would often long for Clandeboye, lost to her through primogeniture.

The history of great families has always held a fascination. For Caroline Hamilton Temple Blackwood, the family that nourished her imagination was not the brewery Guinnesses, but her father's family of Blackwoods, who traced their lineage back to sixteenth-century Scotland. The Blackwoods and the Hamiltons emigrated from Scotland to Ulster in 1586 and settled in the soft rolling lands ten miles from Belfast, in Northern Ireland's County Down.[14] Today the Guinnesses are far better known than the Blackwoods—for their wealth, their flamboyance, their Book of Records, their "curse," and of course for their dark brown stout—but the ancient line of Blackwoods anchored Caroline in Clandeboye.

In 1604, James I granted James Hamilton a sovereign charter over the land, castles, and possessions of the Irish family of O'Neills in Upper Clandeboye.[15] The Blackwoods were originally tenants of the land-rich Hamiltons, but when Henry Hamilton, Lord Clanbrassil, was forced to sell his lands to pay off gambling debts in 1688—and was later poisoned, possibly by his wife—John Blackwood acquired the Hamilton lands and a peerage that would be passed down through the generations.

As in many families of property and high social standing, some intermarriages were arranged to keep the wealth in the family. The Blackwoods and Hamiltons were united when John Blackwood of Ballyleidy married his cousin Anne Hamilton and fathered two sons. By the end of the seventeenth century, the Blackwoods were no longer tenants; they were firmly entrenched owners of an estate of more than six thousand acres scattered throughout North Down. Their 340-acre estate near Belfast, then called Ballyleidy, held a small, two-story house, now replaced by the large, gray, ivy-covered Georgian mansion where Caroline, Perdita, and Sheridan were born.

Caroline's three most notable ancestors on her father's side were Richard Brinsley Sheridan, his granddaughter Helen Selina, and Helen's son, Frederick, who would become the first Marquess of Dufferin and Ava.

Sheridan, the Irish playwright best known for *The School for Scandal* and *The Rivals*, contributed his iconoclastic wit and literary talent to the Blackwood gene pool. And if there is a genetic predisposition to alcoholism, Caroline may also have inherited this from her brilliant ancestor. It was to blight many of the important relationships in her life. It had marred Sheridan's spectacular career in the London theater with long periods of financial disaster and personal difficulties. He wrote *The Rivals* in just a few short weeks when he needed money; it was produced at Covent Garden in 1775 and was a great success. Though he claimed to loathe the theater and seldom saw plays, he bought out David Garrick's half-share of the Drury Lane Theatre and attempted to manage it—disastrously. Even the financial success of *The School for Scandal*, which opened in 1777, did little to ease his overwhelming debt, accumulated through his poor management of the Drury Lane and his penchant for entertaining fashionable society on a grand scale. His true love was politics, and he was elected to Parliament, but his personal disasters and lack of fortune derailed that career as well, though he won a reputation as a brilliant orator in the House of Commons.

When the rebuilt Drury Lane was destroyed by fire in 1809, Sheridan was relieved of its management. In 1811 he lost his seat in Parliament; in 1813 he was arrested for debt. When his house was opened to his creditors, it was "found to be filthy and denuded of almost all furnishing."[16] He died in 1816, but instead of being buried next to his political ally Charles James Fox, as was his wish, Sheridan was given a grand funeral and laid to rest next to Garrick, the greatest English actor of his day. He may have disdained the theater for politics, but it was theater that claimed him.

Caroline was fascinated by Sheridan and took him as a patron saint. Sir Harold Nicolson, in his biography of Caroline's great-grandfather Frederick, wrote that "in my uncle's own veins the Sheridan blood seethed and tingled like champagne," a phrase Caroline was fond of quoting.[17] The name Sheridan in fact crops up two more times in the Blackwood line: it's her brother's name and the name she and Robert Lowell gave their son, Robert Sheridan Lowell. "The Sheridans are still dominating sea and land in our household," Caroline said. "We're all very Sheridanish."[18]

In *Great Granny Webster*, Caroline described the Sheridan blood and its effect on at least one member of the family. In an interview she gave to the writer and editor Steven M. L. Aronson three years before her death, Caroline confessed that her novel *Great Granny Webster* was "all too real." The story about her grandmother, Brenda Woodhouse, trying to smash her infant grandson against a stone during his christening "really happened," Caroline said. Her grandmother was afraid that Caroline's brother would have "the bad Sheridan blood."[19]

Caroline, in due time, would have her own reckoning with "the bad Sheridan blood."

Sheridan entered the Blackwood line through one of his three beautiful granddaughters, Helen Selina, who is remembered for writing a popular lyric called "The Irish Emigrant." A brilliant, beautiful, but penniless young woman, she married Caroline's great-great-grandfather Price Blackwood, a union that displeased the dour, Calvinist Blackwoods. After generations of careful acquisition and husbandry, Price Blackwood had gone and married a poor woman who sang, danced, and wrote poetry, and whose grandfather was, yes, a famous Irish playwright, but also a philanderer, a drunk, and a bankrupt. The Price Blackwoods banished themselves to Italy for two years, until Helen's charm and beauty—and the birth of their first son and heir, Frederick—softened the hearts of the elder Blackwoods.

Then mother and son began to make frequent visits to the grand but gloomy mansion at Ballyleidy, and Frederick would prove the most illustrious Blackwood of them all.

An 1842 portrait of young Frederick reveals a doe-eyed young man with a sensitive face and glossy black hair, a far cry from the august, patriarchal figure in military coat and bristling white whiskers he would become. Frederick, Caroline's great-grandfather, would master a romantic and dreamy temperament and be known as a highly accomplished politician, ambassador, paterfamilias, man of letters, amateur architect, collector, and part-time watercolorist.

The dreaming boy in the portrait became the fifth Lord Dufferin and sole heir of Ballyleidy at the age of fifteen, when his father died in 1841 during a stormy Channel crossing; it was thought that he took an accidental overdose of morphine to treat a headache. Frederick would grow up to be "the foremost imperial administrator of the late Victorian era,"[20] according to one historian. The ancestral home is still filled with the curling irons, bobsleds, Mohawk and Ojibwa hunting bags, Cree showshoes, and paddles garnered from his travels in British Columbia, when he served as Governor-General of Canada in the 1870s. Queen Victoria later appointed him ambassador to Russia, Turkey, Italy, and France, and then made him Viceroy of India.

Caroline believed that his appointment as Viceroy of India was the high point of her great-grandfather's life: "He loved the pomp of power . . . Can you imagine him sitting on his throne, with yaks' tails and peacock-feather fans waved above him, while guns thundered?"[21]

Caroline enjoyed satirizing her ancestor, but she was captivated by the rumor, passed down through her family, that this paragon of Victorian industry and virtue was really the illegitimate son of the Jewish prime minister and novelist Benjamin Disraeli. She told Aronson that Frederick did indeed resemble Disraeli and that Disraeli had helped her great-grandfather in his rise to prominence by whispering in Queen Victoria's ear. But at least one chronicler of the Blackwoods, Sir Harold Nicolson, checked Disraeli's diary and ascertained that his first meeting with Lady Dufferin took place six years after Frederick's birth.

For his role in the British annexation of Burma during his term in India, Lord Dufferin would acquire his second title, the name of Burma's ancient capital. Advancing from baron to earl to marquess, Lord Dufferin became the first Marquess of Dufferin and Ava, a name—and a place—that would later prove fateful to Caroline's father, the fourth marquess, who was known affectionately to his friends and family as Ava.

Besides being the first Blackwood to gain international prestige and augment the family's title, Frederick is noteworthy for restoring the name Clandeboye to the ancestral Ulster home and for turning the house into a grand repository of Victorian plunder. Indeed, the vast interior of the great house helped to shape Caroline's gothic imagination: a blackened rhinoceros head rested on an ancient, sacrificial stone in the entrance hall; a museum room contained the mummified hand of an Egyptian and six-thousand-year-old Egyptian ropes once used to lower corpses into their tombs. As a child, Caroline was convinced that she could hear the restless ropes thumping against the walls at night. There were also countless weapons brought back by the viceroy from India and Egypt—cutlasses, pistols, daggers, spiked balls, and lances—all hanging from the walls and the stairs like ancestral portraits, still and alive with their aura of violence.

It was Frederick's love, suitably Victorian, for the poetry of Sir Walter Scott that may have sparked his reclamation of the ancient name Clandeboye, which means Place of the Yellow-Haired Hugh, a reference to Hugh O'Neill, one of the original inhabitants of Upper Clandeboye. Sir Walter Scott "celebrated the mood of resentment" over this usurpation with the following lines from *Rokeby*, memorized by Frederick:

Ah Clandeboye! Thy friendly floor
Slieve Donard's oak shall light no more . . .

And now the stranger's sons enjoy
The lovely woods of Clandeboye.[22]

That Frederick was one of the stranger's sons must have added a bitter-sweet taste to the lyrics, or at least an ironic one.

Frederick's sensitivity and, later, his long list of truly remarkable accomplishments as diplomat and administrator have been attributed to the strong influence of his mother, Helen Selina Blackwood. Frederick would memorialize his mother by erecting a tower on the grounds of Clandeboye, an architectural folly called Helen's Tower, which would give its name to Sir Harold Nicolson's biography of his uncle-by-marriage, published in London in 1937.

Helen's Tower, Nicolson's tribute to Lord Dufferin, is a kind of biography-cum-memoir, inspired by Proust's *À la recherche du temps perdu,* in which Nicolson begins by trying to capture early childhood reveries experienced during school holidays at Clandeboye. Nostalgia has been described as a mild form of depression; Nicolson's text is an odd combination of melancholy for his lost youth and a litany of praise for his uncle, whom he seemed to have hero-worshiped his entire life. He wrote to his wife, Vita Sackville-West, on a return visit twenty-five years after his youthful sojourns there: "And yet everything Clandeboye [once] meant to me has disappeared beyond capture, and it now seems a muggy, ugly place entirely hedged in by damp overgrown trees . . . This *à la recherche* business is not really much fun when the *temps* is as *perdu* as all that."[23]

The tower that lent its name to Nicolson's book is still a well-known landmark in Ulster, built not only as a tribute to Frederick's mother but also to help relieve the misery and unemployment caused by the potato famine. Lord Dufferin seemed to have been a conflicted landlord who loved Clandeboye yet was genuinely horrified by poverty wrought by the great famine of the 1840s and by the role of landlords in the misery of Irish tenants. Nicolson wrote delicately that his uncle "was not unaware that his ancestors had obtained these lands by spoliation, nor had he anything but contempt for those absentee landlords who allowed their agents to oppress the peasantry. Yet he was a man of great possessions and he felt a need of loyalty towards his caste."[24]

The situation in County Down was somewhat less severe than in western Ireland, yet there was still great destitution, even at Clandeboye. "Lord Dufferin salved his aching conscience," wrote Nicolson, with

> *gestures of wild and romantic generosity to his own tenants. On coming of age he presented them with remissions of rent amounting to £2,000 for the improvements they had effected. He spent some £78,000 in bettering the conditions of his farms without in a single case increasing his rent charges. He dug the two vast lakes at Clandeboye; he constructed a fantastic folly in the shape of a two-and-a-half-mile avenue connecting the demesne with Helen's Bay, in the hope of relieving unemployment.*[25]

Helen was still living when the tower was completed in 1861. As a final act of filial devotion, Lord Dufferin asked a number of eminent Victorian poets to dedicate Helen's Tower with verses, which were engraved on metal plates and hung in a Gothic paneled room on the third floor of the tower (there is a sumptuous room on each of the tower's three floors), and then collected them in a manuscript called *The Book of Helen's Tower*, which now resides in the Public Record Office of Northern Ireland. In it are poems by Alfred Tennyson, Thomas Carlyle, G. F. Savage, and Richard Garnett. Written after Helen's death and given to Lord Dufferin for Helen's Tower are lines by Robert Browning, Rudyard Kipling, Sir Edwin Arnold, H. Montague Butler, and Wilfrid Scawen Blunt. The most famous of these dedicatory poems is Tennyson's:

> *Helen's Tower here I stand,*
> *Dominant over sea and land.*
> *Son's love built me, and I hold*

Mother's love in lettered gold.
Would my granite girth were strong
As either love, to last as long.
I should wear my crown entire
To and thro' the Doomsday fire,
And be found of angel eyes
In earth's recurring Paradise.[26]

There was in fact a similar tower that Caroline and her sister and brother would have seen on a daily basis as they were growing up in Clandeboye. A Londonderry family built a duplicate tower, which the Blackwood children invariably referred to as "the copycat tower."[27]

Caroline could be quite comic about the gold-embossed plaques of stiff Victorian verse in the top chamber of Helen's Tower; she was especially fond of quoting the first two lines of Browning's dedicatory poem ("Who hears of Helen's Tower may dream perchance / How that great beauty of the Scaean Gate . . ."). She told Aronson that her third husband, Robert Lowell, was "astonished" when he read those Victorian verses, and exclaimed, "What has the viceroy done to these very great writers!"[28]

When Helen died, in her eightieth year, Lord Dufferin was devastated. According to Nicolson, her death long affected Frederick and the atmosphere at Clandeboye: "There was the whole hushed tradition of some great bereavement associated with Helen's Tower. And there were occasions when visiting ladies would sing 'The Irish Emigrant' in the saloon, and my uncle would cover his eyes with his hand."[29]

It was Nicolson's belief that Frederick's adoration of his mother is what kept him from marrying until the rather advanced age of thirty-seven (that, and an attachment to one Lady Jocelyn, a married, older woman to whom Dufferin was devoted for some time).[30] Lord Dufferin would eventually marry a woman eighteen years his junior (the same number of years separating himself and his mother, Nicolson noted). In the tradition of Blackwoods, Lord Dufferin married a Hamilton cousin, Hariot Rowan Hamilton, a diffident, adoring young woman who would prove her mettle by providing Lord Dufferin with seven children; by holding her own in the courts and high offices of British Columbia, France, Italy, India, and Russia; and by living to be ninety-three. She provided the filial link to Harold Nicolson, who knew her affectionately as Aunt Lal.

Caroline actually met her great-grandmother Hariot Hamilton Blackwood. She remembered being taken to tea in London, when she was three or four years old, and being kissed by the ninety-year-old woman. The kisses were wet and unpleasant; Caroline remembered wiping them off and later feeling guilty about it. "She loved me, you see, and I couldn't love her back because she was too old."[31]

Helen Selina, who was after all a Sheridan—the eldest of the three beautiful Sheridan granddaughters—is represented in *Ireland's Women*, a recent anthology of works by Irish women writers.[32] In addition to "The Irish Emigrant" and other poems, Helen wrote *Lispings in Low Latitudes*, a gentle parody of her son's *Letters From High Latitudes*, published in 1857 and considered a minor classic in the genre of travel writing. In 1894, twenty-seven years after her death (she underwent surgery for breast cancer in 1866 and died the following year), Frederick collected his mother's poems in a light green binder embossed with gold coronets and the title *Songs, Poems, and Verses*. Though mother and son were both literary, Helen discouraged Frederick's more refined interests and encouraged his political career.

Frederick, unfortunately, would crown that career as a Victorian colonial administrator with a series of domestic setbacks and disappointments. In response to William Gladstone's Irish Land Act,[33] he sold most of his eighteen thousand acres, forcing his tenants to emigrate, rather than pay the high taxes levied on Irish landowners once it became clear that the tenant farmers could not pay. Frederick may have believed that emigration was a better fate for the Irish than eking out a living in Ireland in the wake of the famine. He lost his first son and heir, the Earl of Ava, to the Boer War, and a finance corporation to which he had lent his name crashed in 1900, ruining thirty members of the stock exchange and numerous small investors. Lord Dufferin was blamed, and he died, disheartened, two years later. His literary talent—shared by but ultimately discouraged by his mother—would emerge four generations later in Caroline Blackwood.

Caroline was the namesake of Helen Selina's younger sister Caroline, also a writer, though Nicolson sniffed at her accomplishments, describing her as possessing "a flashy literary talent." According to Nicolson, she was bitter, unfriendly, malicious, and brilliant, and she poured out her grievances "in volume after volume of Byronic verse."[34] Her marriage to George Norton, brother of Lord Grantley, ended in 1836 in a spectacular divorce suit, which named Lord Melbourne as co-respondent.

The next ancestor important to Caroline was her grandfather, named Frederick after his father and portrayed as Dunmartin in *Great Granny Webster*. Frederick was the youngest of the viceroy's four sons; the first died in the Boer War, the second produced no male heirs, and the third was killed in the First World War. Thus it was the fourth son, Caroline's grandfather, who inherited the title and the now diminished lands. Frederick became the third Marquess of Dufferin and Ava (his eldest brother had, briefly, been the second), inheriting a vast house that had fallen into disrepair, a demesne of imported trees and plantings that had become gnarled, overgrown, and diseased, and a lack of means to restore Clandeboye to its earlier grandeur.

To worsen matters, the woman he married, a lovely, fragile Scotswoman named Brenda Woodhouse, would suffer frequent periods of insanity.

Caroline claimed that most of her writings were not particularly autobiographical, with the clear exception of *Great Granny Webster*, published in 1977 and short-listed for the prestigious Booker Prize. (In fact, it was on the grounds that Caroline's novel was really a lightly disguised memoir that Philip Larkin cast the deciding vote against Caroline—but more of that later.) It's clear from Caroline's own statements and from those of her sister, Perdita Blackwood, that the Great Granny Webster of her novel is based on Brenda's mother, Caroline's great-grandmother, a stingy Scottish heiress named Woodhouse who lived in a forbidding Victorian mansion in Hove, near Brighton.

"We were told to be very, very nice to her," recalled Lady Perdita, who lives on a fifty-acre horse farm, Cavallo Farms, on what was probably part of the original Clandeboye estate.

> She was supposed to be very, very rich, and we were told she would leave us money. But we dreaded those visits. I'm sure she dreaded them every bit as much as we did. She had the most terrifying maid, who wore a black patch over her eye—she looked like a pirate. We would spend weekends there. It was terrifying. There was a butler who had one leg—he was terrifying, too. The house was dark, dark, with plum colored walls—lit by gas lamps, probably. The house creaked, and there were wooden shutters that banged.[35]

Perdita said that during those early visits, she and Caroline and their brother, Sheridan, would mope around the dark house, terribly shy and afraid of their great-grandmother and her one-eyed maid. Great Granny Woodhouse would ask Sheridan, who never spoke a word to her if he could help it, "Darling, we have to get you something. What would you like?" And he'd study his shoes and mumble, "Comics." So Great Granny Woodhouse—having but a dim idea of what "comics" were—would dispatch the one-eyed maid to buy comic books. Perdita and Caroline would try to make conversation with their stiff, remote, and terrifying great-grandmother while Sheridan buried his nose in his comics. So they were all surprised when Great Granny Woodhouse bequeathed to Caroline a narrow Queen Anne's bedstead, to Perdita a carriage clock, and to the antisocial young Sheridan £45,000—"quite a fortune in those days!" But, then, in those days, if there were males around, women rarely inherited; Great Granny Woodhouse had cut her own daughter out of her will. As it was, the old woman had been amused by Sheridan. "Isn't it funny the way he sits and never speaks!" she said to her scowling maid, whom Caroline called Richards in her novel.[36]

It was to damp, gloomy Clandeboye that Brenda Woodhouse was brought as a young bride. A character named Tommy Redcliffe, based on one of Caroline's father's Oxford friends, possibly the poet John Betjeman, felt that the isolation and general decay of Dunmartin Hall had so depressed the young woman that it had driven her into lunacy. Like Edgar Allan Poe's House of Usher, Clandeboye worked on the febrile imagination of its most vulnerable inhabitant, a situation Caroline saw as a grim retribution for the viceroy's role in England's colonial aspirations. Dunmartin had become a kind of Roderick Usher, tending a mad wife—a cousin instead of a sister—in a decaying manse.

Caroline's portrait of Brenda Woodhouse is both comic and harrowing. It's probably exaggerated, as Caroline's gothic imagination saw the inherent drama—and comedy—in every situation, but its essential truth has been verified by at least one other source: John Betjeman. Betjeman was a close friend of Caroline's father and had visited Clandeboye as a young man. His daughter, Candida Lycett Green, noted in her edited volume of her father's letters that "JB stayed at the Dufferins' Northern Irish seat, Clandeboye, County Down, at the end of August [1928]. He got on well with Basil's mother, Brenda, who was faintly off her head and thought she was Queen of the Fairies."[37]

"Unlike her morose-faced mother," Caroline wrote, her grandmother had been pretty, with "bright gold curls and an impish expression."[38] But well into her marriage, this frail, pixilated woman was unable to manage the household and spent her days hidden away in her room, restlessly wandering the house at night and appearing not to recognize family members. And then, fatally, she began to indulge her overly keen interest in fairies. "She claimed that she could understand the language of the fairies, that they were continually sending her messages, that it was important only to listen to the instructions of the good ones for they could help you avert the terrible spells that might be put on you by demons."[39]

Poor Brenda Woodhouse would spend hours in her room, cutting pictures of fairies from children's books. Even more frightening, she began to resemble a fairy, of the Christmas-tree-ornament variety. Her face became frozen in a childlike expression; she whitened her already white face and combed her blond curls in fairy tresses; she wore diaphanous gowns and silver shawls; she flitted around the cold rooms of Clandeboye in bare feet, astonishing her guests. Basil and his sister, Veronica (Ivor and Aunt Lavinia in Caroline's novel), seemed to have been acutely embarrassed by their mother's eccentricity, so much so that they never discussed or referred to it, in the great Anglo tradition of keeping the upper lip stiff. Caroline's grandfather apparently adored his childlike wife and made every excuse for her, but eventually she wandered too deep into her enchanted world and never found her way out again. She's the grandmother who tried to snatch young Sheridan from his cradle and smash his head against the wall on the day of his christening, in order to purge "the bad Sheridan blood."

Great Granny Woodhouse—who had so approved of Brenda's marriage to her prominent Anglo-Irish cousin—never helped her daughter and son-in-law, according to Caroline, preferring to live alone in her frozen mansion (heating oil was expensive) while her daughter sank deeper into fantasy and her son-in-law lived in the crumbling ruins of his household. *Great Granny Webster* would be the first, but not the last, book by Caroline in which she condemned the utter selfishness of a rich, mean-spirited matriarch, an evil witch who sat and watched over the destruction of her beleaguered child.

Caroline's father, named Basil after an uncle and known familiarly as Ava or Dufferin, became the fourth Marquess of Dufferin and Ava when his father, Frederick, died in an airplane crash in 1930. He was also portrayed in *Great Granny Webster*, though Caroline later admitted that she knew very little about her father.[40]

Basil seems to have been universally admired for his attractiveness, his brilliance, and his flair for politics. The historian William Maguire described him as "a gifted young man of extraordinary charm; like his grandfather [the viceroy] he combined intellectual, literary and artistic gifts with ambitions in public life, and as Under Secretary of State for the Colonies from 1937 to 1940 while still in his twenties, he was talked of in some circles as a future Conservative prime minister."[41] He was handsome and athletic, with a large head and large eyes—Caroline clearly inherited those penetrating, saucer-like eyes from her father. His nickname at Oxford had been Little Bloody, given to him by his friend, the future poet laureate John Betjeman.

Basil Ava and Betjeman became close friends at Oxford. Basil was a Brackenbury Scholar of classical languages at Balliol College, where he made a strong impression on his peers and on Oxford dons alike. Sir Roy Harrod, one-time president of the Royal Economic Society and one of the premiere dons at Christ Church, wrote, "Basil Ava, although he was at Balliol College, happened for a time to be my pupil, and was, in some respects, the most brilliant one I ever had."[42] His friend Edward James, who had been with Basil at Eton and at Lockers Park, was "told to look after him," because he was older by one and a half years, but Basil "was so much more intelligent and alive than I was," James recalled, "that it ended by him looking after me."[43] Bevis Hillier, the author of *Young Betjeman*, compared Lord Dufferin to that "nonpareil undergraduate," the superior Duke of Dorset, in Max Beerbohm's satire of Oxonian manner, *Zuleika Dobson.*

The Dufferins were originally Scots, but Edward James thought Basil "very Irish . . . He had this round Irish nose, like a sort of Paddy caricature; beautiful brown eyes, very alive and deep and large; very quiet and reserved, beautiful manners. And I was in love with him. And John [Betjeman] was, too. And I suppose we both told him we were. Anyway, he asked us over to Clandeboye."[44]

In a letter, Betjeman described Basil during a happy visit to Clandeboye in August of 1928, calling him "the most intelligent conversationalist for his age":

Oh how peaceful were those first few days . . . laughing at Edward James' poetry . . . :

> *Lord Ava had enormous eyes*
> *And head of a colossal size*
> *He rarely laughed and only spoke*
> *To utter some stupendous joke*
> *Which if it were not understood*
> *Was anyhow considered good.*
> *He was so very good at games*
> *He'd even beaten Edward James*
> *And others of the wealthy set*
> *Who fill the pages of Debrett.*

. . . I am glad you like Bloody—what an admirable sterling character is his![45]

Betjeman's letter went on to recount his dancing the Charleston at Clandeboye to the strains of a new gramophone record, the fledgling poet paired with Basil's formidable sister: "I found that by altering my plane of thought I could get on quite well with Veronica."[46]

Randolph Churchill was part of the Betjeman-Dufferin-James

circle. He described Basil as "the most lovable man I met at Oxford. His liquid spaniel eyes and his beautiful, charming manner, commanded affection. He was the most brilliant of all my contemporaries at Oxford." However, Churchill added a somewhat cautionary note, all the more ironic because of his own proclivities: "An undue addiction to drink blighted what might have been a fine political career."[47]

That Betjeman was in love with Basil seems clear, though whether there was any physical expression of that love is unclear. Betjeman himself was fond of analyzing "what percentage of homosexuality" ran through predominantly heterosexual men—a category in which he placed himself more often as his Oxford days receded. According to Hillier, Betjeman's "own percentage probably remained above the average," but he quoted Alan Pryce-Jones, also of their Oxford group, as protesting (perhaps too much) that Betjeman's "absurd emphasis on his queerness, in conversation, really has no foundation or literal meaning, I would think. It's a kind of protect [sic] against being dominated by anybody . . . I mean, he had crushes on people at Oxford, like the late Lord Dufferin, but it had no meaning; it was never intended to be translated into any form of action."[48]

Although Basil seemed to inspire love in men and women alike, it may also have been the aristocratic Dufferin bloodline, even the creepy, spoiled magnificence of Clandeboye, that excited young Betjeman. Tennessee Williams once remarked that poets are especially attracted to ruins. The son of a manufacturer, who disdained the suburban middle-class comfort he was heir to, Betjeman—like Harold Nicolson before him—never forgot his visits to Clandeboye.

Though its Victorian plunder and grand entrance hall gave Clandeboye an imperial splendor, the plumbing never worked; the best one could hope for was a "peat-brown trickle of a bath," Caroline wrote in *Great Granny Webster*.[49] Basil's mad mother, the unfortunate Brenda, added to the gothic atmosphere, though she and Betjeman appeared to get on well. Betjeman was used to humoring his own hypersensitive, hypochrondriacal mother, according to Hillier, so "he was quite equal to chatting with [Brenda] about the Little Folk, just as he had discussed the 'fairy rings' of Ireland . . . Had not his first poem been about 'fairy folk so wee'?"[50]

But Basil was extremely leery of his mother, and not only because Brenda at times was convinced that her two children were not hers at all but were changelings switched at birth by malevolent fairies. To escape her flitting and sudden, eccentric appearances, Basil would hold court with his Oxford friends in a cozy attic room, where he had dragged up a bamboo table and a couple of chairs. It was the only place where he could hide from his mother and relax with a snifter of brandy.

Basil's marriage to Maureen Guinness—a beautiful, prank-playing young woman and, incidentally, a cousin—would dramatically change the atmosphere at Clandeboye, not at all to Betjeman's liking. Basil and Maureen were married in July of 1930 and spent part of their honeymoon in Burma, visiting the ancient capital of Ava, which Basil's grandfather had annexed. The couple toured Burma and arranged for a shooting party in Gwalior, and then spent Christmas as guests of the Maharajah of Mysore, wearing evening dress while dining in the jungle and observing all the formalities of their class.[51] Ava would return to Burma fourteen years later, under vastly different circumstances.

Basil was a young man when he came into his inheritance. His father's death in the airplane crash occurred when Basil was on his honeymoon. The post-marriage atmosphere at Clandeboye that Betjeman so objected to was probably brought about by Maureen, who lived for all varieties of amusement. The poet visited Clandeboye in 1931 on summer holiday and described in a letter a raucous party he attended: "There were too many smart, bright young people to suit me. I feel obliged to write so soon on top of the other letter simply to complain of the hellish people staying at Clandeboye . . . I can't understand why Little B[loody] surrounds himself with them . . . all the richest & most titled of the Guinnesses.[52]

Maureen, a stylish beauty with disturbingly pale blue eyes and golden hair—not unlike a wholesome version of poor Brenda Woodhouse—

has been described as the only Guinness daughter who truly enjoyed her wealth. A controversial figure, Maureen indulged her delight in practical jokes and bawdy stories, which certainly enlivened the gloomy halls of Clandeboye. The house continued to fall into disrepair under its weight of inherited debt and Basil's gambling debts. To her credit, Maureen used her considerable Guinness fortune to restore Clandeboye to a cheerful beauty, but at least two of her three children—Caroline and Perdita—would despise her for her complete and utter fatuousness.

"She only wanted one thing in life," Perdita believed: "to be thought of as the most beautiful woman in the world. That, and playing bridge—she was absolutely mad for bridge!"[53] She also lived for her annual dinners with the Queen Mother, and on certain days Maureen would take to her bed, pretending to be the Queen Mother herself.

While Maureen threw lavish parties in London, making infrequent visits to Clandeboye, Basil's drinking increased. Photographs of the couple in the middle years of their marriage show a bloated Lord Dufferin with a sullen, resentful look. He still managed to cut a dashing figure; he attended the horse races at Ascot in top hat and tails, with Maureen on his arm in chic finery and a fabulous hat. Their three children were born in the first eight years of their marriage: Caroline in 1931, Perdita in 1934, and their only son and heir to the title and lands, Sheridan, in 1938.

One reason for Basil's sullen look, perhaps, is that he was rumored to have fallen in love with another woman. The painter Anne Dunn Moynihan, Caroline's friend and contemporary who was once married to the brilliant and erratic painter Michael Wishart, was convinced that Caroline's father was in love with Anne's older sister, Joan Dunn. Joan, born in 1908, was twenty-one years older than Anne and was already married, to Charles Dutton, the Earl of Sherborne. "Basil and Joan were making plans to leave their spouses and marry each other," Anne believed. "Their greatest romance was with each other; all their love letters were burned about six years ago by Joan's family."[54] Basil's early death ended those plans.

One of the life-altering events of Caroline's childhood—one she never wrote about—was the death of her father when he was thirty-five years old. "The women in my family live long," Caroline said once; "all the male ones go young."[55] The irony of Basil's death was that it took place near Ava, his namesake, during the battle to drive the Japanese from Burma. Caroline, years later, observed that Basil's death was considered a "curse" by everyone who knew him, because it was Basil's grandfather who had presided over the two-week battle that vanquished Burma, and who had annexed it for Britain.[56] Caroline considered the decline of the great house at Clandeboye to be retribution for her great-grandfather's colonial aspirations; she may have also believed, on some level, that her father's early death was one more act of retribution. After all, hadn't he been called Ava his entire life, as if he had been born to fulfill that destiny?

Lord Dufferin was thirty at the outbreak of the war, and, in the tradition of his forebears, he held the office of Under Secretary of State for the Colonies. According to Frederic Mullally's *Silver Salver: The Story of the Guinness Family*—a history of the several branches of the Guinnesses and all their illustrious (and not so illustrious) heirs—Basil "saw the war not only as a summons to personal sacrifice but as an opportunity to 'prove himself' to Maureen and his children."[57] That interpretation was no doubt supplied by Maureen, who, alone among her sisters, allowed herself to be interviewed at length for Mullally's history. Maureen blamed Basil's drinking for "causing unhappiness" between them; his heroics on the battlefield, she believed, were intended to restore Basil's image in her eyes. Others have disputed this view, claiming that Basil had developed such an intense dislike of Maureen that he once went into her closet and slashed all her clothes. Another source claimed that, out of disenchantment with his wife, he left nothing to Maureen in his will except for "the contents of the boot of my car."[58]

No matter his feelings for Maureen, Basil demonstrated the courage and patriotism of many of his class by volunteering for active duty on a dangerous, "hush-hush" mission. He persuaded the War Office to let him go to Burma on "an operation aimed at demoralizing the advancing Japanese troops."[59] With the aid of a Japanese-American recruited from San Francisco, a handful of men moved through the Burmese jungle, broadcasting in Japanese through loudspeakers, a " 'personal message' from the Emperor of Japan," urging Japanese soldiers to put down their arms and return home at once to protect their wives and children. The disinformation campaign did not work, and Operation Burma had to be carried out the old-fashioned way: through the peril and hell of battle.

In a letter to Maureen belying rumors of unhappiness between them and written near Ava on March 17, 1945, Basil wrote:

Darling Maureen,

I am on the last camp of one of my journeys across Burma of which I have now made several. I certainly have seen more of the various fronts in the time I have been here than most people have. I have not enjoyed myself so much since the war began.

Fort Dufferin is still . . . but tonight Ava is said to have been recaptured. So after 3 years Sheridan's earldom is once again in the family. Please congratulate the little fellow on the successful recovery of his property from the invaders.

I am now halfway between two battles and there is a hell of a glare in the far distance, but whether it is Mandalay or Meiktila I am not sure. The only fly in the ointment is that the road I am taking tomorrow was cut yesterday and I shall have to go in a convoy which means very slow travelling and for a nervous old politician some anxious moments on some of the narrower portions . . .

I was so hopelessly wrong about the German war that I don't suppose my stock as a prophet is quoted on the market at all, but it really looks as though the Jap has just about had it in Burma, though how long it will take and how much he will be able to salvage from the wreck is another matter . . .

All my love, darling. I must stop now as it is dark and I ought not to have a light considering all the circumstances tonight. I love you very much you silly old thing and don't forget what I said in my last letter about looking after your inside. I hope we and all the children will be very happy after the war and that in the meanwhile . . . be good as gold and very faithful.[60]

Whatever his motives for persuading the War Office to send him on so dangerous a mission, his last letter to his wife reveals a genuine tenderness toward Maureen, mother of his three children. If similar letters were written to Joan Dunn, they have not surfaced.

Another letter from Lord Dufferin was dashed off and mailed from the jungles of Burma, this one to his children:

I address this to Perdita because she is in the middle!

> *P.O. Box 10207*
> *Calcutta*

Darling Perdita & Sheridan & Caroline,

At the moment I am in a camp in a plain which has got the Japs all round it, so we have to get all our food and ammunition and things dropped to us from aeroplanes every day. But we get plenty so we are all right . . . I was just about the last car to get through on the road before these Japs closed it, so I was in luck.

So now we are like a besieged city in olden days (like Troy) . . . I am writing this in a slit trench as it is six o'clock and the sun is going down so the Japs are shelling us as I'm afraid they are going to attack us again tonight. They attacked us the night before last and got into the middle of our position but we drove them out and counted 300 dead bodies next morning which was jolly good, though they killed a few of ours which was very sad.

Last night nothing much happened but tonight I'm afraid they are going to try again as they are shelling so much. But if you get

this it will mean that I am all right, so don't worry as you will
know before you get it if I'm not. (Later. *And I am!*)

   God bless you my darling Perdita and Caroline and Sheridan
whose town I am so near. Fort Dufferin in Mandalay was captured
yesterday which was nice. Be very good girls, and a good boy.
Work hard, love your mother and daddy, but above all, all of
you, work hard all your lives. I'll write again soon,

Daddy [61]

This letter was dated March 25, 1945, by the censor, the day Lord
Dufferin was killed in action.

John Betjeman, stunned by the death of his friend, helped Maureen write and design a memorial stone to be placed in the family's
Campo Santo at Clandeboye. It read:

IN MEMORY OF

BASIL SHERIDAN,

4TH MARQUESS OF DUFFERIN AND AVA

CAPTAIN, ROYAL HORSE GUARDS

A MAN OF BRILLIANCE

AND OF MANY FRIENDS

HE WAS KILLED IN ACTION AT LETZE ON

MARCH 25TH 1945 AT THE AGE OF THIRTY-FIVE,

RECAPTURING BURMA THE COUNTRY WHICH

HIS GRANDFATHER ANNEXED

TO THE BRITISH CROWN[62]

To express his private grief, Betjeman wrote a haunting elegy, "In
Memory of Basil, Marquess of Dufferin and Ava," published in *New
Bats in Old Belfries.*

   Friend of my youth, you are dead!
   and the long peal pours from the steeple

And you my friend were explorer
and so you remained to me always
Humorous, reckless, loyal—
my kind, heavy-lidded companion.
Stop, oh many bells, stop
pouring on roses and creeper
Your unremembering peal
this hollow, unhallowed V.E. day,—
I am deaf to your notes and dead
by a soldier's body in Burma.[63]

A poem far better, more genuine than any inspired by Helen's Tower.

Two

THE PARISH OF RICH WOMEN[1]

The Guinnesses have been good to the people of Dublin,
but then the people of Dublin have been good to the Guinnesses.
—Brendan Behan[2]

The sisters are all witches—lovely ones to be sure,
but witches nonetheless.
—John Huston[3]

Once, when asked about the origins of the Guinness family, Caroline said that, compared with most Irish families, which can trace their roots back to the oldest families of Ireland, the Guinnesses' earliest traceable ancestor was Arthur Guinness, "who set off in 1750–something clutching a recipe for a black beer with a lot of foam."[4]

But the Guinnesses can in fact boast a three-hundred-year-old family business that has, according to Frederic Mullally's history of the Guinnesses, "survived and flourished through the Napoleanic Wars, the Crimean War, the Boer War, the Irish civil wars and two world wars."[5] The art critic and Picasso biographer John Richardson, who has been on close terms with many Guinnesses throughout his life, described the dynasty and Caroline's relationship to them in the following way:

> *Brewers or bankers, aristocrats or plutocrats, the Guinnesses are apt to be a law unto themselves. This Anglo-Irish dynasty is famously cultivated, brilliant, profligate, witty and beguiling. Caution and abstemiousness are not their forte. Caroline upholds her family's reputation for courage, eccentricity and subversive humor. She most certainly does not hold with the ultraconservative views of some of her cousins.*[6]

Mullally, however, did point out that Ernest Cecil Guinness's appropriation of the ancient Irish title Earl of Iveagh, in 1897, was based on dubious claims, and a number of Guinnesses down the line have used the stepping-stone of their wealth to buy titles or to marry into English and Anglo-Irish aristocracy. (" 'Two things worth living for,' " Gerald Seymour of the banking Guinness line was reported to have said: " 'Finance, and—' banging his fist on Burke's [Peerage]— 'this!' ")[7] Arthur, the Guinness who invented the dark brew that made him and his heirs very rich, was, according to Mullally, "an Anglo-Irish rent collector born about 290 years ago."[8] So the great Anglo-Irish family of Hamilton-Blackwoods could afford to sniff at the parvenu Guinness line, if they were inclined to sniff. In Caroline's case, it was probably her antipathy toward her mother's plans for her, rather than a yearning for ancient bloodlines on both sides of her family, that prompted her dismissive remarks about the Guinness line. That—and her natural tendency to satirize pomp wherever she found it. Didn't she, after all, also make fun of the irreproachable Frederick, Lord Dufferin and Viceroy of India, being fanned by yaks' tails?

There are the banking Guinnesses and the brewing Guinnesses and the less famous missionary Guinnesses. Edward Cecil, the Unionist Protestant who laid claim to the title Earl of Iveagh "to [strengthen] the family's roots in Ireland,"[9] left an enormous sum to his three sons and their children, as well as office buildings and a hotel in America, an oil field in Canada, an African diamond mine, a New Zealand sheep farm, and townhouses and country estates throughout Britain and Ireland. When Edward Cecil died in 1927, he was said to be the second wealthiest man in England.[10]

Caroline's maternal grandfather, Arthur Ernest Guinness (known as Ernest), was Edward Cecil's middle son. He and his brothers, Rupert Edward and Walter Edward, owned three great mansions, each facing the western wall of the gardens at Buckingham Palace. They entertained royally throughout the 1920s and 1930s and launched their remarkable daughters—Rupert, Ernest, and Walter fathered seven girls in all—into London's *haute monde.*

Maureen, Caroline's mother, was the most flamboyant of the Fabulous Guinness Girls, which is how Ernest's three beautiful daughters were described in the society pages (or sometimes as the more alliterative Golden Guinness Girls). Caroline's maternal grandmother was Marie Clothilde "Chloe" Russell, a descendant of Charles II; her father was the fourth baronet, Sir Charles Russell. Maureen was fond of telling people that Chloe's maternal grandfather's sister's great-grandson was the eighth Earl of Spencer, father of Diana, which meant that Maureen and her two sisters, Aileen and Oonagh, could "claim cousinship" with the late Diana, Princess of Wales.[11] Maureen, obsessed by bloodlines, would cling throughout her lifetime to her connections to royalty, particularly her friendships with the Queen Mother and Princess Margaret. In a letter to Caroline she tried to establish that the Boston Brahmin Robert Lowell, Caroline's third husband, was actually a distant relative. ("James Russell Lowell claimed Sir George [Russell] as a kinsman," she wrote to her daughter on August 29, 1973. "Do ask Cal if we were already his kinsmen.")[12]

Like most women of their class and their generation (and this was true of Caroline's generation, as well), the Guinness girls were given numerous coming-out parties and balls in lieu of university education. During their coming-out season in London, the Golden

Guinness Girls, who outshone their four female cousins, threw themselves into the good works that were expected of their class. Maureen showed great enthusiasm for transporting hot meals from London's soup kitchens to invalids living in the slums around Paddington. The sight of this lovely, high-spirited, rich young woman being ferried around London's slums must have baffled and delighted the objects of her charity. Maureen obviously derived great satisfaction from her charitable works and would, later in life, use a portion of her wealth to establish a home for patients suffering from arthritis.

Aileen, the eldest, was the first to marry. In the tradition of Guinnesses and Blackwoods, she married a cousin, the Honorable Brinsley Sheridan Plunket. When the Plunket estate and barony passed to the eldest Plunket son, bypassing Aileen's husband, Ernest Guinness gave the couple a magnificent Gothic castle, Luttrellstown, complete with an ornamental lake on a vast estate bordering the Guinness family seat of Farmleigh. Poor Plunket would die in combat as an RAF flight lieutenant at the age of thirty-eight, a year after his divorce from Aileen. The couple had already produced two pretty daughters, Neelia (Aileen spelled backward) and Doon, both of whom spent much of their childhood in the homes of their cousins, first at Oonagh's Irish estates at Castle McGarrett and Luggala, and later at Clandeboye. Their living away from home may have been a means of shielding them from the marital unhappiness that led to the Plunkets' divorce in 1940, or from the sorrow caused by the sudden death of a third child, Marcia, at the age of three, about which little is known. The art dealer, publisher, and poet Stanley Moss, who was a longtime friend of Caroline's, has intimated that "bad things happened to children on those Irish estates," though no foul play has ever been documented.[13] There would be a tragic and early death among Oonagh's children as well. Perdita thought that her cousin Neelia lived with them because "their mother went to America and abandoned her children. No one ever explained why."[14]

At Luttrellstown Castle, in the discothèque created in the castle's cellar, Aileen Plunket entertained the glamorous, the wealthy, the celebrated: the Aga Khan, Prince and Princess Rainier, the Maharanee of Jaipur, Ursula Andress, Jean-Paul Belmondo. Her guests, however, often had to undergo the indignities of Aileen's practical jokes, a fondness for which she shared with Maureen. Mullally wrote, "The jolly japes practiced on unwary guests might include a bowl of artificial vomit placed at their bedside or a realistic stuffed dummy 'asleep' between their sheets."15

In her late forties, the eldest of the Fabulous Guinness Girls began to cast around for a second husband, whom she discovered in 1956 in New York: a Yugoslavian interior decorator named Valerian Stux-Rybar, upon whom Aileen lavished a great deal of her wealth. The fact that Stux-Rybar was gay didn't seem to deter Aileen, and the marriage lasted seven years before ending in divorce. Stux-Rybar eventually died of AIDS, and Aileen reclaimed her earlier and more respectable married title, the Honorable Mrs. Aileen Plunket. Aileen's grandfather, the Earl of Iveagh, "structured the family trusts pretty tightly. If he had known his granddaughters would bring a Cuban dress designer and a Yugoslavian interior decorator into the family, he'd have cut them off without a penny."16 By the late 1980s Aileen was no longer rich and was being pressed by the Guinness Trust to put Luttrellstown Castle up for sale.

Maureen Constance Guinness, born in 1907, grew up on her father's estate at Glenmaroon with her two sisters, but when the Troubles worsened in 1919, the girls were sent to England. In 1925 she and her sisters came out in London in a series of lavish debutante balls. The most vivacious of the three, Maureen appeared often in the gossip columns; she once gave Sir Oswald Mosley a black eye when he made a pass at her and she swung her handbag in his direction. She married Basil Ava Blackwood, Lord Dufferin, in 1930 and took up residence in Dufferin's gray Georgian house at Clandeboye. A year after her marriage, she acquired an elegant house at 4 Hans Crescent, in the Knightsbridge section of London, and spent as much time as possible in town because she found the decaying Irish mansion gloomy and depressing. "My mother didn't like the country," Perdita remembered.[17]

When she did spend time in Northern Ireland, a new social whirl came to Clandeboye, as John Betjeman noted with distaste. Perhaps he was one of the many guests baffled by her bizarre practical jokes, such as disguising herself as a slatternly servant and asking her male guests, in a thick Irish accent, "D'ye want to *go*, surr?" while directing them to the lavatory.[18]

John Richardson recalled that she always told bawdy stories.

> *The only example I can remember is a story about the beginning of the war . . . about a railway carriage full of slum children being evacuated to the country. And there was no lavatory the children could go to, so the woman in charge had to open the windows and hold the children so they could pee out the window . . . Somehow in this particular carriage was a jockey, and so—Maureen's hooting with laughter at this point—this woman holds up the jockey and tries to get him to pee out the window.*

Perdita observed that, later on, her mother's conversation with her dinner guests "was always about when she was seventeen to twenty-three: 'I was one of the great beauties, with my two sisters, and we were known as the beautiful Guinness girls. I'm sure perhaps you've heard. Every man in London was in love with me, and every man wanted to marry me. The Duke of Devonshire . . . the Duke of ————. Everyone was just mad about me.' " As Maureen grew older, Perdita believed, "she never made anything of her life. She would have liked to be famous. She would have liked to be known as somebody famous of some sort—outside of the society pages."[19]

When Robert Lowell wrote "she loved to lick the palate of her Peke, / as if her tongue were trying a liqueur—"[20] in a poem about Caroline called "Artist's Model," he was satirizing Maureen as a representative of a whole class of Barbara Cartland–like dowagers, according to Caroline. The line actually refers to a Guinness cousin, but Caroline explained that Lowell was lampooning the society matron who lavishes attention on her Pekingese but is just dreadful to her children. Maureen, she said, always had "a Peke . . . you might say, a permanent Peke."[21]

Richardson came to know the three Guinness sisters during the visits he made with his cousins to Oonagh's country house at Luggala. "Maureen was, basically, a perfectly loathsome woman, really monstrous," Richardson believed. "She was grotesque and amazing and rather fascinating." This opinion, extreme as it sounds, was echoed by a number of Caroline's friends, and by Caroline and Perdita themselves. "Caroline loathed her mother," remembered Jonathan Raban, who was a close friend of Caroline's in the 1970s and who now makes his home in Seattle, Washington. "But, then, everyone loathed her mother."[22]

Of course, that was not always the case. Caroline's generation didn't know Maureen in her heyday, when she was one of society's "bright young things" in London between the wars, when every man she met wanted to marry her. But as Maureen aged, the luminous blonde charmer of London society became a parody of her former self, dressing outlandishly, flirting with much younger men, wearing mini-dresses, bedecking herself in heavy makeup and outrageous fur stoles. Richardson crossed paths with her several times on her frequent visits to the States in the 1960s and 1970s. He recalled that "she liked to go to the Miami airport, where she'd buy her shoes . . . which had transparent plastic heels with plastic goldfish in them . . . She was very made-up—a lot of blue eyeshadow, lipstick put on rather badly. A great friend of mine . . . used to hate to go out with her in public because people always turned around and stared. She had blue foxes biting their tails, you know . . . she looked like a whore—an old whore." And yet, it was she who saved Clandeboye from ruin.

After Basil's death, Maureen discovered that Clandeboye had been heavily mortgaged to pay off Basil's disastrous gambling debts. Maureen, in essence, redeemed the estate—the house, the gravel paths, the rolling hills, the forests, the man-made lake in the shape of a shamrock, and the "immense lands and properties beyond the walls, including the town of Crawfordsburn, the seaside resort of Helen's Bay and one half of Killyleagh."[23] Maureen—always shrewd about money and property—bought the estate for £192,000, creating the Clandeboye Estate Company, along the lines of the Iveagh Trust, which had been set up to protect the Guinness fortune and interests. She also made sure that her three children, when they came of age, would inherit a substantial amount of money from her third of the Iveagh Trust, set up by her grandfather. She settled an annual income of £17,030 on each child, as well as income from Canadian holdings, and she gave £50,000—and Clandeboye—to her son as a wedding present. Sheridan had inherited the lands and title at the age of seven, when his father died; Maureen essentially safeguarded his inheritance until he came of age. At twenty-nine, Sheridan married his cousin Serena Belinda ("Lindy") Guinness, the sole daughter of Loel Guinness of the banking line, and took possession of Clandeboye. Caroline and Perdita retained the right to live there as long as they wished.

But if Maureen hoped to express love for her children by seeing to their financial security and making it possible for Sheridan to live the life of a landed aristocrat, her actions came too late. As young children growing up in the nanny's quarters at the back of the house, Caroline, Perdita, and Sheridan had little to do with their mother. Their antipathy toward Maureen was based not only on her vanity and selfishness but on her apparent lack of any maternal feelings toward her three offspring.

Richardson told this story about Sheridan:

Caroline used to say that Sheridan could have been a great tennis player—you know, he was absolutely marvelous, almost up to Wimbledon level—except that he had problems with his adenoids,

and, Caroline said, this was because Maureen was too stingy to have
his adenoids tended to when he was young, so nothing was ever done
about it, and that's why he didn't become a tennis champion . . .
They all had a very rough time with the appalling Maureen.

Perdita felt that Maureen's influence on their childhood was neg-
ligible, because they rarely saw her. "I would say we were not unique
in being reared like this," Perdita recalled. "I mean, you came down
at five o'clock, you went into this room where the grown-ups were
playing bridge. Who they were and what they were I can't remember.
And at six o'clock you went upstairs again . . . You know, children
were seen and not heard. And so long as there was someone upstairs,
theoretically keeping them in line . . . but of course that wasn't always the case." Indeed, the people hired to "keep them in line"
turned out to be, for the most part, neglectful at best and sadistic at
worst, and Maureen seemed not to know or care that some of the nannies she hired were starving and abusing her children. No wonder
Caroline thought of Aunt Oonagh as her ideal of a loving mother who
adored spending time with her children, though Oonagh herself was
eccentric and childlike.

There is much to be said about Oonagh, "far and away the nicest
of the three sisters," according to Richardson, and the one to whom
Caroline was closest.[24] Oonagh was "the least worldly, the most quirk-
ish and odd, and in a way the most bohemian . . . My cousins and I
used to go there and stay [with her] all the time." Oonagh, the youngest of the three, married an English peer, the Honorable Philip
Kindersley, youngest son of Lord Kindersley. Philip and Oonagh had
a son, Gay, who inherited his father's keen skill as a horseman, and a
beautiful daughter named Tessa. Their union, however, ended in divorce in 1936, when Philip abandoned his wife for another woman.
Not to be outdone, Oonagh quickly married the shy, stocky fourth
Baron Oranmore and Browne, and moved her two children from England to the family's Irish county seat in County Mayo. Oonagh saw

to it that Gay and Tessa became Irish citizens, but Philip waged a bitter court battle over their decampment, which resulted in Gay's being sent to his grandparents Lord and Lady Kindersley, so that he could be educated in England. So Oonagh, in effect, lost her first son through divorce; she would soon lose Tessa as well.

Oonagh's love of children was practically "an addiction," according to Mullally, and she soon brought into her family her two nieces—Aileen's daughters, Neelia and Doon.[25] Not long after relocating at Castle McGarrett with her new husband, Oonagh gave birth to another son, whom she named Garech, and, finally, a third son, named Tara. Her boisterous household soon comprised five young children (six, when Gay Kindersley visited on school holidays), headed by Oonagh, a playful, childish woman who earned the reputation of "London's oldest teenager."[26] Since Castle McGarrett, belonging to the Oranmore and Browne family, was modest by Guinness standards, Oonagh's father gave his youngest daughter the lakeside country house at Luggala, in a dramatic setting south of Dublin in the Wicklow Mountains. In this beautiful country house Lady Oranmore entertained artists, writers, and personalities, such as Francis Bacon, John Huston, Cyril Connolly, Brendan Behan. When she wasn't entertaining at Luggala, she flitted from London to Dublin to Paris to New York to Venice, and to her villa at Cap d'Antibes. But Christmas was always spent at Luggala.

John Huston, the rugged American film director who owned a country house at St. Clarens in Galway, was a frequent guest at Luggala. Oonagh and her sisters made a dramatic impression on Huston, a character, by the way, so worldly, bullying, and masterful that he was difficult to impress. Huston described the three sisters:

In 1951, just before starting work on The African Queen, *I went to Ireland for the first time on an invitation from Lady Oonagh Oranmore and Browne, one of the three Guinness sisters. The sisters . . . are all witches—lovely ones to be sure, but witches nonetheless.*

They are all transparent-skinned, with pale hair and light blue
eyes. You can very nearly see through them. They are quite capable
of changing swinish folk into real swine before your very eyes, and
turning them back again without their even knowing it. Or chang-
ing people's shoes—left shoe to right foot and vice versa—so that
they become awkward and stumble about. Or putting the wrong
words into the mouths of pretentious persons, so that everyone, in-
cluding the victim, is appalled at the nonsense they talk.[27]

Oonagh's Christmases were the liveliest; her dinner parties lasted
for days; champagne endlessly flowed; marriages were made and unmade on her beautiful grounds. And then tragedy struck.

In the summer of 1946, the family was at Castle McGarrett, wel-
coming Gay and Tessa home from their English schools for a holiday.
Tessa, just fourteen, was given a routine injection for diphtheria on
August 2 and went upstairs to her room to lie down. Two and a half
hours later she died from cardiac arrest. On that summer afternoon
Oonagh lost her only daughter, a loss from which she never recovered.
She had Tessa's body moved from Castle McGarrett and buried at
Luggala, and she erected a white obelisk beside Luggala's black lake
to commemorate her daughter—not unlike the hovering presence of
Helen's Tower, which had cast such a somber spell over Frederick,
Lord Dufferin, at Clandeboye. The Gothic house, the white sandy
beach, the black lake, the steep granite cliffs of the Wicklow Mountains: Luggala seemed to arrange itself around the obelisk that signi-
fied the grief of the Oranmore and Browne household. At the age of
thirty-six, Oonagh would sometimes dress like Tessa, as if to embody
the memory of her lost daughter. Her marriage became strained and
ended in divorce four years after Tessa's death. Eight years later, Oonagh would marry again, making what her family considered a singu-
larly inappropriate choice: a Cuban dress designer named Miguel
Ferreras, who was several years younger than she, and who, like her
sister Aileen's second husband, would take Oonagh for a great deal of
money.

But, then, Oonagh had never had to worry about money. Her grandfather had set up the ironclad Guinness trusts, reported as worth £200 million in 1945, which would enrich her, her sisters, and all their children. And her father, Ernest Guinness, had given approximately £1 million to each of the Golden Guinness Girls so that they could avoid the steep inheritance taxes levied by England and Ireland.[28]

In 1958, two years after Aileen decided to marry Valerian Stux-Rybar, Oonagh, at the age of forty-seven, secretly married Ferreras in New York. Her marrying in secret showed that Oonagh must have known her choice would stir up disapproval among Guinnesses. Not only was Ferreras foreign, of unknown background, and given to dressing like a matador ("ornamented with gold rings, bracelets and pendants"),[29] he was also a Roman Catholic. And, according to John Richardson, Ferreras was, like Stux-Rybar, "totally gay." Richardson remembered that Oonagh "backed him in a couture business in Paris. . . He took her for the most amount of money!"[30] Shunned by many of her friends and extended family, Oonagh moved abroad with Miguel, and they divided their time between Cap d'Antibes, Venice, and Paris.

They continued to spend Christmases at Luggala, however, and on one occasion Miguel had a serious run-in with the hard-drinking Irish playwright Brendan Behan. Behan was "a regular house guest [at Luggala] from 1955 until his death," wrote Behan's biographer Michael O'Sullivan.[31] According to the story—which Mullally also recounted—Behan was in his cups when he was caught making overtures toward Tara, Oonagh's youngest son.

Behan had been introduced to Oonagh and the festivities at Luggala just before *The Quare Fellow* opened in Dublin, and, indeed, the playwright became a close family friend of long duration. Oonagh herself never believed that Behan was trying to seduce her son, but Miguel Ferreras—perhaps to demonstrate his devotion to Oonagh's large brood, or to demonstrate his manliness—took offense. He invited the very drunk and boisterous writer to step outside and then knocked him to the ground.

Brendan Behan, however—with all his outrageous charm and bad behavior—turned out to be a more enduring houseguest than the unfortunate Señor Ferreras. Oonagh had their marriage dissolved when she discovered that the dress designer was not who he claimed to be. Born José María Ozores Laredo, he had served on the Fascist side in the Spanish Civil War, and later "as an Unter-lieutenant with the German S.S."[32] And he had apparently taken the name Miguel Ferreras from the deceased brother of an old friend. Oonagh's divorce was based on the grounds that "their marriage was never valid, [because] at the time of the ceremony, Lady Oranmore and Browne was, in effect, marrying a man who was legally dead."[33]

If the dissolution—and disillusion—of Oonagh's third marriage seem comic, one more tragedy would be sprung upon the most loving and loved of the Golden Guinness Girls. Tara—handsome, blond, and high-spirited, like his mother—married secretly at nineteen and fathered two children. The marriage broke down, and Tara found himself in court battling his soon-to-be-ex-wife, Noreen "Nicky" Macsherry, for custody of the children. One night, in the midst of the court case, Tara fatally crashed his sports car in the Chelsea district of London. Oonagh was devastated.

Always the mother figure, Oonagh got custody of her grandchildren. She had also adopted two Mexican boys during her marriage to Ferreras, so Oonagh replicated her earlier life at Castle McGarrett, this time in a villa on Cap d'Antibes—entertaining lavishly, devoting affection on four small children, throwing parties that "were led by the pipers and their hostess in prancing, singing 'crocodiles' throughout every room of the villa."[34]

Caroline described Oonagh in a haunting short story called "How You Love Our Lady," which was first published by *London Magazine* and reprinted in *For All That I Found There* in 1973. "How You Love Our Lady," Caroline admitted, was based on the festivities at Luggala, where artists and painters reveled, drank, and talked—endlessly talked. Significantly, the character based on Oonagh is transformed into the narrator's mother. The events, told in flashback, center on school holidays that the narrator, Theresa, spends at Luggala, when the house is filled with guests who quote poetry throughout the night. Theresa's mother can bear the company only of artists.

In Caroline's story, Theresa's mother is romantic, flamboyant, self-destructive, and sad. The carpets in her Georgian mansion are stained with the spilled drinks of her perpetual guests; one room is strewn with mattresses for drunken friends who need to spend the night; she gives herself over to rapturous interludes at the piano, dressed in a velvet dress, with her long hair streaming down her back, as if enchanted by the music. In contrast, painfully shy Theresa feels like a painted Easter egg whose dye comes off in the hand, exposing the drab shell underneath.

Theresa is enchanted and seduced by the poetry and magic of her mother's world, particularly in contrast with her later, grown-up life in New York, when she is married to a banal advertising executive who spends his evenings writing copy for menstrual pads. Her husband accuses her of living in the past, in the Celtic twilight of her enchanted childhood. On one level, the story indicts modern urban life and its debasement of language, but it also dramatizes the danger of living for Art and Beauty. Theresa's mother, in a scene that eerily foreshadows Caroline's description of her mad grandmother conversing with the fairies in *Great Granny Webster*, discourses on elm trees as "the great tutors" of life:

> *Have you ever seen the way that an elm dies, Theresa? An elm doesn't die like other trees . . . An elm dies in secret . . . Once they are dead you can see how the rot has eaten into them so hideously that they are completely hollow.*[35]

At the end of the story, Theresa's beautiful mother inexplicably commits suicide by slashing herself with a carving knife.

In life, as in fiction, Caroline became something of a surrogate daughter to Aunt Oonagh after Tessa's death; the fictional name Theresa is even suggestive of Tessa. Caroline visited Luggala often as a young girl and later during her first marriage, no doubt relishing her aunt's flamboyant affection, and Oonagh would appear at several crucial moments in Caroline's life. Despite Oonagh's childishness and folly, she became the mother Caroline wished she had had, and Oonagh's love of poets and artists would, subliminally, lay the groundwork for Caroline's own choices in life.

Another motif that emerges in "How You Love Our Lady," and also in *Great Granny Webster*, is Caroline's self-portrait of a morbidly shy, deeply silent young girl. In a world in which her mother loves poets and talkers, Theresa feels that her drabness exiles her from that enchanted world, and thus from her mother's affection and regard. She seems to please her mother only when she's reciting a poem for the gathered guests; the rest of the time, Theresa feels she disappoints her mother by her tongue-tied shyness. Teresa's mother tells her that the only sin is to let "the humdrum" steal over her spirit.[36] Brendan Behan himself observed that the only rule at Luggala was not to be tedious. "You may say whatever you like so long as you don't take too long and say it wittily."[37] Drabness, banality—and silence—were the only crimes.

In *Great Granny Webster*, Caroline created an unforgettable character in Aunt Lavinia, based on her Aunt Veronica Blackwood, Basil's only sister, but with a great deal of Maureen, Aileen, and Oonagh weighing in. Lavinia is a *jolie-laide* given to telling outrageous stories, living far beyond her means, engaging in countless affairs with men of all persuasions, lavishing kisses on Poo Poo, her fluffy white poodle. Lavinia's suicide attempt in her elegant marble bath is comic in Caroline's telling ("I had it perfectly planned, darling. It couldn't have been more Roman"),[38] as is an attempted rape of Lavinia by the head psychiatrist at the hospital where she is sent to recuperate from her wrist-slashing.

Like the Oonagh figure in "How You Love Our Lady," Aunt

Lavinia also cherishes her ability to shock and dismay through her outrageous stories, and she too takes aside the young narrator—clearly Caroline—and admonishes her for her silences. "Shyness is all right. But only to a point, and yours can sometimes seem quite oppressive."[39]

Perdita remembered that when she was a young girl, Aunt Veronica took her aside one day and gave her advice about how to conquer shyness. She suggested "the alphabet game" when stuck at a dinner party and at a loss for conversation: simply run through the alphabet in your mind and light on a topic of conversation for each letter. It was a trick Perdita found useful; Caroline, however, suffered terribly for her silences. Ned Rorem remembered meeting her for the first time in Paris in the 1950s and spending a long afternoon in her company, during which time she smoked furiously and never uttered a word. Alan Ross, editor of *London Magazine*, remembered Caroline's phone calls: "After she said 'Hello, it's Caroline,' there would be a long, long silence that it would be up to me to fill. She was very silent until drinking suddenly switched her on, and then she was very dramatic and overelaborate in her conversation."[40]

"After the war there was no longer any doffing of the caps; the war changed all that," remembered Perdita. "That was the best thing to have happened to Northern Ireland. There was more work after the war, and better wages." The Second World War democratized an almost feudal system. Caroline's great-grandfather, the eminent Viceroy of India, had dreamed up projects for the Irish tenants on his estate so that they would not starve. Perhaps it's an irony, then, that the great-grandsons and great-granddaughters of Lord Dufferin's tenants would in their day help keep Lord Dufferin's great-grandchildren from going hungry, for Caroline, Perdita, and Sheridan were being starved by their nannies.

The most sadistic of the lot was a woman remembered only as Miss Alley. Miss Alley may have seemed worse than she was, however, because she was preceded by a much more "nannyish" nanny, a Miss

Barthlomew, remembered affectionately as Nannie Bartie. Perdita recalled her as being "very old, and very nannyish, and very cuddly," all of which Miss Alley was not. When Nannie Bartie left the Blackwoods' employ (probably in a coffin), she was replaced by Nanny Gray, about whom the children had no complaints. "She was nice," Perdita said, "but she surprised us all by getting married at the ancient age of thirty." The next nanny, her name lost to posterity, was carted off to the local mental hospital shortly after joining the household, a scene that struck the three Blackwood children as unbearably funny.

And then came Miss Alley.

Miss Alley—her full name forever repressed by the last living Blackwood—had spent most of her life in India, and she was huge. Her arms were huge; her head was huge; her voice was huge. Her arms were red and covered with the scars of scratched mosquito bites, a legacy of having lived in the tropics. Her hair was pulled back in a tight black bun. With her red arms, her black bun, and her strict, authoritarian ways, she was born to terrify children.

During the war, food was rationed, but Miss Alley would order for breakfast an egg for each of the three Blackwood children, an egg for their cousin Neelia when she was living with them, an egg for herself, and one for the maid. She would then mash up the six eggs with bread and portion off one third of the mixture to be divided among her charges and the maid. She would eat the rest. "She would have four eggs for breakfast," Perdita remembered, "and we would starve!"

Everyone got a pot of jam as part of the war rations, and Miss Alley helped herself to the children's jam. For the early evening meal, she would fix them an undressed salad of lettuce and raw carrot—a "Russian salad," she called it. That was dinner. So of course the Blackwood children and Neelia roamed the vast grounds of Clandeboye—about 5,400 acres then, dwindled from its original 18,000—pestering the tenant farmers and staff on the estate for food. According to Perdita:

The workers really liked us children. They were somewhat permanent—you know, the woodsman and his wife worked in the house, cleaning . . . [there were] carpenters and painters, laundry women, like your own private village. I remember we had this gardener who gave us fruit. He had a lovely name—Isaiah Howe— and his son was named Willie. They would sort of doff their caps when we children came by and he would give us plums.

But one day when they returned to the great house with fruit in their pockets, Miss Alley caught them and accused them of stealing. She threatened to take the children to the head gardener and make them pay for the fruit, and she told them that they would go to hell. Although the children were terrified, they continued to supplement their meager diet with fruit and soda bread given them by workers on the Clandeboye estate. Even so, it didn't keep Sheridan from developing rickets. In photographs of him as a young boy, his legs and arms are woefully thin. Miss Alley was also given to hitting and slapping. "She would hit my brother a lot. She would slap his hands," remembered Perdita.

It was probably Miss Alley who held Sheridan out of the second-floor nursery window by his feet for humming loudly in bed. Sheridan described the incident in an essay, written in 1985, two years before his death, about growing up at Clandeboye.

To most people Clandeboye would seem to be an extremely large house. As a child, however, my personal world was reduced to approximately three rooms at the far end—my bedroom, the day nursery and the night nursery. This was the kingdom of my nanny.

As a child I was extremely frightened of the dark and sought to allay my terror by humming myself to sleep. The noise irritated my nanny . . . and I remember being snatched out of bed at one o'clock in the morning and held out of the window at arm's length with the threat that if I didn't shut up she would drop me . . . I got

my revenge later by peeing on that particular nanny's hatbox—
with the hat in it.[41]

Because the three girls—Caroline, Perdita, and Neelia—were off
at the Rockport Preparatory School during the day, Sheridan bore the
brunt of Miss Alley's sadism. Long after her eventual departure,
Perdita was able to scare Sheridan by threatening to "go get Miss
Alley!"

Meanwhile, their father, when he wasn't drinking heavily, was
kept busy as the Under Secretary for the Colonies and Speaker of the
Senate of Northern Ireland, until he set off for Burma on his fatal
mission. And Maureen was often in London, or was busy entertaining
naval officers headquartered near Clandeboye at Helen's Bay, or planning parties, or indulging in her favorite pastime—bridge.

"We never questioned anything," recalled Perdita. "Nannies
would come and disappear. Things were just the way they were. We
didn't know anything different." She remembered being asked as a
child—probably at one of Maureen's bridge parties—if she was
proud of being a Guinness. Perdita responded, "I'm not a Guinness.
I'm a Blackwood!"

Brendan Behan's cheeky definition of an Anglo-Irishman as "a
Protestant with a horse"[42] underlined the importance of horse breed-
ing and horse riding in Northern Ireland, particularly among the upper classes. Caroline was a naturally good rider. Her special horse was
Silver Millar, and with this spirited creature she won in the class of
riders under twelve at the Balmoral Horse Show in Belfast, in 1942.[43]

"Caroline was a far better rider than I," said Perdita, "as was
Sheridan, but Caroline didn't like all the work that was involved—the
grooming, the caring for the horse. She was what we called 'a front
door rider'; she liked the horse to be brought round to the front door
so that she could mount and then be taken away afterwards. My
mother was like that, too . . . I was the only one who did the work!"[44]

Indeed, Perdita's love of horses led her to use her inheritance, while
still a young woman, to buy the fifty-acre farm practically next door

to Clandeboye, where she now breeds and trains racehorses. Lady P, as she's known locally, is revered in County Down for her horse sense, her kindness, and her charity in conducting riding classes for disabled children from Belfast.

Caroline and Perdita and Sheridan used to ride every afternoon. Caroline's pony, Silver Millar, was hitched to a trap each morning to take the girls to school. "The trap was so dangerous," Perdita said, "it could have toppled over at any minute. We were driven to school in that trap by our groom, not a very nice fellow." Caroline later wrote a sinister, short memoir, "Never Breathe a Word," about this groom and an aborted attack he made on her one night. Perdita did not recall anything about an attack, but she remembered that he used to give young Caroline pills—whether they were vitamins or amphetamines, she didn't know. He may have seen in Caroline the makings of a champion rider and wanted to improve on nature, but the children never figured out what the pills were for, nor did they ever tell their parents. "I don't think he ever molested Caroline," Perdita said, "but he was creepy."

Neither Maureen nor Basil especially liked to ride or hunt. "My love of horses came from Aunt Veronica's genes," said Perdita. "We were never *taught* to ride. Nobody of that generation was ever taught. We just fell off until we stuck on! I think I was seventeen when I had my first riding lesson." In fact, the girls fell off their horses so often that they sustained numerous small fractures, which went untended. Perdita broke her collarbone in a riding accident and never had it set. The bone eventually healed, but it remained crooked. When she went for X rays some years ago, the surgeon asked, "What happened to you? Your vertebrae—every one is chipped!"

"It was from falling off horses. We used to fall off all the time. When we'd come in for lunch, if we *hadn't* fallen off—that was news!" Caroline's left foot was turned inward, and she walked with a slight limp, possibly from a fall.

Their parents were inattentive, and their nannies were horrible, so the Blackwood children had a wild and unsupervised childhood. They were pretty much allowed the run of the estate, sometimes riding their bicycles the two and a half miles along the dual carriageway to the town of Bangor, where they spent the day, bicycling back after dark. Perdita said she was once stopped by a policeman for not having a light on her bicycle.

The two sisters were very close. Caroline's nickname was Ceeje, for "Caroline's joke," and Perdita's was Peeje, for "Perdita's joke." They kept pets, which they adored ("I had my poodle and Caroline had a mouse"). Given their parents' preoccupation with other matters, and given the high turnover of nannies, the children had a lot of freedom. "We children really did just what we wanted to. We ran wild, because nobody knew where we were—they just didn't know or care!"

The great house of Clandeboye infected the imaginations of the three children in different ways. For Sheridan, despite his mistreatment at the hands of Miss Alley, Clandeboye remained for him "an enchanted place," rich with the scents and secrets of a well-run kingdom. There was the "magical workshop reeking of fresh wood shavings and paint,"[45] presided over by Mr. Docherty, the estate carpenter, and even more enchanting was Mrs. Docherty's cottage, where the baking was done and where the always starving Sheridan would be treated to thick slices of warm soda bread. Sheridan learned to ride and to hunt, encouraged by Perdita's passion for horses, though it was an enthusiasm that would leave him by the time he was sixteen, to be replaced by a passion for collecting paintings and objets d'art.

One of Caroline's favorite youthful pastimes was to draw caricatures and cartoons. Perdita thought that Caroline might have grown up to be a cartoonist or an artist. She didn't seem to have any special interest in books, although there is a photograph of her, around the age of three, reading Beatrix Potter in her baby carriage. Her wicked sense of humor came out in her funny drawings of family and friends, and especially of the dreaded schoolmasters and mean boys with whom she and her sister and cousin had to contend at school.

Because gasoline was rationed during the war years, the girls were sent to the closest private school, Rockport Preparatory School, a boarding school for boys, which Perdita, Neelia, and Caroline were allowed to attend as day students. The school provided another dosage of life's daily horrors. Housed in a large gray stone building, not unlike a smaller version of Clandeboye but surrounded on two sides by Belfast Lough, Rockport is now coeducational and, by all appearances, a cheerful, modern school. But in Caroline's day the schoolmasters were harsh, and an inflexible pecking order dominated the schoolyard. Perdita thought that perhaps all the best teachers had been conscripted into the army and were fighting the Germans. What was left were those unfit to serve—or to teach.

There were more unhappy children in that school than I've ever seen since. We were lucky to get out alive. One schoolmaster used to pick me up by my hair and swing me against the desk, and shout, "You will do your math!" The headmaster was frightfully old and didn't seem to know what was going on there. The most brutal teacher later moved away and ended up committing suicide.

Caroline held her own by winning the cup for being "the best all-around" athlete, beating out all the boys. But her account of life at Rockport, in her short memoir called "Piggy," describes her initiation into adult cruelties at the hands of the school bully.

"Piggy" is by far the most disturbing of the four short prose pieces included in the section called "Ulster" in *For All That I Found There.* Renamed the Stoneyport Preparatory School in her memoir, the piece is probably an exaggeration of the nastiness of school-aged boys, but even if the details are embellished, the story has the ring of truth. In it, Caroline tells of taking part in the ritualized tormenting of new boys by aligning herself with a repulsive bully named McDougal, even going so far as to take part in the stoning of a Catholic family living in a run-down cottage near the village of Ballycraig, not far from the school.

The memoir astutely describes the psychology of a bully, who condemns the new boys for "blubbing" and for being "feeble," yet gets his comeuppance by displaying those same behaviors. The two most disturbing aspects of "Piggy" are Caroline's going along with McDougal's cruelty in order to save herself from being his victim, and her description of McDougal's cronies holding down a new boy so that Piggy can pee in his mouth:

> *"Someone hold his nose!. . . Make him open his mouth."*. . . *The golden jet of McDougal's urine would sometimes miss his mouth, splash on to his hair, or his spectacles, trickle down over his tear-stained cheeks.*[46]

In order to keep herself from being victimized by Piggy, who thinks that the presence of a girl at Stoneyport makes the school look feeble, Caroline steals cigarettes and sweet-ration coupons from home to give to her would-be tormentor. She laughs at his cruel jokes and plays the sycophant to avoid his wrath. Ironically, the very fact of Blackwood's being a girl helps bring about Piggy's downfall. He comes to fear her, as if she had "the evil eye."[47]

One of Caroline's earliest prose pieces, "Piggy" has all the hallmarks of her later style and sensibility: her willingness to examine the nastier aspects of human behavior; her matter-of-fact narration of outrageous events; her willingness to reveal her own baser instincts; her mingling of the grotesque and the comic. And even though the story was written in the 1960s, when Caroline was a young woman, "Piggy" suggests that even as a schoolgirl, she already had a sense of the atavistic power her femaleness held over males.

Caroline's memories of growing up in Ulster are further captured in *For All That I Found There*. She was keenly aware of the entrenched prejudices of her Protestant tribe, such as never drinking from a glass "that a Catholic has drunk from. Any such glass should be broken immediately."[48] She also weighs in on what she perceived as the relentless boredom that hung perpetually over Protestant Ulster: "In the wealthy suburbs of Belfast the wives of industrialists went on reading the Bible, drinking their sherry and eating scones."[49]

Caroline then poses the provocative, and unanswerable, question: "If there had been no Catholics, would the Ulster Protestants have found it necessary to invent them," just to relieve the boredom and monotony of everyday life in Ulster?[50]

Perhaps, then, it was liberating for her to leave the horrors of Rockport, and the boredom of Ulster, when, at the age of twelve, she was sent to boarding school, first in Switzerland and then in England. Sheridan had already been sent to school in Switzerland at the age of nine. Perdita would be sent to yet a different school in Switzerland, one that was "so cold that when we woke up in the morning, there was frost on the counterpane." Caroline later claimed that she was sent away in order to recover from a botched tonsillectomy. "I was ill and sent to Switzerland because of health reasons. I had my tonsils out—which was an operation everyone had in those days—and the surgeon was drunk when he operated, and he split my adenoids. It set off a haemorrhage which you can't get at, don't you see? The surgeon's wife had left him that day and he got drunk."[51] Perhaps that's why Maureen had a horror of dealing with adenoids.

In this 1995 account, Caroline displayed her storytelling gifts: wresting horror from a routine childhood experience; depicting the surgeon as drunk; even finding a cause for the hapless surgeon's error. Whether this was a family story, an actual childhood event, or a typically dramatic Caroline invention is unclear. But she did attend Brilliantmont in Lausanne (where, she recalled, all the girls ever did was shampoo their hair and paint their nails) and the Downham School for Girls in Essex.

At least Caroline was not alone at Downham, for her girlhood friend Anne Dunn was there, as were her cousins Neelia and Doon Plunket. Caroline became especially close to Doon, perhaps in part because they looked so much alike—both fresh-faced blond gamines. (In her early photographs, Doon resembles a young Grace Kelly.) However, all three girls were remembered by at least one other boarder at Downham as "unusually slovenly and wild for this boarding school for young ladies. The three Guinnesses always stuck together, and they seemed both wild and clannish to the rest of us."[52] Anne Dunn recalled that Caroline was "very, very shy in those days, very silent and uncommunicative. But she was clever and got the best marks. She and another girl were always at the top of the class."[53] Anne felt that she and Caroline were both eccentric, and therefore were always paired. "We were so unpopular," she recalled, "we always walked together; all the girls were supposed to pair up when walking from their rooms to the school."

Caroline's short story "How You Love Our Lady" is a harrowing account of life in a girl's boarding school. Some of the other girls were sadistic, forcing the newcomers to place their breasts over a towel rack and pricking their nipples with safety pins. The newcomers who screamed were pricked even harder. For someone as modest as Caroline, the ritual must have been as humiliating as it was painful.

Caroline's formal education was completed at Miss Cuffey's finishing school on Merton Street in Oxford. Caroline thought the place was silly, but Perdita, who was also sent to Miss Cuffey's, remembered it as worthwhile and genuinely educational:

> *My mother didn't know quite what to do with me, so she just shoveled me into another school and another school. I should be the most educated person in Europe! Caroline and I were at [Miss Cuffey's], but not at the same time. She was French, and she had this shock of white hair. Somebody set her up in this little house in Oxford with about eight students. Miss Cuffey was very keen on literature and architecture. She was good at making it interesting . . . And there were lots of university things anybody could go to . . . lectures and that sort of thing, with people like David Cecil.*

Caroline claimed that she dressed as a boy in order to attend Oxford lectures while she was a student at Miss Cuffey's, which Perdita thought may have been true, simply to disguise the fact that she wasn't a matriculating student at any of the Oxford colleges. Among their friends, it was still considered unusual for a young woman to pursue a university degree. "I remember one girl went to university and we all talked about her," Perdita said. "We all knew her, and we thought she was quite a weirdo: 'She's going to do what?!' "

While at Miss Cuffey's, both girls were closer to London and to Maureen's immaculate house. Miss Cuffey's was considered the right finishing school to ensure a successful debutante season, and the girls were often invited to weekends at their friends' country homes. But that always posed a problem. Perdita remembered that Maureen usually neglected to give them money for the train fare, and the poor girls would arrive penniless and have their fares paid by their friends' parents. Not only that, but Perdita also recalled that the London house never had any food. "I'd come home for weekends and I'd starve— there would be nothing, and the kitchen would be locked up. Maybe some stale old cornflakes. 'The Mother' was completely indifferent to food. And this was in a double house with two formal dining rooms, one suitable to seat forty!"

It also bothered Perdita that Maureen never went to the "plane or the train or the bus or wherever" to greet them or, later, to see them off when they returned to school after a holiday. "She had absolutely no interest." But Maureen did take a keen interest in the thing she cared most about: launching her marriageable daughters into London society.

In 1949, Caroline made her debut at a series of balls arranged by her mother. "Caroline didn't resent it as much as I did," said Perdita. "She was much more social than I was. She didn't want to be in the country with animals, you see, so she didn't fight it. I think she did like London life; I never heard her say she didn't." But Caroline did say that she was always miserable at debutante balls, and there was one in particular that she would never forget. It was a grand affair given by the legendary hostess Lady Rothermere (who soon after became Mrs. Ian Fleming), with Princess Margaret and the Queen Mother in attendance, and, of course, Lady Dufferin, with her new husband in tow. The previous year, Maureen had remarried a man "young enough to be Caroline's boyfriend," according to Perdita, an antiques dealer and retired army officer named Major Desmond "Kelpie" Buchanan. Maureen, ever mindful of her place in *Burke's Peerage*, however, continued to use the title Marchioness of Dufferin and Ava. Lady Rothermere's ball was, as far as the guests were concerned, great fun. But for Maureen, the evening would be a disaster.

"Princess Margaret was among the guests," Caroline later wrote in a memoir about the event for *The New York Review of Books*, "and could immediately be seen on the parquet floor wearing a crinoline and being worshipped by her adoring set, who were known at the time as 'the Smarties.' "[54] Because Princess Margaret was a devotee of popular music who also smoked, drank, and flirted, she was by far the most approachable of the royal family and was popular with London's social set. She was indulged and pampered and treated like a pal, that is, until she would suddenly draw herself up to full height and snub "the socially inept," letting them know that they had just "offended the daughter of the King of England."

Late in the evening, according to Caroline, Princess Margaret was seized by a desire to add to the festivities by singing a medley of Cole Porter tunes, which she sang "hopelessly off-key." Her audience was nonetheless cheering and asking for more, when, suddenly, a hiss emanated from the back of the ballroom. Someone was booing the princess!

Princess Margaret left the stage amid a flurry of ladies-in-waiting, while the astonished revelers looked around for the source of the jeering. Caroline felt that the bejeweled ladies and the gentlemen in white tie and tails had been just as appalled by Princess Margaret's singing as had the mysterious heckler, but they had been too "gagged by snobbery" to protest.

Two arty guests had showed up—gate-crashed, by some accounts—and one of them had booed the princess. For Caroline, the two bohemian guests had turned a stuffy bore of a ball into a chaotic and delightful event. For Maureen, it was the beginning of trouble, real trouble, between her and her firstborn, because the fellow who had booed Princess Margaret was the iconoclastic Anglo-Irish painter Francis Bacon. And Bacon had arrived with his young friend and fellow artist, the wolfishly handsome Lucian Freud.

Three

WHEN CAROLINE
MET LUCIAN

One of the joys of art is that it introduces a
new hierarchy into the world.
—Christopher Bram[1]

Lady Rothermere—Ann Fleming—took Caroline under her wing and became, for a short while during Caroline's early years in London, another surrogate mother, temporarily replacing Aunt Oonagh, who was spending more time away from England. Lady Rothermere, born Anne Charteris, was a landed aristocrat whose parents had been part of the privileged intellectual set known as the Souls. Because her mother died at a young age, Anne was raised mostly by governesses and by her beloved grandparents, the Earl and Countess of Wemyss, at whose country seat—the beautiful Gloucestershire estate called Stanway—Anne had spent her childhood. The dark-haired, sharp-profiled, green-eyed Anne—she later dropped the *e* for the less formal spelling Ann—was elegant, witty, intelligent, and highly social. The insouciant art curator Roy Strong, who knew everybody in London, described her as "tall and commanding, almost gaunt to look at, with marvelous eyes. She looked as though she disapproved of everything and everybody as she presided over those gatherings, swooping from time to time as it were from her perch, cigarette in hand, her arm and hand movements at angles to her body in the manner of the twenties."[2]

She was to become one of the most celebrated hostesses of her day.

Her first marriage, at nineteen, to the sporty Baron Shane O'Neill, was anything but a love match. She had two children with O'Neill, but came close to divorcing him in order to marry the second Viscount Esmond Rothermere. At the same time, however, she was carrying on a serious dalliance with the very dashing Ian Fleming, who was smitten but wary of marriage. The three managed a sociable *ménage à trois*, dining together and playing bridge while Baron O'Neill saw action in Italy. His death on the battlefield in 1942 freed Ann to marry Lord Rothermere three years later, though she said that if Ian Fleming had proposed marriage, she would have immediately canceled her wedding to Esmond. In any event, the marriage proved but a small obstacle, and Ian and Ann continued their affair. In 1948, Ann became pregnant by Ian, but her premature daughter died eight hours after a cesarean delivery. Grief for their lost daughter drew Ann and Ian closer. Ann became pregnant again in 1952, divorced Lord Rothermere, and she and Ian were married at Fleming's villa in Jamaica. Some of Ian's friends and family felt that Ann had "trapped" Ian into marriage by allowing herself to become pregnant again; having lost their daughter, Ian finally had to do the honorable thing. But others felt that Ann was Ian's one true love. Her marriage to Fleming, however, like her first two marriages, was troubled. (A friend once said about Ann's marriages that "something seems to go wrong in the taxi from the registry office.")[3] The Flemings' life together in Jamaica, their flirtations and affairs among the English "ex-pats"— millionaires and black sheep who owned homes in and around Montego Bay—became the backdrop for Noel Coward's late play *Volcano*. Their marriage produced a son, Caspar Robert Fleming, and lasted until Ian Fleming's death in 1964. Caspar, at twenty-one, would die by his own hand. "I suppose that Ann must have been a terrible if memorable mother," Strong said. "She was a woman of great loves and hates."

Before her marriage to Fleming, Ann had been attracted to the newspaper baron Lord Rothermere in part because of his ownership of the *Daily Mail* and her keen interest in the newspaper business. She felt that her husband's journalistic connections would supply her table with a rich coterie of writers and intellectuals, for Ann was an inspired hostess, mixing political figures and aristocratic bridge-players with bohemian artists, writers, and generally flamboyant characters. "[Her] gatherings did have the quality of a work of art which was peculiarly English," Strong recalled, mingling such personages as Lady Diana Cooper, Roy Jenkins, Peter Quennell, Cecil Beaton, Cyril and Barbara Connolly, Alan Ross, Claud Cockburn, T. S. Eliot, Stephen Spender, Evelyn Waugh, Somerset Maugham, and Noel Coward (whose villa Fleming had purchased in Jamaica and rechristened Goldeneye). Like a less eccentric Lady Oranmore, Lady Rothermere opened her homes to literary London, receiving their confidences and dining out on their troubles. "Acid and sharp-tongued"—Strong again—"she liked to be given as much as she gave, and nothing pleased her more than a verbal fracas at her table as two *éminences* would set out to demolish each other." Talent, beauty, and wit really won her heart, which is how Lucian Freud entered the picture.

Far from being a gate-crasher, Freud was an adored young friend of Ann's, one of "Ann's gang," though some of her well-born family and friends took offense at her mingling of the socially superior with the artistically gifted. At one of Ann's dinner parties, "Ann's querulous brother-in-law, Eric Dudley, express[ed] disgust at the sight of the painter Lucian Freud absent-mindedly munching a bouquet of expensive purple orchids."[4]

It was probably Ann Fleming who helped to arrange Caroline's first job as a journalist. After leaving Miss Cuffey's in 1949, at the age of eighteen, Caroline began working for *Picture Post*, a popular magazine published by the Hulton Press, along the lines of *Paris-Match* and *Look*, but with a more political bent. *Picture Post* published "picture-stories" on current events and social issues, including articles and interviews by a number of prominent writers, such as H. G. Wells and Cyril Connolly (who interviewed Aldous Huxley for the magazine in 1948, in part to make amends for having earlier savaged Huxley's *Point Counter Point* in *The New Statesman*).[5] Its founding editor was Stefan Lorant, a Jewish refugee from Hungary. *Picture Post* had been especially strong in its coverage of the war and its encouragement of England's war effort (Stefan was worried that "the democracies intended to deal with Hitler" and that he would be "handed back" to the Germans).[6] Decidedly anti-Fascist, the magazine earned a reputation for being provocative and left-leaning, which would have appealed to Caroline; perhaps it laid the groundwork for Caroline's own socialist tendencies—or at least for her reputation for having them.

Caroline described her job as writing articles on a whole range of subjects, from politics to horse racing—articles that were then severely criticized by the editors. She later said the training taught her discipline. Though it would be several years before she began to write seriously and think of herself as a journalist, the job at *Picture Post* was her introduction to the writing life.

Caroline later claimed that the demise of *Picture Post* ended her job at Hulton Press, but she actually left long before its last issue, in May of 1957. (The magazine went out with a whimper, having lost its focus and its gravity.) She appears to have left her nine-to-five job as a fledgling journalist because something far more exciting was unfolding in her life: Lucian Freud had begun to pursue her.

Smitten at their first meeting at Lady Rothermere's ball, twenty-six-year-old Lucian began to drop in on eighteen-year-old Caroline at the Hulton Press offices. Ann encouraged the match, even though Freud was still married to Kitty Garman, the illegitimate daughter of Kathleen Garman and Jacob Epstein, England's most famous sculptor.

Lucian had married Kitty in 1948, and the couple had their first child, Anne, the same year. But by 1951, Lucian had fallen seriously in love with Caroline.

Lucian had always been attracted to waifish women with large eyes—his early portraits of Kitty Garman are disturbing explorations of her wide-eyed vulnerability. Caroline herself thought that Lucian was in search of a girl with *les yeux grandes* to use as a model, but it was, of course, much more than that. At eighteen, Caroline was fair-haired, disheveled, slender, athletic, intense, puckish, and shy. She no doubt satisfied Lucian's aesthetic sense, but she also possessed intelligence and courage. And, perhaps equally important, she was an aristocrat and a Guinness heiress. Hovering around her like an aura was the prospect of some part of her grandfather Ernest Guinness's £200 million trust.

"There's no greater snob in England," according to Jeremy Lewis, Cyril Connolly's most recent biographer, "than an aristocratic bohemian. And the aristocrats who hobnobbed in bohemian circles were tremendous snobs. It was a kind of symbiotic relationship: the aristocrats paid for things and funded the artists, the artists provided entertainment and danger."[7] Freud definitely provided entertainment and danger for the Ann Flemings of London society, but as a painter, a "foreigner," and a German Jewish émigré, Freud had an insecure foothold in that world during the late forties and early fifties. First, there was the problem of money, since it was long before the days when a Freud canvas would command $3.3 million.[8] Lucian once took the boat from England to Jamaica to visit the newly married Flemings at Goldeneye and arrived with just ten shillings in his pocket—"his last."[9] And his German Jewish status, complete with middle-European accent, made him a fascinating but slightly suspect creature among the well-born. The frightful snob Evelyn Waugh early on took exception to Freud's presence at Ann's social gatherings. He had long disliked Lucian, whom he considered an upstart, a parvenu, a foreigner, "a jew." In 1951 he wrote to Nancy Mitford:

I went to London for the General Election—just like last time, same
parties and same parties . . . [Duff] Cooper got veiners with a jew-
ish hanger-on of Ann [Rothermere's] called "Freud." I have never
seen him assault a jew before. Perhaps he took him for a Spaniard.
He has very long black side-whiskers and a thin nose.[10]

In October of the same year, Waugh again wrote to Mitford: "Yes,
I don't like Freud. I knew him before he got into society & didn't like
him then."[11] And, in November, "Freud takes Princess Margaret to
night clubs in saffron socks."[12] He complained to Ann Fleming about
several of her closest friends—Cecil Beaton, Alistair Forbes, Peter
Quennell, as well as Freud, calling them "her fuddy-duddies."[13]

Lucian's social climbing had a Proustian scent; like the Narrator
of *À la recherche du temps perdu*, he would spend his youth in the
service of society, art, and love. The combination of wealth and title—
especially to a disenfranchised émigré who had to earn his British citizenship—was all the more seductive, because the Freuds had
been driven out of a once secure world in which the Freud patri-
arch had exerted a sublime influence. Lucian's social climbing may
also have come about when he realized that in a society as hierarchi-
cal as England's, talent—even genius—is not enough. An indefatiga-
ble worker, consumed by his painterly ambitions and well aware of
his gifts, Lucian perhaps launched himself into society in service
of his art. Or one can interpret his willingness to suffer the anti-
Semitism and snobbery of Waugh and his ilk because, as the grandson of one of the premier intellectual shapers of the twentieth
century, Freud knew that his lineage was as good as—better than—
that of many of the social luminaries around Ann Fleming's table.
The subtle war between aristocracy and meritocracy continues. Although he has lived in London since 1933 and became a British subject in 1939, Lucian is still thought of in some quarters as a foreigner.

Though many of the men in Ann's circle were suspicious of young
Freud (including Ann's husband, Ian Fleming), the women felt

differently. To his great advantage was Freud's fatal attraction for upper-class women.

Freud's models were usually the wives and daughters of England's titled aristocrats. His collectors and patrons were from the same interconnected, even cloistered milieu. Among them was Lady Jane Willoughby (Baroness Willoughby de Eresby, "one of the most ancient [titles] in England"),[14] who is Freud's "Woman in a Fur Coat, 1967–8." Penelope Cuthbertson, before her marriage to Caroline's cousin the Honorable Desmond Guinness, sat for "The Naked Girl" and other paintings (jokes were later made about the portrait depicting "Penny's parts"). The Honorable Jacquetta Lampson, who married Viscount Eliot, the tenth Earl of St. Germans, was also a frequent model and close friend of the painter. Freud painted Lady Annabel Goldsmith's two daughters, Janie Longman and India Jane Birley.[15] Another aristocrat, Susanna "Susie" Chancellor, wife of Alexander Chancellor, the former editor of *The Spectator*, has been identified as the lady with the whippets ("Double Portrait").[16] Lady Belinda "Bindy" Lampton sat for a number of Freud's paintings in the early 1960s and later served as the model for "Woman in a Butterfly Jersey."[17]

Daniel Farson, the late photographer, writer, and media personality, believed that Lucian simply "cultivate[d] the aristocracy because he [found] the people more interesting,"[18] a view shared by Lucian's friend Catherine Lambert, former director of the Whitechapel Art Gallery and one of the women who posed for Freud: "A pattern began in the early 1940s that demonstrates how consistently Freud has made his best works from people he wants not to disappoint or bore."[19] But the attraction seems to have been deeper than that and more complex than the usual patron-artist relationship. Even if Freud had been temperamentally suited for the role of faithful husband, which he apparently was not, Kitty Garman's biggest drawback as a wife for Freud may simply have been—in the opinion of one of Freud's former paramours—her Cockney accent.

"He was a snob," one of his former girlfriends has anonymously offered. "He was always put off by the fact that the Epstein girl—Kitty—had a Cockney accent. Of course, Caroline was just the opposite. And he never stopped thinking about his famous grandfather. All the time quoting his grandfather . . ."

As one of Freud's critics observed, "Freud has had a definite class system of women in his life—strong aristocrats and feckless waifs."[20] In Caroline, he found a rare combination of both. And, as the ultimate "insider's outsider," in the art critic John Russell's phrase, Freud was, at least at first, drawn to the "insider" status Caroline was born to.[21]

A friend of Caroline's later testified, "Oh, Lucian's a *frightful* snob! That was never in dispute. Right from the beginning he wanted Society with a capital S and he probably thought of Caroline as his entry ticket."[22] Another close friend of Caroline's, Cornelia Foss, felt that "Lucian was in love with Caroline and everything she stood for."[23]

But if others saw Lucian's interest in Lady Caroline as part of the symbiotic relationship between aristocrats and artists, Caroline did not. She had been amused and impressed by the iconoclastic behavior of the raffish Bacon and the dandyish Freud at Lady Rothermere's ball. At one point, Caroline recalled, Lucian had tipsily fallen over a sofa that Princess Margaret was sitting on and toppled right into her lap. Just as Freud needed the patronage of English aristocrats, Caroline needed whatever it took to tear down the gates of "the Mother's" bridge-playing, upper-class, Anglo-Irish world. If given a choice between casting her lot with those "gagged by snobbery" or going with those who could provide entertainment and danger, her choice was clear.

And then there was Lucian Freud's devastating beauty.

Caroline described Lucian as Byronic, a man whose very presence transformed daily life into something magical. His disturbing blue-green, close-set eyes gave him an expression of marked intensity. He didn't have to assert his personality to be noticed; he had the fine, sharp features of a bird of prey. Women of all social strata—and men, too—were drawn to him. Caroline's girlhood friend Anne Dunn, who had had an affair with the painter before his marriage to Caroline, believed that "a lot of men and women were in love with Lucian. They would then fall in love with Lucian's girls if they couldn't be with Lucian, as sort of the next best thing."[24] Ned Rorem, who met Lucian in London and then again in Paris at the salon of the aristocratic doyenne Marie-Laure de Noailles, thought him "solemn, smart, and fetching . . . (was he queer? could one ever tell with the English?)."[25] Simone de Beauvoir, having spotted him in the Gargoyle Club in Soho, indicated that he "was the only man present she found attractive enough to go home with."[26] His handsomeness was overcast with a tragic glamour, an aura made of the evocative power of the name Freud and the vestiges of Lucian's childhood as an émigré, a Berliner with a slight foreign accent making his home and reputation among the English. *Paris-Match* called him "*un dandy tragique nommé Freud.*"[27] Stephen Spender described him as "totally alive . . . like something not entirely human, a leprechaun, a changeling child, or, if there is a male opposite, a witch."[28] Freud's fellow Soho habitué Daniel Farson described him as a creature who "slide[s] into a room with an air of apprehension and a sideways glance in case a crucifix or ray of sunlight might suddenly appear."[29]

Lucian was born in Berlin on December 8, 1922. In 1933, while Caroline was starving on the ancestral Dufferin estate among the ancient forests and man-made lake, Lucian was escaping, with his brothers and parents, from a Berlin threatened by the rise of Nazism. The Freuds were well-to-do bourgeoisie who vacationed in the Alps and lived near the Tiergarten. Ernst Freud, Sigmund's second son and Lucian's father, was an architect. When the Nazis came to power, in 1933, Ernst and Lucie Freud had the foresight to move with their three young sons to London and settle in Hampstead with other European émigrés.

Lucian, the middle child, was named after his mother, Lucie Brasch, who would later be the subject of many of his paintings, including a drawing he made of her right after her death ("The

Painter's Mother Dead") in 1989. Lucie Brasch absolutely doted on her middle son. Caroline later described Lucian's relationship with his mother as "fraught," and she found his many paintings of her, many done after she became ill, "terrifying."[30] Lucian can also be compared with Proust in his devotion to his mother. She coddled and cossetted him and denied him nothing. In later life, Lucian, like Proust, would seek to captivate those he loved through the obsessive use of his art.

Bruce Bernard, one of Freud's oldest friends and coeditor of the most complete published catalog of Freud's work, wrote briefly about Lucian's childhood, noting that Lucian and his brothers were not really brought up as Jews. They didn't understand that German anti-Semitism and the rise of Nazism had anything to do with them. In fact, Freud's mother "once had to tell Lucian to stop drawing swastikas, which he was doing in imitation of his schoolfriends."[31]

Though young Freud grew up protected in a comfortable, upper-middle-class family, the mere fact of his immigrant status in London must have left its mark. If nothing else, Lucian would have absorbed some of his parents' anxiety as they made up their minds to leave Berlin.

The anxiety of middle-class Jewish Berliners in the years before the war was widespread, and would be expressed outright in a number of Lucian's earliest paintings. The fear and uncertainty of immigration may have been the catalyst that jolted Lucian into art: he produced his first drawings at the age of twelve. At fifteen, he studied sculpture with John Skeaping at the Central School of Arts and Crafts in London and began working in oils. When he was seventeen, his drawings were reproduced in an issue of *Horizon*, the literary magazine founded by Cyril Connolly and Peter Watson.

An early, almost crude painting of Lucian's called "The Refugees" depicts an ill-assorted "family" of seven refugees of different nationalities: an Asian woman; an older, Eastern European male wearing the dark glasses of the blind; figures with varying shades of dark skin, including two youths and a hideous child sticking out its tongue in a menacing grimace. (At least one critic suggested that the hideous infant is Lucian's jeering self-parody.) The figures are stiff and distorted, against a flat, black sea, upon which are two fragile wisps of boats. The painting, executed in 1941–42, when Freud was about twenty, evokes the grim wartime caricatures of George Grosz and shows no trace of the consummate realist Freud was to become. Except for the exhausted faces of his subjects, there are no other signs of life; none of Freud's iconic birds or his botanically accurate renderings of plant life. "The Refugees" is expressionistic, ugly, and powerful. Equally disturbing is Freud's "Evacuee Boy," also painted in 1942. Again, the face and figure are distorted. The boy's teeth resemble jagged rat's teeth; the close-set eyes are crazed with exhaustion. The heavy black background, with faint smears of oxblood, makes the somber portrait—or self-portrait?—even more oppressive. Though the painting is called "Evacuee Boy," Freud was painting his counterlife—his life in Nazi Germany if Ernst and Lucie hadn't had the funds, the connections, and the foresight to escape.

Lucian's famous grandfather was brought safely to London by Ernst and Lucie Freud, and was settled in a house in Maresfield Gardens, near their apartment. Sigmund Freud encouraged his grandson's artistic leanings; he gave him reproductions of Pieter Brueghel the Elder's "Seasons." Caroline always thought that Lucian was especially close to his grandfather, whom he remembered as funny, quick-witted, and fond of jokes, not the grim, Jewish paterfamilias he's been made out to be. It's perhaps a testament to how deeply Lucian felt about his grandfather that he didn't attend Sigmund Freud's funeral in 1939, a year after the doctor left Vienna for London.

Lucian was the most spoiled and protected of the three brothers. Bruce Bernard observed that Lucian liked being known as bad-tempered, more at home with animals than with humans.[32] His father once introduced him to a friend by saying, "This wild animal is my son."[33] Lucian was sent to Dartington Hall in Devon, a progressive, coeducational boarding school, where he learned English and developed a passion for horses and horseback riding. His brothers, Stefan and Clemens, were enrolled with him. (Clemens is now Sir Clemens

Freud, a popular broadcaster, gourmet, and former Member of Parliament. The two brothers are said to be estranged.) The parents later sent Clemens and Stefan to St. Paul's preparatory school in London, and Lucian to Dane Court, Bryanston, in an attempt to instill more discipline in him than he had received at Dartington.

While at Bryanston, young Freud made a remarkable sandstone carving of a three-legged horse, which his father submitted to the Central School of Arts and Crafts in Holborn. Lucian was admitted to the school on the basis of this single, and singular, piece of sculpture.

After taking classes at the Central School of Arts and Crafts, in 1939 he enrolled in the East Anglian School of Drawing and Painting in Dedham, where his mentor was the artist and horticulturalist Sir Cedric Morris. Morris, born in Wales, was the ninth Baronet of Clasemont, and he would have a discernible influence on young Freud. Morris had founded the East Anglian School with his lifelong companion, the artist Arthur Lett-Haines, and it was run in a private house in a loose, unstructured manner for a handful of students.

Sir Cedric Morris's interest in botany and botanical drawings may have inspired Lucian's precise renderings of flowers and plant life. His work would also stand in stark contrast to English "tastefulness" in painting, an attitude that would be executed with even greater effrontery by his most famous pupil. As Catherine Lambert observed, Morris's own cartoon-like figures, with large, exaggerated eyes, probably influenced Freud's early drawings and paintings of flattened, staring creatures, like his series of paintings of Kitty Garman ("Girl With Roses," "Girl in a Dark Jacket," "Girl With a Kitten," "Girl With Leaves," and "Girl in a White Dress").[34] Like his teacher, Freud experimented with abstraction and expressionism in his early work, but he steadily moved toward strict representation, even when it meant going against the prevailing movement and, for a time, being considered retrograde. ("Freud has been described as both the *greatest* and the *only* Realist painter of our time," Bruce Bernard wittily observed.)[35]

Morris's affection for and devotion to his young charge are

suggested by a portrait he made of Lucian in 1940, now owned by the Tate Gallery in London. And his devotion was proved in another way. One night when Lucian was up late, smoking in one of the studios with a friend, the building caught fire and burned to the ground. The incident has always been called an accident. It foreshadowed a disturbing quality associated with Freud his entire life: a brooding sense of danger. Rather than expelling him, Morris invited young Freud to stay at his private home at Benton End, Hadleigh, Suffolk, where he bred irises and where he and Lett-Haines would reestablish their school. But Freud had had enough structured schooling, even in unstructured places like Dartington and East Anglian, and in 1941 he took off for Liverpool and joined the merchant navy. He then spent a few miserable months at sea before receiving a medical discharge for tonsillitis.

Far from being condemned for his carelessness in burning down the school, Lucian found that an older generation of gay artists, intellectuals, and patrons were fascinated by him and by the very "bad boy" qualities that would no doubt have gotten a less attractive pupil expelled. Bruce Bernard, no stranger to Soho's demimonde in postwar London, wrote, "Freud became involved with the important homosexual stratum in British cultural life . . . part of a discreet faction which would exercise an increasing influence in the British equivalent of avant-garde culture."[36] Besides Sir Cedric Morris and Lett-Haines, the group would soon include *Horizon*'s financial backer, the elegant art patron Peter Watson.

Watson subsidized a number of young artists living in London and Paris. During the war he had supported the London painter Graham Sutherland and the Glaswegian painters Robert Colquhoun and Robert MacBryde ("the two Roberts," as they were known in their Soho haunts). As a cofounder of *Horizon*, Watson provided the funds and the perfect working partnership for Cyril Connolly, preferring to stay in the background and granting Connolly complete editorial control. *Horizon* published Lucian's drawings in 1939 and again in 1944. "The Refugees" hung in the magazine's office.

Watson, the son of a baronet who had made his fortune in the manufacture and sale of margarine, was devoted to pleasure, including London's rough trade. He was melancholy, generous, and well-liked. Cecil Beaton, who fell in love with him, wrote, "Peter's acute sensibility, subtlety of mind, wry sense of humour and mysterious qualities of charm made him unlike anyone I had known."[37] Edith Sitwell once playfully referred to him in a letter as "Trumpet Lips";[38] in his photographs he resembles a sensuous, canny elf. Another of his protégés, the painter Michael Wishart, who chronicled his sentimental education in his memoir *High Diver*, wrote, "Peter was a dandy and dilettante *par excellence* . . . [He] spent a lot of time in the pursuit of love; a thankless task for so fastidious a homosexual, despite his haunted beauty. By no means an optimist, he aspired to a *protégé* whose beauty and sex appeal matched his own creativity."[39]

Lucian promised to be just such a protégé, and in 1943 Peter Watson set up Freud and another handsome young painter, John Craxton, in a studio in the then-derelict Paddington section of London. It was a part of London that appealed to Lucian, with its postwar destruction of once grand Georgian houses, now broken up into bed-sitters and inhabited by the working poor and—in Catherine Lambert's phrase—"costermongers, villains and thieves."[40]

John Richardson, who has remained a lifelong friend of the painter, wrote that "Paddington permeates Freud's painting as deeply as Tahiti permeates Gauguin's. Whether or not it manifests itself in Lucian's imagery, the funkiness of the place, as of an unmade bed, and its slightly shabby light seep into virtually all his work and Londonize it."[41]

Michael Wishart, then just twelve but already an artist, spent a lot of time at Lucian and Craxton's Paddington studio, sleeping over during school holidays on the floor. Freud made a number of pencil drawings of young Michael: "Boy With a Pipe," "Boy on a Bed" (in which Wishart lies recumbent, nude, holding his penis), and "Boy With a Pigeon." ("When the bird died," Wishart later wrote, "he went on drawing until it stank and turned to mould.")[42]

In 1944 Lucian had his first exhibition, at Lefevre Gallery. Because the wartime blitz was still going on, his show did not attract a great deal of attention, but those who noticed it felt that Freud's was definitely a talent to watch. Caroline later said:

> *He had a reputation in Soho—people thought he was going to be a great artist. But he wasn't much liked by the galleries. Everyone thought his work was too ugly, even the work we now think of as really pretty. They thought the portraits were hideous. Everyone said, "Oh, the nightmare would be to be painted by Lucian, because he makes everyone so ravaged."*[43]

Freud's early work was indeed disturbing, having moved from the grotesque but powerful expressionism of paintings like "Evacuee Boy" to more placid surfaces, which focused on brilliantly drawn dead animals, with deadpan titles like "Dead Bird," "Dead Monkey," and "Rotted Puffin."

Following Sir Cedric's example, Freud in the fall of 1946 left for Paris, a city that embraced him wholeheartedly, and he settled in the Hôtel d'Isly on the corner of the Rue Jacob and the Rue Bonaparte. Michael Wishart was also in Paris, and for a while the two shared Freud's hotel room. "The arrangement worked well," Wishart later wrote, "as usually either Lucian or I did not return overnight."

> *During the days I explored Paris, or sat to Lucian. He painted me as a birdseller in the Marche aux Oiseaux on the Ile de la Cité, where we went every Sunday morning. Sitting to Lucian is a trial comparable to undergoing delicate eye surgery. One is obliged to remain absolutely motionless for what seems an eternity. He was distressed if I blinked while he was painting my thumb. However, the extraordinary wit and originality of his conversation . . . was so rewarding that I underwent this torment willingly, quite apart from the great admiration I have always felt for his work.*[44]

While in Paris Lucian met the painfully young *poète maudit* Olivier Larronde and made a witty painting of two stiff parrots in a red birdcage, called "The Birds of Olivier Laronde" *[sic]*. Larronde was a tragic figure—an opium addict, a drunk, a sad dandy devoted to Cocteau and Mallarmé. He was a friend of Picasso's. Giacometti completed more than fifty portraits of Larronde, who would die at the age of thirty-eight. Cyril Connolly would publish his poems in *Horizon*, accompanied by Lucian's drawing of a rose.

Young Freud also met Marie-Laure de Noailles, Picasso, and Giacometti. An anonymous friend offered this description of Freud's Parisian hiatus: "While, in Paris, some of us hung out at the Café de Tournon and wondered if we dared call on Giacometti, Lucian was spending his time with Giacometti, [Boris] Kochno, [Christian] Berard and Marie-Laure de Noailles."[45] John Richardson worried that "Lucian appeared to fit so naturally into the postwar avant-garde Left Bank life that some of us were afraid dismal, philistine London would lose him."[46]

Peter Watson financed a trip to Greece for his two protégés; the location cure worked on John Craxton, who would ultimately make his home in Crete, where the light is beautiful and abundant. But some part of Lucian craved the dilapidated gloom of Paddington, and he returned to England and to his studio on Delamere Terrace.

It was around this time that Lucian met and had a brief romance with Joan Wyndham, the diarist who wrote three wartime journals about her madcap life among artists and bohemians in London. What Lucian "really liked," according to Joan, was to pick up young women waifs in the park and "bring them home like stray kittens."[47] Joan, who met Lucian at a party given by the poet William Empson, remembered her first glimpse of him. "He was thin and hawklike with hair growing low on his forehead and eyes that darted furtively from side to side."[48] After giving Empson's party the slip, the two made their way back to Lucian's studio and then to bed. "In an icy bed I made love to an intriguing mind and a finely chiselled face," Wyndham wrote, "but no more."

Lucian haunted London in a great black coat with a fur collar that had belonged to his famous grandfather. He also kept a morose-looking hawk—John Richardson identified it as a kestrel—which he carried around London tethered to his wrist by a leather thong. "It didn't seem to like Lucian very much," Joan thought.[49] (Lucian's kestrel has become somewhat mythologized over the years. Waldemar Hansen, one of Peter Watson's friends, described Lucian's Paddington studio: "There is a zebra-head on the wall, an old-fashioned phonograph with a huge horn, and a live falcon which swoops around the room and alights on the master's wrist!")[50] Freud's fierce interest in animals—especially horses and birds—has been well noted. As a youth he was obsessed with drawing bird people.

A woman from Freud's Soho days, who wishes to remain anonymous, is convinced that Lucian had formed a friendship with the notorious Kray brothers, the twin gangsters of 1950s London who moved easily through the city's social strata. Another friend anonymously contributed an essay on Freud for the Robert Miller Gallery catalog: "Lucian courted danger and tempted fate in ways of his own invention. There were the intimate acquaintances with the members of a razor-slashing gang."[51]

Almost as soon as Lucian's dalliance with Joan began, it came to an unceremonious end, ushered in by Kitty Garman. Kitty had her mother's large, soulful eyes, shoulder-length dark hair, and Slavic cheekbones. She had grown up with artists and bohemians. In many ways Lucian was like her father: Jewish, brilliant, immensely talented, and sexually adventurous. As Epstein's daughter, Kitty brought to the relationship an artistic lineage that must have appealed to Lucian, so when she began to show up at his flat in Delamere Terrace, Joan Wyndham took note. "Every morning she'd come along with a cuppa tea," Joan remembered, "and ask if I wanted some, and finally

I realized it was going to end up with *me* on the sofa and Kitty in Lucian's bed, sooner or later."[52]

Though Joan characterized Freud as "threatening" and "dangerous," she also wrote, "One thing I liked about Lucian was that he always told me the truth, no matter how painful."[53] Lucian was wholly in the business of telling the truth, in life and in art.

Freud married Kitty in 1948, and in June of that year the couple's first daughter was born. Kitty's mother, Kathleen Garman, wrote to a friend about Lucian's new state of fatherhood: "I know it will amuse you to think of your old schoolfellow as a husband and a father."[54] Kitty and Lucian lived in St. John's Wood after their marriage, but he kept his studio in Paddington. Epstein at first welcomed his son-in-law and made a powerful sculpture of Lucian's head and torso. But when Lucian divorced Kitty four years later, and Caroline began living with him in his studio, Epstein naturally changed his mind. In a letter, he wrote that Kitty "divorced the spiv Lucian Freud," who had "turned out a nasty piece of goods."[55]

When Lucian and Francis Bacon showed up at Ann Fleming's ball in 1948, Lucian was already recognized as a painter with the mark of genius. Yet there was still the problem of money. He was always out of pocket, despite Peter Watson's patronage, despite his having taken a job teaching at the Slade School of Fine Arts. Helping Lucian may have been Ann Fleming's motivation in encouraging a match between her favorite young artist and her favorite young debutante.

In February of 1953, Raymond O'Neill, Ann's son from her first marriage, was entertaining his great-uncle Lord Wakehurst, who had become Governor of Northern Ireland the previous year, and Northern Ireland's prime minister, Viscount Brookeborough. He hosted them on a pheasant shoot in Ulster, to which Lucian and the Dufferins had been invited, probably arranged by Ann, so that Lucian could try to win the Marchioness's approval. The outing, however, was a disaster. Ann Fleming wrote to Cecil Beaton on February 6, 1953, "Lucian has had a curious holiday with Raymond in Ulster, he was in pursuit of Lady Caroline and was socially a disaster . . . and of course I am blamed for encouraging bizarre tartan-trousered eccentric artists to pursue virginal Marchionesses' daughters."[56] Ann further described, somewhat cattily, how "Lucian retrieved the birds faster than any retriever, which shocked them deeply," conjuring up an image of Freud in tartan trousers panting after the aristocrats' bloodied pheasants. Caroline had already had the experience of retrieving freshly killed birds for her father.

When Maureen Dufferin abruptly left the shooting party to set off for Switzerland, Lucian apparently took the occasion to bed Caroline. Ann wrote that Caroline "was discovered with Lucian on the hearthrug beneath dimmed lamps by the agent; the agent is a pompous ass and he told R[aymond] that that kind of thing would do him no good. Oh dear."[57]

Perdita remembered that visit, or at least the impression Lucian made on her in his tartan trousers. "He was so terribly shy, he couldn't look anyone in the eye. He stood with his head down, eyes darting from side to side."[58] But Perdita liked him, sharing in particular his intense love of horses. The Mother, however, was not amused. The marchioness had taken one look at the Jewish foreigner in his open shirt and tartan trousers and never recovered: Lucian Freud was not and never would be a suitable match for her daughter. "She didn't like him because he was really bohemian looking," Perdita said.

I mean, he had a shirt open and no tie . . . and so Mother used to get mad at him . . . He never wore a coat as far as I know and I don't think I ever saw him in a jacket. And of course he was just thirty years before his time—now everybody else dresses that way. But that was not suitable and she wanted a duke's son—any duke's son will do for her daughters, you know.

So Freud's beauty, wit, and talent made no headway with Maureen. Nor did his famous grandfather, whom Lucian was fond of quoting and whose name he often mentioned in social circles throughout London. Caroline later told Steven Aronson that Maureen had "never heard of Sigmund Freud, and to this day she doesn't understand that he was really very distinguished,"[59] but she would find herself in hot water for making that statement. She also insisted that Maureen had reported Lucian's father to the police as a German spy in an attempt to prevent the marriage. It was a nightmare for Ernst Freud, Caroline said, who was understandably "very paranoid about having police pounding at his door," after having lived through the early stages of Nazi Germany.[60]

Maureen's antipathy to Freud was put into words by two distinguished members of Ann Fleming's set: Randolph Churchill and—again—Evelyn Waugh. Randolph, Sir Winston's son who became a journalist and a Conservative Member of Parliament, was by many accounts "an impossible guest, rude to servants and often to everyone else too . . . often, but not always, forgiven his excesses."[61] But this was one occasion, according to Caroline, when his excesses were not forgiven. Caroline brought Lucian to Maureen's house in Knightsbridge for a cocktail party, which upset her mother. When Randolph Churchill saw Freud, he exclaimed loudly, "What the bloody hell is Maureen doing—turning her house into a bloody synagogue?"[62]

Caroline and Lucian both pretended they hadn't heard the remark, but the next time their paths crossed, Freud knocked Churchill to the ground. "It was the fashion in those years," Caroline said. "That was postwar intellectual behavior—a lot of punching . . . Lucian anyway was terribly aggressive—he tended to knock down anyone in a bar."[63]

Waugh wrote to Nancy Mitford, after Lucian and Caroline ran off to Paris together, "You know that poor Maureen's daughter made a runaway match with a terrible Yid? Well this T. Y. has painted a portrait of Ann Fleming with a tiara all askew, obviously a memory of his mother in law."[64] A nasty, if ironic, little reference, yet containing some insight: Freud's painting of his social mentor Ann Fleming with a tipsy tiara does have a hint of parody, and Freud may have wanted to subtly skewer not just English aristocrats as represented by Ann Fleming but his mother-in-law as well, the implacable Maureen.

Under the shadow of Maureen's deep disapproval, Caroline left her mother's house on Hans Crescent and lived with Freud in his Paddington studio. And then they took off for Paris, to live for a year at the Hôtel La Louisiane above the Buci market.

"Lucian was *mad* about Caroline, and Caroline was mad about him," a friend of Caroline recalled. "So she more or less did a flit to Paris to live with him—bearing in mind that what were called nice girls in those days did not go and live with people."[65] In Paris, they saw a lot of Michael Wishart, now married to the beautiful Anne Dunn, who was pursuing her own career as a painter.

Lucian's three paintings of Caroline done in Paris remain among his most tender and beautiful works: "Girl in Bed," "Girl With Starfish Necklace," and "Girl Reading." Caroline described what it was like to sit for Lucian: "Not only is it slow, but after six months you can be back where you started." Not only did he paint "the anguish of our age," Caroline joked, he painted the "anguish of his sitters."[66]

Caroline remembered that she was reading Dostoevsky's *The Idiot* while posing for Lucian, and she would sometimes read aloud to him. Henry James's *The Tragic Muse* kept them company while Caroline sat for "Girl Reading."

The most striking aspect of "Girl in Bed," oil on canvas, is the luminosity of Caroline's large, blue-gray eyes, which give her a look of extreme youth. The painting is reminiscent of the staring portraits Freud painted of Kitty Garman, but without their flattened, almost surreal quality. In these more realistically rendered paintings (and in one drawing, "Girl's Head"), Caroline seems a child—tentative, untried, wary. In contrast to Caroline's fragile vulnerability in "Girl in Bed" are her large hands, the nails squarish and the skin coarse— almost the hands of a laborer. Caroline's large hands and long fingers throw the painting off kilter in interesting ways: they belie the apparent youth of the sitter (is she a child? is she a woman?); they undercut the sense of Caroline's aristocratic nature; they reveal her to be both unbearably tender and irrefutably tough. The beauty of the "girl" is unmistakable, but it's almost her least interesting aspect.

It was in Paris that Caroline first met Ned Rorem, the American composer and master of the art song, and an ingenious diarist who has chronicled his picaresque life among the artistic and homosexual demimonde on two continents. They were introduced at the apartment of Vicomtesse Marie-Laure de Noailles, the wealthy society doyenne who seemed to have lived her life for and among the avant-garde artists of her day (she called herself "Cocteau's Lolita"; her portrait was drawn by Picasso; she was the first to show Salvador Dalí and Luis Buñuel's *Un Chien Andalou* at a private screening in her home).

Rorem had met Freud at a London restaurant some time earlier, but they were introduced again in Marie-Laure's elegant home in the Place des États-Unis. The composer described that first meeting:

> . . . *Lucian brought his fiancée for lunch. Lady Caroline Blackwood was heart-stoppingly beautiful, but vague. There she sat, in Marie-Laure's octagonal drawing room, on the edge of a sofa, legs crossed, one knee supporting an elbow extending into a smoking hand, which flicked ash abstractedly onto the blue Persian rug. Caroline, very blond, with eyes the hue of the Persian rug and large as eagle eggs, uttered nary a word, neither approved nor disapproved, just smoked. Marie-Laure was wary of her, as of all attractive females.*[67]

Years later, he would recall her as "one of the two or three most beautiful women I have ever seen. There's always something askew about great beauty. In Caroline's case it was her eyes, which were unusually large. I would see her again later, after she moved to New York, and I'd see her down on West 4th Street haggling with the butcher."[68]

With all her beauty, and having just created the scandal of running off with Lucian—the *enfant terrible* of London society—Caroline was probably too intimidated to hold up her end of a conversation. So she sat, and smoked, and dropped her ashes on Vicomtesse de Noailles's Persian carpet, and remained silent.

In 1945, Maureen had settled upon her three children income from the family's Iveagh Trust, reportedly £17,030 a year, a healthy sum at the time, as well as income from Canadian holdings. But Caroline claimed that, because she'd run away with Lucian, Maureen cut her off financially. That would later be disputed. Maureen insisted she never disowned her daughter, although she may have held back Caroline's money while she was living in Paris with Lucian; at one point Lucian had trouble paying the hotel bill. Maureen later wrote in a private letter that it was Lucian who did not allow Caroline to see her, a situation that pained her greatly.[69]

By the end of 1952, Lucian and Caroline, still in Paris, were indeed running out of money. In November, Caroline telephoned Cyril and Barbara Connolly, whom she had met through Ann Fleming, and asked them to buy one of Freud's paintings of her. It was Fleming's idea; she suspected that Cyril was infatuated with Caroline and would be willing to buy one of Lucian's stunning portraits.

Barbara Connolly, however, was not taken by the idea. She wrote in her diary on November 24:

> *Caroline Blackwood telephones. In a state about Lucien* [sic] *Freud who is stuck in Paris unable to pay the hotel . . . Caroline and Lucien to get Cyril to buy Lucien's latest portrait of Caroline. Cyril*

*feels paternal towards them both and is keen on Caroline. I say it is
not worth putting himself in a state of debt for the whole of the
next year.*[70]

Despite Barbara's misgivings, the Connollys bought "Girl Reading,"
signaling the beginning of a fascination with Caroline that would
have serious repercussions.

After nearly a year of living in Paris on little money, Caroline and
Lucian returned to London. Freud, having secured his divorce from
Kitty, wed Lady Caroline Blackwood on December 9, 1953, a day after his thirty-first birthday, in a civil ceremony at the Chelsea Registry Office. Lucian joked that he had wanted Ann Fleming "to be the
best man at their wedding,"[71] but she was not present. In the London
Times announcement, Caroline was described as "a 1949 debutante
[whose] debut was attended by Princess Margaret. Her mother is a
close friend of Queen Mother Elizabeth"—two details probably supplied by Maureen—and Lucian was described, simply, as an "artist,"
though the announcement carried the headline FREUD'S GRANDSON
WEDS (which must have galled Maureen, who would have no doubt
preferred the headline MARCHIONESS OF DUFFERIN AND AVA'S DAUGHTER
WEDS).

Despite her antipathy to Lucian, Maureen showed up at the Registry Office and got involved in a shoving match with Caroline's
cousin Doon Plunket (now Countess Granville) over who was to serve
as witness to the marriage. Both Lucian and Caroline felt it would
be an ill omen to have Maureen as an official witness, so Caroline
enlisted Doon's help. After elbowing her aunt out of the way, Doon
signed the registry.

As is true of power struggles between mothers and daughters,
Maureen's disapproval most likely deepened Caroline's desire to be
with Lucian. And though some people thought that Lucian originally
pursued Caroline because of her family's wealth and title, he soon
found himself in love. Joan Wyndham said:

*Caroline was the great love of Lucian's life. With Caroline he be-
haved terribly well. Very unusual. He didn't love any of us . . . He
must have known that she loved him, which was a great thing.*[72]

Bruce Bernard agreed: "Lucian was in love with two women in his
life: one of them was Caroline Blackwood."[73] (The other woman,
Anne Dunn Moynihan has said, was probably Lorna Wishart, Michael's beautiful mother, whom Lucian had loved before his marriage
to Kitty Garman. Kitty—besides being Jacob Epstein's daughter—
was Lorna Wishart's niece.)

Now safely married, the couple made their home in Soho, in a
Georgian house they bought on Dean Street. Despite Maureen's disapproval, Caroline must have continued to draw on her share of the
Iveagh Trust, because in addition to their house in Soho, the couple
bought a stone priory in Dorset, Thomas Hardy country, where Lucian immediately bought a horse and took up his lifelong love of riding bareback. It was perhaps the most idyllic time in their married
life. Perdita visited them on occasion in Dorset and in London, and
Lucian began a painting of the sisters. He planned a large, full-length
portrait of the two, his most ambitious painting yet in terms of size,
but he never finished any of it except one of Caroline's eyes. The double portrait was abandoned.

The couple continued the intense round of socializing that Lucian
had been accustomed to before he met Caroline. They cavorted with
Ann Fleming's crowd of politicians, aristocrats, and intellectuals and
took up with Soho's demimonde of artists, musicians, homosexuals,
hangers-on, drunks, and geniuses.

Caroline introduced Lucian to her favorite aunt, Lady Oranmore
and Browne, and to the pleasures of Luggala. The two made the trip
to Oonagh's Irish country house during the Christmas festivities of
1955. Among the guests were the writer and editor Francis Wyndham, the novelist Derek Lindsay, and Brendan Behan and his new
wife, Beatrice. Behan would later commemorate the flavor of Christ-

mas at Luggala (and a drunken fall down the stairs) in a bread-and-butter note he sent to Oonagh:

> *Lady Oonagh, Garech, Tara,*
> *Three bright heads be twice as fair*
> *This time twelve months (and*
> *as hard a curse of mine lies on that stair).*
>
> *The girl that danced* The Blackbird *lightly,*
> *Michael Wilding, Harold Lloyd,*
> *Tara's bow to shine as brightly,*
>
> *Bless Caroline and Lucian Freud.*[74]

And, for a short while at least, their life together did seem blessed.

· *Four* ·

THE SOHO CIRCLE

It's a dangerous place . . . if you get Sohoitis . . .
you will stay there always day and night and
get no work done ever.[1]

I had dinner with [Francis Bacon] nearly every night for more or less the whole of my marriage to Lucian. We also had lunch,"[2] Caroline said about the three years she lived with Lucian Freud in Soho, the colorful London district that lies squarely between the boundaries of Wardour, Dean, Frith, and Greek streets. In postwar London, Soho was as much a state of mind as a place, and Bacon, the legendary Anglo-Irish painter, was its resident genius.

It may seem odd that a young woman like Caroline, who had lived a fairly sheltered life on a country estate in Ulster, would become a good friend of Bacon, the sacred monster of Soho whose flamboyant homosexuality, penchant for sadomasochism (the receiving end), and ruthless paintings disturbed more seasoned souls. In part, the friendship flourished because Lucian and Francis were, in those years, extremely close. Anne Dunn Moynihan, then married to Michael Wishart, thought that Lucian had "a kind of hero-worshiping crush

on Bacon, though I don't think it was ever consummated."[3] Admirers
of each other's work, the two had the wary intense friendship of men
who recognized the other's genius at the sullen craft and art of apply-
ing paint to canvas. As Bacon's biographer Michael Peppiatt observed,
their friendship was strengthened by their being figurative painters in
a time when abstract expressionism was considered the only exciting
and legitimate style of painting.[4] Each appreciated the other's wit and
passionate curiosity; each had a fondness for poetry. (Freud was an
inveterate quoter of T. S. Eliot, which must have delighted Caroline,
who had a sense of familial security when quotations were traded over
dinner. Bacon admired the modernist poet's work for its "total atmosphere of despair.")[5] Freud was thirteen years younger than Bacon, yet,
in the 1950s, was the more established artist of what R. B. Kitaj
termed "the London School of Painters," a group with diverse styles
who flourished in and around Soho. Among them were Bacon, Freud,
Kitaj, Michael Andrews, and Frank Auerbach. Bacon, however, was
the "acknowledged leader, due to the sheer force of his personality,"
according to Daniel Farson, who first met Bacon in 1949 in the dark-
ened cavern of Muriel Belcher's private drinking establishment at 41
Dean Street, known as the Colony Room.[6]

When the club opened in December of 1948, above a little Italian
trattoria, its barstools were covered with leopard skin, and bamboo
adorned the walls. Farson lovingly described the afterhours drinking
club as "little more than a small and shabby room with a telephone
and a lavatory . . . [and] a battered upright piano" at the top of
"filthy, ill-lit stairs." Yet the powerful personality and character of
Muriel Belcher made the Colony Room the place where reputations
were made, friendships were forged and broken, and where the London School of painters were so much in residence they were often referred to as Muriel's Boys.

"She has a tremendous ability to create an atmosphere of ease.
After all, that's what we all want, isn't it? A place to go where one
feels free and easy," Francis Bacon said about Muriel and the Colony
Room. Not unlike a demimonde counterpart of Ann Fleming, she was

described as "grandeur personified" by Farson: "Chin tilted upwards, cigarette in raised hand, she gave an impression of haughtiness, an eagle surveying the carrion of her membership."[7]

She was also tough as a sailor and given to referring to her homosexual customers as "she" and "Miss," as if they were drag queens; Muriel herself was bisexual, maternal, rough, shrewd, and loyal. She detested pretension, including pontificating about art; she proclaimed loudly that she wasn't the least bit interested in discussing art or artists, and her artists adored her for it. She strictly maintained the "members only" nature of the club, but she liked painters in part because they were lively and gregarious and brought in paying customers. Freud, Bacon, Auerbach, and Andrews were among her first regular members, and Bacon made the club his second home. Farson suggested in his memoir of Bacon that Lucian was accepted as a member because of his friendship with Bacon, hinting that there was some initial resistance on Muriel's part. But Lucian figures prominently in Michael Andrews's painting "The Colony Room"; indeed, he is the central, dominating figure of what amounts to a group portrait, in which a number of the figures are seen from the back and are barely distinguishable. That group includes—besides Freud, Bacon, Muriel Belcher, and Bacon's friend and favorite model, Henrietta Moraes—the brothers Jeffrey and Bruce Bernard and the gifted but doomed photographer John Deakin, whose career was destroyed by paranoia and alcoholism.

Farson said the Colony was a second home to artists, drinkers, and homosexuals, because "we could be ourselves, and that is one of the hardest things to achieve in life."[8] Muriel contributed to the campy atmosphere, cajoling and teasing her customers, addressing them as "cunty" or "sweetie," and, at eleven P.M., closing time, announcing "Back to your lonely cottages!"—a reference in the parlance of the day to the public lavatories where gay men picked up tricks.

Not all of her customers were enamored of the Colony's charms, however. Colin MacInness described the Colony Room and Muriel

Belcher—whom he disguised as "Mabel"—less favorably in an essay in a March 1957 issue of *Encounter*:

> *Of course the spell of the drinking club is partly morbid. To sit in Mabel's place with the curtains drawn at 4 P.M. on a sunny afternoon, sipping expensive poison and gossiping one's life away, has the futile fascination of forbidden fruit: the heady intoxication of a bogus Baudelairian romantic evil.*[9]

Another detractor was Barry Humphries, who, before his "Dame Edna" fame, once suffered Muriel's insults; she could be brutal to anyone wandering into the club who didn't suit her fancy. According to Farson, Humphries maintained that the Colony Room was "one of the nastiest places he has known."[10]

Caroline and Lucian lived conveniently nearby. Lucian—ever watchful and self-protective—was not a big drinker, as were Francis Bacon, the suicidal painter John Minton, the outcast *Vogue* photographer John Deakin, and "the two Roberts"—all fixtures of the Colony. But they dropped in at the private drinking club on a daily basis. Caroline herself described her marriage to Lucian as "a whole kind of Soho life. Going out to Wheeler's, and then the Colony and the Gargoyle, was the thing with that crowd—Francis Bacon, James Pope-Hennessy, Johnny Minton, Cyril Connolly . . ."[11]

Wheeler's, on Old Compton Street, is an oyster bar and restaurant once owned by Bernard Walsh. In the 1950s the atmosphere was congenial, the decor spartan, the fresh oysters briskly opened by white-coated waiters. Served at plain wooden tables with brown bread and butter, radishes, and spring onions, Walsh's fresh oysters and house Chablis provided one of the culinary delights of Soho, especially in postwar London, when "British food was at its dreariest," according to Farson.[12] Like Muriel at the Colony Room, Walsh created a congenial atmosphere for the artists and poets and talkers who congregated there. He welcomed Bacon and his crowd, allowing the painter—who was frequently broke—to run up huge tabs until he sold a painting or won at the roulette wheel and was able to settle his bill, at which point Walsh would send around a bottle of champagne to celebrate the artist's good fortune—and start the cycle all over again. Wheeler's was more expensive than most Soho eateries, but Bacon usually footed the bill for his friends, enjoying the role of host and knowing that Walsh would carry him for as long as necessary. It was the custom to have lunch at Wheeler's, followed by the afternoon at the Colony, then on to the Gargoyle for late-night revelry, dancing, more talk, and more drink. Having since been sold to a chain of fish houses, the Wheeler's that occupies the same space on Old Compton Road today seems to cater mostly to well-heeled tourists, and no longer exudes bohemian conviviality.

The Gargoyle was a holdover from the post–World War I era of Bright Young Things, a private nightclub that opened its doors at midnight to a mix of royalty, titled aristocrats, bohemians, drunks, and hangers-on. Founded by David Tennant and his wife, Hermione Baddeley, the ballroom was designed by Henri Matisse. In 1952 it was bought by John Negus, who expanded the membership to include writers and artists. A low-ceilinged room lined with mirrors, a small dance floor, a lively band led by Alec Alexander (with pencil-thin mustache), all created an atmosphere that was, according to Farson, "a sort of upper-class Bedlam, though the difference between the drunks and the lunatics was imperceptible."[13] On a typical night Lady Diana Cooper (the socialite celebrated for her beauty and a close friend of Ann Fleming's) might be seated cheek by jowl with the homosexual painter John Minton, who was usually surrounded by his entourage of art students, admirers, and rough trade. Caroline recalled that "everyone there would be a bit drunk. You could wander in any night and find the cleverest people in England"[14]—Graham Greene, Cyril Connolly, Peter Watson, the poets Louis MacNeice and Dylan Thomas, Michael Wishart, George Weidenfeld, Peter Quennell, Elizabeth Smart, Stephen Spender. There were also the beautiful people; besides Diana Cooper, there was Michael Wishart's wife,

Anne, and his mother, Lorna, as well as Cyril Connolly's wife, Barbara Skelton, Antonia Fraser (then Pakenham), and Caroline and her cousin Doon Plunket. The music was kitschy, much to the dislike of Lucian Freud and John Craxton, who preferred good American jazz, but the Gargoyle's brilliant clientele and shabby-genteel air of past grandeur made the music sound sublime.[15]

John Minton was a tragic figure, a talented graphic designer and painter who had lost faith in his talent, who felt that "after Matisse and Picasso, there is nothing more to be done."[16] Tall, thin, horse-faced, he had an undisguised homosexuality that could have flourished, at the time, only in a place like Soho. A respected art teacher at the Royal College of Art, Minton seemed embarrassed that his commercial success as a designer, as well as inherited family wealth, kept him well-heeled and well-fed while so many of his colleagues scrounged and starved. Thus, he paid for drinks and helped out his friends; his generosity was couched with the cry "Let's spend the rest of my trust fund!" That same generosity and fear of displeasing made it impossible for him to break off with former lovers, so he was often surrounded by an entourage of young men—past, present, and future. Eventually his melancholy and alcoholism overcame him, and he committed suicide at the age of thirty-nine by taking a massive barbiturate overdose. But not before Lucian Freud painted a disturbing portrait of his friend and fellow artist, one that seemed almost to predict poor Johnny Minton's fate. It's as though Freud painted not only "the anguish of the sitter" but also the future of the sitter—the subject as corpse. As many have observed, Freud's famous portrait captured Minton's "inner melancholy."[17] It also added to Lucian's growing reputation for being sinister.

Given the demanding round of Soho social life, Lucian painted at night and, vampire-like, slept during the day—or seemed to go without sleep. Caroline embraced this life wholly, and for a while Lucian and Caroline were a stunning couple in Soho: young, beautiful, fashionable, clever. Freud appeared to have everything he desired: recognition as one of England's best young painters among people whose opinion mattered, and acceptance at the homes of the well-born, whether at Ann Fleming's table or Lady Oranmore's, or dancing with Princess Margaret at the Gargoyle. But the intense socializing, odd hours, and heavy drinking would, for Caroline, begin to take their toll. A photograph of her getting out of a taxi on a Soho street, taken during the early years of her marriage when she was still in her twenties, shows a woman who looks aged. There are deep circles under puffy eyes; her features are heavy; her hair is disheveled—she looks drunk in broad daylight. The contrast between this picture and photographs taken just a few years earlier is surprising.

Freud and Bacon had a charged friendship, one that would finally break, but not before Caroline and Francis formed their own bond that would last their whole lives. It was partly because each had had an upper-class, Anglo-Irish childhood—what Caroline called Bacon's "unlikely and horsey Irish upbringing"[18]—and a horror of that time-honored expression of Anglo-Irish society, the fox hunt. Many years after their first meeting, long after Caroline had made her reputation as a journalist and novelist, she would write *In the Pink*, a controversial book on the pros and cons of the hunt. Francis Bacon's unpleasant childhood memories supported her claim that the enthusiasm for fox hunting among the upper classes could be detrimental to the health and well-being of children. She quoted Bacon as saying, "Of course they forced me to hunt. I really *loathed* it . . . But those hunting people are so cruel to their children. They are ruthless about making them hunt. And I suspect that the Anglo-Irish may be even more ruthless than the English in that respect."[19]

An allergy to horses made the sport all the more unbearable to young Francis, and his horse-training father's penchant for humiliating his son made the boy's childhood a torment. Caroline told Farson that "a homosexual friend had told her that Francis admitted that his father had arranged for his small son 'to be systematically and viciously horse-whipped by his Irish grooms.' "[20] In his biography of the artist, Peppiatt gives no other corroboration of this story, but it's persuasive and helps to explain Bacon's self-proclaimed sadomasochism. For as much as Francis detested fox hunting, horses, horse training, and his horse-training father, he was aroused by Edward Bacon, père. Farson wrote:

> *His father had little time for his awkward son . . . Yet Francis admitted that he was sexually attracted to him, even if he scarcely understood his feelings at the time, and recognized the truth only after he had been "broken in" by his father's grooms and stable lads.*
>
> *"How many of them?" I asked, amazed, for Francis could not have been older than fifteen.*
>
> *"Several."*[21]

Another bond between Bacon and Caroline was Caroline's fascination with homosexuality and with cruelty. She was fascinated by all things that went against propriety and that required daring and imagination. Her experiences with the pecking order of Rockport Preparatory School, and with sadistic nannies, had early acquainted her with cruelty. Bacon, who came of age when homosexual acts were against the law and who saw friends ruined by jail terms or blackmail, was defiantly homosexual. He was fond of wearing makeup, shoeblacking his hair, and was usually seen in a black leather jacket he'd bought in the South of France. Farson wrote that Bacon was

> *the embodiment of all that was advantageous in being homosexual, and it has to be admitted that it frequently enhanced as well as shadowed our lives. Though he might have appeared effeminate as a youth, this was the effeminacy of leather. In spite of his exaggerated mannerisms, no one ever called him a queen. He moved alone, cutting his particular swatch of calculated chaos, and his homosexuality was an irreversible part of both his life and his art.*[22]

Peppiatt referred to Bacon's "lifelong preference for dressing up in female underwear . . . Disguise and transformation were clearly as essential to his artistic attitudes as to his sexual ones."[23]

Caroline's fascination with transsexuality and homosexuality would be explored in her writing—first in an early unpublished short story, and, at the end of her life, in an unfinished profile of a post-operative transsexual. Her research for that article would bring her to haunt the rough gay bars of lower Manhattan.

The untitled story is among Caroline's earliest attempts at fiction, written around 1957, when Caroline was twenty-six. It involves one Humphrey Tompkins, an unmarried, forty-year-old man living with his mother in the country. Mrs. Tompkins is outraged one morning when she reads that a local woman who had gone to school with her son has turned herself into a man. Humphrey, who has always lived in the shadow of his oppressive mother, has a different reaction: he begins to speculate about "Angelica" and her sex change, and discovers that the girl who never attracted him at school now seems strangely desirable in her new incarnation. The unfinished story brings Humphrey to the point of recognizing his repressed homosexuality, but stops just short of the revelation. The sympathetic portrayal of a gay protagonist may have had its roots in the temperament and disposition of Caroline's brother, Sheridan, who came out as a homosexual shortly after his marriage to Lindy.

Caroline's intense interest in transsexuals was unusual in the 1950s. When the story of Billy Tipton, the female jazz trumpeter who lived as a man, became public in 1988, Caroline avidly read any piece of information she could find about the musician's secret, star-crossed life.[24] It's one of the "modern" themes that separate Caroline from Anglo-Irish novelists like Elizabeth Bowen and Molly Keane (although Keane raised the subject of homosexuality and its effect on family in *Good Behaviour* and *The Rising Tide*). Caroline was certainly not the only member of her social set to be fascinated with homosexuality and, in some ways, eager to compete with young men for the romantic affections of her gay friends. The sexually adventurous Barbara Skelton, after her marriages to Cyril Connolly and George Weidenfeld, embarked on a short-lived but intense affair with Michael Wishart, the self-described defector from gay life during his marriage to Anne Dunn and briefly thereafter. The experience was unsatisfying, and Michael felt that Barbara had actually been

> *gathering material for a short story about an innocent girl's bewil-*
> *dered failure to convert a drunken homosexual, who was rapidly*
> *going to pieces in the rather hackneyed luxurious surroundings of*
> *Cannes and St. Tropez. The research was accurate; those who*
> *thought that the publication of the story would upset me were dis-*
> *appointed. With leaden irony, Barbara called the story* Count on
> Me, *presumably a reference to my independence.*[25]

Years later, in her whiskeyish, gravelly voice, Caroline would tell Steven Aronson about the three Francis Bacon paintings she owned and eventually sold to the Tate Gallery, including "The Wrestlers," which she gleefully referred to as "The Buggers." But she pointed out that whereas she sold her Bacon paintings, she only lent the paintings by Freud. She could not bring herself to part with them.[26]

Francis Bacon would be present, like a bad angel, at two crucial passages in Caroline's life: her flight from Lucian and the devastating illness several decades later that would nearly end her life.

There's another arresting photograph of Caroline in Soho: in a plaid wool coat, her hair characteristically parted on the left, she is standing with Cyril Connolly in front of Wheeler's. Daniel Farson took a number of photographs of Caroline and Cyril in front of the glass-and-wood-frame façade of the Soho establishment—Cyril with his characteristic scowl, Caroline looking a little weather-beaten. (Igor Stravinsky, after dining with Cyril one evening, described him as having "a disproportionately large head, like a Bacchus, a flat pro-file with a Pekinese nose, flat ears with sprigs of hair growing out of them—'earbrows.' ")[27]

Connolly had helped Lucian out of a jam when he purchased "Girl Reading." Ann Fleming had made an effort to befriend the acerbic, jowly critic, in part to develop a new circle of friends who would appeal to Ian Fleming, since he disliked most of his wife's crowd. Ian respected Connolly—the two had discussed starting a magazine together—so Cyril and his new wife, Barbara Skelton, were among the first to be invited to the bungalow in St. Margaret's Bay, Jamaica, which the Flemings had taken over in 1951. The Connollys were an important addition to Ann's soirées at her homes in Kent, St. Margaret's Bay, and London's Victoria Square. In 1953 she hosted a gala dinner party, in honor of Cyril's fiftieth birthday, to which Caroline and Lucian were invited. Also present were Francis Bacon, Stephen Spender, and Cecil Beaton, who later described the event in *Self-Portrait with Friends*: "Cyril was radiant and feeling very warm-hearted at such a genuine display of affection. His heart and greed were equally overflowing at the tributes given to him."[28] Lucian, Caroline, and Bacon each presented Cyril with a pot of caviar. Lucian's affection for Connolly, however, would soon be shattered.

In March of 1954 the brilliant young theater critic Kenneth Tynan wittily described Connolly in *Harper's Bazaar* as "either a *bon viveur* with a passion for literature, or a *littérateur* with a passion for high living. He has never quite made up his mind, and his biography will be the story of his indecision."[29] Connolly was equally indecisive about his love life. Having spent part of his youth involved with the homosexual crushes that were fairly typical at Eton and Oxford, Cyril would marry three times and carry on numerous flirtations with the women in his social set, including his friends' wives. Though he transferred his deep romantic crushes from young men to women, he seemed to be driven as much by the desire to create a family as he was by sexual desire. It's possible he never got over the sentiments that were fashionable in his time at Oxford. In a youthful letter to his friend Noel Blakiston, he wrote, "I find the male form more beautiful, the male mind more true, and in the love of friends more good—a certain austerity of taste has made me always revolt from the curves of the feminine shape and the professionalism and the wiles of the daughters of Eve!"[30]

His second marriage, to the cat-eyed seductress Barbara Skelton, ended in part because of Cyril's reluctance to have sex with her, though by all accounts Barbara was a strikingly beautiful woman. He claimed that sex "was sapping his mental energy, that it was bad for him."[31] Connolly "would often only make love once a month in the hope of increasing his literary output."[32] (Ironically, it was the sexually aggressive Barbara Skelton who prompted Ian Fleming to quip that her presence at Ann Fleming's salon "rescued London's literary world from the taint of homosexuality.")[33]

Connolly, however, found it more satisfying—or less challenging, perhaps—to fantasize about and pursue young women than to make love to his wife, and if the young women in question were already married and unattainable, all the better. Caroline was one of those young women.

It's not clear whether Barbara embarked on her love affair with the wealthy publisher George Weidenfeld (who was Cyril's publisher and who had contracted to bring out Barbara's first novel) because of Cyril's schoolboy crush on Caroline, or whether Cyril pursued Caroline as retaliation against Barbara's infidelity. The two events coincided, and the Connolly marriage—already characterized by boredom, frustration, and strife—quickly unraveled.

Cyril had long been interested in Caroline. The Christmas before Caroline's marriage to Lucian, the Connollys attended a luncheon at Ann Fleming's house in Kent, where her usual crowd had gathered. Ann was quick to notice Cyril's interest in Caroline, having already discerned that Cyril might buy one of Lucian's beautiful portraits of her.

Connolly was probably attracted to Caroline's half-Irishness (which Connolly shared, on his mother's side), her wealth and title, and—not surprisingly—her beauty, despite Caroline's already noticeable tendency to go about unwashed. Barbara Skelton recorded part of the luncheon conversation in a diary entry for December 25, 1952: "The inevitable topic . . . Lucian Freud. Caroline was severely criticized for looking dirty; 'She needs a damned good scrub all over,' Ian [Fleming] said, in his blokey manner . . . he couldn't bear to see bitten-down fingernails."[34]

Caroline's father, Basil Dufferin, had been Cyril's contemporary at Eton, one of the young men Cyril had been attracted to in his youth. And the kind of Anglo-Irish, aristocratic life Caroline was fleeing from had immense appeal to Connolly, who, according to the novelist Anthony Powell, entertained a fantasy that one of Ireland's grandest mansions, Castletown, belonged to him.[35] Castletown had been built by Joseph Connolly, a Member of Parliament and possibly a distant relative of Cyril's; Caroline, during her third marriage, would live in a flat in Castletown. She considered Cyril "a raging snob" and "a brilliant manipulator of other people's emotions,"[36] yet she tolerated his attention at dinner parties and luncheons and accepted his gifts and letters, which he began sending to her in the summer of 1953 and continued through 1959, the whole duration of Caroline's marriage to Lucian, and beyond. In one such letter he complained of getting the Guinness brush-off from her and said he was upset that she never answered his letters. He comically pointed out that their age difference was the same as that of the notorious Latin American playboy Porfirio Rubirosa and his fifth wife. He even encouraged Caroline to divorce Lucian, offering himself as the necessary co-respondent. Caroline was not persuaded.

She neither encouraged nor discouraged him, but people began to gossip, and Lucian decided the matter had gone far enough. One day he discovered Cyril hanging around outside their Dean Street house, waiting for a glimpse of Caroline. He ambushed Cyril—whom he had once admired—from a doorway and kicked the older man in the shins, driving him off.[37]

Not to be deterred, Connolly soon confessed his one-sided love affair to Barbara: "I like lunching alone with [Caroline] very much—she is now my only friend."[38] Barbara recorded her response to Cyril's declaration in her diary:

> *Then, one day, Cyril confessed he had become infatuated with Caroline Freud and had been for some time.*
> *"In that case," I said, "I shall have to find somebody."*

> *Using the very words of my mother, Cyril replied, "So long as*
> *he is a gentleman, I won't mind."*
>   *"Whom do you consider a gentleman? Weidenfeld?"*
>   *"Too continental. But, so far as a continental Jew can be a*
> *gentleman, he fits. And . . ." Cyril added, "I would prefer him to*
> *most people."*[39]

If Cyril had consciously set out to use his infatuation with Caroline as the means of driving Barbara away, thus ending the unbearable intimacy of his marriage, the ploy succeeded. His pursuit of Caroline faded to a whisper, as he fought unsuccessfully to keep Barbara from Weidenfeld's bed. After much *Sturm und Drang*—and a great deal of gossip among literary London—the Connollys divorced, and Barbara married Weidenfeld. Cyril would later try to revive his interest in Caroline when cracks appeared in her marriage to Lucian.

Ann Fleming, somewhat hypocritically, had no trouble laying the problem with Caroline and Lucian's marriage at Cyril's feet, although she herself had slyly encouraged Cyril's infatuation. But Caroline never took Cyril's protestations of love all that seriously, nor would she ever consider him as having a role in the unraveling of her marriage. When pressed, she would blame Lucian's penchant for gambling, an addiction well documented by Lucian's friends and detractors alike.

Lucian's passion for gambling was Dostoevskian, Caroline felt. He was a committed risk-taker, whose "horror [was] breaking even."[40] It was dangerous to drive with him, she later said, as he'd routinely risk head-on crashes at every intersection. His risk-taking was terrifying, but it probably contributed to the brilliance and daring of his work. It's doubtful that Caroline even knew the full extent of Lucian's gambling; certainly not during their early days of living together at the Hôtel La Louisiane. But once they were married and living in London, Lucian's recklessness asserted itself. It was a passion he shared with Francis Bacon, whose gambling obsession was legendary, as were the illegal gaming parties he set up at his flat in Cromwell Place. (Bacon employed his ancient and beloved ex-nanny, Jessie Lightfoot, as

hostess, hatcheck "girl," and partner in crime.) Michael Wishart described Bacon's attraction to

> the weary glamour of those hotels in and around Monte Carlo
> where Francis had spent so much time during a period of disillu-
> sion and self-doubt. . . . He was happier among the ghostly clients
> of the casinos, whose life-styles, conditioned by the crazy whim of
> a little ball, veer from extravagant opulence to abject poverty.[41]

Anne Dunn Moynihan thought that Lucian "started gambling
while under Bacon's influence."[42] Farson wrote that Lucian's "recklessness as a gambler is alarming and has led to trouble with book-
makers and casinos. It seems that he is excited by the danger of losing
large sums of money as a form of catharsis."[43] Alan Ross, the worldly
editor of *London Magazine*, said that Lucian "invested huge sums.
He lost enormously." Ross also remembered an incident he found
disturbing:

> I was very annoyed with [Lucian] because after not seeing him for
> about ten years (we were never very close friends), he suddenly
> rang up one morning about half past eight and said, "Is your horse
> going to win today?"
>
> I had a horse running, but I thought it was cheeky to ring up af-
> ter ten years' silence, and I thought to myself, "If I say, it's got no
> chance, and it wins and Lucian is surrounded by these hooligans
> and bounders—would he come and kill me?" And if I said, "It will
> win"—and it doesn't, I'm in trouble!
>
> So I said, "Yes, it's going to try very hard indeed." And actually
> it won. And I have a feeling he put on a lot of money. And I never
> spoke to him afterwards.[44]

Caroline later implied that Lucian's gambling and general
recklessness—not Cyril Connolly's attempt at wooing her—led to the

Clandeboye House, the Dufferin ancestral home on 3,000 acres in County Down, Northern Ireland. Guinness wealth rescued the Georgian mansion from its period of decline. *Dufferin and Ava Archive*

Maureen, fourth Marchioness of Dufferin and Ava, was one of the "Fabulous Guinness Girls" of the twenties. John Huston described Maureen and her two sisters as "beautiful witches." *National Portrait Gallery*

Basil "Ava," fourth Marquess of Dufferin and Ava. Lord Dufferin's early death in World War II robbed Caroline of a father. *National Portrait Gallery*

Maureen with Caroline, who would spend many years in fierce rebellion against her mother. *National Portrait Gallery*

A precocious Caroline in her pram, reading Beatrix Potter.
Copyright Hulton Getty/Liaison Agency

Blackwood family portrait at the christening of Caroline's infant brother, Sheridan. Caroline is seated next to Maureen, in a fabulous hat; Aunt Veronica Blackwood, in furs, stands behind Maureen and next to the Hon. Mrs. Ernest Guinness, Maureen's mother. Perdita sits next to Basil Ava in the front row. *Dufferin and Ava Archive*

Caroline's debutante photograph, 1949. Lord Gowrie called her "one of the most beautiful women of her generation." *Copyright Hulton Getty/Liaison Agency*

"Miss Fireworks and Miss Icicle," Robert Lowell's description of Caroline (left) with her cousin Doon Plunket (Lady Granville, right). 1951. *Copyright Hulton Getty/Liaison Agency*

Lucian Freud, smoking. Caroline met Lucian at Lady Rothermere's ball, where Freud appeared with another great bohemian painter— Francis Bacon. 1952. *Copyright Hulton Getty/Liaison Agency*

Freud with the boisterous Irish
playwright Brendan Behan, 1952.
Both men attended Christmases
at Lady Oranmore and Browne's
country estate in the Wicklow
Mountains of Ireland. *Copyright
Hulton Getty/Liaison Agency*

The day after Caroline and
Lucian's wedding at the Chelsea
Registry Office, 1953. *Copyright
Hulton Getty/Liaison Agency*

Cyril Connolly wooed Caroline unsuccessfully while she was still married to Freud and he was still married to Barbara Skelton. Pictured outside of Wheeler's, the popular oyster bar in Soho. *Daniel Farson/National Portrait Gallery*

Caroline and Lucian spent much of their marriage living in Soho, carousing with painters and artists at bohemian hangouts such as Wheeler's, the Colony Room, and the Gargoyle. Caroline's problems with alcohol began to surface. 1955. *Copyright Hulton Getty/Liaison Agency*

Alan Ross, editor of *London Magazine*, helped launch Caroline's career by publishing several of her short stories.
Courtesy of Alan Ross

Caroline left Freud in 1956 and moved to Los Angeles, where she began a long on-again, off-again relationship with the screenwriter Ivan Moffat. *Ivan Moffat (detail) by Don Bachardy, 2 June 1977, pencil and ink on paper, 23" x 19"*

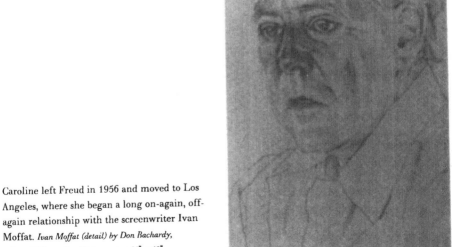

break-up of her marriage. She once asked Farson, "Have you ever driven with him?"

"Yes," he answered. "I was so terrified that when he stopped at a red light, for once, I threw myself out."

"Exactly . . . That's what being married to him was like."[45]

But Alan Ross, who would enter into an affair with Caroline in the dregs of her marriage to Freud, felt in retrospect that Caroline left Lucian because of other factors:

> *I remember Caroline saying all the time it was impossible being married to Lucian, because he'd work all day and he didn't want a relationship with a woman. He had to go from one place to another, all night—one club to another. He's a very restless figure. . . . Caroline just got fed up with it.*[46]

Others have supposed that Lucian's well-known womanizing contributed to the dissolution of the marriage. Lucian allegedly fathered numerous children, eight of whom he's acknowledged—a rumor oft quoted but impossible to prove or disprove. Anne Moynihan, who was married to Michael Wishart at the time Lucian and Caroline first ran off together, was one who thought that Caroline's marriage "broke up because Lucian was a very unfaithful husband. Lying awake at night, it's like counting sheep, trying to work out who his children are."[47]

But it's just as possible that Lucian was completely faithful to Caroline—he was certainly in love with her—and that it was Caroline's youth, Lucian's recklessness, and the seedy glamour of Soho that undermined what turned out to be a doomed relationship.

Caroline later described the night that crystallized her decision to leave Lucian, claiming that she left him over something that might seem trivial but really meant everything. It had to do with Lucian's indifference to a meal she had gone to great lengths to prepare for him. She had spent the entire day shopping and cooking an exquisite meal for the two of them, and when they sat down to dine, Lucian simply pushed his plate away. She knew that he seldom ate when he felt his work wasn't going well, but she was deeply hurt by the gesture. She left their home and checked into a hotel. As far as she was concerned, the marriage was over.

The Freud-Blackwood marriage lasted from 1953 to 1957, though Caroline left Lucian in 1956, one year before the official plea for divorce "for mental cruelty" was filed. John Craxton, Lucian's former roommate, was surprised that she had lived with Lucian for as long as she had.[48]

Once Caroline's marriage collapsed, Cyril Connolly began writing to her again, hoping against evidence that he could transform their friendship into a deeper bond. In an undated letter, he wrote, rather disingenuously, given his long wail of misery at Barbara and George Weidenfeld's marriage:

We are the weather in each other's hearts. I helped Barbara to marry Weidenfeld so as to free myself for you. This was a miscalculation apparently—but I believe the real miscalculation to have been yours in disguising the tie between us . . . you know you really want to settle down and have a child as much as I do.[49]

Years later, Cyril Connolly would sometimes pore over his unsuccessful love letters to Caroline, whom he described as "a femme fatale with large green eyes, a waif-like creature who inspires romantic passion,"[50] and for whom he would carry an unfulfilled yearning.

Caroline remained unmoved by Connolly's entreaties, even though Cyril had, perhaps unconsciously or through the projection of his desire, touched on one of Caroline's concerns. She did indeed want children—particularly if they were fathered by men of genius—but she felt instinctively that Freud was "not the sort of man one could have children with."[51] Given Freud's prodigality and Caroline's desire for children—she would later bear three girls and a boy—their lack of offspring does seem surprising. Joan Wyndham, who had had her brief affair with Lucian years earlier, testified that Lucian was known for his aversion to any kind of birth control. "One of his most dangerous things was that he never allowed himself or the women to use contraception. He had an absolute veto . . . Lucian wouldn't have let Caroline use anything. I can't imagine why she didn't conceive."[52] (This reckless aversion—given Freud's proclivities—may have stemmed from Lucian's desire to conform to the upper classes. Nancy Mitford, in her witty article "The English Aristocracy," lists an aversion to birth control as decidedly U as opposed to Non-U.)[53]

Lucian Freud's fourth and last painting of Caroline, "Hotel Bedroom," executed in 1954, seems to contain veiled information about the failure and dissolution of their marriage—almost as if, once again, Lucian had the power through his art to see into the future.

The date of 1954 ascribed to "Hotel Bedroom," a year after they married, is surprising, in that the painting is often considered one of the group Freud made of Caroline the previous year, before their marriage, while they were living in Paris. Yet the tone and mood of the painting are far different from "Girl in Bed" and "Girl Reading." Caroline lies on a bed, fully clothed, apparently benumbed by grief or anxiety. She looks prematurely aged. A distraught and watchful Freud looms in the background, hovering over his beloved. What is he afraid of? Anne Dunn Moynihan thought the painting was made in Paris, in the same small, long room they had previously shared at the Hôtel La Louisiane. "It was the coldest winter in history," she recalled. "Caroline was frozen, and depressed by then. She knew her marriage was starting to get unfixed at that time."

Through the open window of the opposite building, one can just make out a few simple objects: a pitcher, a white cloth, a table—iconographic objects associated with the Virgin Mary in Northern Renaissance paintings. However, in Freud's canvas, they may suggest a birth, or a miscarriage, or an attempt to explicate the disappointments of his marriage.

Art scholars and critics have been intrigued by this unusual painting. Bruce Bernard described Lucian's self-portrait in "Hotel

Bedroom" as "unlike any other figure he has ever painted," and
the painting itself he sees as a commentary—a kind of French film,
perhaps—on the difficulty of living in close quarters with a loved
one, in Paris, in the early fifties. He calls it "a unique kind of intimate
autobiography."[54]

The art critic John Russell was also taken with "Hotel Bedroom."
He offered this analysis in his introduction to the catalog of Freud's
1974 retrospective at the Hayward Gallery:

> *"How much can one know of another human being?"* . . . *when
> [Freud] put himself in the picture as he did in* HOTEL BEDROOM
> *(1954), he looked as if he had been skinned alive with his own hand;
> suddenly we realized that there is a point beyond which interroga-
> tion and torture are one and the same thing.*[55]

The point where "interrogation and torture" combine has been
noted in feminist criticism as "the male gaze," in which the artist's
scrutinizing eye is compared to the invasive, hypnotizing gaze of a
predator.

The art scholar Lorraine Karafel pointed out that Freud admired Northern Renaissance painting, particularly Grünewald's Isen-
heim altarpiece, a work that includes scenes of the Annunciation and
Birth of Christ. Karafel saw a possible parallel between that work and
the unoccupied interior glimpsed through the window of "Hotel Bedroom":

> *The room and its furnishings may hold a clue to the foreground
> scene of Freud and his wife Lady Caroline Blackwood—an image
> of separation, even alienation, painted in cool, gray tones. A large
> basin is at the center, a light glows overhead, and a clean cloth
> hangs neatly by the door of the mysterious room. These details are
> curiously reminiscent of elements in Northern Renaissance paint-
> ings . . . symbolizing the purity of the Virgin Mary and heralding
> the coming birth of Christ.*

The meaning of the unoccupied room, though, remains unclear.
How is it connected with the foreground drama? Does it signify a
birth, or a death? The answer, and the story behind this intriguing
painting, remain to be discovered.[56]

The meaning of the unoccupied room may have been Freud's
ironic recognition that the muse he had hoped to find in Caroline—
an embodiment of the sanctified feminine—was not there. Caroline
had fallen from that archetypal mode into mere human frailty.

Xandra Hardie, the literary agent who befriended Caroline in the
1960s, found the portrait disturbing for other reasons. "I think it reveals Caroline as a depressive," she admitted, "Lucian realizing that
she is a damaged soul, that he'll never be able to make her happy . . .
Caroline just lying on that bed drunk."[57]

Two years after Lucian painted "Hotel Bedroom," Caroline left him.
Oonagh, who had visited Caroline in Paris, saw how unhappy her
favorite niece was. It was probably Oonagh who encouraged Caroline
to leave Lucian and flee to Rome, where Oonagh was renting a villa,
in an effort to put distance between Caroline and her husband.

By many accounts, Lucian was devastated by Caroline's departure.

However one interprets "Hotel Bedroom," the change in Freud's
depiction of females—from the wide-eyed, lyrical girl-women to the
splayed, corpse-like nudes in Freud's later work—arguably begins
here. "Starfish Necklace," "Girl in Bed," and "Girl Reading" were
executed with a tenderness that now seems rare in Freud's *oeuvre*.

"Lucian's painting changed violently after I left him," Caroline
believed. Lucian himself confessed to the art historian Lawrence
Gowing that "my awareness that I wanted to work in a different way
was fired by a period of unhappiness,"[58] an oblique reference, perhaps, to Caroline's departure. Caroline later observed that "Lucian
painted me in a different way to how he's painting other people.
There's much more lyricism in these early works. Then his vision of

women changed radically, didn't it? Now the girls know they will be painted with their legs apart, which he didn't used to do . . . No wives are ever nude."[59]

Caroline and Alan Ross maintained their friendship throughout the break-up of her marriage to Lucian and her escape to Italy. She returned to London, Ross remembered, "and then just one day she went off to America, and then a different bit of her life started."[60] If he was hurt by her departure, he took it in stride, realizing that Caroline was in flight from a difficult marriage and at a loss as to what to do with her life.

Ross found Caroline reticent, challenging, but very much worth the struggle:

> *The thing is, you had to be very loving of her to get the best out of her. I think otherwise you might find yourself in all sorts of chaos. She wasn't usually wooed by people—she was a louche, skittish sort of girl. She wasn't easy socially—everything was in little jerks and silences. And then, sort of passionate changes and things . . . She was very silent until drinking suddenly switched her on, and then she was very dramatic and over-elaborate in her conversation. But very funny.[61]*

Her relationship with Ross would prove beneficial once Caroline began writing short stories. In Ross's opinion, Caroline was "a bit like Barbara Skelton, another figure of that kind, not natural writers but who became very interesting because they weren't facile at all." Alan would later have to pester Caroline to send stories to *London Magazine*, once she traveled to America and began to pick up the threads of her writing career. "After she left Lucian," Ross noticed, "what she'd been living began to work into her writing."

Caroline never uttered a word against Lucian in the years after she left him, though one family friend believed that she feared him and was glad not to have borne his children. But she had loved him, and she recognized his genius, and she was loyal. And, as the interior designer Nicholas Haslam and others have observed, Freud's paintings of Caroline "glamorized her, as in the sense of 'made fatal.' He bewitched people, and Caroline was bewitched by Lucian."[62]

Given Freud's mesmeric power over the many women in his life, it probably took a tremendous amount of will—and courage—for Caroline to leave him and the seductive world he inhabited. Alan Ross felt that Lucian's personality was so overwhelming that Caroline would probably never have become a writer had she stayed with him.[63] Anne Dunn Moynihan thought so, too. "When she was with Lucian," Anne said, "he wouldn't have wanted her to do anything. He was a control freak."

But Caroline did take some of Freud's strength and originality with her. Though she would never return to Soho to live, her life among the London bohemians sparked in her the desire "to never be ordinary, like everybody else. It's important to try to live the life of an artist."[64]

Her Soho years wrought a sea change in Caroline, a change that had, perhaps, waited in her genes for the right combination of events to unleash its force. Though she would never have used the word to describe herself, Caroline emerged from her marriage to Freud an alcoholic in the first stages of the disease.

· *Five* ·

THE HORROR OF HOLLYWOOD

In L.A. I felt like a goldfish going nowhere
down very, very ugly roads.[1]

I went to Italy, alone—do you know that kind of mood?" Caroline said about the demise of her marriage to Lucian. She claimed that Lucian followed her and entreated her to return to their home; it was all she could do to convince him that she was not going back. Lucian, Caroline later said, even tried to get Francis Bacon to play Cupid, but Bacon recognized—and tried to explain to his friend—that "things end, and this has ended."[2]

Caroline accepted Aunt Oonagh's invitation to go to Rome, because there was no point in returning to 4 Hans Crescent and crying on Maureen Dufferin's shoulder about the break-up of her marriage and admitting that her mother's opinion of Lucian may have been justified. Oonagh would comfort but not judge.

In Rome, Caroline met the poet and actress Iris Tree, daughter of the celebrated Shakespearean actor Sir Herbert Beerbohm Tree. Oonagh was fond of Iris and her son Ivan Moffat. Witty, high-

spirited, peripatetic, Iris married twice, moved often, and finally settled in Rome, abandoning Hollywood, where her eldest son pursued
his screenwriting career among the English colony of writers, directors, and actors. Ivan's father, Curtis Moffat, was an American. In the
1920s Curtis had been a popular fixture of London's bohemia, turning his Fitzroy Square house into "an Aladdin's cave filled with ori-
ental carpets, African sculpture, T'ang dynasty horses."[3] In 1938 he
returned to America, and Ivan inherited the spacious, top-floor apartment of his father's sumptuous house, where he continued in the
pleasure-loving tradition of Moffat père. Ivan befriended a number of
Gargoyle habitués, such as Dylan Thomas and Philip Toynbee, son of
the eminent historian Arnold Toynbee. Ivan and Philip had both been
involved in leftist student politics; Philip was the first Communist to
be elected president of the Oxford Student Union. Both Moffat and
Dylan Thomas were working as filmmakers for Strand Films, which
produced government-sponsored documentaries. Like *Picture Post*,
the documentary unit promoted the war effort and tried to wake up
England's social conscience. When America entered the war, General
Eisenhower created the Special Coverage Unit of the U.S. Army Sig-
nal Corps, known familiarly as the Hollywood Irregulars, to improve
film coverage of the war, and he asked the American film director
George Stevens to organize it. Stevens assigned a writer to each unit,
thereby helping to launch the careers of the novelist Irwin Shaw, the
storywriter and playwright William Saroyan, and, from London, Ivan
Moffat. That stroke of luck would bring Ivan to Hollywood after the
war, where he would contribute to the screenplays of two celebrated
George Stevens films.

It's surprising that Caroline did not meet and befriend Moffat
at the Gargoyle, where he had "played a seminal influence in peo-
pling the place with 'young turks,' "[4] noted Michael Luke in his history of the Soho nightclub. By the time she did meet him, in 1956,
Moffat had been living for some time in Hollywood and was visiting
his mother in Italy.

Alarmed at how unhappy Caroline was, Oonagh encouraged her

friendship with Ivan, and it was soon decided that Caroline would fol-low him to Hollywood and pursue—if somewhat vaguely—an acting career. If nothing else, it would remove her from the baleful en-treaties of Lucian Freud.

Moffat's first marriage had ended a few years earlier. His wife was a stunning but unstable Russian woman named Natasha Sorokin, re-puted to have been involved in a *ménage à trois* with Jean-Paul Sartre and Simone de Beauvoir; Christopher Isherwood described her as "verging on insanity, very beautiful."[5] Their union had produced a daughter, Lorna. Like Lucian, Moffat had a roving eye and would make a career out of bedding interesting and beautiful women—women like Caroline.[6] Isherwood, at the center of Hollywood's colony of ex-pats and a friend and neighbor of Ivan's, described him in a September 1955 diary entry: "He is always so pretty and bright-eyed and clean—he has to be, for I imagine his evenings usually end, if they don't begin, visiting some girl. He has the slightly guilty grin of the accepted lover."[7]

Tall, aristocratic, attractive, Moffat worked in 1951 with George Stevens on *A Place in the Sun*, the film adaptation of Theodore Dreiser's *An American Tragedy*. Moffat in fact supplied the film's ti-tle; the screenwriters had agonized over a suitable title change, fear-ing that the novel's title would turn away potential audiences. When Moffat fell asleep one afternoon and dreamed of Kaiser Wilhelm giv-ing his speech about Germany's "place in the sun," he woke up know-ing that he had the perfect title for the movie.

In 1953 Moffat was assistant producer on *Shane* and in 1955 co-wrote the screenplay for *Giant*, the big, gorgeous epic starring Eliza-beth Taylor, Rock Hudson, and James Dean. (Moffat told Isherwood that the film's success was entirely due to George Stevens and that James Dean was a selfish actor. "He did nothing whatsoever to help the girl"—"the girl," of course, being Elizabeth Taylor.)[8] Ten years later, Moffat would write the screen adaptation of Lawrence Durrell's *Justine*, a big, gorgeous flop starring Anouk Aimée as the doomed

Egyptian beauty. Moffat also wrote screenplays for *Bhowani Junction*, *Boy on a Dolphin*, and *Tender Is the Night*.

Iris Tree was fond of Caroline. She had been a friend of Edith Sitwell's, who had published her poems in the literary journal *Wheels*; by the time Iris met Caroline, she had published two volumes of poetry. She was just the kind of company Oonagh delighted in: aristocratic, bohemian, poetic—a flirtatious and lively *artiste*. Ivan recalled, "My mother liked Caroline very much—that's partly how Caroline and I met . . . But a curious thing happened . . ."[9]

When Iris Tree was dying of cancer, the family hired an attractive young woman as a live-in nurse to administer the patient's intravenous morphine. His mother was heavily sedated, remembered Ivan many years later. "The nurse gave her these strong intravenous treatments probably as much to finish the matter as to relieve pain. My mother was semiconscious much of the time." Since the young nurse did not wear a uniform, when she approached Iris near the end, Iris mistook her for Caroline.

"Is that you, Caroline?" she asked. Iris Tree had mistaken her deathbed ministrant for the young woman whom she had befriended years earlier and who would become deeply involved with her son.

Ivan Moffat returned to the States, and Caroline made plans to move to Hollywood. Oonagh encouraged her and then phoned Ivan to tell him to buy Caroline an overcoat once she arrived, typically fulfilling her maternal role, since Caroline showed little interest in clothes, fashion, or even the practicalities of keeping warm. Ivan promised to do so, even though he knew the last thing Caroline would need in Los Angeles was an overcoat.

When Caroline arrived, with a vague ambition to become an actress—that was certainly one way she could live the life of an artist—she checked into the Beverly Hills Hotel, and she and Ivan began their long, off-and-on-again affair. (In an undated letter to Caroline, Cyril Connolly, ever hopeful, was somewhat dismissive of

Caroline's new lover, arguing that she had taken him on simply to put Lucian behind her.)

Caroline soon left the hotel and moved in with Moffat, who was living in a tiny modern house overlooking Santa Monica Canyon on Adelaide Drive. They called it "the glass house," and it was small but charming, perilously perched on an embankment as if hung from the sky, with a view of the Pacific and the careless sweep of a canyon dotted with beach houses. Christopher Isherwood and his young companion, the artist Don Bachardy, lived nearby and would eventually move to a cunning little house on Adelaide Drive a few doors away.

Caroline was made to feel at home among Hollywood's thriving English colony, which included, besides Isherwood and Bachardy, such luminaries as Elsa Lanchester and Charles Laughton, Aldous Huxley, Basil Rathbone, Nigel Bruce, and Hermione Gingold. Stephen Spender, Terence Rattigan, Cecil Beaton, and Elaine and Kenneth Tynan made frequent visits from London. Evelyn Waugh's *The Loved One* blithely parodied a number of fish-out-of-water, upper-crust Englishmen clinging to the prerogatives of their class while the rest of the Hollywood community—crass vulgarians— ignored them.

Having divorced Natasha in the early 1950s, Ivan, in Isherwood's opinion, seemed bent on remaining single. Isherwood wrote in his diary, on May 30, 1956:

> *What an interesting figure Ivan is! I feel I would like to know much more about him—what he really wants, what he hopes for. Is it to be a good writer? A good director? He seems to be avoiding marriage, and he repeatedly says that one of the great advantages of his house up on Adelaide is that you couldn't possibly share it with anyone else.*[10]

But share it he did.

Isherwood's feelings about Moffat were complicated. Katherine Bucknell, who edited the first volume of Isherwood's published diaries, noted that Isherwood "admired Moffat's considerable wit and charm" and based the main character in the first draft of *Down There on a Visit* on the screenwriter; he identified with Moffat "as an expatriate and as a romantic adventurer,"[11] even though Moffat was clearly heterosexual and Isherwood clearly was not. But Isherwood sometimes tired of Moffat's company, especially at social gatherings when Ivan performed his mimicries of friends and famous people (including a particularly unwelcome imitation he did of his host, at Isherwood's own table). In a February 1958 diary entry he compared Moffat to a cat:

> . . . *one of the big ones; a heavy old panther sitting patiently in a tree, waiting for his prey. He has a heavy-jowled face, grave with patience. He is cruel in a sense, but not fierce. He even waits with humour. "I've had everything I wanted," he said, "even the most unlikely things."*[12]

In many ways, Ivan was an ideal mate for Caroline, one whom even Maureen would have approved of: attractive, English, aristocratic, intelligent, and—at the time—unmarried. Like Lucian, Ivan inhabited a world of glamorous and creative personalities. He also had leftist credentials from having worked for Strand Films, which would have appealed to Caroline's *Picture Post* sensibilities. Jessica Mitford caught the charm when she described Ivan as "span[ning] the gap between left-wing politics and the deb dance scene."[13] But the arrangement proved problematical for him and Caroline. "It became a bit sticky," Ivan said, when "a gossip columnist wrote something about 'Lady Caroline and Ivan Moffat . . .' It just didn't look quite right in the press. After all, Caroline was still married to Lucian at the time." No one in Soho would have blinked, but this was America in the mid-1950s, and Hollywood was still a small town. Moffat did not want a scandal.

Giant was nominated for several Oscars, and Ivan took Caroline to the 1956 Academy Awards. She liked the glitz of the occasion, but

Hollywood's patina quickly wore off. "Caroline wasn't easily impressed," Moffat recalled. "She had a clear eye—it later became a jaundiced eye—although she may have been intrigued by the possibilities in Hollywood." A screen test was arranged for Caroline, but it never came off. She was supposed to have appeared in a film, but that didn't materialize either. Caroline later claimed that she had landed a bit part in the television series *Have Gun Will Travel*, a Western morality tale showcasing the brilliant, if hammy, Richard Boone, in which the few roles for women were mostly decorative. But, finally, Caroline in Hollywood was like a graft that didn't take; part of the problem, thought Ivan, was Caroline's personality. She simply refused to gush.

> *She had a personality that was inconsistent with Hollywood, you see. She didn't have that style at all—no question of "how lovely your hair looks . . ." So she didn't go out of her way to make friends. There were people she liked very much and who liked her . . . but she didn't make a lot of friends.*

On one occasion Moffat took Caroline to a party at the house of Merle Oberon, the English actress, born in India, who had starred opposite Laurence Olivier in *Wuthering Heights*. Oberon was known not only as an important star in Hollywood but as a prominent social figure who was obsessively devoted to preserving her youth. Moffat brought Caroline to the party because a number of directors had been invited—Henry Hathaway, for one—and he thought it would be good for her stalled acting career. "It was beyond my expectation that she might actually enjoy something!" Moffat said. But for Caroline, the party was a disaster:

> *There was a game proposed after dinner with semi-spiritual undertones . . . not exactly the Ouija board, but something akin to it. Well, Caroline refused to play, which made a stir at the party. She said,*

"We're all too old to play this game!" And Merle, who prided herself on the perpetuity of her own youth, was not happy with that.

Isherwood, like Moffat, noticed Caroline's tendency toward gloominess. First, there were her famous silences, but what Isherwood found more noticeable was Caroline's tinge of upper-class disaffection toward all the low-brow delights of mid-1950s Hollywood—a place as glorious and tacky and full of diversion as a hungry soul could hope for. "Caroline was round-eyed as usual. Either dumb or scared,"[14] Isherwood wrote in describing a dinner party to which he'd invited Caroline, Moffat, and Shelley Winters. And later, in February of 1959, when Caroline embarked on her first journalistic piece since leaving *Picture Post*, Isherwood observed, "Caroline was dull, too; because she is only capable of thinking negatively. Confronted by a phenomenon, she asks herself: what is wrong with it?"[15] Even a dinner party with Laurence Olivier and Richard and Sybil Burton as guests did not thaw her. "Caroline was a frost, as usual," Isherwood recorded.[16] In her defense, Caroline was still probably hiding behind a mask of impassivity; she had not yet found her voice, and in the heady environs of Hollywood's English colony—which could be as arch and witty and vicious as any Soho gathering at the Colony or Wheeler's—she was overwhelmed. Or perhaps it was all that sunshine; Caroline just didn't like too much sunlight. She didn't know what she wanted from Ivan; she was ambivalent about chasing an acting career; she still had a desire to write. In fact, Don Bachardy could hardly remember Caroline as ever having a genuine desire to act. "She always presented herself as a writer—I mean, we always knew that's what she wanted to do. I'm surprised to know she ever went so far as to get herself an agent for acting jobs, or to suffer a screen test! She just always seemed a writer, even then."[17]

In an effort to deal with her sometimes crippling shyness, or perhaps to satisfy her curiosity, Caroline embarked on a radical form of therapy that was becoming fashionable in Hollywood. She undertook

a six-week series of lysergic-acid therapy with Dr. Mortimer Hartman, an early experimenter with this discredited psychoanalytic
treatment. It was risky and untried, but Isherwood was an enthusiastic proponent of LSD and mescaline, and Caroline was intensely curious about it.

Isherwood and his circle were fascinated by the possibilities of
spiritual enlightenment. Cary Grant had already undergone the treatment and was raving about the results, claiming that it had helped
him bridge the puzzling gap between his "real life" as Archie Leach
and his debonair film persona, and had also helped him to "conquer"
his homosexuality. One day he lunched with Caroline and Ivan at the
20th Century–Fox commissary, and Moffat recalled that the actor "introduced Caroline to this course, which was indescribably difficult. I
used to pick her up at the doctor's office on Lasky Drive after her sessions." Caroline, who had learned how to drive in California, had
bought herself a Thunderbird, but she knew she wouldn't be able to
handle the drive back to Santa Monica after her LSD course with Dr.
Hartman.

Moffat remembered:

*She described these tortuous waking dreams. The office was in
semidarkness, music playing, and he'd hold her face down while
she went through these mental convulsions. Her fantasies were
extraordinary—grotesque, Brueghel-like dreams. She didn't seem
to mind it, and she quickly recovered. She'd be quite cheerful.*

Moffat thought that the course actually did Caroline some good, that
it helped her to concentrate: "Her thoughts did seem more collected,
more focused afterward."

One of Moffat's close friends was the composer Leonard Rosenman, whose powerful, modernist film scores for *East of Eden* and
Rebel Without a Cause made his reputation in the mid-1950s. Rosenman later won an Oscar for composing the film score for Stanley
Kubrick's *Barry Lyndon*, and Aaron Copland would credit him with

bringing film music into the twentieth century. Rosenman's wife, Kay Scott, was an actress and a gifted pianist and composer herself. She was also high-strung and sensitive, like Caroline, and the two women became friends. In the closed circle of Hollywood's intellectual and artistic elite, perhaps it's not surprising that before Kay married Leonard Rosenman, she and Moffat had been lovers.

Rosenman remembered his first meeting with Caroline in Los Angeles. She had come with Ivan to his apartment house, which was across the street from the Beverly Hills High School. "She was very naive then, very sheltered," Rosenman recalled. "She was impressed with where we lived because she thought the entire apartment building was our house. She couldn't stop admiring it. Of course, she grew up in mansions, so it's not that surprising."[18]

He also recalled that whenever she came to visit, he and Kay would cover up all the furniture, because Caroline "was drinking then and she was so sloppy—cigarette ashes, spilled drinks. She was a strange girl, but absolutely gorgeous."

Caroline was not making much progress with her acting career, but her more fundamental problem was what to do about Ivan. Ivan believed that one reason he got on so well with Caroline was that he never tried, at least at first, to define their relationship:

> *With certain people, you don't want to put them on the spot. She hated when people asked her, "How long are you going to be here?" I tried to fend that off. We never discussed what the future of our own relationship was going to be. She felt irresolution about it all— she didn't want to set a priority for why she came here, whether to be an actress or to see me. It was awkward for everybody.*

Part of the problem for Caroline was that she was still married to Lucian Freud. She finally decided to go back to London and resolve that issue by divorcing him.

Caroline stopped in New York on her journey home, but when she arrived and learned that Oonagh had taken a townhouse in Manhattan, she decided to stay with her aunt for a while. Oonagh was being courted by the man who would become her third husband, the dress designer Miguel Ferreras. They would marry in 1958, though Caroline voiced her objections, as did many of the Guinnesses.

Meanwhile, Ivan Moffat had begun to work for the tyrannical Harry Cohn, head of Columbia Pictures, so he couldn't follow Caroline to New York. Moffat was apparently more in need of assurance than was Caroline. He pursued her by telephone, but she remained "undefined," and Moffat didn't want to force her to make a decision about their relationship. He complained to Isherwood, who wrote in his diary on March 28, 1957, "Ivan Moffat is in a sad state because Caroline prefers to stay in New York. If she really loved him, he says, she'd stay here with him no matter how much she hated the place. He's right, I fear."[19] Moffat recalled that some time in May 1957,

> *I went back to the glass house and fixed myself a light supper of cold chicken and sat down and wrote a letter summarizing my feelings about Caroline. I started writing this letter about seven or eight in the evening. By about five- or six-thirty in the morning, when the sun was coming up . . . I was still at this letter. By then it was becoming a self-serving, self-pitying epistle . . . many pages torn up and crumpled all over the place.*

He mailed it. Three or four days later, he called Caroline and asked, "Did you get my letter?"

There was silence at the other end of the line.

Finally, in a crisp voice, Caroline said, "I think we'd better forget that letter."

Moffat laughed. It served him right, he felt, for writing such a pathetic plea. He had his answer . . . and yet he would prove his patience by waiting, waiting for Caroline to change her mind. He would "wait with humor," as Christopher Isherwood had predicted.

Caroline confessed to Ivan that she missed him but that she did not want to return to Hollywood. Ivan convinced her to meet him halfway, which turned out to be Denver (an act of generosity on Caroline's part, Ivan thought—clutching at straws—because Denver is much closer to Los Angeles than to New York). So they met there, and it was lovely.

"We stayed in the Grand Palace Hotel," Moffat recalled. "I've never been there since. We drove around. I bought her an overcoat [at last fulfilling Oonagh's request]. We went to Saks and bought her a very nice coat, something like fur but it wasn't . . . she wore it all the time, like a sort of carapace."

But Caroline was not persuaded, and she returned to Manhattan, where she had taken a two-bedroom apartment on the eleventh floor of a small building in the East Fifties. She shared it with a distant cousin, Lord Beaverbrook's vibrant granddaughter Jeannie Campbell, an arrangement probably designed by Oonagh. Jean, a tall, dark-haired, voluptuous young woman, was involved in a two-year affair with Henry Luce, the powerful newspaper magnate and owner of Time-Life, Inc. Like Caroline, Jean was an heiress dabbling in journalism, but on a lower rung; she worked in the photographic department of *Life* magazine. She had grown up in a drafty castle in Scotland, and she very much wanted children, which is one of the reasons her affair with Henry Luce ended.[20] Luce was married to the formidable writer Clare Boothe, and he continually postponed divorcing his wife. Jean would eventually leave Luce for the brilliant, pugilistic writer Norman Mailer, with whom she would have her first child, a daughter. Lord Beaverbrook advised Jean to have the child but not to marry the brash novelist. Heiresses in the 1950s had more allowance to fly in the face of convention, but Jean married Mailer after all, even though Luce seemed to have been the love of her life—and she of his.

Caroline realized that she preferred New York's dense interior life to the serene unrealities of Hollywood. She later dismissed her Hollywood interlude with a mixed metaphor: "In L.A. I felt like a goldfish going nowhere down very, very ugly roads."

In New York, Caroline met two men who intrigued her, the second of whom would finally make it impossible for her to return to Ivan Moffat. But the first of her new acquaintances was Walker Evans. The legendary, quintessentially American photographer—best known for the photographs of Depression-era families that accompanied James Agee's text in *Let Us Now Praise Famous Men*—was fifty-three when he and Caroline met at a party. He was living in a cold-water flat on York Avenue, and his greatest work was behind him. Caroline sensed that Evans "was ashamed of working for *Fortune* [magazine]; it was just a way he had to make money. The success of *American Photographs* seemed to be forgotten, and he thought he would not really be noticed until after his death. He accepted this rather bitterly."[21]

Evans had been married to Jane Smith, a Midwestern beauty with Southern roots, but the marriage had ended. He seemed to be sexually ambivalent—he tended toward passivity—but he was drawn to Caroline's striking appearance as well as to her wit and intelligence. The poet Jane Mayhall, a close friend of Evans's, recalled that "Walker met her one day, said he wanted to marry her the next. He thought she was divine."[22] In her biography of the photographer, Belinda Rathbone noted that Evans "lacked confidence about his masculinity. His sex drive was inverted into a purely visual lust."[23] And although he was, in his photographic subjects, drawn to America's underclasses and to the humbler artifacts of American culture, Walker Evans, like many artists, "had a sweet tooth for the aristocratic."[24]

Caroline would be introduced to the city by this sublime interpreter of deep-grained American life. One of his passions was to rummage in out-of-the-way shops for discarded treasures—odd lamps, Depression-era signs, simple tools, odd bits of Americana—a habit Caroline enthusiastically took to, scouring junk and antique stores for the unusual artifact. She later told Belinda Rathbone, "There couldn't be a more wonderful person to show you New York. Walker made you feel as if you were going through life blind—his brilliant eye would notice the tiniest detail."[25] For several months that year, Evans took on the role of Caroline's mentor and, after a fashion, her suitor, suggesting books and articles for her to read, preparing intimate, candle-lit dinners for the two of them in his tiny, walk-up apartment. When Caroline found herself short of cash, Evans would send money to her by cab, though he could ill afford it. They spent several weekends together, at the Coggeshalls' home in Newcastle, Maine, and with the Voorheeses in Old Lyme, Connecticut—close friends of Evans. They assumed the two were lovers, though Caroline later said it wasn't so, that Walker was more a "fantasist" in his relations with women, inclined to boast about sexual conquests that may or may not have taken place.[26] She said that she was not sexually attracted to him, perhaps in part because of the difference in age; she was twenty-six, his junior by twenty-seven years. Perhaps she had been spoiled by Lucian Freud's beauty and by Ivan Moffat's sexual confidence; her lovers now had to be handsome as well as brilliant and artistically gifted. If Ivan failed as a lover because he was not, after all, a great writer, then perhaps the great photographer fell short of the mark because he lacked personal attractiveness. Caroline rather uncharitably described him as looking like Mr. Magoo.[27] On the other hand, Caroline was often coy about her sexual encounters, and it's possible that the two did have an affair. Evans was certainly smitten, and he took many striking photographs of her.

Caroline, still in search of a calling, began photographic modeling for *Vogue*, but she didn't enjoy the work; she found it mind-crushingly boring. Walker Evans, who disliked fashion photography and thought color photographs were vulgar, lampooned the stiffness of her professional photographs. On one of their weekends in the countryside, he made her sit on the grass and pull her T-shirt down around her shoulders while he took her picture. The T-shirt was miraculously transformed into a gown, as if by the wave of a wand. Though Evans never published his photographs of Caroline, he would on two other occasions take several informal and striking pictures of her. Their friendship remained strong, and Evans's own skill as an essayist may have rekindled Caroline's interest in journalism. She obviously trusted him, because when she began to venture into the less secure waters of fiction, she sent him her first two unpublished stories.[28]

Both manuscripts are coffee-splattered and show sparse comments from Evans—a redundancy crossed out here, a word change suggested there. They're surprisingly accomplished stories for first efforts, and they set forth two themes Caroline returned to in later works: an abandoned wife grappling with self-loathing in "The Shopping Spree" and, as described earlier, a transsexual who brings about an awakening on the part of a sheltered "mama's boy" in an untitled story. Both manuscripts are signed "Caroline Freud," as Caroline had not yet secured her divorce from Lucian.

It's interesting that "The Shopping Spree" was written from the point of view of a forty-year-old woman whose husband of ten years had just divorced her. Caroline would often write about abandoned wives long before she had occasion to feel abandoned by husband or lover. Her first published novel, *The Stepdaughter,* was about an unhappily divorced woman. Ivan Moffat and Alan Ross have both noted that Caroline was always the one who left, the one who ended the relationship, but that didn't prevent her from feeling, at times, that she had been abandoned. After all, her father had left her by dying when she was thirteen. Moffat remembered that when he had to leave Caroline alone in Los Angeles while he traveled to Europe to work on a film, "Caroline didn't like it. Even though at that time we weren't so intensely involved, she didn't like people leaving. And people who leave don't like being left. Caroline was a great leaver."

"The Shopping Spree" describes an encounter between Mrs. Williamson, a depressed, recently divorced woman, and Miss Estelle, an imperious saleslady who deepens the divorced woman's sense of shame. The saleslady's attentions at first comfort the divorcée, as she suggests that the woman is better off without her loutish husband. She lovingly handles the warm garments the divorced woman has just removed in the changing room. Mrs. Williamson realizes that her ex-husband had treated her garments quite differently whenever he had found them on the floor, and she suddenly wonders whether her husband was an insensitive boor, and that she may really be better off without him. But when she confronts her image in the dressing room mirror, her brief optimism is dashed: she is overcome by hatred of her flesh. She wishes she could tear it off her bones, in an effort to punish herself for her profound failure.

At that point, the saleslady tactlessly tries to interest Mrs. Williamson in a "foundation garment." Caroline manages to punctuate her character's morbid self-loathing with humor. "The Shopping Spree" is a tightly constructed, two-character story that economically explores a range of emotions: elation, distrust, betrayal, and outrage. It's sophisticated in that Caroline began by adopting a persona who is, on the surface, different from herself.

In June 1958 Caroline returned to Los Angeles for a month-long stay at the Château Marmont, a famous hotel on Sunset Boulevard. She was still toying with the idea of an acting career and had half-heartedly engaged an agent, but with little hope. She wrote to Walker Evans in Manhattan, asking about his ulcer and describing the Château Marmont as a "castellated" architectural monstrosity. She then wrote about the red, aged face of Maurice Chevalier, a fellow guest, as he lounged poolside; in general, her letter invoked the seedy, unreal glamour of Hollywood in terms Nathanael West might have used.

That Caroline was no longer staying with Moffat on Adelaide Drive suggests how much the relationship had changed. "Caroline was critical of men, you know," Moffat later said. "She had no heroes. She was very, very critical of anyone she was close to, more so than is usual. I certainly was no exception."

But it was not only that. One of the two men she met in New York had displaced Moffat in her affections, which was ironic, because it was Ivan, through his friend Leonard Rosenman, who helped arrange her introduction to the man who would become her new lover and her second husband—the composer, music critic, and pedagogue Israel Citkowitz.

"I was responsible for Caroline's meeting Israel," Moffat said.

"Leonard Rosenman had this friend in New York, Israel Citkowitz, and it occurred to him that, since Caroline was going back to New York, they might meet. And of course they did."

They did so at the home of the legendary acting coach Stella Adler. One of the things Caroline did on returning to Manhattan was to take lessons at the Academy of Acting, founded in 1949 by Lou and Stella Adler. When she first met the handsome composer at one of Stella Adler's dinner parties, Caroline was interested. It didn't matter that Citkowitz was twenty years her senior and had been married once before.

Citkowitz is something of a mysterious figure in the history of modern American composers. A Polish-born Jew who emigrated to Brooklyn at the age of three with his parents and sister, Citkowitz overcame poverty to become, briefly, one of Aaron Copland's protégés. He also studied with Roger Sessions in New York and with Nadia Boulanger in Paris—two rites of passage for modernist composers of the day. Copland, who had great confidence in Citkowitz's abilities, invited him to the first Festival of American Music at Yaddo, in upstate New York, in 1932, where his string quartet was performed. As a composer, Citkowitz is still spoken of in reverent tones for his brilliant setting to music of several poems by James Joyce ("5 Songs from Chamber Music," 1930). He also wrote song cycles for poems by William Blake (1934) and Robert Frost (1936). The modernist composer David Diamond described Citkowitz's settings of Joyce's songs as "beautifully wrought . . . he had such an ear for prosody, for rendering English into song,"[29] which is not surprising, given that Israel's first ambition was to be a poet. Besides Joyce, Frost, and Blake, he also attempted to translate into song the plain-spoken free verse of William Carlos Williams, but apparently abandoned the project.

Caroline would not have known of Israel's music when she met him in 1958, but she was struck by his Byronic appearance. He looked like a darker, more seasoned, and more benign Lucian Freud. (Perdita also commented on the physical resemblance between the two men.)

The editor and critic Karl Miller thought that Israel looked like "an old-style movie actor. He wore open-necked shirts and scarves. He was handsome and dashing, but old by the time I met him. They seemed a slightly incongruous partnership, except that Caroline liked Jewish intellectuals, and Israel was very intellectual, a brilliant critic of music."[30]

There's a photograph, taken in the mid-1950s, of Israel Citkowitz sitting with Leonard Rosenman and James Dean on the roof of the Museum of Modern Art. Citkowitz must have met Dean through Rosenman, who was writing the film score for *East of Eden*. The picture is a dazzling convocation of male beauty—this group of friends sunning themselves in the middle of Manhattan on a fiercely bright day. Rosenman's and Citkowitz's strong features are every bit as glamorous as the boyish James Dean's.

The mystery surrounding Israel is why he stopped composing. His intellectual acumen and gifts as a pedagogue have been well noted. He taught piano at Carnegie Hall and counterpoint and composition at the Dalcroze School of Music on East Fifty-ninth Street; he published astute criticism of the new music that Copland had helped launch in the twenties and thirties. "Israel developed a special piano technique when he taught at his piano studio in Carnegie Hall," David Diamond remembered, but, in Diamond's opinion, Israel

> *just didn't have the drive to be a composer. . . . Aaron Copland used to say "He's just lazy," but I don't think so. He was "all brain," and once he'd worked it out in his mind he sort of lost interest. That's why he was such a terrific chess player. He used to go all night to the chess room on Forty-second Street.*

Moffat had the same opinion of Citkowitz, who, though a romantic rival, became a close friend:

> *Israel was a delightful man. I had my own theories about him. He was hypercritical about everything, including himself. Israel was a*

sort of perfectionist and didn't exhibit more of his work because he felt it had shortcomings; that was my feeling about him. We became very good friends, by the way, during that time. Israel and I would have lunch and discuss Caroline, among other things. That's what he liked to talk about. And, of course, we played chess.

Leonard Rosenman felt that, ultimately, Citkowitz "wasn't really a composer. He loved music; he was an extraordinary musician. He was talented, but he didn't do anything. He had a promising career, and then he just sort of fell asleep. This was before he married Caroline. People say he was lazy, but there's no such thing as laziness. It has to do with fear."[31]

When Caroline first left Hollywood on her way back to London to get her divorce from Lucian, Ivan had a special gold band made as a friendship ring, though "its purpose was ill defined." They had discussed marriage, but it became more and more an abstract idea. Nonetheless, Ivan had a jeweler make a band of 24-karat gold. "The jeweler didn't want to do it," Moffat remembered. "He said, 'It's too soft; it'll wear away.' But I said, 'If it wears away before Caroline's affection for me wears away, then so be it. Go ahead and make it of 24-karat gold.'"

Caroline loved the ring and wore it, but it never became a wedding ring. In August 1959 Isherwood wrote in his diary that the English actress Joan Elan "is said to be pregnant, by Ivan Moffat."[32] And in 1961, Moffat, forty-three, married Katharine Smith, the twenty-eight-year-old heiress to the W. H. Smith book and stationery fortune and a lady-in-waiting to the Queen Mother.[33] Caroline and Ivan remained close friends. Ivan sometimes seems wistful about their not having married. "Caroline had great curiosity," he recalled. "She loved to laugh. I was sometimes capable of making her laugh. More than sometimes . . ."

The end of their romance was officially signaled in Italy, where it had begun three years earlier. Moffat recalled,

Oonagh had returned to her palazzo in Venice, in September of 1958, I think. I joined Caroline there . . . We had a nice time, nice enough, but Venice is so romantic, so marvelously beautiful, that any ill matching on the part of the emotions of two people would show up more than they would elsewhere . . . Needless to say, Caroline's and my relationship . . . well, it became obvious.

Ivan, however, apparently resumed his relationship with Caroline while she was married to Citkowitz. When Caroline's third daughter was born in 1966, she was called Ivana, named after the screenwriter Caroline had loved, but had decided not to marry.

Ivan recalled a meeting with Caroline, in Rome, in the early days of their courtship, which revealed to him an essential aspect of Caroline's nature.

She had met a lot of people in Rome—signore, as they're called, these sort of amorously forward people. She hadn't liked any of them, but one of them went around to where she was staying. He was parked in the front, and he took her by her bare arms, you see, and stroked them, and said, "Morbida," which actually means soft.

But she thought it meant morbid. She couldn't speak Italian, really. So she thought, "Ah, here's a man who knows what he's talking about! Psychological insight!" She thought she'd made a mistake about him, so she invited him up . . . It wasn't until the next day that she came to know what he meant—he was commenting on the softness of her arms. A very disillusioning story—but funny! It told me a lot about Caroline Blackwood.

· *Six* ·

SAUVE QUI PEUT:
CAROLINE AND ISRAEL

Somehow I feel that something very fantastic is in store for me.[1]
—Israel Citkowitz

Ellen Adler—the striking, socialite daughter of Stella Adler—
met Caroline in Paris in 1952. Ellen had just returned from a sojourn in Haiti and was sitting at a sidewalk café with Sonia
Orwell, *Horizon* magazine's noted editorial assistant, and a French
poet. She was describing how "uniformly beautiful" the Haitians
were when the French poet looked across the square and said, "Now,
that's what I call a beautiful woman!" Sonia Orwell turned and saw
Caroline Blackwood sitting in another café.

"I know her! That's Caroline," Sonia said, and Ellen remarked
that Sonia seemed to know everybody.[2]

Indeed, Sonia did know everybody. She had cut her teeth running
the now-defunct *Horizon* office for Cyril Connolly and Peter Watson,
two men she revered, and her confident opinions were heard throughout literary London. Sonia Brownell (who in 1949 married George
Orwell when he was on his deathbed) was loud, intelligent, and good-

looking, with a mane of light brown hair and a full figure bordering on the zaftig. She drank and gossiped with equal gusto. Jeremy Lewis described her as "warm-hearted, hard-working, and tireless" in promoting her favorite artists and writers, whom she had championed at *Horizon.*[3] Ned Rorem, who knew her when she was a freelance editor, found her to be

> *vivacious, grand, grossly pretty . . . with long fair hair coiffed all in a swirl over her left ear, leaving her right ear free for a bangle. She was smart without depth, cultured without creativity, heterosexual but with mostly gay friends . . . She drank too much and was bitchy, knew everyone and went everywhere.*[4]

The Canadian writer David Plante portrayed her, years later, as one of three "difficult women" in his eponymously named book.

Sonia was devoted to Cyril Connolly and very much disapproved of his infatuation with Caroline, but nevertheless she introduced Caroline to Ellen Adler. They would meet again in Venice when Caroline was staying with Lady Oonagh and her handsome son Tara, shortly before his untimely death. And when Caroline moved to New York at the end of the decade, she renewed her friendship with Ellen Adler, who, through her glamorous mother, had already met Israel Citkowitz. She thought it ironic that Israel fell in love with Caroline, because Stella Adler had intended to introduce Israel to Lady Oonagh. Oonagh and Israel were both in their fifties, and Oonagh had not yet embarked on her unfortunate third marriage. Instead of desiring the older woman, however, Citkowitz "took to Caroline," as Leonard Rosenman put it.[5] But Rosenman was surprised by their budding romance.

At the time, Stella Adler, in her late forties, was still a handsome woman. Ned Rorem described seeing her at a performance of Samuel Barber's *The Serpent Heart* at Columbia University's MacMillan Theater, on the Upper West Side of Manhattan, angrily pacing the aisles during intermission. Wearing a beige pillbox hat and flame-colored scarf, Stella Adler was "very blond, all alone, overly made-up but saved by her theatrical beauty." (Rorem's companion James Holmes remarked that her chiffon scarf was of "the cheapness that only money can buy.")[6] Citkowitz had been Stella Adler's piano teacher at his small studio in Carnegie Hall; Rosenman thought that he and Stella "may have been lovers." Indeed, Citkowitz seemed to specialize in wealthy and attractive women students of a certain age. They tended to be intelligent and well-fixed; some were talented amateur pianists, one or two at concert level; and they all fell in love with him. Ellen remembered that Citkowitz "was a tremendously beautiful man, really intelligent, who was worshiped by his piano students."[7]

Israel also had the glamour of his past accomplishments: a protégé of Aaron Copland, an important member of the short-lived Young Composers' Group, and a composer of a handful of art songs still spoken of in hushed tones by devotees of song in America. But by the time Caroline met him, twenty years had passed since he had written any music. Ellen said, "I think that [Caroline] very much liked the idea that he had been this great composer, and then for some reason, through depression or what have you, he had stopped . . . She was obviously very interested in geniuses. She thought she could get him to go back to composing."[8]

Citkowitz, at the age of sixteen, had met Copland in New York in 1926, when he was writing romantic poetry and involved in leftist politics. (Roger Sessions considered him a Trotskyite.) He lived with his sister and parents in three miserable rooms over his parents' store in the Williamsburg section of Brooklyn, and in his middle teens he was helping to support the family by, among other things, modeling. It was partly his male beauty that attracted Copland's attention, but it was clear that the handsome Jewish youth with dark curly hair was also brilliant and gifted. It was Copland who encouraged Israel to study with Boulanger in Paris; he even helped to raise the necessary funds.[9] Israel entered into a passionate correspondence with Copland, alternately entreating and chastising his mentor for failing to pay enough attention to him. His letters were so obsessive and full of yearning that music scholars have wondered whether Israel and Copland had had a sexual relationship as well as an intellectual one. In September of 1927 Israel wrote:

> *[A] good deal of time has passed since we were last together these same cold winter nights, when you would stretch out in your own chair and with the light falling from above . . . and I on the other side of the room railing against the Fates . . .*
>
> *And then the early Spring days, and lovely walks down the Riverside Park . . .*
>
> *The deepening of our friendship did a great deal to steady me. The loss . . . of a friend is much more disastrous to me than the loss of a woman I loved. What places our friendship in such a curious position now is that it was just beginning to ripen when we were forced to part. And all we can do with our friendship is to write it on a sheet of paper and mail it across the ocean . . .*
>
> *You'll never be completely rid of me, Aaron, not even if you die.*[10]

Copland dedicated his Nocturne for Violin and Piano to Citkowitz in 1926, and "Poet's Song" in 1927, a setting of an e. e. cummings poem for voice and piano, which he copied out for Israel on his birthday.

But Howard Pollack, Copland's most recent biographer, said that "Copland fell for Citkowitz—no doubt early on—though such affection by all accounts went unrequited."[11] The two men did spend a summer together in the small French town of Juziers, a hiatus marred by Israel's struggle with depression, which he wrote about at some length in his letters to Copland. On October 26, 1929, for example, he wrote, "I think it's one of the most unfortunate things in my life that the first time we two lived together should have coincided with such miserable depression on my part. An invalid is an impossible person to live with, and spiritually sick as I was, it must have been trying for you."[12] Their friendship would wax and wane throughout the early 1930s; by 1934 Citkowitz would virtually stop composing.

Rosenman believed that it was Copland's intense interest that had coaxed Israel into composing in the first place, and without his mentorship, Israel ceased creating his beautifully crafted art songs. Ned Rorem, while acknowledging Israel's reputation as "a song composer's song composer,"[13] wondered whether

> *maybe he wasn't really a composer in the first place. Nearly every performing musician has written some music at some time or other. I think that if you counted the number of minutes of music that Israel had produced, it might add up to an hour's worth . . . Maybe he didn't like to compose; maybe Aaron Copland forced him to write those songs.*[14]

From the mid-1930s on, Citkowitz devoted his time to writing and to teaching counterpoint and composition at the Dalcroze School. His essays on the new music championed by Copland are considered brilliant. As Rosenman observed, Israel was so intellectual that once he had solved a compositional problem in his head, he didn't feel the need to write it down. Pollack, noting Israel's struggles with depression, thought that the end of his composing career "apparently brought him some peace of mind."[15]

Two other activities now occupied him: playing chess and playing the stock market. He was skillful at both. And his interest in the stock market prepared him for his two marriages to wealthy women. On September 16, 1935, Citkowitz married Helen M. Simon, the daughter of a man who was a real estate mogul and president of Carnegie Hall. Helen was also a grandniece of Henry Morgenthau, Sr., former ambassador to Turkey, and a second cousin of Henry Morgenthau, Jr., Secretary of the Treasury.[16] So Israel's brilliance and beauty were put to use in the making of a "good marriage," one that produced two children before ending in divorce. Citkowitz wound up with a permanent studio in Carnegie Hall, where he often lived and where he gave private lessons to talented pianists.

In 1959, in a private ceremony at his Orthodox parents' home in

Yonkers, Citkowitz wed Caroline Blackwood. Leonard Rosenman was astounded when he heard of the marriage. "They were entirely different people," he said. "They didn't have any relationship in terms of *talk*. I didn't think for a second that they would get married."[17]

Caroline was still dividing her time between her life with Israel in New York and her unproductive acting career in Los Angeles, which she finally gave up. One of the last things she did before leaving Los Angeles for good was to get her divorce from Lucian Freud. On April 23, 1959, the London *Daily Mail* reported:

> *Lucian Freud, 35, grandson of psychoanalyst Sigmund Freud, was divorced in Los Angeles today by Lady Caroline Freud, 27-year-old Guinness heiress. She was granted a decree on grounds of mental cruelty, after testifying that her husband told her he did not care what happened to their marriage.*

So Caroline's liaison with Lucian had ended. On paper, her marriage to Freud had lasted seven years. A close friend of Caroline's would confide that it had been "a totally ill-conceived marriage . . . a very unpleasant experience for her. It wasn't until many, many years later that she would even speak to him again."[18]

With her inherited share of the Iveagh Trust, Caroline, who always loved houses, bought a brownstone at 250 West Twelfth Street in Greenwich Village. It was a lovely shaded street with a uniform row of private houses, where Greenwich Avenue and West Fourth Street converge. Rorem remembered looking out the window from his third-floor apartment, on the corner of West Twelfth and West Fourth, and seeing Caroline on the street—still beautiful but disheveled and definitely bohemian. Rosenman visited his old friend and marveled at the change in his circumstances: "Israel used to live in one room in Carnegie Hall, and, suddenly, he lived in a fabulous house."[19] Ellen Adler recalled that the brownstone was full of "beautiful furniture and wonderful paintings."[20]

If Caroline had hoped to inspire her husband to begin composing again, she was disappointed. The reverse happened: Israel encouraged Caroline in her writing. During one of her visits to Los Angeles, probably at a dinner party given by Isherwood, Stephen Spender asked Caroline to review some films for *Encounter*, the political and literary journal Spender edited. The results so impressed Ivan Moffat that he wondered whether Israel had written them himself. But her next article for *Encounter* was a breakthrough piece of journalism for Caroline, establishing her signature style and sensibility. As Rorem and others have pointed out, one thing Caroline had going for her was a distinctive voice; Rorem later described it as "savagely original."[21]

In the early 1950s Spender and the conservative writer and editor Irving Kristol started the political and literary journal *Encounter*, sponsored by the Congress for Cultural Freedom. (Spender was to learn later that funds for its support were channeled from the CIA.) The first issue was published in October 1953; Spender described the journal's point of view as "anti-communist in policy, but it was not McCarthyite, and its pages were open to political debate of Left as well as Right. Its title was meant to indicate its openness to clashing views."[22] Nancy Mitford's essay "The English Aristocracy," on the distinctions between U and Non-U, appeared in September 1955 and helped put the journal on the map. The witty essay, comparing class distinctions in manners, diction, and forms of address among the upper and middle classes, and written from a decidedly U perspective, was based largely on the observations in an academic monograph by a Birmingham University professor named Ross. "Our fortunes were made," Spender later wrote, "by the obscure pamphlet of the obscure professor."[23]

Spender asked Caroline to write about the Beat movement in Venice Beach, California. It would appear in the same issue as C. P. Snow's "The Two Cultures," Philip Larkin's "The Whitsun Weddings," and W. H. Auden's essay on Hannah Arendt.[24]

In researching the article, Caroline dragged Christopher Isherwood and Don Bachardy to a number of Beatnik bars in Santa Monica and the adjoining beach community of Venice—then, as now, a down-at-heels beachfront town with lively street life and a community of artists, drifters, petty criminals, craftspeople, poets, and personalities. They visited one Beatnik bar called Venice West and another on Sunset Strip called the Renaissance. Isherwood, Bachardy, and Caroline were not favorably impressed.

Caroline's essay "Portrait of the Beatnik" was a wickedly satiric report on the life of the denizens of Venice Beach, in general, and of one self-described Grand Lama of Beatdom, the little-known poet Lawrence Lipton, in particular. She began with the usual attack on Beatniks by those inclined to support establishment views, describing them as black-clad poseurs who would rather sleep than work and who spoke an argot so opaque and truncated that it was unintelligible to the uninitiated ("I dug giggin' for bread to wail").[25] "Beatific talk," Caroline wrote, "is the very soul of brevity, if not wit."[26] She also covered the Beatnik wars, mentioning Kenneth Rexroth's envy of Jack Kerouac's title as Father of the Beat Generation, and Lawrence Lipton's claim that he was the true Beat champion of the future.[27] She was appalled that these society dropouts eschewed alcohol.

Though written with considerable verve and wit, Caroline's appraisal seemed peculiarly judgmental for a woman who had spent the first half of her twenties living in Soho, making the rounds of fashionable dives like the Colony, where bad behavior was tolerated—except banality and bad art. In her essay, the London bohemian met the American Beatnik and found him wanting.

But what Caroline missed in her narrowly conducted research was any brush with the genius that spawned the movement: a Jack Kerouac, an Allen Ginsberg, or a William Burroughs. And she did not notice that some of the most intriguing actresses of the fifties—Leslie Caron, Jean Seberg, and Kim Novak, for example—saw themselves more as Beatniks than as starlets. What Caroline missed was that Beatnik culture in Los Angeles did offer a viable alternative to Hollywood cheesecake, but her gift for satire saw only what was easy to mock, and her essay fit in quite well with *Encounter's* political perspective.

There was another curious element to "Portrait of the Beatnik," an accidental prophecy that would come uncomfortably close to being true. She concluded her interview with Lawrence Lipton with his suggestion that she go around Venice and visit the starving artists who were, in his opinion, America's most creative talents:

> *I saw that "The Lama" had already, mystically, ruthlessly, appointed my future Duties . . . like a Florence Nightingale, or a conscientious Inspector of an Insane Asylum, making daily rounds of condemned Artists in padded cells.*[28]

Caroline would later gain firsthand knowledge of a condemned artist in an asylum, if not a padded cell.

Caroline made a lasting friend during her marriage to Israel: Cornelia Foss, a talented painter and the wife of the composer and conductor Lukas Foss. Lukas Foss was a friend of Israel's, and on meeting Caroline, he knew that she and Cornelia would get along well. "We had just moved to New York," Cornelia recalled from her summer home in Bridgehampton, Long Island, "and I was pretty much tied up at home with my baby, when Lukas said, 'How wonderful; this could be a new friend for Cornelia, someone European.' And indeed it turned out to be just like that. Caroline and I became very, very close friends."[29]

Cornelia was struck by how beautiful Caroline had made their home in the Village.

> *She had a talent for making the most beautiful houses I've ever seen. They were so incredible! The colors that she chose for her rooms, and the infinite care she took with things! There was nothing sloppy about her there, and that house was a miracle. You'd walk through and just gasp. She had a wonderful eye, and the heart of our friend-*

*ship was that she admired my paintings. She was a wonderful per-
son to show my paintings to.*

Caroline soon confided to her new friend her complicated feelings
about her mother. Cornelia felt that Caroline didn't hate her mother,
but "was deeply, deeply wounded by her, and by her mother's inability to love her." Cornelia knew that Caroline had had a neglected
childhood, had been left in the care of unsupervised nannies, and that
she felt emotionally abandoned. "She had been terrorized," Cornelia
believed. Caroline's marriage to Israel, and the birth of her first child
in 1962, however, would bring about a temporary rapprochement between Caroline and Maureen.

Caroline and Israel named their daughter Natalya. Walker Evans
took a number of striking photographs of the mother and baby, in
which Caroline looks beautiful, angry, and depressed all at once. Indeed, her postpartum depression was severe, no doubt deepened by alcohol, but throughout the ordeal of birth and its aftermath, she
managed to keep her sense of humor. Shortly after Natalya's arrival
she wrote a letter to Maureen that suggests a certain closeness in their
relationship—or perhaps Caroline's forgiveness. She joked that she
was spending a great deal of time examining the baby's stool and trying to match it to the precise greenish hue in the baby manuals. She
complained about the overwhelming chore of hiring a suitable baby
nurse; she had mistakenly hired three, all of whom were to show up
on the same day. She revealed how depressed she was—how the
breaking of a zipper or the loss of a bedroom slipper could bring her
to tears. She wrote that she cried for a month after Natalya's birth.

The trauma of hiring a nurse for the baby—that is, three
nurses—would stay with Caroline for some time and form the basis
of a grim story called "The Baby Nurse," first published by *London
Magazine* and included in her 1973 collection *For All That I Found
There.* The story has her usual hallmarks of dark, gritty humor and
monstrous characters casually destroying one another. In "The Baby

Nurse," Stephen Richardson's actress-wife, Arabella, suffers severe depression after the birth of her first child. It's up to the puzzled husband to hire a baby nurse, who appears in the stern form of one Miss Renny; she quickly fills the vacuum left by Arabella's retreat into depression, bullying and dominating Arabella and her husband. Stephen is absolutely terrified of her.[30]

Miss Renny was probably based on the horrifying nanny of her childhood, Miss Alley, the huge, unmarried, middle-aged woman of enormous selfishness who bullied everyone around her. Like the legendary Miss Alley, the greedy Miss Renny is excited by "meats, and cakes, and puddings . . . She plotted to get very large shares of them . . . Miss Renny had seemed to swell until she filled the whole flat with her combative and competitive competence."[31]

Miss Renny is also a tremendous snob, crowing about the important families she has worked for, such as Lady Eccleston and Sir Keith, who often had grand dinner parties for sixteen guests. "The Baby Nurse" exposed the vulnerability felt by upper-class families in relying on hired help to perform the most basic functions. In Caroline's story, Miss Renny runs the household and consumes most of the family's goods. The husband, Stephen, caters to her and allows her to dominate him. Arabella becomes a helpless child, retreating into depression, languishing all day in her bedroom, and padding out to the kitchen in the dead of night to polish off the whiskey. It's a frightening household. Stephen rids himself of Miss Renny only by resorting to a little old-fashioned adultery with his secretary, which offends the nurse's inbred prudery. Meanwhile, Arabella virtually disappears into a black *cafard*, dismissed by her doctor as nothing more than "the old post-natals!"[32]

Arabella is clearly an extreme version of Caroline in her postpartum depression, down to her big, green, staring eyes. Caroline the writer was hardest on this particular character; Arabella is described vividly but with little sympathy. We are given a powerful image of depression: "It's as if an ink-fish," Arabella says, "had squirted black poisons into my brain."[33] Arabella can muster no interest in her new-born girl as she retreats deeper and deeper into insomnia, depression, and drink.

Part of Caroline's daring and originality as a writer was her willingness to explore, and expose, uneasy subjects, such as a mother's rejection of a child. It's a theme she would later explore, head-on, in her first published novel.

Two years later, in 1964, Caroline gave birth to another girl, whom Caroline and Israel named Evgenia and called Genia. Soon, the beautiful townhouse on West Twelfth Street, with its good furniture and paintings by Francis Bacon, began to look more like a bohemian household with young children—which is exactly what it was. It was chaos.

John Richardson remembered visiting Caroline and Israel. "It was a nice Village house, sort of typically bohemian, masses of books and a mess everywhere. We always had a good time—it was fun . . . the children were young and all over the place."[34] Leonard Rosenman, however, was bothered by how his friend Israel had changed. Rosenman was surprised to see that Caroline "had Israel doing laundry. It just wasn't him. There were the kids everywhere—it was just so weird."[35] Israel—the brilliant, promising composer, the beloved piano teacher with the handsome profile—was becoming Israel the caretaker. He devoted himself to the children while Caroline drank and smoked—and wrote.

As it became clear to Caroline that her brilliant husband would never return to composing, the fissures in their domestic life deepened. It was during this time that the Gowries moved to the United States and began seeing Caroline on their trips to New York from Boston.

Greysteil "Grey" Gowrie, until recently the head of the British Arts Council, was a rare bird—an Irish earl enamored of the American avant-garde poet Charles Olson, founder of the Black Mountain Group of poets. Gowrie earned his doctorate at Harvard and became friendly with another midcentury American poet, Robert Lowell, whose creative writing classes at Harvard Gowrie sometimes attended.

By the mid-sixties, Lowell was already established as the dean of American poets, with a Pulitzer Prize and dozens of other honors under his belt. Despite harrowing episodes of bipolar illness that required almost yearly visits to private psychiatric hospitals, Lowell was a distinguished professor at Harvard when the Gowries met him.

Gowrie and his tall, striking wife, Xandra, both stemmed from the Anglo-Irish aristocracy in Northern Ireland. Gowrie was extremely fond of Caroline; he and Xandra visited Caroline and Israel's Greenwich Village home on several occasions throughout the sixties and sometimes spent weekends there.

"The first time I met Caroline," Xandra recalled, "was in that house. She sat in bed in the middle of the day, talking endlessly, smoking Gauloises. She was writing essays then, some of those gathered in *For All That I Found There*. I always thought that was her best work—it showed her complete fearlessness."[36] Xandra observed that Caroline had "her tribe's fearless, arrogant authority" when it came to writing. "When she thought of an idea, she didn't say, 'I wonder if I can do that.' She said, 'Of course I can do that!' "

The two women shared an interest in writing and writers; Xandra would later become a literary agent in London. She remembered that Caroline

was very, very sharp about writers. What I admired about Caroline is . . . she was a learner. She learned from her husbands. She had that magic thing that crossed the line of fantasy and metamorphosed into something creative. She loved to tell stories and anecdotes—always with a bad ending! It had to have that kick. A story or anecdote to Caroline was like a drink of brandy—it's pain, but it's life! That's what words were for Caroline—they were life!

But Xandra witnessed some terrible scenes, and it became clear to her that the Citkowitz marriage was unraveling. "I think she had left Israel," Xandra recalled, "but he was around all the time." Indeed, by the mid-sixties Israel often returned to his secure quarters in Carnegie Hall, though he continued to visit the Village house. "He was very motherly, and he wanted to keep an eye on the children to make sure they were being looked after," Xandra noted.

She recalled one evening when she and her husband were staying at Caroline's house while Caroline was away for the weekend, possibly visiting Cornelia Foss on Long Island. "Israel came round. The house was very bleak by that time. We were staying in the basement, and there was white powder all around. Israel was concerned. 'Oh, my God!' he said. 'It's rat poison! The children! They're going to come back and be poisoned!' "

The cleaning lady was due before the children returned, so Xandra thought Israel's panic was unfounded. But on that weekend, she came to believe that Israel and Caroline's relationship was based in part on mutual "fantasies of terror."

That's the key to Caroline. If you sat in a car with her, and you were driving, and she was a passenger, at every crossroad she saw someone being run over and being mangled. Almost every minute of her life she saw an appalling disaster happening right in front of her eyes . . . That's the line of somebody who's involved with alcohol.

During the dissolution of the Citkowitz marriage, Xandra spent a lot of time with Caroline; she had lunch with her every week and often looked after the little girls. It became clear to her that Caroline's abuse of alcohol was putting the children in danger, and yet it was the very stuff that made Caroline who she was. At thirty-five, Caroline could neither admit that she was an alcoholic nor give up drink. For one thing, said Xandra, "I think Caroline would rather have died than admit to powerlessness." She would not allow herself to recognize that alcohol had power over her, and her addiction did bring secondary gains. Xandra believed that "alcohol *fired* her—it fired her talent. If she couldn't drink, she couldn't write, she couldn't talk, she couldn't sleep, she couldn't fuck, and she liked to fuck—she liked all those things. She did them because of alcohol. What she would have been without it, I really don't know."

After the birth of Caroline's third child, Ivana, in 1966, she and Israel separated, although they remained legally married until 1972. Caroline began to look elsewhere for romantic companionship. As to why the marriage failed, perhaps one need seek no further than Caroline's drinking and Israel's passivity. Two such personalities living together with small children under one roof—regardless of money, style, beauty, talent, and even love—was a recipe for disaster. *Sauve qui peut.*

Israel chose to save their daughters. "An alcoholic can't love her children," Xandra said. "I think all her children felt rejected by her. If it's true that we treat other people the way we treat ourselves, then Caroline treated herself immeasurably cruelly, and she treated everybody cruelly." Caroline would always maintain that her children were important to her, but her ability to look after them was becoming impaired. Israel knew it. He may also have guessed that Ivana was not his daughter.

Cornelia Foss believed that the age difference between Caroline and Israel was one of the main reasons that their marriage foundered. In fact, Foss thought that Israel had gone to some lengths to conceal the truth about it. She said that throughout the marriage, Israel pretended to be ten years younger than he was, and because he was handsome and youthful in appearance, Caroline never knew his actual age until he died. "She went through his papers and his passport and discovered that he was ten years older than he had told her. There was a twenty-year, not a ten-year, difference. She was astonished."

Foss claimed that there were other problems in the marriage as well.

Eventually, she found other people more interesting. There were many other liaisons . . . You have to remember this was the 1960s, when everyone was cavorting around like mad. There was just something in the air that made it possible. No one frowned on it—

the possibilities seemed endless. No one understood yet what harm
it could do, not simply to oneself and to one's partner, but to the
children. And Israel? He probably took it in stride. He became the
nanny—he was incredibly sweet with the children. He took care of
*them.*³⁷

Even as their marriage unraveled, Caroline continued to socialize
with those whom she'd met through Citkowitz, members of New
York's intelligentsia such as Dwight Macdonald, the founder and editor of *Politics Literary Review*, Philip Rahv and William Phillips
of *Partisan Review*, the critic and novelist Mary McCarthy and her
then husband, the actor Bowden Broadwater. She also met Lionel and
Diana Trilling. Caroline's apprenticeship in the bitchy Soho world of
artists and writers prepared her well for this brilliant, backbiting
crowd.

At a party given by *Partisan Review*, Caroline ran across a former
acquaintance from her London life, Cyril Connolly's ex-wife, Barbara
Skelton. Barbara had moved to New York after her divorce from
George Weidenfeld and embarked on two harrowing years in that
city. Having reverted to "Miss Skelton," Barbara found her situation
clearly diminished and a tad desperate. She lived a picaresque life,
holding—and losing—a series of sales and secretarial jobs while she
made her way through New York's café society. She drifted from job
to job, from apartment to apartment. The low point was Christmas of
1963, which she spent as a baby-sitter to earn her keep, quite a come-
down for a woman who had been married to two of the most formidable men in London, and who had been given a fabulous jewel by
King Farouk. Now she scrounged for places to live; she once inhabited
a fifth-floor walk-up just a cut above squalor. Once a darling of London's literary coterie, many had vied for "the danger of her hand."³⁸
As far as Barbara was concerned, neither Connolly nor Weidenfeld
had provided generous alimony in his divorce suit. In some ways she
was a lot like Caroline—Caroline without money. And they were dis-
tantly related: Barbara's grandmother was a descendant of Richard

Brinsley Sheridan.[39] Like Caroline, Barbara wrote memoirs and short stories with the encouragement of Alan Ross and Stephen Spender. Ross published Skelton's 1965 collection of short stories, *Born Losers.*

The title story of *Born Losers* is, in fact, a vicious little tale about Israel and Caroline. Barbara would describe in glowing terms, in her memoir *Weep No More*, evenings spent with Caroline and Israel. But she painted a grim picture of their marriage in "Born Losers." She said of Caroline, named Grace in the story, that she chose her men for their instability and their looks. "She created shambles wherever she went," Barbara wrote; "[cigarette] stubs were chucked across a room and left to smoulder . . . as if she reveled in being a fire hazard."[40] She described Israel as "a wan handsome man" in his fifties who was emasculated by his wife. "[He] hovered about the trash bins rankly overflowing under the sink. His black eyes on Grace, he said eagerly, 'Like me to vacuum?' "[41]

Even harsher was her depiction of Grace's attitude toward her husband and their disintegrating marriage. Grace tells her friend Judy (Barbara's counterpart in the story) that her husband has "refused the good settlement I offered three months ago . . . He doesn't seem to realize I've got all the trumps . . . the house . . . the money . . ."[42]

In another story, "Sour Grapes," Barbara wrote of an affair with a dashing editor who would become a serious suitor of Caroline's as well. The brilliant and roguish editor, called Ben Gold in Barbara's story, is probably Robert Silvers, a founding editor of *The New York Review of Books*. In her memoir, *Weep No More*, Skelton described Silvers, then an editor at Harper's, as one of "the two most sought-after about-town bachelors of that period."[43] Silvers had the kind of movie-actor good looks that Caroline and Barbara were drawn to; like Israel, he was dark, Jewish, with aquiline features. Though Barbara's memoir was short on details, she did say that Silvers taught her to do the Twist, the dance craze then sweeping the country: "He counselled me to imagine I had just stepped out of a bath and was briskly towelling my buttocks," Barbara wrote.[44]

According to Barbara's memoir, one summer Silvers invited her to live with him in a large apartment over Carnegie Hall, lent to him by Peter Duchin. Silvers often worked throughout the night at his editorial duties, slipping into bed with Barbara in the early morning hours. In "Sour Grapes," Ben Gold remains an elusive lover, quick to wriggle out of entanglements and remain uncommitted. At one point, Barbara compared Silvers's lovemaking to George Weidenfeld's. Curiously, Weidenfeld would try to lure Silvers away from Harper to work for his publishing firm, but Silvers refused: the English house couldn't match the salary paid by Harper's.

After a printers' strike briefly shut down newspaper publication in 1963, *The New York Review of Books* was founded to fill the gap in book reviewing. It was spearheaded by the *Partisan Review* critic Elizabeth Hardwick with help from her husband, Robert Lowell, and the book editor Jason Epstein. Silvers left Harper's to become an editor of the new review, which quickly filled the vacuum created by the strike and earned a reputation for serious critical essays.

After a promising start, Barbara's rediscovered friendship with Caroline proved to be short-lived. Around Christmas of 1960 she had written to Cyril Connolly, "The first snowy night I spent with Caroline in her cosy Greenwich Village house, with the Bacon paintings and baby taking an active part in a babychair next to the fire. I like both her and her husband, Israel Citkowitz. He is very sympathetic with a wry sense of humour."[45] But a few years later, she called Caroline a heartless harridan, who, "on hearing of someone's ghastly misfortune . . . would double up laughing."[46]

Caroline tried to help Barbara in a number of ways. She got her a job as an assistant to her dentist, and she referred Barbara to her psychiatrist, Dr. Hartman, who had moved to New York. Barbara recorded his name in her memoir as Longman and—gleefully— as Maudman in her short story "Sour Grapes." As he had in Los Angeles, Dr. Hartman used LSD as part of his practice. After a harrowing LSD session with the doctor, Barbara would walk downtown to spend the evening with Caroline, and the two women would sit up "half the night, ridiculing Longman and comparing [their] reactions [to the drug]."[47] Her description of those re-hashing sessions is vivid in "Born Losers": "Grace had been going to Maudman for years. Grace had lived out every fantasy of cannibalism . . . excretal omnipotence . . . and parental assault, and was thoroughly primed for the right Mr. Right."[48]

The friendship ended in 1963, around the time Caroline and Robert Silvers began seeing each other. The two women were, perhaps, too much alike. They had shared the affections of at least two men: Connolly and now Silvers. Barbara broke with Caroline, complaining that they were "no longer friends for, from being a delightful companion, she had begun to turn into an angry lady wielding a ferocious pen."[49] Caroline's anger aside, Barbara's envy of her former friend's romantic conquests—and of her reliable income and "cosy" house in Greenwich Village—may have sabotaged that friendship. At one point, Barbara took a job modeling the latest fashions in the Junior Miss department of Bergdorf Goodman's. She described a grueling schedule of smiling on demand for fussy shoppers and trying to stay out of the way of Miss Eric, the head of the department. And then one day Caroline waltzed in and decided to torment Barbara. "Dressed in one of the latest models, a hat dangling with price labels, I'd get into the lift and tour the other floors . . . The last straw was when Caroline came in pretending to look for a bargain on one of the rails and I was ordered to twirl."[50]

Caroline and Silvers embarked on a relationship that would last throughout Caroline's life. Cornelia Foss characterized it as "a sweet friendship. They had an affair and they stayed friends . . . He's a very loyal person, and so was she, and they remained loyal to each other."[51] Their romance, however, did give rise to the rumor among several of Caroline's close friends that it was Silvers, not Citkowitz and not Moffat, who had fathered Caroline's third daughter.

John Richardson believed the rumors that Ivana was not Citkowitz's daughter:

She's either Ivan Moffat's daughter or Bob Silvers's . . . In theory, that's why she's called "Ivana" . . . because Caroline wanted, as it were, to hide the fact that Bob Silvers is really the father, so she called her Ivana so that everyone would think Ivan's the father. I'm convinced that Bob's the father. I've never discussed it with Bob; he hasn't acknowledged it; but Bob's lady friend, Lady Dudley, has always treated Ivana [well], even when she was a girl and had her terrible scalding. She was always taking her to doctors to see what could be done about it.[52]

But the scalding of Ivana would come much later, long after Caroline left both Citkowitz and Silvers and returned to London—after Silvers introduced her to the man who would become her third and last husband, the poet Robert Lowell.

· Seven ·

"MERMAID EMERGING": CAROLINE AND CAL

One wondered who would see and date you next,
and grapple for the danger of your hand.
Will money drown you? Poverty, though now
In fashion, debases women as much as wealth.
You use no scent, dab brow and lash with shoeblack,
Willing to face the world without more face.
—Robert Lowell, "Mermaid"[1]

When Robert Lowell's and Caroline Blackwood's paths crossed in London—as if for the first time—it's been said that, in terms of class and bloodlines, Lowell had met his match.

Caroline first met the poet in 1966, the year of Ivana's birth, at the West Sixty-seventh Street apartment Lowell shared with his second wife, the writer and critic Elizabeth Hardwick. Hardwick, as a founding editor of *The New York Review of Books*, was a colleague and friend of Robert Silvers, and Silvers had brought Caroline to a number of dinner parties at the Lowells' as his guest. Caroline was uncomfortable at those dinners, suffering her chronic troubled silences, and it didn't help that both Hardwick and Lowell—known by his childhood nickname Cal, after Calvin and Caliban and mostly the mad emperor Caligula—were brilliant and loquacious. She later re-counted one such evening to Lowell's biographer Ian Hamilton:

> *I couldn't speak. I'd been told—which was nonsense—that Cal couldn't speak about anything except poetry. That was the legend about him: everything else bored him . . . So there were these ghastly silences. . . . I just used to sit absolutely silent. I was always put next to him. And it used to be my dread. To break the silence once, I said I admired the soup. And he said, "I think it's perfectly disgusting." And then we had a silence.*[2]

On another occasion, the taxicab Caroline was in nearly ran Low-ell over, one of those random events that would later take on an em-blematic significance. Lowell had absentmindedly stepped in front of Caroline's cab in the middle of a traffic-clogged street, and Caroline was afraid for him. "I remember thinking, 'He's not going to last very long,' and feeling awfully sad."[3]

At the end of the decade, Israel and Caroline were still nominally married. Perhaps because she was impatient with her relationship with Silvers—Caroline *liked* being, if not married, at least in a do-mestic situation—she decided to pack up her children, move back to London, and lease the New York house. In her absence, according to Caroline, the rental agency unknowingly leased her house to a prosti-tution ring. When she was called back to New York to sort out the mess after the tenants fled, she found whips and chains tucked away in corners. She later described in enthusiastic detail what she had found in her abandoned townhouse: "There was a rack and a crucifix and a stocks in the basement; everything in the house down to the last kitchen utensil was for a sinister purpose. What's more . . . the phone kept ringing, with men wanting the most disgusting and unprintable things."[4]

Caroline enlisted her friend Stanley Moss, the poet and art dealer, to help her field calls from would-be clients. Moss remembered that Caroline was highly amused by it all.[5] At one point, as the calls from avid customers kept coming, Caroline pretended to be the madam and coolly discussed prices for various acts of bondage and discipline, hooting with laughter when she hung up the phone. "I used to quote prices according to my mood—50 dollars, 200 dollars, no one ever quibbled," she explained.

Caroline claimed that she then got the wicked idea of forwarding calls to Silvers at his office. She gave callers a secret password, "Chambers Dictionary," and told them to ask for Silvers, "who would give them exactly what they wanted." Caroline recalled that Silvers "got so angry that I had to stop. The children used to call it Mummy's brothel."[6]

In 1970 Caroline sold the brownstone in New York and bought a five-floor house in London, on a corner at 80 Redcliffe Square in Chelsea. At the time, the area was somewhat down-at-heels, and the house had already been broken up into flats; an aged Anglo-Indian woman lived in one of the two basement apartments. Caroline rented the other basement flat to the young writer Jonathan Raban and took possession of the top two floors, which included an enormous room for entertaining. Israel Citkowitz, rejected as a husband but still avidly concerned about his children, trailed his family to London, where he occupied the middle flat, with the children and their succession of nannies living in a large flat below. Raban recalled that "the Anglo-Indian tenant lived in misery. No one wanted to deal with her; I was sometimes sent to her because Caroline couldn't bear it."[7]

Ivan Moffat, whom Caroline had continued to see whenever he was in New York, may have influenced her decision to return to London. By then he was married to the heiress Katherine Smith and had moved back to London, but he maintained a close friendship, with the usual romantic undertones, with Caroline. The Moffats lived in a grand house near Redcliffe Square, and Ivan saw a lot of Caroline. He noticed a change in his former lover: she had begun to drink more heavily, and vodka had become her drink of choice. He noticed something else that he had not seen before:

*I saw her anger bubbling up. She would sometimes squat on the floor
with her glass beside her and pound her fists on the floor . . . By
then she was getting more and more involved in politics, she was becoming indignant about things. I don't think she was politically
aligned, although she was probably more for Labour than Conservative. She had a rather strident indignation about things, during
and particularly after her marriage to Israel.*[8]

Israel, it seems, had begun a downward slide as his marriage to
Caroline ended. He was distraught when she left him, and, unasked,
moved to London to keep an eye on the children. And there was another reason, thought Cornelia Foss, for his following Caroline. Without her, Israel had little income. "She left him absolutely nowhere,"
Cornelia believed. "He was devastated."[9] When Caroline sold the
house in Greenwich Village, Israel had no place to live except his tiny
studio at Carnegie Hall, so he was grateful for the opportunity to
live rent-free in her Redcliffe Square house until he found his own
apartment.

In London, Ivan frequently saw Israel, who was looking distracted
and eccentric, an image contributed to by the belt strung with keys
that he often wore. No one ever knew what all those keys were for. "I
was deeply fond of Israel," Ivan maintained, "but he *was* fussy. Caroline always called him a 'fusspot.' He was such a loving father, but he
couldn't drive, and occasionally I'd drive him to the market, thinking
it would be five or ten minutes, but he'd carry out huge cases full of
food and stuff. It always took a long time, and there were heavy car-
tons that had to be taken up to his flat." The two men often met at a
little French club off of St. James's Street, which used to be a place
for exiled Frenchmen but had become a kind of afternoon club. They
would play chess—Israel always brought his own board—and sometimes talk about Caroline.

Ivan's relationship with Caroline continued to be ambiguous. "She
didn't like my having married Kate," Ivan said. "Not that we were

involved then, but she didn't approve of the match. They were very unalike, but Caroline had good manners; she was never rude. She and Kate would observe the amenities, but I don't think Kate liked me to see Caroline alone."

In the fall of 1969 Lowell had accepted an invitation to be a visiting fellow at All Souls, Oxford, for the 1970 spring semester. He had been teaching creative writing at Harvard and working on the revisions of *Notebook 1967–68*, with the editorial help of an intense, devoted, and gifted student, the poet Frank Bidart. Lowell's yearly breakdowns, due to his almost uncontrollable bipolar illness, had landed him in various private institutions and had put a tremendous strain on his marriage to Elizabeth Hardwick. No less harrowing than his bouts of mania were his symptomatic infidelities, often rampant flirtations and affairs with much younger women, some of them his students, often carried out right in front of his wife. His mania took several forms, usually focusing on a particular obsession and often characterized by sexual adventurism. One of the mysteries among the intelligentsia of New York was Hardwick's continued devotion to her dangerously troubled, frequently unfaithful husband. Hardwick, a brilliant woman, originally from Kentucky, and a writer of ferocious intelligence (her caustic book reviews for *Partisan Review* were much feared by those under her scrutiny), seemed willing to pay the price of living with genius. Lowell's status as, arguably, America's preeminent midcentury poet, certainly raised her status. His capacious mind met her own. She clearly loved her husband, but her submitting to repeated humiliations at his hands, and enduring the dangers of his mania, cause one to wonder why Hardwick was willing to martyr her peace of mind to her husband's genius. Lowell's infidelities were not simply manifestations of his illness; Ian Hamilton, in his biography of the poet, distinguished between Lowell's manic and "non-manic attachments."[10] Both were legion. Nonetheless, Lizzie Hardwick acted as Lowell's wife, friend, and caretaker, helping him keep mind and body together, ever vigilant for signs of the breakdowns that had become a yearly event by the late 1960s.

Lowell was that rare bird among American poets and academics: a genuine American aristocrat, and that was, no doubt, part of his tremendous appeal to women. Among his ancestors were James Russell Lowell and Amy Lowell; his family history had been entwined with the history of Harvard, America's oldest university, for generations. The revered English novelist Anthony Powell rather caustically noted that "Lowell is an interesting instance of the American self-deception as to no class existing in the US; Robert Lowell never on any occasion being mentioned without his precise standing within the Lowell family, as a Lowell aristocrat, albeit a minor one, being gone into."[11]

Though Lowell's father was from a relatively poor branch of the family, the whiff of great wealth clung to the Lowells and to his mother's family, the Winslows (though it would be Lowell's Aunt Sarah who would inherit most of the Winslow wealth). Lowell's charm and his frazzled, nearsighted good looks—he was handsome as a movie star in his youth—made him all the more irresistible. The American pianist and wit Oscar Levant once described Lowell as "a gentile Clifford Odets" in appearance, noting his large head, black-framed glasses, and unruly hair. "He looked the way a poet should look," Levant wrote, describing him at a dinner they shared in the Oak Room of the Plaza Hotel in New York in the 1960s. Lowell, "slightly sloshed and garrulous," engaged in good-natured competition with Levant, another manic-depressive who had been frequently hospitalized. " 'I've been committed to twelve sanitariums,' [Lowell] announced with an air of triumph. 'How about you?' "[12]

Lowell was a poet in America at a time when accomplished poets still had mainstream status. Throughout the 1950s and 1960s his influence in the intense, small, academic world of poets and critics was supreme; he was the figure around whom the "confessional" school of poetry congregated. Sylvia Plath and Anne Sexton had been his students; Plath credited Lowell's blatant use of autobiographical material as having opened the floodgates to her own shattering and highly personal poems. Having already won a Pulitzer Prize for *Lord Weary's Castle* in 1947 and a National Book Award for *Life Studies* in 1960, Lowell's involvement in the anti–Vietnam War movement had brought him higher national attention. As a protest against the war, he had publicly refused President Johnson's invitation to the White House, and he had marched on the Pentagon with Norman Mailer, who rightly observed that Lowell's stature as a Boston Brahmin, as well as a distinguished man of letters, added credibility to a peace movement that had egregiously divided the nation. Lowell had even been invited to join Senator Eugene McCarthy's presidential election campaign in 1968, and it crossed his mind that he might be offered a post in McCarthy's cabinet if the senator from Minnesota won the presidency. John F. Kennedy had apotheosized Robert Frost at his inaugural address eight years earlier; Lowell might have enjoyed the same kind of high public stature had things gone differently. Still, among poets, Lowell reigned supreme.

Part of Lowell's tragedy was the manic-depressive illness that, even with lithium, was hard to control. He was probably an alcoholic as well. But there were other issues that drove him and became the subjects of his autobiographical poetry: he was the unwanted child of a particularly loveless marriage. His father, Robert Spence Traill Lowell, a naval officer, was sad, inept, and henpecked. His mother, Charlotte Winslow, was a pretentious, bullying snob. Robert— Bobby—was their only child. Several of Lowell's later poems testify to the guilt he felt over his capitulation in his mother's systematic undermining of his unfortunate father. Lowell's groundbreaking autobiographical essay, "91 Revere Street," describes the humiliations Charlotte heaped on the father in front of their son, and the contempt Lowell felt for a father who could neither stand up to his wife nor pursue his own modest interests without being ridiculed for them. Lowell's poem "Anne Dick 1. 1936" expresses his guilt about having knocked his father down in a heated argument over a girl—a guilt that would take a lifetime to resolve. "I knocked my father down / . . . Their glass door locking behind me / . . . no retreat."[13]

Before leaving for England in 1970, Lowell, then fifty-five, had become involved in what was apparently a "non-manic attachment" to Martha Ritter, a twenty-one-year-old poetry student. Ritter, who had been in Lowell's creative-writing class at Harvard the previous semester, had begun a thesis on Lowell's work in progress, *Notebook,* and was therefore invited to sit in on the weekly editorial sessions Lowell held with Frank Bidart, after being somewhat humorously cautioned to keep quiet, listen, and take notes.[14] Martha described how she gradually fell in love with her professor during the fall term and visited his rooms at Harvard's Quincy House. It was, for her, an idyllic interlude, in which she would cook little meals for Lowell and type his poems. Throughout their involvement, Lowell made it clear that he had no intention of leaving Lizzie. He acknowledged that Martha's love for him was greater than his love for her, but he was fascinated by Martha's virginity; he told her that he had never slept with a virgin. "I think for him women were somehow distant, mythological, as if they were to be studied—as if he was watching, like a child . . . He was conscious that he was treading on dangerous ground," Martha recalled.[15] Indeed, the danger was, in part, what attracted him; it contributed to his necessary sense of renewal with each new romantic entanglement. Ritter planned to follow Lowell to Oxford once she'd completed her course work at Harvard; Lowell may have been aware of her plans, though he neither encouraged nor discouraged her. Elizabeth Hardwick and their thirteen-year-old daughter, Harriet, meanwhile, made their own plans to join Lowell in England. Lizzie gave up her teaching job for the year at Barnard College, took Harriet out of school, and sublet their apartment.

Lowell settled into life at All Souls, a place he found "elderly and stiff, yet a pleasant seat on the sidelines to watch the storm."[16] Six days after arriving in Oxford he was invited to a party in his honor at Faber and Faber, his English publishers.

Xandra Gowrie, now living in London, had known Lowell in the States through her husband, Grey Gowrie, from whom she was now separated. She had always liked Lowell, who turned up one day on her doorstep.

"Oh, hi, honey," Lowell said to Xandra in his curiously Southern inflection (picked up, no doubt, from his marriage to Elizabeth Hardwick and perhaps from his friendship with the Southern writers John Crowe Ransom, Allen Tate, and Peter Taylor).[17] "Fabah is giving a pahty for me tonight. Do you want to come?"

Xandra recalled the evening:

It was in the old Faber building, upstairs, in a large room with big Georgian windows. A crowd of people had gathered, and I watched Cal being lionized while he backed off, and I was afraid he was going to fall through the window. He was smoking two cigarettes at once as people talked and talked around him. I was there with Lizzie Spender—Stephen Spender's beautiful daughter. Eventually the party slowed down and we left—Lizzie, me, Grey, Caroline, and Cal.

Caroline was pretty drunk. We went to Woo's, an old-fashioned restaurant, and had a lovely dinner . . . And then we went to a party at [Caroline's brother] Sheridan and Lindy's. It was a great big party, with Mick Jagger and Liberace and everyone under the sun. We all stood around and had some drinks, and Cal, because he was living at Oxford, said to me, "Can I come and stay at your place?"

I said, "No, you really can't, because you'd have to sleep with me, and I don't think you really want to do that . . . Stay with Grey."

"Oh, honey, there's such a lot of stairs. I couldn't do that—and it's too far off."

And I turned to Caroline and said, "Caroline, you've got lots of room; you have him." And they left together, and that was that.[18]

What had begun as a practicality became a cataclysm that would wrench apart one marriage, feed the flames of a new book that would win Lowell his second Pulitzer Prize, and bring into Caroline's life her third and final marriage, her "main marriage,"[19] to a man who was her equal, her soulmate, and her tormentor. Far from sitting on the sidelines and watching the storm, Lowell would become the storm.

After a night at Caroline's Redcliffe Square house, Lowell virtually moved in. Caroline later explained that he was suffering under the delusion that Robert Silvers had tried to bring them together, but, in reality, "that was the last thing Bob wanted. But Cal persisted with that fantasy always—that this was fate, organized by Bob."[20] The two immediately began their grand affair, with Caroline at times sneaking into the august, all-male establishment of All Souls to sleep with Lowell. At first, they made an attempt to keep their relationship secret, while Elizabeth Hardwick, no doubt sensing that something was amiss, sent her husband "boiling messages" about her and Harriet's prospective move to join him in England and Lowell's tardy efforts to find them a house.[21] A few weeks after meeting Caroline, Lowell wrote to his lifelong friend Blair Clark that he was house-hunting and expecting Lizzie and Harriet to arrive soon, as if all was well and the three would resume family life. But that was not to be.

Lowell was offered another academic post in England, this time at the University of Essex, to begin later that year. The University of Essex was middle class, built in Colchester after the war, and was the scene of violent student protests in the 1960s—violent enough to have driven the conservative poet Donald Davie out of Essex, out of England, and into a teaching post at Stanford University in California, in a department made safe for academic poetry by the ultraconservative poet and critic Yvor Winters. Lowell was invited to replace Davie and thus boost the morale of the beleaguered English department.

When Elizabeth first heard, in June, that Lowell had moved in with Caroline Blackwood, whom she knew only as a friend of Silver and an occasional dinner guest, she at first suspected that her husband was on the verge of another manic phase, which usually began with a sexual folly. On at least three earlier occasions, Lowell had become sufficiently infatuated with another woman to talk about divorcing Elizabeth, but those episodes coincided with Lowell's bouts of dementia, when he was fighting for his freedom on all fronts from private psychiatric institutions. Elizabeth was time and again cast in the role of protective wife and jailor, two roles she despised. Once his madness subsided, Lowell would usually return to domestic tranquillity with Elizabeth and Harriet. So Elizabeth immediately suspected that Lowell was entering another manic phase, and she knew she would have to go to London to see him through it and have him hospitalized if necessary. What Elizabeth didn't know in June of 1970, however, was that Lowell's attachment to Caroline was a non-manic attachment, and it was genuine, deep, and life-changing, even though a manic phase would soon follow.

Xandra, in recalling the Faber party, marveled at the attraction between Cal and Caroline. Xandra thought that Caroline, ever the bohemian, took so little care of her personal hygiene and appearance—"You use no scent, dab brow and lash with shoeblack, / willing to face the world without more face"—that she often appeared grimy. Xandra noticed that "they both smoked endlessly and didn't wash much. They were very much alike—they were both drinkers, and clever, and had tons to talk about. They loved jokes. And both lived very near the cliff edge. As Cal said at some point, near the end, 'We're like two eggs cracking.' "[22]

For Lowell, Caroline's ancient bloodlines and titled status were surely part of the attraction. The democratically minded Lowell had not capitalized particularly on his own Brahmin status, but he could not have grown up as Charlotte Winslow Lowell's son without gleaning some of her tremendous satisfaction in being a member of an exalted tribe. If anything, an attachment to *Lady* Caroline would, once and for all, trump his mother's pride in being both a Winslow and a Lowell, though it had been clear to Cal for some time that Charlotte had most likely married his father only to secure the Lowell name. (It was a prize she paid for dearly, extracting payment from husband and son.) By attaching himself to "royalty," he would "do better" than even Charlotte Winslow. Both of Lowell's parents were deceased by the time he met Caroline, but the specter of his mother's grand expectations and his father's inability to live up to them still haunted him. In Boston, Lowell's Winslow relatives would soon be referring to Lady Caroline as "the Countess," which must have struck Lowell as demented, hilarious, and yet somehow satisfying.[23] Lowell would have especially appreciated Caroline's literary ancestor Richard Brinsley Sheridan, and, like Caroline, identify with the "Sheridanish" qualities that "seethed and tingled like champagne" in the blood— like madness or genius.

And despite her often boozy dishevelment, Caroline did possess the lines of unusual beauty: the "curve and bone from crown to socks,"[24] the "*bel occhi grandi . . ./* bright as the morning star or a blonde starlet,"[25] as Lowell would describe her in the series of poems called "Mermaid." Caroline was highly sexual, and for the aging poet—whose poems sometimes revealed a fear of impotence ("I lack manhood to finish the fishing trip")[26]—their early sexual life was a wellspring of renewal. "[H]ow often I made the woman bathe in her waters" was a line of sexual celebration that he wrote in "The Serpent," part five of the poem "Redcliffe Square."[27]

As for Caroline, she saw in Lowell the lionized poet whose mastery of classical languages recalled her lost father's linguistic gifts. (Basil had held a scholarship in classical languages at Oxford.) She had grown up with poetry at Oonagh's table and had always loved poets. Hadn't John Betjeman himself memorialized Basil, shot down in the unfathomable Burmese jungle? Lucian Freud had possessed the promise of genius when she married him but had not yet realized his great style; Israel Citkowitz had been living on the embers of his gifts, unable or unwilling to rekindle them; but Robert Lowell was at the peak of his reputation, still mad for poetry and writing in a white heat.

Even their illnesses dovetailed, in ways that would at first delight the poet. "I'm manic," Lowell would say, "and Caroline's *panic*."[28]

Early on in her relationship with Lowell, Caroline and her three girls visited Aunt Oonagh at her villa in Cap d'Antibes. In a letter to Lowell she revealed how much she was already in love. "Darling Cal," she began, and went on to describe Oonagh's beautiful villa, dripping with bougainvillea and mimosa and staffed with a chef hired from Elizabeth Taylor and Richard Burton (who had let him go because he was too expensive). The meals were so sumptuous, the villa so grand, and the gardens so luxurious that Caroline complained that having everything one wants in life is, in fact, boring. She couldn't wait, she said, to leave Oonagh's claustophobic villa, with its eleven children in residence, and return to Lowell. She longed to be back at his side— "revising."[29]

When she returned to London, Caroline continued to write, this time with more fervor, purpose, and satiric glee than ever before. Jonathan Raban believed that Lowell's influence on Caroline was the full flowering of her talent:

> *Living with Lowell made Caroline a writer; Lowell spotted the genius in Caroline. It was liberating for her to be with him. He was entranced by the stories she told and by her way of putting things—she told wonderful, scandalous stories—feats of exaggeration! She didn't distinguish between life and fiction. She was surrounded by Lowell's belief in her ability to write.*[30]

In May 1971 Sonia Orwell invited Caroline and Cal to attend an avant-garde play, "A New Communion for Freaks, Prophets and Witches" by Jane Arden, founder of the Holocaust Theatre, to be performed in London and followed by a panel discussion led by Sonia herself. This early piece of women's lib propaganda rather appalled both Caroline and Lowell. In spite of their left-leaning political sympathies, they were not prepared for women behaving badly. Caroline's hilarious and biting review, published in the June 3 issue of *The*

Listener—actually more of a review of the disastrous panel discussion than of the play itself—caused a furor. She wrote, "Where there had just been eight extremist women writhing naked while they moaned and masturbated, and complained that they were oxen and had 'holes inside,' there were now four more women . . . If they had holes inside, one sensed immediately that they would be the very last to mention them."[31]

After savagely lampooning the muscular, close-cropped women from Gay Liberation who disrupted the too-genteel panel discussion, she concluded her review with an interview with the author of the play, in which Jane Arden complained bitterly about how Sonia Orwell and her liberals had ruined the play's "vibes."

And then Caroline shrewdly looked around Jane Arden's opulent house on the Little Venice Canal, near Lady Diana Cooper's, and forced the playwright to admit that, although she didn't *look* exploited, she *felt* exploited. With that one observation, Caroline undercut the pretensions of Arden's revolutionary rhetoric. When the piece was published, Lowell wrote to his friend Peter Taylor that "menacing and armed bull-dykes" had begun to picket Caroline's house in Redcliffe Square.[32]

That spring, the manic high that Elizabeth Hardwick had detected in Lowell began to manifest itself. His conversation at high table at All Souls became incoherent, even boorish, and he had "made not altogether unrequited overtures to one of the dons' wives."[33] In July, four months after the Faber party, Lowell inexplicably locked himself and Caroline in their upstairs flat and forbade her to call anyone. She was terrified about the children two flights below. "I simply didn't want him in the same flat as the children in the state that he was in," Caroline told Ian Hamilton. "Neither did I want to be locked in with him. It was the longest three days of my life."[34] There was no solution other than to hospitalize Lowell; he was admitted to the rather dingy Greenways Nursing Home in St. John's Wood. Word of his illness reached Hardwick, by way of Sonia Orwell, raising in Hardwick's mind the possibility that Caroline would never take on Lowell, now that she had witnessed the terrors of his breakdowns. But, instead, Caroline wrote to Lowell at Greenways declarations that Lowell would use, verbatim, in one of his poems: "I think about you every minute of the day, / I love you every minute of the day."[35]

She also wrote to Lowell that she agreed to consider his breakdown *their* affliction, not just his. The idea of a "simultaneous sickness"[36] greatly appealed to Lowell, as the psychic borders between their two personalities wavered and merged. It was part of Lowell's sickness that he had difficulty separating Caroline's suffering from his own; it also strengthened his belief that he and Caroline were meant to be together. At last, here was someone with whom he could share his worst suffering, someone who could help him bear the loneliness of his unbearable breakdowns. Caroline wrote that she knew it would be better for her not to see Lowell, but life without him already seemed *"hollow, bor[ing], unbearable"*—more words Lowell would use in his poems.[37]

Meanwhile, Elizabeth's letters and cablegrams from the States became more strident. She wrote to Lowell just before he entered the hospital that her "utter contempt for both of you," for having caused her and Harriet so much unhappiness, "knows no bounds."[38]

When Lowell wandered away from Greenways one afternoon and showed up on the steps of Caroline's house, his wild appearance so terrified the cleaning lady that she ran off screaming. But it was Caroline who was really frightened. She packed up her children and left for the country, to an eighteenth-century house she had recently bought in Maidstone, Kent, about fifty miles southeast of London.

Hardwick arrived in London and spent a few days visiting Lowell in Greenways, reassuring herself that he was being well cared for, though the fate of their marriage and Lowell's attachment to Caroline were still far from being resolved. Then she flew back to New York. When Caroline returned to London, she refused to allow Lowell to move back to Redcliffe Square. Lowell was devastated; he had hoped to lodge in one of the other flats. Instead, he was installed in a nearby apartment on Pont Street. Israel, too, had moved into his own flat off Grosvenor Square, though in future months he would move back to Redcliffe Square whenever Lowell seemed about to slip into a manic state. "I wanted Israel to be in the house, because I couldn't deal with it alone," Caroline later admitted. "Not that Cal would have hurt the children; he wasn't murderous. But I had to watch him all day and all night because a manic never sleeps."[39] Israel was willing to take on the task.

Restored to a state of relative good health, Lowell settled into his new apartment and prepared to begin teaching at Essex in October. He was passionately in love with Caroline but was still suffering guilt and loss over his abandonment of Elizabeth and Harriet. He thought he should make a return visit to New York to see them over Christmas, and agonized over whether he should go with Caroline or go alone or go at all. His letters to Elizabeth were full of vacillation, self-recrimination, and regret. Finally, on October 18, 1970, Lowell wrote that he didn't think he could return to Elizabeth, but he begged for more time to make up his mind. Lowell admitted that by choosing Caroline, he was turning his back on the "most loved fragment" of his life.[40] A few days later he wrote to persuade Elizabeth that his love for Caroline was different from the crushes he had had while ill. He stressed Caroline's sturdiness and stability, and he admitted that they had already "been together" for some time—"often and intensely."[41]

He left for New York in December, still not having resolved anything, still wondering whether he could "pull this new marriage off,"[42] and also wondering whether Elizabeth would take him back, as she had so many times in the past. That might, after all, be the safest and most expedient solution. Caroline, sensing the danger, wrote to Lowell as soon as she returned from seeing him off at the airport. She told him that two of her girls, Evgenia and Ivana, cried over Lowell's departure, and her description of London as "Chinese gray" or "oyster gray" wound up in another of Lowell's poems, as did her reaction to his leaving, even temporarily. "If I have had hysterical drunken seizures, / it's from loving you too much," Lowell wrote, cannibalizing Caroline's letter.[43]

Lowell continued to vacillate, preferring to stay with Blair Clark, the journalist and writer whom Lowell had known since their school days at St. Mark's near Boston, than attempting to move back into the apartment he had shared with Elizabeth. Before setting off for New York he'd written to Clark that he was "haunted" by letters from Elizabeth and Harriet, which varied from "frantic affection to frantic abuse." Lowell confided in his old friend that, despite the misery he was causing his family, he had found happiness with Caroline. It helped that Caroline exerted no pressure on Lowell to marry her—quite the contrary. Not only was she doing her own vacillating, aware of how dangerous Lowell could be during a manic phase, but she had always been a woman ahead of her time on matters of marriage. Lowell appreciated that Caroline was leery of marriage; not being bound by legal ties somehow loosened the "self-killing desire to master the other."[44]

While in New York, Lowell asked Frank Bidart to fly in from Boston to help him sort out the ninety or so poems and drafts he had written since July. A new book was taking shape in his mind, and once again he would rely on Bidart's expert help as editor and guide. Bidart later described that December meeting:

> *I think I went to see him around December 28—though it may have been before Christmas . . . We talked a little about his personal situation, but he had the beginning of* The Dolphin. *At that time, there was no image of the dolphin in it, so the whole controlling symbolic scheme was not there. It was more nakedly a ninety-odd sonnet narrative, but very much without an ending.*[45]

Like a man condemned to want only what he does not have, Lowell resolved that he would return to London and Caroline. But in January, back in London, he was pursued by the old doubts. He wrote to Hardwick that he missed her steadying—at times "chiding"—

influence, and that surviving without her was going to be difficult.[46] What is clear in Lowell's letters to Elizabeth is that he needed her familiarity and her strength, especially during his manic phases, but their twenty-year marriage no longer held the thrilling excitement he found in Caroline. Caroline—her lineage, her sexuality, her ragged beauty—completely enchanted him. And when she discovered in February that she was pregnant at the age of thirty-nine, Lowell finally made up his mind (though he would tell Bidart that he intended "to stay with Caroline regardless of the pregnancy").[47]

Lowell was pleased. If he had sought spiritual as well as sexual renewal in Caroline, the birth of a child was the proof and flower of that renewal. In March of 1971 he described the calm that had come over him during the early months of Caroline's pregnancy, in a letter to his friend, the playwright William Alfred. He compared his state of expectancy to "walking through some gauze screen"—a screen that allowed him to see but not touch the world around him.[48] In an exuberant letter to Blair Clark, Lowell described Caroline's "blooming health, [her] sheer woman humanity."[49] And, finally, to his friend Peter Taylor, whom he had known since their undergraduate days at Kenyon College, Lowell wrote triumphantly that he and Caroline "haven't quarreled for four months"—a record for Lowell—and that he'd just finished a book of poems. He added that he and Caroline were both "slovenly, but essentially sane."[50]

Lowell moved back into the Redcliffe Square house, with Caroline, in the top-floor apartment. Israel was still a frequent visitor, keeping an eye on the children, since Caroline could never seem to hire a proper nanny or keep one in her employ. They often entertained, and when Israel showed up during parties, looking disheveled and jangling the keys on his belt, Caroline's guests sometimes mistook him for the caretaker. "I couldn't have borne being Israel, turning up at his former home with Caroline and Cal there, entertaining guests," remembered Jonathan Raban.

Raban noticed that Israel's health was deteriorating, and his apartment off Grosvenor Square "was catastrophic."

> *It always looked burgled: upturned chairs in the middle of the room, rows of empty yogurt cartons, papers everywhere. Once I stopped by and couldn't find him, so Caroline said I should call the police. I did, and when they came they were alarmed and thought the place had been burgled. I told them he always lived like that. He had gone to the hospital, probably because he had a small stroke, though he said it was something else.[51]*

To anyone who had known Israel in his heyday, Israel at sixty was a sad sight. The writer and broadcaster Jonathan Fryer knew Israel and Caroline in the early 1970s and thought that Israel still loved Caroline but was terrified of her, and used to shake when the phone rang in fear that she was calling.[52] Israel had been unable to leave Caroline, mostly because of the children, and he was now condemned to live in the long shadow cast by her and her famous consort, who seemed to slowly replace him, even in his children's hearts. Caroline had Evgenia, Natalya, and Ivana busily writing fetching little cards and poems "to Robert" when he was in New York, begging him to return.[53] And with preparations now being made for the birth of Lowell's child, Israel became more and more marginalized. Partly to escape his somewhat oppressive appearances at Redcliffe Square, Caroline and Lowell made arrangements to move more or less permanently to the country house in Kent.

The calm that Lowell had written about to William Alfred, however, was short-lived. Raban lunched with Robert Lowell that spring, after favorably reviewing the English edition of *Notebook* in a radio broadcast, and noticed Lowell's enthusiasms heating up. The two men had visited the London Dolphinarium on Oxford Street, where Lowell was instantly smitten. As with previous enthusiasms, Lowell became obsessed with the sublime creatures ("bigger brained than man and much more peaceful and humorous"),[54] and bought stone dolphins for hundreds of pounds, placing them all around the house in Kent—in the garden, in the bath, guarding the front door. Lowell now had his theme, one that would give shape and meaning to the fourteen-line, unrhymed "sonnets" that his new book, *The Dolphin*, would comprise. It was an image and a symbol that expressed Caroline as the ineffable Other: a sensuous, enchanted being belonging to a mythic world, friend to man, a creature straight out of Ovid:

> "*I am a woman or I am a dolphin,*
> *the only animal man really loves,*
> *I spout the smarting waters of joy in your face—*
> *Rough weather fish, who cuts your nets and chains.*"[55]
> —"*Mermaid Emerging*"
>
> *Any clear thing that binds us with surprise,*
> *Your wandering silences and bright trouvailles,*
> *Dolphin let loose to catch the flashing fish. . .*[56]
> —"*Fishnet*"

Raban, observing that Lowell was able to maintain his equilibrium and prevent his high enthusiasm from careening off into mania, said,

> *This was early in his relationship with Caroline. She was two or three months pregnant, I think. Cal was able to hold off the mania by some kind of effort of will—hitting the brink of it and being able to voluntarily draw back, in a way he wasn't able to later . . . Cal holding himself back because he saw the panic in Caroline, and Caroline in a way holding herself back from her . . . fear of Cal. They treated each other with an almost drunken delicacy, and you could feel a massive amount of self-restraint on both sides, and terror—terror that if one of them flipped, the whole thing could crash.*[57]

Milgate Park, the early-eighteenth-century house in Kent, was, like Clandeboye—like most centuries-old country houses—a grand, shambling edifice in constant need of repair. Lowell relished his new role as country squire and described the house as "very old-South messy." As Ian Hamilton observed, "The gentle crumbling interior and the blithely overgrown fields and gardens in which the house was set presented a comic and endearing challenge to his 'New England creed that morality is tidiness.' "[58] Tidiness, in fact, was the first thing to go, once he traded in Elizabeth Hardwick's "guiding and chiding hand" for Caroline's more laissez-faire companionship. Caroline, as if doomed to relive the discomforts of her childhood at Clandeboye, discovered that the house was impossible to heat in the winter, requiring all combinations of coal, oil furnace, and electric heater. Xandra Gowrie, who often visited Milgate out of her affection for Lowell, remembered the house as "chaotic—there were electric wires all along the floor." Xandra found the meals served at Milgate particularly unappealing. She described a comic scene that could have come straight out of *Great Granny Webster*:

> *Caroline used to cook these appalling meals. They had very flat plates, sort of leftovers from a grander life: fine china, very flat, the sort footmen were supposed to carry away. And Caroline would slop onto these plates a sole really burned on the top, maybe some grapes chucked in with it, and some sort of white sauce which was about ninth-tenths white wine, one-tenth cream. And potatoes, and very often there wasn't a vegetable at all, so you had these big white shiny plates, and the white fish, and this sloppy white sauce, which would fall all over the edge, and the white potatoes, as we carried it upstairs on a big, wide staircase with a red carpet. We dined in the sitting room. I don't think there was a dining room at Milgate. The food would just slide around towards the edge of the plate; it was a ghastly scene.[59]*

Lowell described the benign chaos in a poem called "Fall Weekend at Milgate":

Midday heat
Draws poison from the Jacobean brick,
And invites the wilderness to our doorstep:
moles, nettles, last Sunday news, last summer's toys,
bread, cheeses, jars of honey, a felled elm
stacked like construction in the kitchen garden.[60]

As Paul Mariani pointed out in *Lost Puritan*, his biography of Robert Lowell, "maintaining a three-hundred-year-old house was a total mystery to him." He then quoted Lowell's complaints in a letter to William Alfred about the problems of taking care of endless repairs needed at Milgate: workmen huddled in conference with their boss, only to disappear forever after a few hours of labor. The worst annoyance, Lowell complained, was the sandman who arrived at odd hours with "the noisiest machine known to man"—or, even worse, arrived having forgotten his equipment and left again in a pique.[61]

The housekeepers and nannies were usually unprofessional and unreliable, but were often a source of hilarity for Caroline. She could always cope with disaster if she could make an outrageous story out of it. Xandra remembered that "Caroline called me from Milgate one time and said, 'Guess what? Guess what's happened now! The nanny's been shopping in Maidstone and has fallen off her platform soles and injured her ankle! Isn't that the worst!' And she laughed and laughed."[62]

To add to the chaos, the children kept a menagerie of pets: two kittens, a large white rabbit named Snowdrop, a smaller black one named Flopsy, and a gerbil they gleefully named Gertrude Buckman, after the raven-haired ex-wife of Delmore Schwartz, whose affair with Lowell years earlier had contributed to the breakup of his first marriage. Jean Stafford, Lowell's first wife, was, at least superficially, much like Caroline: blond, intense, alcoholic, and a highly regarded writer of fiction. Stafford's merciless short story "An Influx of Poets," about the demise of her marriage to Lowell, blamed a character based on Buckman.

The hardest thing about living in the country, for Lowell, was the two-hour commute back to London and then to Colchester to teach his classes at the University of Essex. He found the students there unprepared and uninterested, compared with those in his Harvard classes, with the exception of one student who suddenly turned up in his classroom, having arrived unannounced from Boston: Martha Ritter, who was still smitten with Lowell. Ritter later told Hamilton that Lowell hadn't known she was coming to England. When she saw him again for the first time, he was wearing a tie she had given him, but she could tell that he was still very much married. She had impulsively flown over in the hope that she and Lowell would pick up their relationship where they'd left off. It was not to be.

Lowell handled this apparently unwelcome complication by turning Ritter into a confidante and airing his unhappiness over the breakup of his marriage and his confused feelings toward Elizabeth and Caroline. He also felt out of place at Essex, an unease noticed by his colleagues and confirmed by Martha.

For a time, Martha and Lowell had lunch every day while he agonized over which woman he should choose—Elizabeth or Caroline. Martha, reverting to her role as handmaiden to genius, thought he was in bad shape, walking the university grounds where no one seemed to know or care who he was. His students appeared interested mostly in having him analyze songs by Bob Dylan and the Beatles. Martha found the experience so disappointing and dispiriting that she finally just left.

On weekends, Caroline and Lowell opened up Milgate to guests arriving by train and filling all the bedrooms—Robert Silvers and Robert Giroux from New York, Xandra and Grey Gowrie, though separated, with their son. Stephen and Natasha Spender, and Mary McCarthy with husband and "a depressed son," arrived for Christmas. The critic and writer Lorna Sage, who was a girlfriend of Jonathan Raban's at the time, occasionally accompanied Jonathan to Milgate. Raban recalled that "she would afterwards marvel over the 'marriage' "—though Caroline and Cal were not yet married—and considered their relationship "blessed." Raban thought so, too: "It looked wonderful—immensely lively, talkative. The weekends were great fun—it seemed like a marriage made in heaven."[63]

Caroline gave birth on September 28, 1971, after twelve hours of labor and a great deal of *Sturm und Drang*. Caroline had been rushed at midnight from the hospital in Maidstone to the University College Hospital in London, because the infant was in a breach position and had to be turned around lest it be strangled. Lowell himself suffered eight days of nosebleed, a chronic condition due to his elevated blood pressure but for all the world an acute case of sympathetic labor pains—like Caroline having her "simultaneous sickness" with Lowell a year earlier. Lowell bled before, during, and after Caroline's bloody ordeal. He wrote in a poem called "Nine Months":

> *Today I leaned through lunch on my elbows,*
> *Watching my nose bleed red lacquer on the grass;*
> *I see, smell and taste blood in everything—*
> *I almost imagine your experience is mine.*[64]

They were delighted with their son. He was named Robert Sheridan Lowell and called Sheridan, after Caroline's brother and her favorite ancestor, the playwright and satirist, the wit, the drinker, the carrier of genius and—possibly—the gene for alcoholism. Lowell, fifty-four when Sheridan was born, was well pleased. Sheridan looked uncannily like his father and would bear that resemblance throughout his childhood. Lowell described his new son to Harriet in a letter—he was trying hard to maintain an affectionate, long-distance relationship with his daughter—as looking like a "lobster-red stiff gingersnap man" or a bartender who "imbibes as well as sells."[65] He would incorporate that description into a commemorative poem, "Robert Sheridan Lowell," published in *The Dolphin*:

> . . . *too much blood is seeping* . . .
> *after twelve hours of labor to come out right,*

in less than thirty seconds swimming the blood-flood:
Little Gingersnap Man, homoform,
Flat and sore and alcoholic red . . .

"If you touch him, he'll burn your fingers."
"It's his health, not fever. Why are the other babies so pallid?
His navy-blue eyes tip with his head . . . Darling,
We have escaped our death-struggle with our lives."[66]

After Sheridan's birth, life at Milgate became even more chaotic. (Lowell would write in "Careless Night": "What is worse than hearing the late-born child crying—.")[67]

Lowell's American driver's license expired and was not replaced; it was decided that, given his high blood pressure and unpredictable manic episodes, it would be better for Lowell—and for everyone else—if he did not drive. Caroline had owned a car in Los Angeles but never liked driving; her youthful car accident with her cousin Doon had left her with a painful back injury that often flared up. Having let her license lapse, she tried twice, unsuccessfully, to get a new license. Instead, the family had to rely on a hired handyman-cum-chauffeur, but when they returned from London with the baby, they discovered the driver had beaten a man in a jealous fit and had to be let go. Since his girlfriend was the nanny, they had to replace her as well.

Caroline had never had the good luck or good judgment to hire reliable help. Lowell wrote to William Alfred in November about the endless couples they interviewed, including a couple of aggressive Italians, a man who "polished silver for Lord Butler," as well as "two Irish fairies" and a pair of "feeble-minded orphans" raised in a Catholic convent.[68] Lorna Sage, who visited Caroline and Lowell both at Milgate and at Redcliffe Square, recalled that Caroline

hired a succession of more-or-less disastrous people ranging from superannuated hippies to drunken professional butler-and-

housekeeper double acts to do the cooking, housework, etc; in London she ate out, or picnicked . . . and occasionally got contract cleaners in. She lived for the most part in grand squalor . . . [but] the conversation was marvelous, and went on well into the night.[69]

Meanwhile, Elizabeth Hardwick filed for separation from her estranged husband. But there was something even more troubling than his abandoning her: she heard that Lowell was weaving her letters, phone conversations, and cablegrams into the text of his new book of poems. She was horrified. Not only had Lowell left her and Harriet, but now her anger and despair and hurt would be paraded throughout America and England. Lowell tried to assuage her fears by writing her solicitous letters, even offering not to publish the book. However, his true intentions were revealed when he again turned to Frank Bidart to help him organize and shape the lengthy sequence into a narrative. In September he invited Bidart to Milgate, where he would be a welcome emissary from Lowell's old life in the States. As Mariani pointed out:

By then it was clear to Lowell that England was beginning to look rather like something out of the Brontës, and within a year he would be anxious to get back to the States to resume his teaching duties at Harvard. The English experiment had lasted so far for only a year and a half, and already America was beginning to have "the glamour of a foreign country" for him, a wildness, an appealing strangeness all its own.[70]

Bidart arrived right after New Year's in 1972 and stayed for five weeks, helping Lowell to shape and edit *The Dolphin*, which would record Lowell's abandonment of his marriage to Elizabeth Hardwick and mythologize his marriage to Caroline. Transformed into a fabulous creature of the deep, Caroline is alternately a dolphin, a baby killer whale, and a mermaid as seductive and dangerous as any of Ulysses' sirens:

None swims with her and breathes the air.
A mermaid flattens soles and picks a trout,
Knife and fork in chainsong at the spine,
Weeps white rum undetectable from tears.
She kills more bottles than the ocean sinks,
And serves her winded lovers bones in brine,
Nibbled at recess in the marathon.[71]

Lowell was hardly prepared for the firestorm that would follow publication of his new book of poems.

· *Eight* ·

DISSOLUTION AND DESPAIR

Surely good writers write all possible wrong—
—Robert Lowell[1]

art just isn't worth that much
—Elizabeth Bishop[2]

S heridan's birth, welcomed by Cal and Caroline, was not universally celebrated among Lowell's extended family. With Charlotte
Lowell deceased, the matriarchal authority of the family now
resided in Charlotte's sister, Sarah Winslow Cotting, Lowell's aunt and
the inheritor of the Winslow wealth. Lowell's cousin, Sarah Payne
Stuart, described in her memoir, *My First Cousin, Once Removed,* the
effect that "Bobby" Lowell's behavior and the birth of Sheridan had
on the family.

> *Aunt Sarah and Uncle Cot refused to speak to him even after he
> and the Countess were married in 1972. When we asked her, she
> would say, yes, she would like to see Bobby, but when he called,
> she wouldn't come to the phone. My mother said the fact that Bobby
> had named an illegitimate child Lowell was what caused Aunt*

Sarah to disown him; the illegitimate child itself was not the sin so much as bestowing on him a legitimate surname.³

Aunt Sarah didn't quite know what to make of Caroline, whom she persisted in calling "the Countess." Stuart recalled that Caroline Blackwood was "the opposite of any woman Aunt Sarah had ever had to tea. Lady Caroline didn't care what people thought of her: an ungraspable concept. She was beautiful, rich, titled, and talented—and she didn't need anyone's approval."⁴ Stuart's mother also found the match hard to grasp when she met the couple in New York just before Lowell's divorce and remarriage:

My mother was impressed that [Caroline] wasn't more chic: She was wearing an ordinary dress. Though she wasn't slovenly, it seemed that she did not care at all about her clothes. Bobby did all the talking as Lady Caroline smoked incessantly, while my mother kept trying to figure out why Bobby liked her better than Elizabeth. Caroline seemed too high-strung, completely dependent on Bobby, whereas Elizabeth had been independent, strong, and supportive. "Elizabeth was one of eleven children from a working-class Kentucky family," my mother said, "and every one of those children went to college."⁵

Lowell was disinherited by Aunt Sarah, who would leave her fortune to her nieces, but he would never know that he was disowned by this highly respectable member of his family, because Sarah would outlive him by many years. Sheridan's illegitimacy would, farther down the road, be the cause of yet another disinheriting, with a greater fortune at stake.

The cost of Lowell's divorce was high indeed. The interest on Lowell's trust fund (about $20,000 a year), his beloved house in Castine, Maine, and the two apartments on West Sixty-seventh Street all went to Elizabeth Hardwick. Lowell would describe it in *The Dolphin* as "a barracuda settlement,"⁶ in keeping with the maritime imagery of the book, and he would later complain to his ex-wife that the divorce had left him only his grandfather's "gold watch and . . . fifteen books."[7] Bidart recognized that

> *one of the ironies is that though Lowell was in conventional terms very well off, in fact the money he got from trusts and things was essentially supporting Lizzie and Harriet. And the only money he had was from his teaching, and in England, that's not very much money! So in a way, the premise of all this happening was actually the fact that [Caroline] had a home of her own and could support herself. So it was not irrelevant that she was an aristocrat with aristocratic means. He could not have done this with someone who didn't have money; he would have been very poor, and would have had to take another teaching job; it would have been a tremendous struggle.*[8]

Anticipating his divorce, perhaps, Lowell became acutely aware that he must write to earn his keep. In "Summer Between Terms," he seems to wince at the drudgery of writing for pay, and the worse drudgery of performing at ill-paid poetry readings:

> *. . . I go on typing to go on living,*
> *There are ways to live on words in England—*
> *Reading for trainfare, my host ruined on wine.*[9]

It was a particularly cold winter when Frank Bidart arrived in Kent, in January of 1972. His first impression of Caroline was that

> *she seemed shy, she was meeting this American who had known Cal before, and I wanted her to like me and she wanted me to like her. She had sort of ravaged looks, but was very striking, in a way a little like Jeanne Moreau in that you can see she'd obviously been very beautiful. I admired the way in which she was not trying to look pretty, she was not trying to be a debutante. She was very contemptuous*

of her mother and her mother's circle who wanted to look as if they
were in their twenties and thirties.[10]

Bidart found Caroline very welcoming, and he thought that Lowell was happy, even though he was surrounded by criticism over the breakup of his marriage to Elizabeth. Lowell seemed "embattled but flourishing," and Bidart was impressed with Caroline's intelligence and sense of humor. He was also impressed by baby Sheridan's resemblance to his father: "I have never seen a child who so much looked like one of the parents. It was eerie. I mean, Sheridan had a face that was just like Lowell's, to an incredible degree. Amazing." Bidart also noticed that among the three daughters, Natalya, the eldest, "was extremely nice and certainly smart, but not bookish, not academically minded," and that it seemed to bother Caroline.

I think Natalya felt undervalued. Unvaluled. Both Genia and Ivana,
who were younger, were much more verbal and were talented—
gifted—and it was hard on Natalya. Natalya got on very well with
her sisters; they were close. But I think she felt that she was not the
kind of brilliant daughter that Caroline would have liked.[11]

For five weeks Bidart worked with Lowell, revising and organizing over four hundred unrhymed sonnets. Those on historical figures would make up *History*. The family drama poems that had not fit into *The Dolphin*, along with a sequence called "Mexico," would be published in *For Lizzie and Harriet*. Mariani has pointed out that a dolphin figure also appears in *For Lizzie and Harriet*, but it represents Martha Ritter, not Caroline: "This would remind Lowell's readers that while the dolphin of the title was Caroline, in a larger sense he was invoking the erotic muse which had renewed him. It was this same muse, of course, which would also help destroy him."[12]

Caroline, working on her own stories and articles in a nearby bedroom, frequently offered suggestions and criticisms as the two men worked side by side. Bidart noted that she "never had the slightest hesitation in saying she didn't like something."[13] Indeed, Caroline was tough on Lowell and often told him his poetry was self-indulgent.[14]

Of the three concurrent books, *The Dolphin* was the most disturbing, going deeper than ever before into the autobiographical, and angering Lowell's friends, admirers, and detractors for its blatant use—and many felt its *misuse*—of Elizabeth's letters and phone calls. William Alfred warned Lowell that Lizzie would be devastated by the book's publication, and he conveyed W. H. Auden's disapproval on hearing what Lowell had done.[15] Lowell's friend Elizabeth Bishop, a woman and a poet whom he deeply admired, wrote a long, gently chastising letter, laying out her moral objections to Lowell's new book:

> *Dearest Cal,*
>
> *I've been trying to write you this letter for weeks now, ever since Frank [Bidart] & I spent an evening when he first got back, reading and discussing* THE DOLPHIN. *I've read it many times since then and we've discussed it some more. Please believe that I think it is wonderful poetry. It seems far and away better than the* NOTEBOOKS; *every 14 lines have some marvels of image and expression. . . It's hell to write this, so please first do believe I think* DOLPHIN *is magnificent poetry. It is also honest poetry— almost. You probably know already what my reactions are. I have one tremendous and awful* BUT.

Bishop went on to quote Thomas Hardy on the "infinite mischief" that follows "the mixing of fact and fiction upon unknown proportions." Bishop, a poet often admired for her reticence, continued:

> *One can use one's life as material—one does, anyway—but these letters—aren't you violating a trust? IF you were given permission— IF you hadn't changed them . . . etc. But art just isn't worth that*

much. *I keep remembering Hopkins' marvelous letter to Bridges about the idea of a "gentleman" being the highest thing ever conceived—higher than a "Christian," even, certainly than a poet. It is not being "gentle" to use personal, tragic, anguished letters that way—it's cruel.*[16]

Lowell wrote back, defending his use of Lizzie's letters by saying that he had edited them "in order to comb out 'abuse, hysteria, repetition.' "[17] But he agreed to make some changes, moving the birth of Sheridan earlier in the chronology of events, making it the reason for Lowell's visit to New York, and giving him a compelling—and more honorable—reason for returning to England and to Caroline.

As if the turmoil surrounding the writing and revising of *The Dolphin* had somehow disordered Caroline and Lowell's universe, another cruel disruption occurred in January. Little Ivana, now six, was seriously scalded when a kettle of boiling water turned over on her lap. She had to spend three months in the Queen Victoria Burns Unit in East Grinstead, a good two hours away from Maidstone and a harrowing drive through the winter snows with Caroline's less than reliable driver. Ivana underwent painful skin grafts, but she was lucky in that the Burns Unit was the best in the country. Its founder and chief surgeon, Dr. McIndoe, had perfected his skills operating on badly burned pilots in the Second World War. A plastic bust of the Burns Unit founder, now deceased, beamed down on distraught family members who gathered in the waiting room.

Xandra Hardie—since divorced from Lord Gowrie—felt particularly protective of Caroline's children and thought that the hired nannies were inadequate at best. She believed that the general disorder of the household may have contributed to the accident. "The house was chaos—there were electric wires all along the floor!"[18] However, Dr. Paul Brass, who was Caroline's general practitioner in London and who treated the children for all the usual childhood complaints, thought the accident nothing more than a stroke of terrible luck.

("The Guinnesses are known for their bad luck," he observed, "and remember, Caroline was a Guinness.")[19]

Children do things on the spur of the moment; it happens so quickly! Caroline often used to come to surgery with the children—she was attentive in that way. To the best of her ability, she did worry about them, she looked after them and made sure they got good medical attention. I think they were more in the hands of the keepers; there might have been some neglect, or she might have thought there was some neglect and felt guilty about it. How do you know what they're doing with the children?

It was an excuse Maureen Dufferin might have used.

Bidart remembered that Caroline insisted on making the drive to East Grinstead every day, even when the roads were icy and dangerous.

Lowell was frightened for her, and he would go with her, but she would get very wild, she was so upset. He became the rather sober one trying to make order and make things happen in as rational a way as possible. It was an example of Lowell turning out to be the one who had to take care of things, rather than being the irresponsible one who had to be watched over. When things were in control, when things worked out all right and were not too wild, he liked that role. He liked not being the sick one. And she was the one, naturally, who was beside herself.[20]

Caroline wrote a chilling journalistic piece about Ivana's experience called, simply, "Burns Unit," which would be published in her first collection of stories and articles. The tone of the piece is, understandably, controlled hysteria, as Caroline recounts in grotesque detail the images of burned patients on television monitors behind the head nurse's desk—"soundless images of burn-blotched stomachs and strapped-apart thighs in close-up . . ."[21] She compares their charred limbs to figures from Francis Bacon's paintings, "women whose breasts were blown up like balloons . . . infants in cots, tiny pieces of purple zebra flesh."[22]

"Burns Unit" contains the antisentimentality of all her journalism, which tends to heighten the horror, as she dispassionately described how one day she recognized her daughter on three different television monitors. Disoriented, she found herself going back and forth between Ivana's room where the *"real"* Ivana lay unconscious, and the television images of her behind the nurse's station.[23] It's as if Caroline forced herself to consider the worst aspects of her child's misfortune rather than put a hopeful face on it; typically, she refused to close her eyes, to avert her gaze. She described another burned child screaming for water, only to be told by the nurse that she can have one teaspoon of water every two hours. She wrote that the patients' screams were amplified over the monitors in the halls. Noticing the seeming indifference of the nurses, Caroline wondered how long it took to become inured to "this chilling broadcast of howls."[24]

As usual, Caroline leavened her grim account with humor, relating how she one day mistook the man who cleans the lavatories for the head surgeon and asked him for her daughter's prognosis.

She then carried on a conversation with the ghost of Dr. McIndoe, the clinic's founder, who, she imagined, shared her mistrust of sentiment, since sympathy is a "wretched substitute for skill." Dr. McIndoe must have known that the true horror of his burn patients would begin after they left the ward and went out into the world, where they would be treated to the real "cruelties . . . pity and horror."[25]

Sympathy being no substitute for skill could well have been Caroline's credo as a writer.

Caroline did not realize, nor would she have been interested in so characterizing her writing, but she was practicing "the new journalism": the journalism of the 1960s in which the writer was very much present, and which relied on the details and dialogue usually associated with fiction. The writer John McPhee's comment that "things that are cheap and tawdry in fiction work beautifully in nonfiction because they are *true*" could have been applied to some of Caroline's prose pieces. The new journalists of the 1960s, such as Tom Wolfe, Gay Talese, Joan Didion, and Norman Mailer, made their voices central to their reporting. Caroline's voice was so powerful in her writing that there was no way she could submerge it in an objective retelling of facts. Without identifying herself as such, and most likely without having read the new journalists of her day, Blackwood wrote essays that contributed to the new hybrid of literature and journalism. It was a contribution stemming, arguably, from the arrogance of her tribe—her confidence in her own voice—rather than from her placing herself within a literary trend. More to the point, the influential editor Colin Haycraft, at the Gerald Duckworth and Company publishing house, was impressed enough by "Burns Unit" that he offered Caroline a contract for a book of her stories and journalism.[26] Caroline accepted, and Ivana recovered from her third-degree burns.

Meanwhile, wild baby Sheridan was terrorizing the household. Lowell ruefully wrote to Peter Taylor in Charlottesville, Virginia, that he feared Sheridan was already a "University of Virginia type"— untidy, boisterous, good fraternity material.[27] He destroyed books, short-circuited a third of the house, and pushed over a section of the fireplace. Lowell tended to stay away from child-rearing, proud of the children but a little baffled and frightened. Stanley Moss, who would later befriend Sheridan and act *in loco parentis* in New York, believed that when Sheridan was growing up, "he was never once said *no* to."[28]

Among the chaos and bursting life of the household, Lowell nursed premonitions of his death, a foreboding that crept into a number of *The Dolphin* poems. Though only fifty-four, Lowell believed that he would die at the age of sixty, as he believed his parents had. In "Plotted," he wrote, "Death's not an event in life, it's not lived through."[29] In "Another Summer," he wrote, "When most happiest / how do I know I can keep any of us alive?"[30] The last section of "Flight to New York" evokes his dread of having to leave one household for another, at the same time suggesting, with a dull thrill, a more final leave-taking:

> *underneath us like a submarine,*
> *nuclear and protective like a mother,*
> *swims the true shark, the shadow of departure.*[31]

And in the long poem sequence called "Marriage," he wrote:

> *now death becomes an ingredient of my being—*
> *my Mother and Father dying young and sixty.*[32]

History filled up with elegies to his friends and contemporaries. John Berryman, perhaps the closest contender for Lowell's crown as America's supreme, mad, scholar-poet, had leaped to his death in 1972 from a bridge over the Mississippi. Seven years earlier, Randall Jarrell had been fatally struck by a car. Lowell elegized both men. "They come this path, old friends, old buffs of death," he wrote in an elegy to Jarrell published in *History* the following year.[33]

In 1972 Lowell and his new family were involved in two automobile accidents, as if Caroline's early experience of her taxi nearly running him over in New York had been an omen. At the end of April he and Caroline were in a taxi on the way to Maidstone, to see a Sunday matinee, when they were suddenly cut off by a turning car. Caroline was unhurt, but the accident raised a lump on Lowell's shin that would bother him all summer, and the shock stayed with him for a long while. Lowell had never been a good driver; accidents formed a *leitmotif* in his life, beginning with the crash in which Jean Stafford's nose was broken and her face disfigured. Ann Hulbert, one of Stafford's biographers, blamed Lowell for the disaster; she described him as "a notoriously bad driver who had probably been drinking that evening."[34] (Aunt Sarah thereafter referred to Jean Stafford as "that girl Bobby married just because he broke her nose," an opinion shared, no doubt, by Charlotte Lowell, who considered her first daughter-in-law "common.")[35] Sinister cars do crop up in Lowell's poems: from the Tudor Ford and hulking "love-cars" parked hull to hull near the graveyard in "Skunk Hour,"[36] to the "giant-finned cars" that circle Boston Common like great sharks in "For the Union Dead."[37] In a poem near the end of *The Dolphin* ("Cars, Walking, etc., an Unmailed Letter"), Lowell remembers an old car he and Lizzie once owned, which now suddenly appears to him as "a warning like Hector's Ghost from the underground."

> *The car graveyard . . . now no longer obsolete.*
> *I do not drive in England, yet in my thought,*
> *Our past years, especially the summers, are places*
> *I could drive back to if I drove a car,*
> *Our old Burgundy Ford station-wagon summer-car,*
> *Our fourth, and first not prone to accident.*[38]

In retrospect, the poem is ominous, as if Lowell knew that death would come to him one day in the backseat of a car. And there would be one more near disaster before the year was over.

In August of 1972 Caroline received a touching letter from her old friend Michael Wishart, ostensibly asking if he could come visit her in Milgate in September, but really taking the opportunity to rail against an Earl's Court nursing home, where his problems with drugs, alcohol, and depression had landed him. Addressing the letter from "Limbo," he began by thanking Caroline for her "characteristically kind" offer of a loan. "I am happy to say that it will not now be needed," he wrote, "as my father, who has grown markedly more benign, and whom I now almost love, is going to pay for this hell."[39]

Wishart's letter, like the painter himself, is full of fanciful and brilliant insights. His devotion to Caroline shines through; one has the feeling that Caroline, though never one of Wishart's lovers, inspired him to unleash unconscious creative ideas and images, as in this passage:

> *I cry a lot, of course, like a baby, as when the sun shines and I think of O. Wilde's "that little patch of blue we prisoners call the sky," and last night I dreamed I was having sex with Esther Williams in an aquarium, very much my schoolboy dreams. Sonia Henje [sic] spinning so effortlessly in her little white fur skirt and white leather skating boots used to give me nocturnal emissions . . . and Sabu and Weissmuller in their exotic loincloths like pansy [Gauguins] . . .*
>
> *I wish my real life were like my dreams under deep narcosis: they are close to bliss.*

Wishart then wrote, "I have not even seen your son yet . . . What is he called? How happy you must both be and that makes me very glad, almost gay, for you." A number of letters he wrote to Caroline in 1972 and 1973 reveal his devotion to her, but he was apparently too ill that summer, and the next, to make his visit.

At the end of that summer Harriet came to Kent for a brief visit, which turned out to be rather pleasant and fortunately uneventful. In September 1972 formal divorce proceedings were drawn up for Lowell and Hardwick, and in October Caroline and Lowell flew to New York to secure divorces from their respective spouses and, at last, marry. It was probably Lowell's idea; Caroline never put a high premium on the wedded state. But as Sarah Payne Stuart observed about her first cousin once removed, when he had tried to run away with Anne Dick, "even at nineteen he was a 'marrier,' unlike most men."[40]

They brought young Sheridan to New York with his nanny, an Australian hippie, and checked into the Gramercy Hotel on Gramercy Park. Lowell flew to Cambridge to see old friends and arrange his teaching schedule at Harvard for the following semester, an undertaking he was eager to resume after a difficult and disappointing year at Essex. When he returned to New York, the couple flew to Santo Domingo to get their divorces in one day. The tackiness of the enterprise was not lost on Caroline, who described the adventure to Ian Hamilton:

Blair Clark arranged the whole thing—it's terribly expensive . . . it was a double divorce, of course, because I was divorcing Israel. The limousine waits and then on to the marriage, which was just a shed with a lot of people typing. The typing didn't stop at all, deafening typing. And the ceremony is in Spanish, of course.[41]

Caroline later noted that she'd never had a traditional wedding; somehow marriage seemed less intimidating if it was more like getting a dog license.

In December—after Ivana's painful scalding, the firestorm over the impending publication of *The Dolphin*, the "barracuda settlement" with Elizabeth, and the hurried divorces and marriage— Caroline and Lowell were relieved to see the year limp to its close. There was yet one more frightening near disaster, however: the children's nurse ("about the best driver we've had," Lowell wrote to Bidart)[42] backed the family Volvo out of the driveway, with the children in the backseat, and was promptly hit by another car. The Volvo spun out of control and ended up on a barbed-wire fence. Three of the windows were smashed, and Ivana's eyelid was cut. The car itself was beyond repair.

Life at Milgate returned to some semblance of normality, with Lowell and Caroline both readying books for publication: Lowell's three new volumes of poetry and Caroline's first collection of stories and essays. The two often worked in the same room, editing and revising, knocking off around six to begin their drinking, sometimes with guests from London who arrived for dinner and stayed until the last train left for the city. Caroline realized that it was unusual to work in the same room as another writer, because most writers need solitude. Lowell would frequently interrupt her, asking her opinion on

various lines. As Lowell was an obsessive reviser, he must have pep-
pered her with interruptions. And Caroline showed him everything
she wrote.

Even with Lowell's assurances, Caroline was nervous about her
first book, to be published by Duckworth at the end of the year.
Lowell wrote to Bidart that Caroline, usually quite formidable, was
sheepish around her publisher.[43] Bidart himself felt that she was def-
erential about her writing because

> she was forty-two when her first book was published, and here she
> was married to a world-famous writer. Of course she was not go-
> ing to talk about her writing and the book, but that doesn't mean it
> wasn't important to her. On the contrary, it probably took her a long
> time to realize that what she wanted to do was write . . . Look how
> productive she was, writing most of her books in about ten years!
> She was nervous about mechanics, not just spelling but punctuation,
> because she'd had this non-education. If you have to do it all your-
> self, you have a lot of fear that you're going to make a fool out of
> yourself. But I think it was very important to her, and important not
> to be merely the wife of Robert Lowell.[44]

Michael Wishart wrote to Caroline in March 1973, announcing
the opening of an exhibition of his paintings scheduled for May.

> I am off all drugs and drink, living like a hermit and working
> from 9 A.M. daily until I drop from mental fatigue . . . The gas
> strike renders arctic my studio as with mauve paws I struggle to
> evoke Africa: land of orange groves, parrots and Arab daydreams
> which is what my exhibition is about, as well as myself. The sub-
> jects are unimportant, an excuse to arrange colours really . . . I
> wonder whether you would make a gesture of great friendship by
> letting me borrow "Flowers and Gardens in Flemish Art" for the
> exhibition. It would be a perfect foil for the new "tougher" work.
> I'm happier than for a long time working under such pressure but

suffer migraines and, except for taking myself to the opera some-
times, I hardly ever leave this fridge where at night I munch cold
suppers in an overcoat . . .

> *Best wishes to Cal + very much love*
> *Michael[45]*

The Dolphin, published in July 1973 (the same year as *History* and
For Lizzie and Harriet), came in for the expected measure of outrage
in the American journals, earning the scorn of Adrienne Rich in *The
American Poetry Review* ("this is bullshit eloquence, a poor excuse for
a cruel and shallow book")[46] and the judgment of Marjorie Perloff in
The New Republic ("Lizzie and Harriet seem to get no more than
they deserve").[47] Hardwick was more incensed and humiliated than
Lowell by the negative reviews. She was in the unhappy situation of
having her *life* placed under review, against her wishes and with
nothing to gain by the book's publication. It was as if punishment
were being meted out by some wicked God of Reviewers, paying back
Hardwick for all the astringent book reviews she'd written. She angrily wrote to Lowell that she never wanted to hear from him again,
and she fired off condemnatory letters to Lowell's American and English publishers.[48]

Caroline herself had mixed feelings about the publication of *The
Dolphin*, but for different reasons. She defended Lowell's use of Hardwick's letters and phone calls, because they had provided the book's
narrative backbone, but she did not like his casting her in the role of
muse. She was unhappy at being exploited by Lowell's poetry, and she
later confided in Andrew Harvey, the young Oxford scholar who
would become close to her after Lowell's death, that she

felt gutted and used by it. She was too loyal to ever complain about
his appropriation of her in The Dolphin, *but she didn't want to be*
the muse of men. She wanted to be creating her own things. But
she did inspire and initiate men in their creativity. It was her des-
tiny to play that role. Look how deep and rich The Dolphin *is,*

compared to Lowell's Notebooks. *He really captured Caroline's complexities.*[49]

Lowell believed that *The Dolphin* was "his last and perhaps best book"; as Mariani observed, it was "a problematic breaking through into a new life."[50] He took comfort there, and in the favorable English reviews (one of which compared *The Dolphin* with the last poems of Yeats) and the support of treasured friends like William Alfred and Frank Bidart.

In August of that year, Caroline received a much welcome and calming visit from an old friend. Walker Evans, her former companion—or beau, depending on whose version of events is true—visited the Lowells in Kent, where he took a number of photographs of Caroline and her family. Evans was trying out a new Polaroid camera, with interesting results. Among the many photographs of Cal and Caroline, among the lively disorder of their household, is a portrait of Caroline staring unflinchingly into the camera, looking forbidding, demonic, and full of rage. Fifteen years earlier Evans had captured her stunning beauty on one of their weekend visits to Connecticut, in which Caroline, bare-shouldered against a wild tangle of foliage, looks like a seductive wood sprite about to enchant the beholder into other realms.[51] It was not just the fifteen years of stress and hard drinking Evans revealed in his later photograph; it was as if he had captured two different people: a beautiful enchantress and a demonic destroyer. And yet they were the same woman.

After leaving Milgate, Walker Evans spent some time in one of Caroline's flats on Redcliffe Square, where he wrote to friends about his impressions of the Lowell marriage:

August 29, 1973

. . . I did go to the Lowells, Milgate, near Maidstone . . . most interesting; at the moment indescribable. All in all a real success, somewhat to my surprise; I mean, Lowell and I got on OK, in fact more than OK. I made many pictures, as I had promised to do,

*mostly for Caroline's coming book. I think they do a lot for each
other, and it is a great pleasure to see. Later probably I can
describe for you what I remember. If not, it will all be in my
memoirs, 1990 about, when we're all gone, for our descendents to
read . . .*

*She flies to USA this Thursday. I must leave Redcliffe Square.
She needs to list and show this apartment, to rent it to rich
Armenians. Wow. The troubles and the cares of the rich! We're
better off poor.*[52]

The proposed memoir went unpublished, and if Walker Evans, then
seventy, had any nostalgic yearnings for Caroline, he did not express them.

Early in September, Caroline and the children accompanied Lowell to Boston; he was to resume teaching at Harvard. It was four years
since Caroline had lived in America. They spent the entire year in
Brookline, in a rented house that Lowell's cousin Sarah remembered
as "Victorian, gloomy, and shabby . . . There were all kinds of nannies and children running around. Empty liquor bottles were scattered everywhere on the floors."[53] On Sarah's first visit to meet
Caroline, she was impressed that "Lady Caroline sat elegantly with an
empty liquor bottle at her feet that she did not even try to kick under
the couch. To me, this made her an aristocrat."[54] Caroline and Lowell
had brought with them Lucian Freud's youthful, staring portrait of
Caroline, "Girl in Bed," and placed it in the living room over the
couch. There the painting hung, its arresting gaze reminding all visi-
tors that, though Lowell was the academic and literary star of the
family, Caroline's spirit nonetheless infused the house.

When the academic year ended, the family packed up and returned to Milgate. Caroline's first book, *For All That I Found There*,
had just been published. The title, taken from an Ulster Protestant
hymn, evoking the boredom of empty Sundays in Ulster among the
Protestant gentry, suggests the importance of Caroline's early years in
shaping her view of the world. Caroline later wrote in *The Listener*

on the subject of boredom, suggesting a Baudelairian connection to the *eerie* (a good Scots word). In describing the "eerie pathos" of bored Anglo-Irish women staring out their windows at gray lakes and gorse-covered mountains, she compared them to ghosts haunting the cold stony halls of their homes.[55]

The critics' response to *For All That I Found There* was mixed. Gabriele Annan wrote favorably in *The Listener*:

> *This book contains five short stories, four bits of miscellaneous reporting and four reminiscences of Ulster: the sort of collection that the publishers of a well-known, possibly even recently dead writer might assemble. But this writer is not dead, though she can be lethal . . . She has power, imagination, wit, and above all, precision.*[56]

The reviewer rightly discerned that "[t]he theme of this rather haphazard book seems to be the unbearable," an assessment that probably pleased Caroline. (She would no doubt have howled at Annan's comment that "this writer is not dead"!) "The stories are mostly dialogues between people tormenting one another," Annan continued; she placed Caroline as existing somewhere between the "horsey world" of Ulster and the realm of the avant-garde, suspended, as it were, like Mohammed's wife.

The London *Times* was more critical. Robert Fisk, in fact, sounded downright repelled by Caroline's tone and subject matter. He wrote that "the trapped claustrophobic atmosphere of her childhood memories seems to have had its effect on nearly all the essays and short stories in this hotchpotch of a book."[57] The reviewer, after mentioning that Caroline was the wife of Robert Lowell, compared her, unfavorably, to Tennessee Williams and Arthur Miller. His biggest objection was to her characters, whom he described as "a sick little crowd of semi-humans with not a scrap of humour in their awful personalities. Of course, they are symbolic creatures, and the vacuity of their lifestyles symbolizes our own trapped existence." Fisk did find persuasive, however, the connection Caroline made between boredom and the Troubles in Northern Ireland.

In the *London Magazine*, Digby Durrant said he was puzzled by the division of the book into three parts: "Fiction," "Fact," and "Ulster." (The section titles may have been suggested by Lowell, whose friend Elizabeth Bishop had earlier published *Questions of Travel*, with only two sections, sweepingly titled "Brazil" and "Elsewhere.") In any case, Durrant remarked on the similarities between Caroline's fact and fiction. "The excellent short story writer she is," he wrote enthusiastically, "turns into an equally excellent journalist with such smoothness there seems little difference."[58] Durrant could hardly anticipate that in future books, and in life, the difference between fact and fiction would blur even more.

In April 1974 *The Dolphin*, with its dedication "For Caroline," won the Pulitzer Prize in poetry—Lowell's second. It had been nominated by Lowell's good friend William Alfred.

In early May Caroline was unable to reach Israel Citkowitz on the telephone. Frustrated and then alarmed, she alerted the police and then the fire brigade and had them break into his apartment. Israel lay dead in his bedroom, among the squalor and debris of his paralyzed life, felled by a heart attack. He was sixty-five years old.

Citkowitz had suffered a stroke earlier that year and had been taken to St. George's Hospital in London. Lowell visited him there, taking Caroline's place because she had a cold and was warned that exposure to her virus might carry off Israel in his weakened state. Caroline recalled that Lowell insisted on bringing Israel two translations of Herodotus, because he believed that Israel, a "Jewish intellectual," would want to have both. Lowell also wanted Israel to confirm his opinion that one translation was brilliant and the other was terrible.[59] Israel, who was reduced to reading with one unparalyzed eye, apparently enjoyed Lowell's visit, and Lowell was moved by the experience. He later described the visit in the poem "In the Ward," published in *Day by Day*: "If you keep cutting your losses," he wrote, "you have no loss to cut."[60] Like many of Lowell's late poems, "In the Ward" is a meditation on aging and death ("Being old in good times is worse / than being young in the worst"), but it ends with a tribute to Israel's spirit, and, perhaps, an understanding of the perfectionism that made it impossible for the composer to fulfill the brilliant promise of his youth:

Somewhere your spirit
Led the highest life;
All places matched
With that place
come to nothing.[61]

Caroline had those lines engraved as Israel's epitaph, after having him buried by Harrods, London's upscale, all-purpose retail store— not far, incidentally, from Maureen Dufferin's house at 4 Hans Crescent. Genuinely saddened by Israel's death, she would nonetheless have a good laugh at the irony of America's "great white hope" in the exalted realm of the art song being buried by a department store.[62]

By the summer of 1974 Lowell had managed to avoid another full-blown manic phase. He had not been in a hospital since his stay at Greenways Nursing Home four years earlier. Lowell's drinking, however, remained a threat to his hard-won sanity, particularly when mixed with lithium, so he self-prescribed himself doses of Antabuse. He thought John Berryman's fatal mistake was going off alcohol completely. Sudden abstinence, Lowell reasoned, had brought on suicidal depression, and Lowell was convinced that it would be dangerous for him to completely stop drinking. Elizabeth Bishop, who also drank heavily, had written to him earlier that year:

I wish you wouldn't drink. I know it is bad for your health, primarily—
I had a lovely time drinking vodka and aquavit while traveling, but
when I'm working here I find it's much better just to stop completely—
that's easier for me than cutting down. I don't know how it works for
you. But I do know I like all my friends better when they aren't

drinking—And now I have said more than enough of my mind for once.[63]

Frank Bidart didn't consider Lowell an alcoholic, but he recognized that Lowell "shouldn't have been drinking at all, because he was taking lithium, and a little alcohol could make him a little manic." Unlike most heavy drinkers, who encourage their friends and loved ones to imbibe with them, Caroline, fearing another of Lowell's manic phases, didn't want him to drink. Her own high alcoholic intake, however, probably made it easier for Lowell to continue. And in the life of poets and writers in midcentury America, alcohol was clearly the drug of choice: socially approved and ordained by Dionysus, god of wine and song. "When seven people went out to dinner," Bidart observed, "six of them were having drinks. But if Cal drank a lot, he would get weird at times. Not always. It was hard for him not to have it; he liked to drink."[64]

At a party at George Weidenfeld's in October, however, Lowell suddenly collapsed. He blamed the dizzy spell on his mixing Antabuse, alcohol, and lithium; he also suffered from high blood pressure and a congenitally weak heart. Dr. Brass, who looked after the entire family when they were in London, wanted Lowell to consider having a pacemaker surgically installed if the dizzy episodes recurred. Lowell, in a letter to Jean Stafford—who was now married to the writer A. J. Liebling and who had undergone hospitalization at least twice for alcoholism—explained away the incident. He wrote that he didn't intentionally drink while taking Antabuse, and he told her that he was alarmed by *her* excessive drinking. He did caution her, though, that it could be dangerous for her to stop completely.[65]

Caroline's drinking had also reached the point where it was making her physically ill, at first masking but then exacerbating her back pain; she was at times unable to sleep unless she lay on the hard cold floor. Lowell wrote to Elizabeth Hardwick that Caroline was having "an acute nervous depression."[66] She had also begun to experience vague gynecological problems, and Lowell wrote again to Elizabeth, asking her advice and wondering whether Caroline, who was forty-three, was entering menopause. Elizabeth—though a year earlier she had vowed to never correspond with Lowell—replied in October 1974 that Caroline was too young to be entering menopause, and made no other references to her complaints.[67] But Caroline was still unwell in January, so Lowell returned to Harvard for the 1975 spring semester without her. In March, however, Caroline could no longer bear being separated from Cal, so she packed up Ivana and Sheridan and flew to Cambridge to join her husband. Natalya and Evgenia were safely away at school. The stress of life with Cal, and the constant flying back and forth between England and America, further exacerbated Caroline's back pain, and, at Cal's urging, she sought medical attention.

Caroline went to Lowell's Boston physician, Dr. Curtis Prout, who recommended surgery, suggesting that her back would never fully heal without it. He wrote to her that it was probably true that all of her troubles stemmed from a bad back.[68] He also recommended that she stop taking Elavil, usually prescribed for anxiety and depression, and switch to Thorazine. He apparently did not caution her about her high consumption of alcohol. Lowell later wrote about Caroline's back troubles:

> *You are very sick,*
> *You remember how the children,*
> *You and your cousin,*
> *Miss Fireworks and Miss Icicle,*
> *First drove alone with learners' cards*
> *In Connemara, and popped a paper bag—*
> *The rock that broke your spine.*
> *Thirty years later, you still suffer*
> *Your spine's spasmodic, undercover life . . .*[69]

Caroline returned to England, and after the spring term ended, Lowell left Cambridge and flew back to Kent. She was relieved to have him back home; she feared that his residing in the city of his birth, so near the scenes of his bitter childhood, might bring on another manic attack; she also recognized that, in Cambridge, he was surrounded by hangers-on who encouraged him to drink and stay up all night, expounding on poetry. Lowell had a powerful constitution, but now Caroline feared for his weakened heart.

They spent a relatively peaceful summer at Milgate, writing throughout the day. Lowell was preparing his *Selected Poems* and composing new poems for what would become his last book, *Day by Day*. Caroline worked on a number of essays and book reviews for *The Listener*, including a scathing—and hilarious—review of Nancy Friday's book of pop sociology, *My Secret Garden*, a painfully detailed compilation of women's sexual fantasies. Caroline gleefully debunked the American best seller, newly published in England by Virago/Quartet, complaining that the sexual fantasies of the women interviewed by Nancy Friday became monotonous when read in bulk.

A Bertha who dreams of being bound and raped by a donkey while three black men are watching doesn't seem significantly different from a Betty who . . . [dreams] of being bound and raped by three black men while a donkey is watching.[70]

She ends her review by soberly listing some of the more bizarre fantasies, the ones that involve household goods and appliances: a vacuum cleaner nozzle, a cucumber, a battery-operated toothbrush.

Poking fun at radical feminists like Jane Arden and more commercial feminists like Nancy Friday made Caroline seriously suspect among that diverse crowd. The previous year, a feminist had written from Charlottesville, Virginia, to *The New Review* to complain about an essay of Caroline's on feminism. The writer, Anne Williamson, felt that Caroline had misunderstood and distorted information; she even accused her of making things up and of brutally lampooning her and a friend who had consented to be interviewed.[71] Williamson was probably right in her judgment, but what she failed to grasp about

Caroline was that she was, in her essays and reviews, fundamentally a satirist. And earnestness is always easy to satirize. Nonetheless, her lack of credentials among feminists didn't prevent her first novel, begun that year, from being hailed as a feminist study of female rage.

Caroline's novel had started out as a short story, a tale probably inspired by her friend Ellen Adler's predicament at finding herself unable to get along with her husband's nearly grown child from another marriage. The protagonist is a thirtyish woman of leisure, in a beautiful New York apartment, who has just been left by her husband. But not before he unloads his miserable, fat, teenage daughter on his about-to-be-divorced wife. It's an angry novel, ostensibly removed from the life Caroline was leading with Lowell—except that, according to two of Caroline's close friends, the depressed, uncommunicative teenage girl in *The Stepdaughter* was based on Natalya, Caroline's eldest daughter.

By November 1975 Lowell's old symptoms began to return. He described his manic phases as always beginning with a tingling at the base of the spine, followed by reduced good humor, then a surge of enthusiasm. Before long, the enthusiasm blossomed into full-blown mania.

Caroline recognized that Lowell's manic episodes were often wound around a theme. At one point he was obsessed with Jacqueline Kennedy; at other times, with Hitler, Mussolini, or Christ. When he was obsessed with Jacqueline Kennedy, whom he had met at the White House at a formal dinner given for André Malraux, Lowell started calling her repeatedly on the telephone, until she had to change her number, Caroline said. Another object of his mania was hardware stores, because Lowell had discovered that T. S. Eliot loved such stores in England. So Lowell made the rounds of the local shops and shoplifted hardware shamelessly, bringing home all kinds of appliances. At one point, Caroline recalled, Lowell's psychiatrists wanted to know whether Cal was handy in the kitchen. "Why do you think the professor loves hardware so much?" they asked. To that, Caroline had no answer, but she later observed, "I'm afraid madness is very comic, isn't it? I mean afterward."[72] In truth, she was terrified. In the depth of his madness, Lowell would lose the ability even to read a newspaper; he was capable of putting his hand into a fire to see if it was hot. Once, he hung out of one of the top windows in the London house and declaimed to the streets below, believing he was Mussolini.[73] Another time he insisted on eating detergent, until Caroline instructed the help to lock up the Cascade. Dr. Brass, who was luckily convenient to Caroline's house, remembered Lowell "in a very bad state . . . digging a hole at their home, digging at a socket with a nail file. He got deep into the exposed wires, and Caroline was absolutely terrified about it."[74] Caroline remembered:

> *Once at Milgate he said he was going to have an attack. And we had one hope: that if he had a massive Valium injection, it might stop . . . So I said: "Let's get right on the train and go to Dr. Brass." When we set off he was talking a lot, but he was making sense. By the time we reached Victoria, he wasn't. He'd gone, flipped.*[75]

Dr. Brass rushed to their home and administered an injection of Valium; he stayed throughout the night, giving Lowell more injections, but nothing seemed to calm him. The doctor did his best to restrain him until an ambulance was called, and he was taken away to a private hospital, the Priory, in Roehampton. When Dr. Brass later visited him there, he found Lowell still manic and aggressive.

> *He threw a piece of paper at me and he said, "Read that. What do you think of that?" I read it through—it was a poem about arriving by ambulance—and I said, "I like it very much." And he said, "No, you don't." He could be very aggressive. I said, "I do, rather; I love your description of the ambulance man, and your being*

removed," and he said, "It's true; I write my best poetry when I'm manic."

Well, I'm not sure that he did write his best poetry when he was ranting. He had quite good insight into his illness; into the way he really got going until he was uncontrollable, so you couldn't stop him. Caroline tried, and she couldn't stop him, and she used to ring me up in fear and enormous anxiety.[76]

Lowell spent two weeks at the Priory and then discharged himself and returned to Milgate, where he remained relatively calm. By the end of December, however, he was out of control and was checked back into the hospital, Greenways this time. But Lowell managed to charm his doctors, who called him "Professor" and sometimes allowed him to leave the hospital grounds for long periods of time. Caroline was upset when he signed himself out of the hospital a few weeks later, still clearly manic. By January 21, 1976, he was readmitted to Greenways, where he told people that he was the King of Scotland; he also showed up with a large knife after a day's outing. Lowell was so physically imposing that there was no way Caroline could have defended herself from a violent attack. And then, of course, she had the added burden of keeping her children safe. Dr. Brass realized that Caroline "just could not take Cal's bipolar illness. It's a dramatic illness—really dramatic, and I don't blame her, poor thing. It was terrible. She definitely couldn't cope with that. There was a lot of stress generated in that relationship."

There was already an undercurrent of violence in their marriage, occasionally acted out when Lowell was sane or on the edge of a manic high. It had been present in his first marriage as well. Once, in New Orleans, Lowell had punched Jean Stafford in the face, breaking her nose for a second time. Peter Taylor's wife, the poet Eleanor Ross Taylor, thought that Lowell "was an abusive husband. I think he was just somebody who got his way . . . . He was very wonderful to me in so many ways, and so important in Peter's life, but there was a side of

Cal that I was afraid of and didn't want anything to do with." Anne Macauley, the wife of Robie Macauley, Lowell's friend and classmate at Kenyon College, told Eleanor that "she and Elizabeth were going up in an elevator once, when Elizabeth said to her, 'Does Robie ever hit you?' And she said, 'No, he never hits me.' And Elizabeth said, 'I told Cal, other men don't hit their wives.' "[77]

Eleanor and Peter Taylor witnessed some of that abuse when they stayed with the Lowells in London. "We were in the children's quarters," Eleanor recalled, "and they had come up from Maidstone. Lowell was locked out because he and Caroline had been quarreling. He had hit her, and she had a black eye. She pushed him out the door and locked him out." Lowell later wrote the troubling lines describing Caroline: "bulge eyes bigger than your man's closed fist, / slick with humiliation when dismissed—."[78]

As the new year dawned, Caroline began to fear not Lowell's hospitalizations, but his release from the hospital. She recognized that he was frequently discharged while still in a mild manic state, and his acute relapses occurred in a matter of weeks. But Lowell, not legally committed to any of the psychiatric hospitals where he took refuge, was free to discharge himself whenever he felt a surge of good health. And when Lowell was in a manic phase, it often took the form of confusing Caroline's identity with his own and not allowing her out of his sight. "It was so claustrophobic," Caroline remembered; "if I went down to the harbour, he would follow me. He would take my books and sign them Robert Lowell. He'd say, 'Cal and Caroline are the same, we are the same,' and I would say, 'No we are not the same' . . . It was hopeless by then."[79]

Caroline became so unhinged by Lowell's illness, she soon lost the ability to distinguish between mad Cal and healthy Lowell. Therein, according to Frank Bidart, lay the tragedy of their marriage:

I think the hardest thing and in some ways I think what destroyed the marriage was that Caroline could not deal with Cal's breakdowns. And I don't mean that therefore it was all her fault, but, unlike Lizzie, who did deal with them year after year, Caroline would get utterly freaked out. Caroline was so threatened by them, in a way so angry because of them . . . and she was afraid of what he would do.[80]

Caroline, desperate because she had no control over Lowell's hospital stays, flew to America and moved into a house Bidart rented for her and Lowell on Sacramento Street, in Cambridge, in anticipation of Lowell's return to Harvard. "She was extremely upset that the doctors were convinced that he was well enough to go home," Bidart explained. "That was a terrible period when she refused to let him come home, and she came to Cambridge. She was very angry at the doctors." When Lowell was released from the hospital, he spent several days alone in their London apartment, calling Caroline and begging her to allow him to join her. Finally, she relented. Bidart and Caroline picked up Lowell at Boston's Logan Airport and took him to the rented house in Cambridge. But according to Bidart the reunion was not a happy one:

This was deeply sad, one of the saddest moments I know of. He was okay, he was well, I knew in my veins he was not manic—he was just nervous, nervous to see her again, and feeling extremely rejected by her. But she was convinced that he was still sick. When we got into the car, she whispered to me, "He's still sick." I didn't think so. And he knew, he could tell from the way she was acting that she thought he was sick. She was rejecting, she was cold; she let him know that she thought he was not well.[81]

Lowell began to fear for Caroline—and to fear her. He recognized that his breakdowns "made her worse—more wild, more destructive, more out of control. She would get extremely agitated," Bidart observed.

And he was afraid of how destructive she could be when she drank.
She was always a very vivid talker, but she got to be much more
flamboyant, and there was a kind of vehemence, an apocalyptic, de-
structive coloration, and one never knew how much would remain
only talk, or somehow would get acted out in her life. She once
threatened to put her children in the car and smash into a wall. Cal
said to me, "I feel I make her sick."[82]

If Caroline was still his erotic muse, his dolphin, she was also "a
baby killer whale . . . warm-hearted with an undercoat of ice."[83] Or
she was a mermaid serving up "her winded lovers" bones in brine.[84]
And yet they stayed together, like drowning persons terrified of letting go, each dragging the other down—drowning, not waving.

In the spring of 1976 Duckworth published *The Stepdaughter*.
Though it was a slim book, a novella of a hundred pages, and one in
which there were no sympathetic characters, *The Stepdaughter* was
well received. *The Listener* reported, "Blackwood has an unblinking,
observant eye, and a penetrating, acid wit . . . *The Stepdaughter*
is like an etching, sharp, precise and sensitive."[85] The *Times* praised
it as "brilliant": "Form, style, content and perception are brought
together so immaculately, with such absence of technical strain by
Miss Blackwood, this little book demonstrates a major talent."[86]

Indeed, the novella succeeded in its singleness of purpose, its Poe-
like, unified mood. Written as an epistolary novel by a character identified only as K, *The Stepdaughter* explores the entwined emotions of
obsession, resentment, and despair. K, abandoned and lonely, despises
the lumpish, sullen, teenage Renata who has been unceremoniously
dumped on her doorstep by her absconding husband. Renata, who has
unattractive personal habits (stuffing the toilet with toilet paper and
never flushing, for example) and whose only solace is to bake herself
fattening cakes from cake mixes, is pathetic and unlikable. But, then,
K, who despises her, is a hard-hearted monster of self-pity. She is particularly unlovable when she begins to neglect her own infant, losing

interest in her and relying on the homesick *au pair* for all the housework and child care. The husband, whom we never see, is an anonymous male getting away with it all.

This is a book full of controlled rage, in which Caroline has the
confidence not to sweeten her tale by giving any of her characters a
shred of goodness. It's hard not to read *The Stepdaughter* as a veiled
account of Caroline's sense of entrapment by her brood of children,
whose constant needs she was often unable to meet. Dr. Brass noticed
that the children sometimes seemed neglected, though they were
extremely close to Caroline and clung to her. K's failure to fulfill
the needs of the two children—one a stepdaughter and one her
own—breeds resentment and depression. And, of course, no help
is found anywhere from the children's father. Similarly, Lowell,
though proud of Sheridan and his pretty stepdaughters, came to
feel overwhelmed by Caroline's offspring. He confessed to Blair
Clark that he "had never been much interested in children"; he
ultimately found them "boring, totally incomprehensible beings."[87]
K's manipulative husband in *The Stepfather* is a smug businessman
and therefore nothing like Lowell on the surface, but Lowell's enormous problems and obsessions made him a father not to be relied
upon.

Peter and Eleanor Taylor immediately recognized *The Stepdaughter*'s originality and strength; they compared it to Henry James's
What Maisie Knew. Peter wrote to Caroline in August,

> *We both like* The Stepdaughter *very, very much. It is certainly one
> of your best . . . a real literary feat, I think. Nobody else could
> have thought of telling the story that way and nobody else could
> have made it work so well . . . . If you haven't ever read* MAISIE, *I
> urge you to do so—just for your own satisfaction. I had never felt
> before that it is one of James' best pieces of writing, but I feel so
> now. The two novels are very interesting put against each other. I
> think* The Stepdaughter *displays your real genius, Caroline—
> maybe better than anything else you've written—and Eleanor and*

I keep agreeing over and over that you do have real literary genius.[88]

That was high praise, coming from Peter Taylor, well on his way, in 1976, to being recognized as one of America's masters of short fiction. Even Gertrude Buckman, still writing to Lowell and now to Caroline, sent her an admiring, envious letter on the publication of *The Stepdaughter.*[89]

Later that year, *The Stepdaughter* was awarded the David Higham prize "for the best first novel or book of short stories of 1976," an award of £350. It was the first public recognition of Caroline's gifts as a writer, and she was well pleased.[90]

In April, Caroline and Lowell flew to New York to attend a production of Lowell's play *The Old Glory*, at the American Place Theater. They stayed with Blair and Joanna Clark, who owned a townhouse on East Forty-eighth Street with a separate, two-room apartment on the third floor where guests often stayed. Blair Clark had never liked Caroline; he believed she had a destructive influence on Lowell, whom he had known nearly all his life and whom he deeply cared about. He also found Caroline difficult to talk to; she was "formal and abrupt, not one for casual conversation."[91] It's possible that Caroline sensed Clark's disapproval, though the two had exchanged friendly letters early on, and Blair and Joanna had visited them at Milgate in happier times.

Like Lowell, Blair Clark is a tall Boston aristocrat; he's also a former newspaperman and a well-respected writer. He maintained a friendship with Elizabeth Hardwick and was on her side during the tumultuous breakup of that marriage; Hardwick, he said, had behaved "with tremendous dignity" throughout the ordeal. It was Clark who had asked Caroline whether she was prepared to help Elizabeth and Harriet financially, which Caroline, understandably, had refused to do. Clark had then brokered the financial settlement so favorable to Elizabeth.

Blair Clark knew that Lowell, the New England Puritan, was

"impressed with Caroline's beauty—he had raved about her beautiful eyes—and by her aristocratic decadence. And there was that erotic attraction—Caroline was loose and sexual in a way that Jean Stafford and Lizzie were not." Despite years of serious drinking, at forty-four Caroline was still striking, bone thin and dramatic, her eyes heavily outlined in black.

Clark believed that Caroline "divided people into those who could help her and those who could not." He agreed with Elizabeth when she wrote to him, as early as 1970, that, in Caroline, Cal had met his match "for unreality and carelessness."[92] And if there were any lingering doubts about Caroline's unreality and carelessness, they were banished by what Blair and Joanna witnessed during the Lowells' brief visit. Joanna went into their apartment after a few days and was shocked by what she saw. "The squalor was unbelievable," she said. "There were bloody sanitary napkins on the floor; cigarette butts, bottles of liquor, and empty pill bottles were scattered around the room. It looked like the room of an addict."[93]

Meanwhile, unbeknown to Caroline, Lowell and Elizabeth had established a rapprochement. He was harboring a secret wish to leave England and resume his former—safer—life in America. The terrors of his English life, and Caroline's inability to cope with his illness, had finally become too much for him. He confessed to Blair Clark that he had wearied of her relentless "drunken aggression."[94] Elizabeth had always known what to do. If the erotic attachment to his former wife was no longer there, Lowell—thoroughly exhausted at the age of fifty-nine—needed forgiveness more than passion: forgiveness not just for the pain his divorce had caused, nor for the publication of *The Dolphin*, but forgiveness for the Puritan guilt, the nursed hurts, real and imagined, that stemmed from his early childhood, when he had sided with Charlotte in the symbolic castration of his father. That was the first sin, the Oedipal one. Elizabeth seemed willing to provide forgiveness. And if passion was gone, at least he and Elizabeth had the archeology of their marriage to sift through, a rich resource for any writer.

In May, Elizabeth Hardwick attended a PEN conference in London and visited Lowell, who was surprised to see how well his ex-wife and his current wife appeared to get along. He confided in Lizzie that he would be better off living in America, but he couldn't face the upheaval of dismantling and resettling their entire household. Caroline, in fact, had begun to discuss the idea of selling Milgate, not to free her to move to America, but because it was too expensive to maintain—£900 a quarter in 1976 just for the electricity,[95] for example. Lowell wrote to Elizabeth Bishop that Milgate now seemed to him a country house straight out of a Russian novel, struggling on the edge of extinction.[96] Lowell shared Caroline's affection for the old house, however, and wrote to Peter Taylor that its loss would be "sad and autumnal."[97] But Caroline was getting used to losing houses. Bidart had stayed up late one night with her in Milgate while she regaled him with her fury at having been passed over in favor of her brother. Bidart recalled:

> *This came up early. And she expressed real rage, and I felt she had a right to express rage. When her father died, the person who inherited everything and who not only had the title but most importantly had the family home, Clandeboye, was her brother Sheridan. It was the son. What naturally would have come to her as the firstborn, the eldest, didn't, merely because she was a woman. And she felt rage against that—a rage that was deep, and it happened early, and I think throughout her life there was a rage at things that women weren't allowed to do or be.*
>
> *I think it was increased by the fact that she was a beautiful woman, and a rich woman. She also had certain kinds of power, but she knew that they were powers that derived from her beauty and not from herself or her soul. And she was very angry about all of it.[98]*

Lowell had earlier described Caroline's resentment in the poem "Runaway," inspired by Caroline's work on *Great Granny Webster*:[99]

Out of your wreckage, beauty, wealth
Gallantries, wildness, came your book,
Great Granny Webster's
Paralyzing legacy of privation . . .
Your father's betrayal of you,
Rushing to his military death in Burma.[100]

With the fate of Milgate still unsettled, Lowell suffered another manic attack and ended up in Greenways. It was his third breakdown that year. Coincidentally, Caroline's old social mentor, Ann Fleming, was staying at the same nursing home, suffering from "permanent nervous gastritis." In a letter to Patrick Leigh Fermor, she described her encounter with Lowell, who arrived at seven-thirty in the morning armed with volumes of Ezra Pound and T. S. Eliot, and proceeded to read aloud until eight o'clock that evening. Once his medication began to work, Ann wrote, "his gait became unsteady and the chain smoking lost its aim so the day was spent extinguishing small bonfires, until Caroline and the psychiatrist called in a special nurse and he was led away, frustrated, sad and distinguished."[101]

This time, Caroline simply could not handle it. The anger she once felt toward his psychiatrists, most of whom she considered softheaded incompetents, she now turned full force on Lowell. She later described his manic attacks to Ian Hamilton: "They destroy me. I'm really better if I'm away if he has one . . . It's like someone becoming an animal, or someone possessed by the devil. And that's what tears you apart. You think, I love this person, but I hate him. So where are you?"[102]

When Caroline heard that Lowell was about to be released, she felt instinctively that her husband had once again charmed his way out of the hospital and was still not well. Unable to face another episode with mad Cal, Caroline fled to America with Ivana and Sheridan, leaving Lowell behind.

Evgenia was attending Dartington, the progressive boarding school in Devon that Lucian Freud had once attended, but Natalya, just fifteen, was left alone in London. Xandra Hardie remembered being called by her in the middle of the night. Natalya wanted to know whether Caroline had left any money for her. In her anxiety over Lowell, Caroline had neglected to look after her oldest girl, who was alone in the London apartment with nothing to live on, a situation that probably deepened Natalya's sense of rejection. It was like a reprise of Maureen's lack of attention to Perdita and Caroline when they were home during school holidays.

By the end of October, Lowell was out of the hospital, feeling healthy, but worried about Caroline's "habitual overdrinking," as well as her mysterious weight loss and stomach complaints.[103] He followed Caroline to Cambridge and stayed with her for three weeks, but her drunken rantings unhinged Lowell to the point that he moved out and stayed with Frank Bidart for ten days, relishing the peace and quiet of Bidart's apartment. Lowell called Blair Clark, consumed with worry, to tell him that Caroline was in serious trouble. Clark recalled that

> the late-night "tirades" after drinking were bad. There was a sui-
> cide attempt. . . . He had a doctor at McLean's who said he might
> be able to help her . . . I got [the] impression Caroline would go
> back to England in a couple of weeks, with Sheridan, but that Cal
> might not go. He said it was bad for her to have to go because of
> taxes (he mentioned eighty percent). He said he was "crazy about"
> her and there was no one else for him, but it was hard now.[104]

Mariani thought that "the strain of Caroline's drunken tirades . . . so shook him that he suffered a mild heart attack."[105]

On December 3, 1976, Caroline returned to England with Ivana and Sheridan; Lowell promised to let her know "if and when" he would follow.[106] Five days later, Lowell was in New York, staying with Blair Clark, so that he could appear at the 92nd Street Y Poetry Center on the Upper East Side. Frank Bidart was to introduce Lowell's poetry reading. Bidart was alarmed at how defeated Lowell seemed, and how grateful he was to be away from Caroline's household and its "terrific turmoil, anger, drama, tension."[107]

At the 92nd Street Y, then one of the most prestigious venues in New York for poets and writers, Bidart was standing in the wings while Lowell took the stage. He recalled:

> *I apprehended how deep the split had become, because of what he chose to read about her. The three poems he read were from the part of* The Dolphin *about being afraid of her, including the lines*

> *I lack manhood to finish the fishing trip.*
> *Glad to escape beguilement and the storm,*
> *I thank the ocean that hides the fearful mermaid—*[108]

> *I think, at the end, he came to that view of her. He'd been scheduled to get on the plane the next day or so; it was on that trip that he told me he was leaving her.*[109]

For Lowell, Caroline had begun as a muse, one who offered a new and idyllic life, a dolphin who "spouts the smarting waters of joy in your face . . . who cuts your nets and chains."[110] But after seven years with Caroline, Lowell saw her transformed into one of the destroying Sirens.

Nine

UNLEASHED

Agony says we cannot live in one house.
—Robert Lowell[1]

One might say of drug-addicts that whereas their birth may be accidental,
their death is never really by chance.
—Michael Wishart[2]

In January of 1977 Robert Lowell had his first serious heart attack. Lowell had followed Caroline to England in mid-December and had spent Christmas with her, before returning to Cambridge for the spring semester. Since Lowell had been too sick to teach in the fall, Harvard had given him courses to teach that spring; Lowell gratefully accepted them, eager to escape the unbearable tensions of his marriage. Caroline was upset about Lowell leaving her again, but she did not follow him, because her own health and state of mind were too delicate.

On arriving in Boston, Lowell stayed with Frank Bidart. One frigid night in January Lowell awoke with chest pains and roused his host. Bidart remembered that it was so cold, his car wouldn't start, so a cab was called to transport Lowell to the infirmary. Lowell had tests done the following Monday at McLean's, a psychiatric hospital near Boston where Lowell had been previously hospitalized. From there, he was taken by ambulance to Massachusetts General Hospital, where he was diagnosed as having congestive heart failure. He stayed there for ten days, in Phillips House, where his grandfather Arthur Winslow had died "in a well-appointed room with a view of the Charles River."[3] Elizabeth Hardwick came to see him; Lowell beseeched Sarah Cotting to visit as well, hoping once again for a rapprochement with his aunt. Hardwick made the arrangements, and after five years of refusing to have anything to do with her famous nephew, Aunt Sarah went to see him.

By then, Sarah Cotting was eccentric, difficult, and possibly in the early stages of Alzheimer's. Her niece recalled that Aunt Sarah sometimes wore bedroom slippers with her evening gowns at dinner, but she managed to wear proper shoes for her hospital visit. Lowell, who continued to smoke incessantly, ignoring his doctor's orders, was delighted to see his aunt, who sat stiffly in Lowell's room and

> began making sarcastic remarks. She was just waiting to jump at him . . . waiting to "pierce his heart with an arrow." Years before, when Aunt Sarah had visited Bobby at McLean's, she had greeted him warmly with statements like, "Well, this is a pretty place." Now her small talk took the form of barbs like "So, how are you? You look old" . . . But Bobby was happy; he thought he had been forgiven.[4]

For Lowell, the idea of death had entered the room, and now he sought, above all else, forgiveness—a state of mind the last poem in *The Dolphin* suggests:

> I have sat and listened to too many
> words of the collaborating muse,
> and plotted perhaps too freely with my life,
> Not avoiding injury to others,
> Not avoiding injury to myself—
> To ask compassion . . .[5]

Lowell did read forgiveness into Aunt Sarah's icy visit—apparently made more out of *noblesse oblige* than any affection she may have still felt for her nephew—but it was Elizabeth's forgiveness he really wanted. He saw her often over the next two months, and on March 1 he spent his sixtieth birthday with Elizabeth and Harriet and the Clarks. Blair Clark recalled that Lowell "was very sweet to Lizzie, calling her 'honey.' It seemed clear that they were getting back together, though Lizzie wasn't sure about how permanent the break with Caroline was. She thought Caroline might try to get him back."[6] Lowell asked his old friend whether he could rent his third-floor apartment, where he had stayed with Caroline the year before.

On his birthday, Lowell received the news from Caroline that she had indeed sold the house in Kent and had packed up and fled to Ireland with the children. She was staying in her cousin Desmond Guinness's grand old Georgian mansion, Castletown, twelve miles from Dublin on the River Liffey. Built in 1722, Castletown was Ireland's "first great house in the Palladian manner."[7] It was restored in 1967 and became the home of the Irish Georgian Society, headed by Desmond himself. The vast mansion was open to the public, but there were small apartments for private use; Caroline rented two of them—somewhat dingy apartments for such a grand house. Still, the proximity to Guinness cousins was a boon to Caroline's children, who occupied their own "teenager flat," and Caroline was able to indulge her love of Georgian houses. Andrew Harvey observed that Caroline "loved the light and space of Georgian architecture; she had a dream of a big grand house filled with light and music. It was the longing of a drowning person for oxygen."[8]

Lowell understood that the move had to do, on one level, with Caroline's establishing residency in Ireland and thus avoiding the high taxes levied in England, but he was wounded by her selling "their" house without consulting him—the shambling old country house where they had sometimes been ecstatic, if not altogether happy. If Caroline had undertaken such a venture to shock Lowell into staying with her, it very nearly worked. What ensued was a repeat of the vacillating turmoil Lowell went through when he left Elizabeth for Caroline; now he struggled with his desire to leave Caroline and return to Elizabeth. He was still erotically in thrall to Caroline; he was still obsessed with her; but he must have known that his heart would give out if he stayed.

Lowell's final book of poems, *Day by Day*, written in the last year of his life with Caroline, opens with "Ulysses and Circe," which predicts Lowell's decision to escape the dangerous enchantments of Caroline and return to Elizabeth, whom Lowell's extended family tended to look upon as Penelope, his "real" wife.[9] Though the aging classics scholar introduced the poem at a reading in New York's St. Mark's-in-the-Bowery with the disclaimer "It's wonderful to write about a myth especially if what you write isn't wholly about yourself,"[10] it's possible to read "Ulysses and Circe" as Lowell's farewell to Caroline, his awakening from the enchantment that had failed to save him. "Why am I my own fugitive," Ulysses asks, "because her beauty / made me feel as other men?"

> *She stands, her hair*
> *intricate and winding as her heart . . .*
>
> *she wants her house askew—*
> *kept keys to lost locks,*
> *unidentifiable portraits, dead things*
> *wrapped in paper the color of dust . . .*
>
> *the surge of the wine before the quarrel.*[11]

Lowell's anguish was revealed in a flurry of letters he wrote to Caroline from Boston in late March and April, proclaiming his love and his desire to do everything he could for her. "What did you mean," he wrote, ". . . that I had nearly lost you?" He demanded to know if she did indeed want him to return.[12]

Lowell flew to Ireland at the end of March to spend Easter vacation with Caroline and the children. The apartment at Castletown struck him as overwhelming and too isolated, except for its relative closeness to the poet Seamus Heaney, who had befriended Lowell during his sojourn in England. By the time the brief visit ended, Lowell had made up his mind that the marriage was over. But he wrote again to Caroline on April 19, hoping, after a fashion, to have it both ways— a life in American (with Elizabeth), and visits to Caroline and the children in Ireland. "[C]an't I be a constant visitor?" he asked, though recognizing that they might be "too heady and dangerous" to ever live together again. Expressing the same anguished indecision he had felt when he first left Elizabeth, Lowell complained about the remoteness of Ireland from his safer life in the States. But he clearly missed their "big winey dinner[s]" with the children, in their "big rotting house."[13]

Caroline, aware that she was now fighting to hold on to her marriage, called Lowell in Boston and announced that she was planning on flying over to see him. But on May 3 Lowell wrote to her that he feared her visit, because "nothing will be done except causing pain." What followed was the usual summing-up of happier times that precedes a final break: "How many lovely moments, weeks, months, we had . . . the long summer of your swelling pregnancy, the rush to London, the little red man's appearance . . ." Lowell contrasted his tender memories of their early life together with the past two years, full of quarrels and ill health. He confessed that he felt Caroline had "ended things" on his last visit to Ireland, and that the two of them could never go back to the life they had once shared.[14]

But Caroline, though she knew she could no longer live with the dread of Lowell's manic attacks, could not bear to be the one who was left. Ivan Moffat had known this about her when he said, "She was always a great leaver, and leavers hate to be left."[15] It stirred up her ancient sense of abandonment—abandonment by her father, whose death she had felt as a betrayal; abandonment by her cold foolish mother, whose earliest photographs taken with Caroline show an aloof woman incapable of affection, as if it were she, not Brenda Woodhouse, who believed that her children were changelings. And though their life together had been derailed by Lowell's mania and Caroline's anxiety and "overdrinking," there had been many good days: the companionable writing in the same room at Milgate, the "big winey dinners," the brilliant friends coming for long weekends and going away convinced they had witnessed a rare kind of bliss. Caroline tried desperately to get Lowell to return to her.

Lowell flew to New York and spent a few days with Blair Clark, confiding in his old friend that his marriage was over, though he was still deeply, fearfully, in love with Caroline. He told Clark that he was "sort of moving back with Lizzie,"[16] planning to live in the studio apartment they bought together years ago, in addition to their larger apartment on West Sixty-seventh Street, which Elizabeth now owned. Blair Clark had been renting the studio at the time, and Lowell asked whether he could take possession of it when he returned from Castine, Maine, that summer. He was planning to spend the summer months with Lizzie and Harriet, instead of returning to Ireland. In all of this, he gave Clark the impression that "he still had romantic-erotic feelings about Caroline. About Eliz[abeth] he talked of what they had in common, mainly literature but also Harriet. He did not talk as if he were formally 'going back to her'; it was some other kind of arrangement, looser, vaguer."[17]

Although Lowell had tried to convince Caroline not to visit him in the States, Caroline insisted on coming to see Lowell receive a $10,000 award from the American Academy of Arts and Letters. The annual literary event took place in New York City, so Caroline flew over and rented a room for herself and Lowell at the comfortable old Gramercy Park Hotel, where they had stayed on past visits to New York. Lowell told a friend that he feared Caroline was suicidal,[18] she was in such an extreme state of mind, so he agreed to spend a week with her in New York. It was a grisly week.

Robert Boyers, a professor at Skidmore College and the editor of the literary journal *Salmagundi*, wrote a thinly disguised—and harrowing—account of meeting Lowell and Caroline in New York.

"The Visit" is called a short story, but both Lowell and Caroline are named, as is their hotel; only Boyers is disguised as the fictional Mr. Salkey.

Salkey, a young professor intent on keeping a nine A.M. appointment with Lowell, anxiously waits for an hour and a half in the hotel lobby. He finally persuades the desk clerk to open Lowell's room to see whether anything has happened to the guest. He knows of Lowell's reputation for alcohol abuse and for the madness that fills his poetry.[19] When he and the desk clerk enter the room, they are shocked at what they find:

Numerous suitcases were open on the floor, their contents spread wildly over the carpets and beds and chairs. Used bathroom towels were hung carelessly over the back of a dark burgundy sofa. Cigarette butts were sprinkled liberally over every surface. Shards of a drinking glass lay on a counter near the windows. Over the dresses and shorts and underwear spilling from the open suitcases were hundreds upon hundreds of colored pills, their vials and compacts elsewhere in the room.[20]

Lowell and Caroline finally walk through the revolving doors of the hotel lobby, Lowell in a worn tweed coat and Caroline in an old silver fur and high-heeled leather boots, the ash from her cigarette dropping onto her sleeve. Lowell is solicitous of Caroline, calling her "darling." When they enter the "charming snake pit" of their hotel room, Caroline puts on a pair of dark glasses, walks over to the bed, kicks the covers onto the floor, and instructs Mr. Salkey to take a seat at her feet. Lowell apologizes for the room's messiness and makes a halfhearted attempt to tidy up. He then begins a frustrating search for the telephone to order some food for their hungry guest, but it's lost in the room's mayhem. Once he finds it, Lowell is "thoroughly out of sorts, and embarrassed, and apologetic, and beginning to feel exasperated with his darling lying before him on her bed of shreds and lumps and pills and patches."[21] Mr. Salkey attempts to engage Caroline in conversation, but she remains silent, lying on the bed in her silver fur and dark glasses. She drops a lighted cigarette on the floor, which Lowell quickly retrieves. Caroline finally speaks:

> *You there, Mr. Salkey, or whatever your name is. You needn't be afraid. I won't bite you. You can damn well come over here and sit down on my bed again. I like you there. It's, you know, comforting, to have a nice young man seated at the foot of one's bed. Don't you think so, Cal?*[22]

Mr. Salkey, unnerved, realizes that Lowell and Caroline "were wickedly practiced at mixing it up, at thrust and parry and cut and slash and tear."[23] Lowell is embarrassed but a little curious to see how far Caroline will go in toying with this earnest young man. Caroline suddenly points her foot at Salkey's face and demands to know whether he likes her boots. Salkey admires them and asks if they're English, to which Caroline replies:

> *What difference would that make to you . . . Do you know the difference between English boots and Italian, or Moroccan, or American? Don't look at me that way, with your mouth half open. I asked you what you know about boots. If nothing, you can say so. That's no shame in it. Now, is there?*[24]

Caroline continues to taunt Salkey, goading him, making fun of his devotion to the great poet, his eagerness to claim new poems for the Lowell anthology he's compiling. After coercing him to read Lowell's poem "Epilogue" aloud, Caroline turns on Salkey, challenging him to interpret the poem and to define Lowell's phrase "living images." Mortified, Salkey finally rises to the occasion. He takes her by the shoulders and pushes her back on the bed. He orders her to remove her sweater. Caroline is compliant. "Surely she was more com-

fortable in her mauve silk tee shirt, the body lithe, the neck gaunt . . .
She would play his game for a while. He could see that it amused her.
If she was frightened, or embarrassed, she wouldn't let on. That
would never do."[25] Salkey then arranges Caroline on the bed in imitation of Lucian Freud's chilling double portrait, "Hotel Bedroom":

> *On your side, defenseless, like that, exactly, just hold that position,*
> *that's how I see you: vulnerable, bitter, exhausted, almost peaceful*
> *but with just a trace of unexpended rage . . . I wouldn't want your*
> *eyes closed, not that, no, I'd want them open, red-rimmed, quite as*
> *they are now, open with fear or revulsion or perhaps a longing for*
> *peace so desperate that peace seems almost at hand—the peace of*
> *the defeated.*[26]

Salkey has almost triumphed, until Lowell begins absentmindedly
picking his nose. He then challenges Mr. Salkey to "corroborate what
I've long believed about nose picking. I don't mean that any one
episode is just like another. Do you know what I mean, Denis, about
the pleasure of picking relentlessly, but slowly, calmly, at tier upon
tier of dry snot?"[27]

Unable to answer, Salkey excuses himself, goes into the bathroom,
which is littered with capsules and blood-streaked towels, and finds
some of Lowell's unmailed correspondence in a briefcase by the tub.
He steals two letters. Satisfied with his small act of revenge, Salkey
leaves the Lowells' room, and in the elevator going down to the lobby,
he rubs his hands over his coat as if he were trying to clean them. In
a Lexington Avenue coffee shop he repeatedly washes his hands, feeling shame at his inability to enter into their cruel games without
flinching.

> *He remembered—how could he not remember—his own long in-*
> *vestment in the poet's vision of decline and fall, and he bit his lip*
> *with furious self-loathing at the thought of his own failure to*

absorb and master ugliness in the way of Lowell's famous skunks,
jabbing their heads in the garbage cans and refusing—refusing—
to scare.[28]

Diane Arbus once commented that in a world where no one escapes human trauma, the deformed are aristocrats because they are
born with theirs. If that is true, then Caroline was a true aristocrat;
she had mastered the art of seeing into the heart of darkness, and
Salkey knew what an amateur, a naïf, a fool, he appeared to be. Was
that the secret of Caroline's muse-like ability to inspire Lowell's great
poems? Was there nothing she had not seen or imagined or experienced? She had mastered the art of negative vision: she could imagine the apocalyptic end of the world, scorched and crawling with
cockroaches, and find in that vision a kind of solace.

Boyers's description of the Lowells' hotel room—the shards of
glass, the scattered pills, the bloody towel, the drapes pulled tightly
shut—suggests the suicide attempt on Caroline's part that Blair Clark
had spoken of. And if not a suicide attempt, then surely rage—the
rage of a woman about to be left by the husband she loved, and rage
at the academics who feasted on his work.

Although "The Visit" is offered as a work of fiction, Robert Boyers later admitted that the story was true, except that he collapsed into
one meeting incidents that took place over time. He met Caroline only
once, at the Gramercy Park Hotel, as described. He recalled, "She was
horrific with me. I think I evoked the awfulness of that meeting in
my story."[29] What Boyers hadn't known was that Caroline and Lowell's marriage was coming apart at a ferocious rate when he met them
that week, and Caroline was angry with those who seemed to be taking Lowell's side.

Caroline insisted that Lowell return to Ireland when Harvard's
spring semester ended, but Lowell had made up his mind. He
could see that Caroline was severely depressed,[30] and he knew his

presence in her life would be likely to deepen her black moods. He
told his friend Esther Brooks that "he did not want to divide what
time was left him 'between two continents and two cultures.' "[31] That
summer he moved into the studio apartment and poured out his grief
to Elizabeth, who—after the seven years of Cal's involvement with
Caroline—was still willing to listen and to comfort. His marriage to
Caroline had broken him.[32]

Years earlier, Mary McCarthy had written a warning to Lowell:
"As for Caroline, I'd already come to the conclusion that it couldn't
work between you. I mean marriage . . . Maybe what I think of as
love can only transcend death and is not much good about life."[33]

Chain-smoking and jittery, Lowell accompanied Elizabeth Hardwick to Moscow as part of a delegation of writers sent by the Ketter-
ing Foundation to the Union of Soviet Writers. After ten days, they
returned to Cambridge, where Lowell had his heart checked again
and this time was given a clean bill of health. He, Elizabeth, and Harriet then went to Castine to spend the rest of the summer. But by mid-
July, Lowell, who had pinned to the wall of his old study the stunning
photograph of Caroline lounging like a mermaid in the bow of a boat,
started writing to her again. He carried her entreating letters around
with him wherever he went, often taking them out and poring over
them, describing her beauty to anyone who would listen. Natalya
called Lowell from Ireland to tell him that, in his absence, Caroline
was on the verge of crying all day.[34] Lowell wrote to Caroline that
some part of him felt "all might be well" if they could be still be together, but another part of him knew that "all would be ruin."[35] Finally, he offered to come see her one last time in September, before
the semester got under way at Harvard. Blair Clark, sensing Lowell's
trepidation, warned him not to go.

On September 2, 1977, Lowell arrived in Dublin for a two-week
visit, with a big model ship under his arm that he'd bought for Sheridan. In a mirror image of his meeting Elizabeth at Logan Airport
in Boston seven years earlier, Lowell quickly announced to Caroline
that he wasn't staying and that he'd be returning to the States. But

Caroline wouldn't hear of it. "He was fine at the beginning when he came," Caroline later told Ian Hamilton about the last time she saw Lowell.

> *He was just totally happy to be home. Like a little boy. And then there was this thing that he'd committed himself to going back to Harvard. And then it started . . . he never stopped moving from room to room. He couldn't make up his mind—he was changing his mind every five minutes. He said, "Will you come with me?" And I said, "But I don't have a house. I can't come with Sheridan and be in a motel." And as he was getting madder, I wasn't sure if I wanted to . . . Would there be more letters, another* Dolphin? *It was too awful. And he knew that.*[36]

Caroline was beside herself—angry, distraught, depressed, and drinking herself into a rage. When Lowell felt he couldn't take it any longer and announced that he was leaving earlier than planned, Caroline flew back to Redcliffe Square, and the children soon followed with their nanny. Lowell, who expected to leave the following day for New York, was left alone that Sunday night in Castletown.

Alone, exhausted, miserable over how poorly the visit had ended, Lowell became lost in the grand old mansion, trying to find his way back to Caroline's top-floor apartment. And then the telephone and electricity failed. He was utterly alone in the dark, unfamiliar house. Caroline would later describe the unsettling atmosphere of Castletown: the dining room had an "eerie and menacing atmosphere. It is certainly not a place where any sensitive person would choose to spend the night."[37]

Unwilling to stay the night, Lowell tried to leave Castletown and make his way to the nearby village of Celbridge, but he couldn't find his way out. By the time he left for the airport the next morning, released by the woman who had come to clean, Lowell was profoundly shaken.

Lowell left Castletown with heavy suitcases and Lucian Freud's lyrical portrait of Caroline, "Girl in Bed."[38] There has been some controversy over why Lowell carted the valuable painting back to New York. Caroline later told Cornelia Foss that she herself had given it to Lowell before decamping for London, as a memento of their life together—as if Lowell would otherwise have forgotten her.[39] Others claimed that Lowell was planning to have the portrait appraised, ostensibly to raise funds for Caroline.[40] (Four years earlier Grey Gowrie had helped her to sell one of her Francis Bacon paintings, as so much of Caroline's income was being eaten away by taxes.)[41] Whatever the reason, Lowell arrived the afternoon of September 12 at Kennedy Airport, "Girl in Bed" clutched to his breast, and hailed a cab to take him back to the studio apartment where he would now reside.

But by the time the taxi pulled up in front of West Sixty-seventh Street, Robert Lowell was dead.

He had suffered a heart attack in the ride from the airport; death had come to him in the backseat of a car, like all the death cars that crept into his poems, like the old car returning to warn him, like Hector's ghost prophesying the sack of Troy. Elizabeth was summoned, and as she opened the door to Lowell's taxi, he slumped over in the seat, Caroline's portrait still in his arms. Elizabeth rode with him to Roosevelt Hospital, knowing that he was already dead.[42]

Lowell had turned sixty in March; he had fulfilled his prediction.

When Caroline got the news of her estranged husband's death, she was not surprised. She called it "a suicide of wish," claiming that he had said certain things at Castletown about impending death.[43] Her relationship with Lowell had lasted seven years. A cycle had come to an end with Lowell's demise. She would know that her youth was gone, and her famished hope for some human love was nearly gone. But what Lowell had freed in her had now come into full flower: her greatest book was about to be published, and it would be followed over the next fifteen years by six original and startling works of fiction and nonfiction.

Sarah Payne Stuart wrote that Lowell's funeral in Boston was held at the Church of the Advent, "a much higher church than the family's socially correct Trinity Church, with swinging balls of incense and chiming bells."[44] Six hundred mourners attended; Lowell's Boston relatives "sat stiffly in the pews, careful not to be too comfortable."[45] Old Aunt Sarah Cotting, now in her eighties, was there, although she had kept her promise to disinherit Lowell and had torn all his photographs out of the family album. Caroline, her children, and their nannies had flown in from London, and sat in the same pew as Elizabeth and Harriet. Sarah remembered that Caroline wore "a chic black hat, like a little top hat," but she later learned that Caroline and entourage had arrived with nothing suitable to wear and were taken by Elizabeth to buy proper clothes for the funeral.[46] Dressed entirely in black, Caroline "looked like a character out of a Greek tragedy, black eye make-up running down her ravaged face. She shook and shuddered throughout the entire service while the rest of us simply stared. Even Elizabeth and Harriet tried to comfort her, but to no avail."[47]

When the congregants were called to take communion, Caroline, who scorned the thin comforts of Christianity, walked out with her children until communion was over and the obsequies continued.[48]

After the funeral, Lowell's body was taken to the Winslow family burial plot at Dunbarton, a two-hour drive from Boston. Caroline rode with Elizabeth. The cortège of black limousines snaked its way out of the city and eventually stopped at a rest area so that the mourners could renew their strength with food and drink. Lowell's cousin Jacqueline Payne passed around sandwiches and little bottles of sherry. Caroline was still shaking. At one point she sent an emissary over to the Paynes to ask whether they had anything stronger than sherry. They did not, but Jackie's husband chatted up a group of picnickers nearby and came back with two airplane bottles of vodka for Caroline. "Soon a tremulous but smiling countess was being taken around and introduced by Elizabeth," Sarah Payne Stuart wrote. " 'This is Lady Caroline . . . Cal's wife.' "[49]

In the end, Lowell's family reclaimed him. He was buried next to his mother, Charlotte, while Caroline, Elizabeth, and Harriet threw flowers into the open grave.

*G*reat *Granny Webster* also ends with an open grave, with Caroline and her great-grandmother's ancient one-eyed maid, Richards, the only mourners at Great Granny Webster's funeral. Caroline wrote that Richards was probably praying for herself, having had a premonition that her employer left her entire fortune to the Society for Euthanasia, leaving poor Richards nothing but Great Granny Webster's favorite chair.

Lowell had recognized that Caroline was engaged in something important when he wrote: "Out of your wreckage, beauty, wealth / gallantries, wildness, came your book, / Great Granny Webster's / paralyzing legacy of privation . . ."[50] though he would not live long enough to see its late-September publication. One of the earliest reviews, published in the London *Sunday Times* on September 25, noted that "Miss Blackwood is Robert Lowell's widow—a wife worthy of him in her accomplishment."[51] That and a slew of other favorable reviews would be Caroline's cold comfort in the months following Lowell's death.

"*Great Granny Webster* is a study in family madness," Anne Redmon wrote in her *Sunday Times* review, "but Great Granny herself is rigidly, horribly sane . . . The narrator, we subtly come to feel, is next in line for the looney-bin, but somewhere off in the distant future."[52]

Caroline's friend from her Soho days, the London *Sunday Times* senior editor Francis Wyndham, selected *Great Granny Webster* as one of the newspaper's Books of the Year, describing it as "funny, frightening and immensely enjoyable . . . The author writes with an appalled, amused intensity that is completely original but without a trace of pretentiousness. The result is unexpectedly powerful, like a box of chocolates with amphetamine centers."[53] The weekly London *Times* observed that "because there is no hint of emotion in the unblinking narrative, the revulsion that is briefly exposed on the closing page constitutes one of the most terrifying moments in fiction I have encountered in ages."[54]

The "terrifying moment" alluded to is when the harassed clergyman, eager to come in out of the cold, rushes through the burial service and hurriedly pours Great Granny Webster's ashes into her waiting grave:

> *I kept expecting her ashes to be a greyish brown, but instead they were dazzlingly white. There was something profoundly unsuitable and disturbing about their brilliant whiteness . . . In no way did it seem at all correct, that Great Granny Webster should look frivolously snowy and sweet, almost like the castor sugar that was being poured into a bowl as an ingredient for a wedding cake.*[55]

Caroline manages to be eerie, ironic, and comic all at once in this passage; the revulsion comes when a blast of sea air scatters some of Great Granny Webster's ashes and they coat Caroline's black funeral clothes. She finds the snowy coating "utterly sickening," but hesitates to brush it off so as not to offend Richards, whose mourning for her stingy employer seems genuine.[56] The coup de grâce, however—both comic and horrible—comes at the end of the novel, when a fleck of the old woman's ashes is blown into her faithful servant's one remaining eye.

In *Great Granny Webster*, Caroline's flat, reportorial style served her well, as the London *Times* reviewer noted:

> *Some may complain Miss Blackwood's style is that of a highly gifted reporter rather than a novelist, but that is to underrate both*

*the imaginative quality of her detail and the architectural subtlety
with which she builds it into her text. I find her unique and utterly
compelling.*[57]

Great Granny Webster was short-listed for the Booker Prize, along
with Barbara Pym's *Quartet in Autumn* and Paul Scott's *Staying On.*
Caroline would remain convinced that Philip Larkin—who had been
a guest of the Lowells at Milgate—was responsible for her losing the
prize to Paul Scott. Caroline later said that she felt she had been
selected to win until Philip Larkin, the jury chairman, weighed in
by saying her book was autobiography, not fiction. The English
critic Karl Miller thought that was typical of Larkin: "He was a mean
sod who came across as an evil civil servant—he loved categorizing
things."[58]

However, Philip Larkin praised the book in his *Miscellaneous
Pieces*:

> *None of us will forget Caroline Blackwood's* Great Granny Web-
> ster, *a matter-of-fact account—and all the grimmer for this matter-
> of-factness—of the temperamental and circumstantial misfortunes
> of an Ulster family. Although it's deceptively concise, it evokes the
> spirits of no less than four ages—Victorian, Edwardian, pre- and
> postwar—in exact and resonant prose . . . a unique literary expe-
> rience in this or any other year.*[59]

Caroline would accept that pat on the head as her consolation prize.

The following year, the novel was printed in America by Scribner's. It was probably Robert Silvers who asked Karl Miller to review
it, along with two new novels by Barbara Pym (including *Quartet in
Autumn*) and one by Emma Tennant, in *The New York Review of
Books.* Miller noted that the novel "has gone down well in England,
where the appetite for the eccentricities and sufferings of the privileged never sleeps . . . Without being, in any extensive way, artless or

careless, it reads like a long and colorful letter, and has the force of eager unburdening."[60]

Jonathan Raban thought so, too:

> *Great Granny Webster is Caroline talking at her brilliant best. I
> have her back again when I pick up that book. It's my favorite of
> her books—in this novel she has a point of view on the world that's
> not derived from literature. She had "the Gothic" naturally, not
> from reading other writers. Her point of view is her great asset—
> and of course, the novel is very funny.*[61]

Great Granny Webster is, among other things, the biography of a
house, which makes for much of the gothic atmosphere of the tale. In
subtle ways, the disarrangements and malice of the Georgian mansion reflect the stultifying, affection-starved, aristocratic family that,
for many generations, has inhabited it. Even those who escape are
doomed: Aunt Lavinia, trapped in the relentlessly pleasure-loving life
of an upper-class flapper in London, slashes her wrists in the bath.
Caroline's father escapes to his death in the Second World War. It's his
absence that haunts Caroline's novel: "I missed my father. Missing
him, I realized that for me he would always be lost . . . Like someone
born before the invention of the camera . . . [n]o anecdotes or reminiscences from his contemporaries could ever give him a face."[62]

It's odd that Caroline had so few memories of her father; she was,
after all, thirteen when Basil was killed. It suggests that even when
he lived, he was not present in her life. The most vivid memory she
retained of her childhood was the pheasant shoot on which she accompanied her father and was sent out to fetch the killed birds. She
remembered thinking that men were cruel, killing birds that seemed
to embody freedom and imagination and beauty.[63] It may not have
been Basil whom she missed—dim and unformed as he was in her
memory—but the idea of a father, a good father who keeps his children safe from the leaking roof and the unpaid bills and the creeping
madness of women who lock themselves in their rooms and learn the

language of the fairies. Caroline had to find some way—or some one—to lead her out of that dark, decaying house.

After Lowell's death Caroline's creative life took root. She developed into a disciplined, hardworking writer, in spite of her mounting losses and the general chaos of her household, in spite of her daily intake of alcohol. But in her private life, the loss of her third husband would pale next to the loss that was to come. It would change her, deepen her belief that the world was a godless place that even her scalding humor could not redeem.

Caroline sent Natalya, Evgenia, and Ivana to be educated at Dartington Hall in part because—as she later told a journalist—"Lucian went there and he didn't hate it and he was certainly well-educated."[64] But by the summer of 1978 seventeen-year-old Natalya was living on her own in a flat she shared with a young man, Daniel Evans, on Colherne Road in Chelsea. Like many of her generation, Natalya began experimenting with drugs. But for Natalya, who had grown up witnessing Caroline and Lowell's high intake of alcohol and reliance on pills—lithium and painkillers and Elavil and Thorazine at various times, in various quantities—what might have been a youthful folly turned lethal. Natalya became addicted to heroin.

It's hard to know whether Caroline knew the extent of Natalya's drug addiction. Xandra Hardie and her then sister-in-law, Lady Adelaide Gowrie, tried to look after the girls as much as possible in the years Caroline was married to Lowell and after his death. Lady Adelaide discovered in September 1978 that Natalya was taking drugs. "She tried to convince me she could control it, but I got her to see a drug expert," she later explained.[65] Hardie, though it still pains her to talk about Natalya, recalled:

I can see those children's faces, I can hear their voices crying on the telephone to me. I can hear Natalya coming round here banging on my window at one in the morning for her money, because they'd left

her in London while she'd gone off with Cal in America. And she
was staying with my sister-in-law but I had her money . . . it was
cruel. I think all her children felt rejected by her. Natalya felt it
most. She happened upon the solution.[66]

The solution was a heroin habit that twice caused her to be treated
for a drug overdose. Natalya had tried to convince Lady Gowrie that
"she was not completely dependent on heroin and did not want to
stop taking it,"[67] yet she knew that she needed help. She entered a
drug treatment program, but discharged herself five days later. "She
was warned of the dangers of returning to the drug after her toler-
ance to it had been reduced, but she said she was aware of the danger
as a number of her friends had died as a result of it," the *Evening
Standard* reported.

One summer night in June, Natalya attended a party at the Not-
ting Hill home of Emma Tennant, the novelist and sister of Colin
Tennant, Lord Glenconner (who, incidentally, had been the first
owner of "Girl in Bed"). She allegedly scored heroin at the party and
returned alone to her flat. One of Emma Tennant's nephews, Simon
Blow, thought it was probably Charlie Tennant, Colin's son, who had
given Natalya the heroin.[68] She drew herself a bath and then sat on
the lavatory beside the bathtub while she prepared to inject herself.
But Natalya had consumed so much alcohol at the party that she
passed out and fell into the tub. She was found dead, with her head
under water, the syringe floating in the bath. "The reasons for the
death of young socialite and Guinness family member Natalya
Citkovitz remain a mystery," the *Evening Standard* reported on
August 7.

An inquest into the 17-year-old girl's death today could not decide
whether she died from the effects of alcohol or the heroin to which
she was addicted. The Westminster Coroner, Mr. Gavin Thurston,
returned an Open verdict . . .

She had been preparing to inject herself with heroin, and a sy-

ringe and heroin were found beside her. But the post mortem re-
vealed that she had not given herself a "fix" and had died proba-
bly as a result of alcohol asphyxiation.

Pathologist Dr. Hugh Johnson said she may also have died in a
state of very high excitement which is known to be a frequent cause
of death in drug addicts.

Natalya's roommate told the coroner's court that Natalya took
heroin once a day. The death was investigated by Scotland Yard's
Drug Squad,[69] which may be one reason that Caroline was represented by counsel and did not attend the inquest into her daughter's
death. The other reason was that, of course, she was devastated by
the loss.

There were three Guinness deaths that summer, fueling the popular belief in a Guinness curse. In May, Lady Henrietta Guinness
leaped to her death from an aqueduct in Spoleto, Italy. Dennis Key
Guinness was found dead in his home in July, an empty pill bottle beside him. And then Natalya's death, which was another kind of suicide, if Caroline's friend Michael Wishart is to be believed. "One
might say of drug-addicts that whereas their birth may be accidental," he wrote in *High Diver*, "their death is never really by chance."[70]

There are those among Caroline's friends who felt that *The
Stepdaughter* reflected Caroline's relationship with her eldest daughter. Jonathan Raban said that "*The Stepdaughter* was a vivid portrait
of Natalya."[71] Grey Gowrie also described *The Stepdaughter* as autobiographical:

With courage and a certain breathtaking cruelty, she followed [For
All That I Found There] *with two autobiographical novels. The*
Stepdaughter *(1976) is a miniature Greek tragedy done as farce,
about an unhappy relationship with your child. The title is the only
figleaf permitted; the book is based on her eldest child, Natalia*
[sic] *Citkowitz, who died through addiction before the book was
published.*[72]

Gowrie continued, "As well as passion, Caroline Blackwood experienced love both giving and receiving. In some ways a difficult mother, she was always close to her daughters Evgenia and Ivana Citkowitz and her son Sheridan Lowell." There are two curious things here: Gowrie omits Natalya's name when describing Caroline's closeness to her children. And he mistakenly places the publication of *The Stepdaughter* after Natalya's death; in fact, Caroline's novel was published by Duckworth in 1976, two years *before* Natalya died. Did Lord Gowrie, either consciously or unconsciously, want to remove any suggestion that Natalya may have recognized herself as the unloved Renata in the novel, and thus turned to drugs as a solace for being rejected? It's a surprising factual error, unless it was made intentionally because of Gowrie's genuine love for Caroline and his hope to spare her any blame for Natalya's death. But even if her friends dared not make the connection between *The Stepdaughter* and Natalya's dreadful end, Caroline probably made it herself. She felt tremendous guilt for her daughter's death—guilt and shame. She later told Frank Bidart that "she was glad Lowell was not there when Natalya died. I think she felt terrible, I think she felt some shame, yet she would have hated for a child of Lowell's household to have died of drugs."[73]

Natalya's end deepened Caroline's pessimism. Before her daughter's death, Caroline tended to see the world as a dark place. After it, Caroline saw herself as part of that world; the darkness she saw in others she now perceived in herself. She had been intitiated into experience at the price of her child's life. "It's no problem to lay Natalya's death at Caroline's feet," Xandra Hardie said years later, a harsh view shared by Caroline herself.[74]

There's another curious suggestion that comes to light when one examines the autobiographical connection between Renata and Natalya. The secret of *The Stepdaughter*, revealed at the end of the novel, is that Renata is illegitimate. Could it be that Natalya was not Israel's child? Could Walker Evans, who took many photographs of baby Natalya with Caroline—certainly not his usual subject—have fathered Natalya? If so, perhaps Caroline never told the photographer, whose aversion to fathering children was well known. Many have speculated about Ivana's parentage, but it's possible that Natalya, born three years after Caroline's marriage to Israel, was fathered by another man. And if he were someone Caroline later rejected as a lover, would that not help to explain her rejection of her eldest daughter?

On this and on Ivana's siring, Caroline remained silent.

Ten

THE FATE OF
MARY ROSE

She had the Black Irish gothic; she had the life the dark cycle wanted.
—Andrew Harvey[1]

The English can't stand happiness.
—Lawrence Durrell[2]

One of the friends who helped Caroline in the dark months after Natalya's death was the novelist Anna Haycraft, who was married to Colin Haycraft, chairman and managing director of Caroline's first publisher, Gerald Duckworth and Company. Haycraft has published novels and nonfiction under the pen name Alice Thomas Ellis. At the time of their meeting, she was employed as a fiction editor at Duckworth's. Like Caroline, she was also a journalist, and she wrote columns for *The Catholic Herald* and *The Spectator*. Each had also experienced the loss of a child. Haycraft lost two of her seven children—a boy and a girl, who both died young.

Born in Liverpool in 1932, Haycraft continues to be an active and prolific writer whose fiction has garnered a number of awards. In 1982 one of her novels, *The 27th Kingdom*, was nominated for the Booker Prize. In 1979, a year after Natalya's death, the two women

embarked on a project that distracted Caroline and allowed many
friends to rally around her, at least symbolically. With generous help
from Xandra Hardie, then an editor at Jonathan Cape, they compiled
a cookbook of shortcut, "cheater" recipes; it was called *Darling, You
Shouldn't Have Gone to So Much Trouble.* (The cheeky title prompted
Caroline to tell a journalist that "we should do one on sex with the
same title.")[3] The recipes were mostly donated by a colorful collection of literary and socially prominent friends of the two women
and their editor. Among them are Sonia Orwell's Tagliatelli with
Truffles, Marianne Faithfull's Different Sweet/Sour Pork, Barbara
Cartland's Filets de Sole Caprice ("cooked by her chef Nigel Gordon
in 10 Minutes"), Quentin Crisp's Tibetan Workhouse Soup, Bernard
Shaw's Vegetarian Salads, Beryl Bainbridge's Stovies, Anne Dunn's
Cold Omelette, Lucian Freud's Tomato Soup au Naturel, Nicholas
Haslam's Fake Mayonnaise for Masking Cold Chicken, Natasha
Spender's Ukrainian Eggs, Jonathan Miller's recipe for coleslaw,
Roald Dahl's Norwegian Cauliflower, Caroline's cousin Doon, the
Countess of Granville's Caviar Soup, and Francis Bacon's Thick, Fat,
Genuine Mayonnaise.[4] It's a *Who's Who* cookbook of London's literary and artistic elite. Interspersed throughout are pithy, culinary-
inspired quotations from an eclectic collection of writers and
philosophers, from Jane Austen to Abraham Lincoln. The book's preface, astute and playful, acknowledges the need for overworked, contemporary women to find culinary shortcuts. ("Dishes that require
her presence in the kitchen—that require her loving surveillance in
case they burn, curdle, shrink, or shrivel, or go wrong in some other
unspeakable way, we cannot recommend.")[5] The authors remind
readers that "cans must be opened and hidden" before the guests arrive, so that the splendid meals retain a certain mystery—advice so
universally sound, it hardly needs mentioning. The preface is rounded
off with a droll anecdote:

Vatel, maître d'hôtel *of Louis XIV, committed suicide on a Friday
because the fish failed to arrive. Much later, Escoffier was asked*

whether, in that calamitous situation, he too would have taken his
life. He shook his head. "I would have served breasts of chicken and
no one would have known the difference."[6]

Indeed, the chief appeal of Caroline and Anna's cookbook is its
wit; unfortunately, many of the recipes leave much to be desired (in
particular Avocados Caroline, a plan for serving to one's children
mushy, overripe avocados disguised with chopped eggs and garlic). At
least one savvy reviewer, however, was not amused. Anita Brookner
expressed her disapproval in the pages of the *Times Literary Supple-*
ment, because she found many of the recipes, with their reliance on
cream, butter, mayonnaise, candy bars, and Cadbury's Smash (potato
flakes), unhealthful as well as unappetizing.

> *This is corrupt food, food intended to impress, to deceive, even in-*
> *tended to inspire fear and loathing . . . Good food does not deserve*
> *this treatment from anyone, however enlightened or liberated she*
> *may be in other areas of her working life. Bad food . . . should be*
> *left alone and not combined with other bad food to produce a memo-*
> *rably awful party piece. People should not eat bad food to save time,*
> *particularly bad food which is rather expensive. Children should*
> *not have their palates ruined before they know any better.*[7]

Brookner mentioned the recipe for upside-down cake ("packet of
cake mixture. Canned pineapple"), which is surprising, given Caroline's antipathy to cake mixes, as expressed in her first novel. In *The*
Stepdaughter, the miserable Renata's reliance on cake mixes is portrayed as a serious character flaw.

Brookner quoted from the cookbook's preface: "It is designed, we
are told, for the woman who does meaningful things all day and who
'wants to be free to drink and talk to her friends without worrying
whether the dinner she is about to produce will be a catastrophe.' "
She concluded by pointing out that "if you are drunk anyway, you
would be well advised to keep what you eat very simple: too much

Hellmann's mayonnaise could land you in bad trouble the following morning."[8]

Brookner's review elicited a stinging letter from Caroline, noting that the writer, having identified herself as one who took cooking "gravely," had taken the entire cookbook much too gravely. She also charged Brookner with willfully ignoring the many recipes by celebrated chefs and focusing only on the oddballs (such as Quentin Crisp's soup "boiled in an unwashed saucepan").[9] Caroline was outraged that Brookner ended her review with her own recipe for a simple, wholesome dish (fillet of beef, rubbed with herbs and oil, etc.). Caroline compared the offering to that of a poetry reviewer who contributes her own stanzas to point up the deficiencies of the poet. Brookner's review prompted another dissenting letter, published the following week, this time from the marketing and sales director of Cadbury Typhoo Ltd.: "I should like to point out that Cadbury's Smash is made from high-grade, fresh potatoes with the addition of milk solids and salt. Any Vitamin C lost during the processing is replaced."[10]

Nonetheless—or perhaps because of the controversy—*Darling, You Shouldn't Have Gone to So Much Trouble* quickly sold out and went into several printings.

Another who came to Caroline's rescue after Natalya's death was her old friend Cornelia Foss, who suggested that Caroline and the children join her for the summer of 1979 in a rented house in Water Mill, one of the lovely, upscale towns nestled among the Hamptons on Long Island. They rented a Cape Cod surrounded by hedges at the end of a long pebbled road. Stanley Moss, the poet and art dealer who renewed his friendship with Caroline that summer, remembered that Caroline's girls were allowed to roller-skate throughout the house, eventually causing thousands of dollars worth of damage to the floors. Caroline had a hard time saying no to her three younger children. "She would give them everything," Moss recalled, "but what they wanted."[11]

Caroline and Anna's cookbook had been a pleasant diversion for

Caroline, but her next book, published in 1981, would plunge Caroline into a world where children are murdered or delivered into danger by a disturbed mother. Caroline's third novel, *The Fate of Mary Rose*, was her darkest. It would become her favorite among her nine works of fiction and nonfiction, the one that most accurately portrayed her bleak view of the world. The rape, mutilation, and murder of a child are at the heart of this novel, which explores the effect of the crime on a particularly ill suited couple. Cressida, an eerily beautiful young woman, is obsessed with the safety of her only child, a passive, adenoidal, and thoroughly bloodless little creature named Mary Rose. But the most repellent character in the novel—at least at first—is its narrator, Rowan Anderson, a cold, detached historian (and would-be biographer) who has married Cressida only to give Mary Rose legitimacy. Their loveless marriage also conveniently keeps his trendy girlfriend at bay. Rowan's cold-blooded seduction of Cressida is particularly chilling:

> *"Am I hurting you?" I asked her. She didn't answer. . . . She seemed to be in agony. Something about her tortured look exasperated me and gave me a spurt of energy. I rammed against her. Something seemed to give. I felt her tearing and Cressida gave a horrible scream. I came very quickly.[12]*

In the novel, six-year-old Maureen Sutton is kidnapped from the working-class council estates on the outskirts of Beckham, a little village so quaint and pretty—and seemingly safe—that it arouses nothing but contempt in Rowan's cold, cosmopolitan heart. The child's murder by an unknown villain "besmatters this idyll," Peter Kemp wrote in *The Listener*,[13] and unleashes an obsession in Cressida that is nearly as destructive as the rape and murder of the Sutton girl. Caroline's novel "aims to show . . . that there are more ways of destroying a child than homicidal assault," Kemp added.

Cressida hovers over the unfortunate Mary Rose, feeding her wheat germ and vitamins but watching over her like a predator, draining all the life from her joyless childhood with her obsessive maternal concern. She renders Mary Rose completely passive, unable to form a thought or voice a wish. As details of little Maureen's murder are revealed over the evening news, Cressida's fear and paranoia grow more intense; she becomes witch-like, stirring boiling clothes in a giant cauldron in order to dye them black, in a bizarre attempt to disguise herself and Mary Rose and thus escape from the evil that has invaded their charming little town. Her obsession turns to madness when she becomes convinced that her husband, Rowan, is the murderer. But is he?

The Fate of Mary Rose, written from Caroline's guilt and despair, is part thriller and part examination of the faces of evil. We are given clues to Rowan's likelihood as the murderer: he has a number of alcohol-induced blackouts during his dutiful visits to Cressida in Beckham, and one morning he awakens with mud on his shoes and trousers, unable to remember how it got there. (Maureen's little body was found, as usual, in the woods.) A nightmare Rowan describes in chapter 4 disturbingly suggests the molestation of a child:

> *I dreamt about Mary Rose's doll. It was lying on an operating table. Doctors were standing round it, their faces half-covered by white masks. . . . The doll's legs were wide apart and kicking in the air. It was wearing a white piece of toweling. . . stained with blood as if the doll [were] menstruating.*[14]

The Fate of Mary Rose was widely and favorably reviewed. Most critics recognized it as a leap forward in Caroline's skill as a novelist, with the novel's clean, driving plot and polished technique. But some noted that the novel didn't quite add up as a thriller, because the carefully planted clues did not lead to the truth or to the restoration of order, a trajectory that usually makes murder mysteries so comforting. *The Fate of Mary Rose* was not made to comfort.

At the novel's chilling close, Rowan has kidnapped Mary Rose in order to rescue her from the smothering attentions of her mother. As he escapes in his car with his terrified daughter, he's pursued by police, whose suspicions have been fired up by Cressida. Mary Rose, too, has been warned, and when Rowan reaches out to touch her, the child flings herself from the car: "And then a sudden blast of cold wind entered the car from the side . . . For a moment I couldn't take in what had happened. Then with a sickening sense of horror, I realized. Mary Rose had thrown herself out of my car.[15]

The novel ends ambiguously, because we never learn whether Rowan murdered little Maureen Sutton. We don't know whether his taking Mary Rose was a heroic attempt to free her from "the demon-infested, murky world of her mother"[16] or a psychopathic attempt to wreak upon Mary Rose the fate of Maureen Sutton. Yet Rowan is sympathetic by the end of the novel, and it's *his* perceptions, not the witchy Cressida's, that we trust. Finally, it is Cressida's soul-killing ministrations that have made her the villain. And because the world Caroline Blackwood explores in the novel is shot through with evil, the police, Cressida's nosy neighbor, even Rowan's girlfriend, all side with Cressida against Rowan.

Caroline's giving the murdered girl the name Maureen, Caroline's mother's name, is curious. A writer angry at her mother might well have named one of her villains after her, but Caroline gave it to the innocent and pathetic victim. Clearly the novel takes a cold hard look at the perils and unpleasantness of child-rearing, from the obsession with cleanliness, health, and safety that blossoms in Cressida, to the slight repulsion toward children expressed by Rowan. ("I rather admired Mary Rose for instantly rejecting the synthetic baby I'd presented her with. If she'd cradled and cooed, if she'd fed the silly object its plastic bottle and burped it on her shoulder, it would have made me very uneasy.")[17] Did her use of Maureen's name for the child victim indicate a softening of her view toward her mother, an identification with the pains and troubles of child-rearing that Maureen could not be bothered with? After Natalya's death, Caroline may indeed have looked on child-rearing as hell, and wondered whether it was worth it.

However, there is a comic passage that also brings Maureen to mind, but in an entirely different light. Describing an "empress" as a woman who believes her very birth entitles her to special treatment, and who demands subservience from everyone around her, Caroline wrote, "In other words . . . an empress is a total nightmare."[18]

More to the point was Caroline's portrayal of Cressida—a wispy, pale young woman with wide eyes, like Caroline's—as a witch. In Cressida, Caroline managed to conjure up images of Maureen as a young beauty, the pale-eyed blonde once described by John Huston (along with her sisters) as a lovely witch. The notion of a witch-like mother haunted Caroline's imagination. During the course of several long interviews she gave to Steven Aronson some thirteen years later, Caroline said that her daughter Ivana had just visited a psychic. "She only went for the fun of it, and he said, 'I see an old woman and she's a witch.' That," she told Aronson, "was my mother."[19] But as Cressida in the novel also physically resembles Caroline, might not that character be a blending of the author and Maureen, a glimmer that the destructive qualities Caroline always feared in her mother she has now discovered in herself?

Caroline said later that she had some hope *The Fate of Mary Rose* would be made into a film, but she realized that the story was too dark, in the year of its publication, for a contemporary audience. It's possible that after creations like Thomas Harris's Hannibal Lecter, the filmgoing population is ready for Caroline's dark tale of rape, murder, and madness.

Rowan's chilling insight at the close of the novel expressed Caroline's state of mind at the end of the terrible decade that brought the ruin of her marriage to Lowell and the spectacular destruction of her daughter: "I wondered . . . if for Mary Rose the plunge towards the tarmac would not always seem safer than life."[20]

There were two Carolines," the Anglo-Indian writer, poet, and translator Andrew Harvey believed. "One was courageous, kind, generous, sympathetic, preternaturally intelligent. The other was obsessed with death. She saw this life and world as hell. She was like the old Jesuit at the end of Joyce's *Portrait of the Artist as a Young Man* who sniffs out evil and sees fire and brimstone wherever he looks."[21]

Caroline first met Andrew Harvey in the mid-seventies, before Lowell's death, at a party given by Faber and Faber for the poet Thom Gunn. Harvey was a classics scholar, a fellow at All Souls (where Lowell had been in residence when he met Caroline in London), and a handsome youth some twenty years Caroline's junior. He remembered his first sight of her: "She looked haunting—a striking, green-eyed woman standing under a tree, who seemed the only person worth talking to at this dry, literary party." Lowell came over and joined them, glad to see that Caroline, usually so shy, was involved in conversation. The three got along well together; Harvey was also impressed with Robert Lowell, who struck him as "tremendously exciting; he had a kind of brooding, wild power."

They met again in 1978, after Natalya's death, at a party in Oxfordshire given by the poet Peter Levi and his wife, Dierdre, who had married Levi after the death of her first husband, Cyril Connolly. Harvey recalled that it was a shock to see Caroline again, just a few years after their first meeting: her hair had turned white from grief. In her late forties, Caroline looked much older; she was haggard, rail thin, but still beautiful. "She seemed incredibly lonely," Harvey said, "but wildly funny! We made a complete connection of spirit and heart, quoting back and forth; it was a joyful meeting." The two became friends. Harvey, in fact, fell in love with her.

It was an unusual alliance. Besides his youth, Andrew Harvey was gay, but that didn't prevent him from having a sexual relationship with Caroline. "She knew I loved her," Andrew recalled. "And she was famished for love—she believed in the transformative power of deep love and sex, its ability to redeem." He said:

We had a happy sexual relationship. Maybe she was attracted to me because I was gay, and she knew that, and she was attracted to a

strong feminine side, although she identified femininity with weak-
ness. She had a rather strong masculine side, but she was very kind,
gentle, and patient with me. There was hope in our relationship—
we had both been wounded. We both loved literature and art. I tried
to help her stop drinking. Perhaps if I were older I could have
helped her more.

He did help her move the rest of her things out of the living quarters she had maintained at Castletown, and he moved into her Redcliffe Square house. Harvey vividly remembered traveling to Dublin with Caroline, driving the twelve miles to Castletown in the rain, and visiting a nearby cemetery where a number of Guinnesses who had died young or by their own hand were buried.

We walked in the rain among all those tombs. She felt strongly,
among the graves of her ancestors, that she had been born into a
whirlwind of fate. I felt I was walking with the spirits of the
dead—we were surrounded by so much tragic loss. There was too
much money, too much power, too much pain among those graves.[22]

Caroline was at a particularly vulnerable time in her life. Harvey perceived that Caroline "recognized that she had been very cruel to Natalya, and had hurt her and insulted her and carped at her. She saw Natalya's death as a suicide she had caused." It was Natalya's death, Harvey believed, that accelerated Caroline's slide. "She couldn't just be the victim anymore; she was now the destroyer. She saw how destructive she was, how cruel she had been, how impatient and angry at Natalya's addiction. The horror of Natalya's death, and of Lowell's madness, had taken their toll on her."

Caroline and Harvey lived together for a year in London, though part of that time Andrew taught at Hobart and William Smith Colleges in Geneva, New York, and he kept his rooms at Oxford. They traveled together, visiting Paris, Venice, and New York. Caroline told Andrew many tales of her childhood—how grown men would come up to her when she was still just a girl and ask to marry her, or offer to give her money and whisk her off to Oxford—or Peru! It frightened her and made her contemptuous of men, who seemed to value her for her beauty when she saw herself as uneducated, frightened, and worth little. And she railed against the lack of education among women of her class. There had been no one around to teach her anything when she was growing up, which is one reason, Harvey believed, that she chose brilliant men who could startle her into creativity and thought, who could wake her up from this tremendous sleep she had been born into. Caroline had a thirst for knowledge; she wanted to be instructed. She thought of her childhood as an upper-class nightmare from which she had to struggle to awake. Harvey said:

> *Her sense of being wounded was at the center of everything. She came from a destroying family. She'd been born into that fatal family, and it formed the core of her vision of men as bizarre sadists. The key to that view is her story about carrying the blood-soaked birds for her father. The dead birds tarnish her, given to her by men. Look at some of Lucian's early paintings of dead birds, like "Rotted Puffin." They are at the core of her psyche.[23]*

Caroline and Harvey settled into a comfortable life together, though it would be short-lived. Caroline rose early in the morning, had a pot of coffee, wrote steadily for three or four hours, then stopped and had a drink for lunch. "She was very disciplined," Harvey said. "She didn't start drinking heavily until later in the day. One of her children told me that she hid bottles of vodka all over the house, but I never saw that. She drank less during the months that we were together."

One of the adventures they embarked upon, in 1980, was research into Caroline's next book, which wouldn't be published for another fifteen years because of legal constraints. *The Last of the Duchess* would be Caroline's last published book, a highly subjective but basically nonfiction account of her attempts to interview the dying Duchess of Windsor, who lay virtually imprisoned, according to Caroline, in her gloomy château in a suburb of Paris, held captive by a tyrannical dragon lady of a lawyer named Mâitre Suzanne Blum. Harvey accompanied her to Paris throughout most of her research, staying with her, incidentally, in a high-class, discreet brothel.

The Last of the Duchess was one more of Caroline's satiric acts of revenge against the English aristocracy, and, by extension, against Maureen. In Caroline's version, the duchess—who once lived for social prestige and the friendship of her few loyal supporters—ended up a prisoner, unvisited and alone, her legs and feet shriveled and blackened like those of a Chinese mummy. And in the person of the duchess's protective lawyer, Mâitre Blum, Caroline encountered a formidable foe she would long after consider the embodiment of evil.

In 1980 the London *Sunday Times* asked Caroline to write an article on Wallis Warfield Simpson, the eighty-four-year-old Duchess of Windsor, who was living out her widowhood in seclusion and silence in her shuttered mansion on the edge of the Bois du Boulogne. The piece was to accompany Lord Snowdon's photographs of the duchess—if, that is, Mâitre Blum would allow the photographs to be taken. Snowdon eventually had to settle instead for a photograph of the formidable Mâitre Blum, and Caroline was reduced to writing a puff piece about Blum to accompany the picture. However, after several interviews with the crafty and ancient lawyer, and with the few remaining friends of the duchess, Caroline wrote an account of the duchess's dying days with "zest and spikiness and outrageous black humour."[24] Her book, like A. J. Symons's *In Search of Corvo*, took a negative and turned it into a positive: Caroline recounted her thwarted attempts to actually *see* the duchess herself, and ended up having to re-create her, from gossip, memory, and myth. If *The Fate of Mary Rose* plumbed the depths of Caroline's despair, *The Last of the Duchess*—though it would not be published until 1995—turned tragedy into wicked, redemptive farce. It allowed her at last to pull down the façade masking the decrepitude, excesses, and venality of sequestered and exalted lives.

As Andrew Barrow observed, years later, in his review in *The Spectator*, Caroline's subjective account of the duchess's last days is written "with a kind of wide-eyed schoolgirlish innocence—and mounting sense of horror."[25] The innocence is a device; Caroline enters into the assignment with firsthand experience of what goes on inside the gated estates and vast mansions of the rich, and we journey with her, marveling at what she finds: this once celebrated (and reviled) social butterfly now "a living cabbage," tended to by a necrophiliac lawyer who is creepily in love with her charge—if Caroline is to be believed.

In the 1996 paperback edition of her book, Caroline added a useful *caveat emptor*: "*The Last of the Duchess* is not intended to be read as a straight biographical work. It is an entertainment, an examination of the fatal effects of myth, a dark fairy-tale."[26] Caroline had anticipated the current debate over the blending of fact and fiction in nonfiction works and the alarums sounded over biographies that blur the lines. *The Last of the Duchess* came in for just such criticism. Lady Diana Mosley, whom Caroline interviewed for her book and who had recently written her own book on the duchess, criticized Caroline's factual and interpretive errors:

> *This book is full of mistakes, as becomes a fairy tale. Unity Mitford shot herself not in 1945, but in 1939 on the outbreak of a war she did not wish to live through . . . The man who got pictures of the Duchess looking half dead took them from the road; he never got near a window . . . I never called the Duchess Wallis, or Hitler "Hittles" . . . As to the description of Michael Bloch, Mâitre Blum's assistant, it is a silly caricature. He is a clever writer who made use of the Windsors' papers for some informative books.[27]*

Caroline's interviews with Mâitre Blum, and with a number of octogenarian friends of the duchess, took place between February and September of 1980. At one point, Caroline managed to get inside the château; Andrew Harvey was present during this attempt to interview the duchess. He recalled seeing her staunchly loyal butler, George, come out of a dark room with his wife, Ophelia, and shut the door behind him. "You could see the dark, closed rooms beyond, with their stench of death," Harvey said. "George's wife looked like a concentration camp victim. Mâitre Blum had told Caroline that the duchess stayed in her room listening to Cole Porter records. Caroline's comment inside the château? 'No sign of Cole Porter!' It was scary inhabiting her world, and having it confirmed by the atmosphere of decay and death."[28]

The biographer Michael Bloch, who was at that time Blum's assistant and who was cruelly mocked by Caroline as little more than a factotum, was naturally hurt by Caroline's portrayal of him in her book. Understandably, he had a different view of Mâitre Blum. "Caroline had a tremendous gift for seeing how people can be made to look ridiculous," he said in his own defense.

> Much of what she wrote had an element of truth to it—my friends recognize me in the portrait she writes—but everything was distorted to make us look ridiculous. And she reported the gossip and speculations of the Duchess's friends—who weren't allowed to see her—as fact. Even Mâitre Blum's middle-class French apartment was interpreted by Caroline as Kafkaesque, with its many doors, but it was a typical French apartment.[29]

Caroline's research was made more difficult by Blum's instant dislike of her, according to Bloch. "Caroline showed up in a slovenly slate," Bloch remembered, "and she always seemed drunk, though she probably wasn't as drunk as she appeared. And she stank. Blum disliked her immediately and wanted nothing to do with her, but I prevailed on her to see Caroline on a few more occasions."

Michael Bloch would come to regret having prevailed. And he was doubly hurt, because he had been rather smitten with Caroline, despite her disheveled appearance. "I found her sexy and still beautiful, with her deep-throated voice, its rich timbre, and hypnotizing eyes." Bloch went to some trouble to introduce her to an eminent friend of his—possibly the architectural historian and diarist James Lees-Milne—who had known Caroline's father in his youth. "Caroline was always hungry to know more about her father," Bloch remembered. "The meeting went very well, and I was happy to have arranged it." Bloch, like Caroline, had been raised in Ulster in Northern Ireland, and he did want to endear himself to Caroline, but she rebuffed him and refused to take his calls. Bloch even felt that an unfavorable review of one of his books on the Windsors by a close friend of Caroline's, Hugo Vickers, was inspired by Caroline's antipathy. (*The Last of the Duchess* is in fact dedicated to Hugo Vickers, who has made his reputation writing about the royals.)

Another aspect of Caroline's behavior that upset Mâitre Blum was Caroline's "morbid interest" in her husband, who was dying while the interviews were taking place. "Caroline was always terrifically interested in death and dying," Bloch said, echoing Andrew Harvey's observations. *The Last of the Duchess,* indeed, can be read as a long meditation on dying, from Caroline's vivid descriptions of "the brown flowers of death" that covered Mâitre Blum's arms, to speculations that the Duchess of Windsor was already dead or had shriveled to the size of a child and turned completely black. Her fiercest criticism of Blum was that, according to Caroline, she was prolonging the duchess's life in a vegetative state, not allowing her to die. And—perhaps even worse—forbidding the duchess, when she was still *compos mentis,* her ration of vodka.

The fact that most of those interviewed in *The Last of the Duchess* were ailing octogenarians looking back on happier times—with the exception of Blum, whose vigor and "step of a girl" made her menacingly youthful—allowed Caroline to declaw a whole class of formidable, outrageously privileged, upper-class women. We see Lady Diana, wife of the disgraced Fascist Oswald Mosley, still beautiful but almost completely deaf, sitting by benignly while her husband airs his ancient Fascist views. ("For no particular reason his half-closed eyes would suddenly open like those of a dozing lizard . . . And then his lids came down again and the beautiful voice continued relentlessly. 'As Hitler said to me, We don't want your British colonies. You can keep them . . . We don't want a lot of niggers who will only contaminate our German blood.' ")[30]

Because of her deafness, Lady Diana was under the impression that Caroline had come to interview her about her own book on the Duchess of Windsor, a misconception that was never entirely put to rest. Lady Diana complained bitterly about the perils of old age: "I loathe being old, I hate every second of my life. My eyes, my ears, are going. Everything is going . . ."[31]

A visit to Lady Monckton was also a lesson in impermanence. Walter Monckton had been one of the few to remain loyal to the Duke of Windsor after his abdication; he had helped the duke write his abdication speech. By the time Caroline went to interview Monckton's widow, she was living in an old people's home near Newbury. Another former beauty, Lady Monckton was by then a doddering woman of eighty-four, being led around by a pair of nurses. Even the home, on a former country estate, belied its former glory:

> There was little evidence that the golden pheasants and the splendour of the trees in the beautiful grounds by which they were surrounded could bring [the residents] much pleasure. Their biggest moment of struggle and drama was the time when two nurses carried them limping painfully to the lavatory and then brought them back to a bed or a chair.[32]

Mrs. Brinsley Plunket—Caroline's Aunt Aileen and a friend of the duchess—was also subtly skewered. Caroline found her in a dithery state, more concerned about retrieving a bolt of "divine" Galway tweed she had given to the duchess long ago than in learning anything about her unfortunate condition. The most telling remark was made by Marquesa Casa Maury, the former Mrs. Dudley Ward and onetime mistress of the Duke of Windsor. "There's something so comic about the situation," she told Caroline; "it's the idea of that horrible old lady being locked up by another horrible old lady."[33] That those society beauties who had flitted from continent to continent and spent lavishly on themselves were all reduced to "horrible old ladies" was Caroline's comic revenge. Maureen—illegitimately clinging to the title of Marchioness of Dufferin and Ava after two subsequent marriages—was indirectly skewered in *The Last of the Duchess*. When the book was finally published, in 1995, after the death of Blum at the age of ninety-five, the *Evening Standard* speculated that it had set off a literary feud between Caroline and her mother:

> *The book is heavily loaded in Wallis Windsor's favour and makes no bones about the Royal Family's hatred of the Duchess. But Lady Caroline fails to mention that both her parents were on the opposite side of this famous feud. Her father . . . was Lord-in-Waiting to King George VI after the abdication. . . . Maureen Dufferin, an intimate friend of the Queen Mother and of Princess Margaret, both of whom were regular guests at her Belgravia dinner parties, is unlikely to warm to her daughter's description of the Queen Mother's gesture in kissing Wallis at the Duke of Windsor's funeral as "plebeian."*[34]

One might argue that Caroline, in *The Last of the Duchess*, sided with her deceased, romanticized father against her flamboyant and vigorous mother—and broke a family taboo in the process. As a child, Caroline was not allowed to know anything about the Duke of Windsor's abdication and the scandal of his love affair with an American divorcée. "In Ulster," she said, "the combination of sex and anything that threatened the monarchy seemed horrifying. I had no idea what [Wallis Simpson] had done."[35]

Michael Bloch also went on record to say that Maître Blum, contrary to Caroline's interpretation, never threatened to kill Caroline if she "got it wrong" and published malicious rumors about the duchess. Bloch, who was present when the remark was made, felt that Maître Blum had been obviously joking when she said something to the effect of "I'll kill you if you get this wrong." The formidable old lawyer's sarcasm was apparently lost on Caroline, who really felt that she had been threatened. In Caroline's dark tale, Blum was transformed into another evil witch—the old crone version of pretty young Cressida in *The Fate of Mary Rose*—and Michael Bloch into the witch's familiar, even referring to Maître Blum as "my Master." Readers should take Caroline's opening disclaimer to heart: she wrote neither memoir, biography, nor factual reportage; she created a fairy tale like one by the Brothers Grimm—or by Charles Perrault, given its French setting—except that there was no happy ending.

Caroline often said to me, 'I wish we'd met ten years ago. I'm such a wreck now,'" Andrew Harvey recalled from his desert home in Nevada.[36] Now the author of numerous books on mystical traditions and spiritual enlightenment, including the highly praised *A Journey in Ladakh*, *The Tibetan Book of Living and Dying* (coauthored), and *Son of Man: The Mystical Path to Christ*, Harvey began his writing career as a poet. Caroline had always depended upon the company of poets. When she and Lowell used to write side by side in their room at Milgate, Lowell would deplore the difficulty he had writing prose while he couldn't stop the torrent of verses. Caroline, who found that prose came easily, felt she could never write poetry. But her standards were high. "She was tough on Lowell," Harvey said. "She told him his poetry was too self-indulgent."

When Harvey, who was born in India and raised and educated in

England, decided to make a pilgrimage to the remote Himalayan region of Ladakh, Caroline was not sanguine about his plans. And when, on a return visit, he underwent a spiritual change and came back in thrall to Thuksey Rinpoche, Caroline was worried about the effect of his spiritual awakening on his standing as a poet and scholar at All Souls. "You must be sophisticated in your writing," she cautioned him.

"But her models were all these London intellectuals and would-be writers," Harvey said, "who felt you had to be witty and clever and unsentimental all the time. Really, except for Lowell, she was surrounded by mediocrities. Caroline refused to examine herself, in life and in literature, afraid she'd be ostracized if she revealed too much." Harvey believed that his spiritual coming-of-age marked the beginning of the end of their relationship.

When I returned from Ladakh a second time, I couldn't share my experiences with her. She couldn't hear what I had to say. She was deeply scared to change her view of the world. She railed against God; she was a Calvinist of Nothingness. She was close to a kind of wisdom because she had had everything and had seen through it all. She saw the emptiness of all those gifts: wealth, position, beauty, talent, opportunity. But she couldn't go beyond it. Life had given her wisdom, but she was caught on the threshold; there was nothing she could do but go beyond her own nihilism, but she couldn't do it. She kept herself in a place where she could not be healed. That's when I knew I couldn't stop her drinking. Drink was her visionary food.

The relationship ended bitterly. For six or seven months after Harvey left her, Caroline would call him on the phone and launch into tirades. "Her verbal cruelty was astounding. She could annihilate you off the face of the earth when she was aroused—it was a murderous anger, without mercy. She would use your frailties and weaknesses against you. She mocked people she didn't like, and she was very accurate in her judgments."

In part, her anger was fueled by her feeling that she had never been loved, Harvey thought. "She *was* loved—incredibly—but she never *felt* loved. You could go to all the trouble in the world to please her, but she wouldn't notice it. She broke people's hearts; she was like a radiant disease."

After leaving Caroline, Harvey continued his spiritual inquiries and began writing novels. He also wrote a fourth book of poetry, his last to date, which was published in 1985 by Houghton Mifflin. *No Diamonds, No Hat, No Honey* would be not only Harvey's farewell to Caroline but his attempt to exorcise her from his life. Caroline was once again cast as a muse in the role of Lydia, a canny, cynical tormentor who by turns humiliates and inspires Fernando, the poet's persona in this collection of thirty-nine verses. We can hear Caroline's contralto taunting Fernando in line after line:

> *"Soak a long time in the black suds*
> *Of disaster and you'll come out—*
>
> *This is Lydia's Law—" she laughs, "not clean*
> *Exactly, but white, white of the ancient lies . . ."[37]*

Lydia's pronouncements in Poem IV could well be Caroline's philosophy of literature:

> *"In fairy stories," Lydia said,*
> *"I'm only interested*
> *In what happens to the villains" . . .*
> *"In the stories I love,"*
> *Said Lydia,*
> *"The wicked stay wicked*
> *And laugh in the face of the Good*
> *And live out to the end of their doom.*
>
> *Stories should make us tremble, like life does—"[38]*

In Poem V, "Lydia as Hecuba," Andrew Harvey perceives how tragedy and humor met in Caroline, how suffering brought her to a place where laughter is the only sane response:

"All suffering to me now is camp, frankly.
When you're changed into a dog, you see
The world hilariously."[39]

In Poem XXXVIII, Lydia/Caroline purrs into the poet's ear: "Won't you miss me? / Who will you talk to when you're holy?"[40] More telling, perhaps, is Lydia's response to the knowledge that her poet is leaving her:

"And so you really think," Lydia says,
"I grieve for your soul . . .
There are weeks, no years
I can't remember your name."[41]

"Caroline must have known that she was Lydia," Andrew Harvey said. "She was touched by my book and thanked me for it. She knew it was a liberating book, and she was complimented."[42] But except for a disastrous dinner party held in New York in the late 1980s, once Caroline left England to live in America, the two would not see each other again. In the years of his absence, she would disparage his importance in her life; perhaps she was embarrassed to have fallen in love with a gay man almost twenty years younger than she. Or perhaps her rage at having been left—the rage Ivan Moffat had seen in her—entirely soured the year-long affair. Older friends, like Peter Levi and Cornelia Foss, spoke of Andrew Harvey as a particularly inappropriate companion for Caroline.[43]

As for Harvey, he concluded that Caroline had a vampirical quality, yet somehow his harrowing experience with her was worthwhile: "She could prey on you, yet she was noble and dazzling in her beauty, wit, humour, and courage. She initiated me—she taught me a huge amount about life." He also felt that because he had been the one to leave, she had to demonize him. "In her madness and rage," Harvey recognized, "she demonized the men who left her, including Lowell. She was furious that her dream of love had not been realized in Lowell."

"*Stories should make us tremble,*" Harvey wrote, perceiving Caroline's love of the Grimms' tales and her identification with villains. He recognized that aspect of her, along with her beauty, as being part of her power. "She kept her beauty for a long time, in spite of all she'd done to herself. Yet she became witch-like at the end. The later photographs reveal no aspect of the stunning girl in the boat. Many wanted to rescue the small, beautiful child trapped inside the body of a witch."

· *Eleven* ·

ON THE
PERIMETER

This morning lying in the bath she had felt
so demented and raw that she had started
to feel sorry for objects.
—Caroline Blackwood[1]

In 1982 Ian Hamilton's biography of Robert Lowell was published
in America by Random House and in England by Lowell's publisher, Faber and Faber. A poet as well as a biographer, Hamilton
had visited Caroline and Cal's country house in Kent in the mid-
seventies, a place Hamilton later described as "always a shambles—
plaster falling down, chaos everywhere."[2] Although Caroline cooper-
ated with Lowell's biographer in the years following her husband's
death by granting him interviews, after the book was published she
denounced it as a distorted picture of her late husband.

"When the book came out, she launched a campaign against it,"
said Hamilton. "She threatened Faber and Faber and got [her friends]
to pan it in reviews." Caroline insisted that her main complaint about
Robert Lowell: A Biography was that Lowell's madness was over-
played and that the book "left out Cal's charm, so there's the mad Cal
but not the one everyone loved."[3]

When Ivana was accidentally scalded, Caroline said that Lowell wanted to stay with her overnight at the Burns Unit, even though Caroline was given a bed for the night and Lowell, the stepfather, was not. Caroline said that Lowell just stretched out on the stone-cold floor, without a blanket. Another example of his devotion, Caroline insisted, was his willingness to buy two of Lucian Freud's portraits of her—painted, as they were, by "the ex-husband."

But Gillon Aitken, Caroline's literary agent at the time, felt that her displeasure with Hamilton's biography was based on something else. "When she saw the larger life of Lowell and the other women in his life, she found her place reduced. She felt slighted. But of course Hamilton had to do that; he was writing a balanced account of Lowell over a long life. And Caroline's part in that life was—well, there were bigger relationships. I don't think she could take that reduction."[4] Because Aitken was Hamilton's agent as well as Caroline's, having represented *Darling, You Shouldn't Have Gone to So Much Trouble* and *The Fate of Mary Rose*, Aitken felt that

> it was difficult for Caroline to remain a client of mine, given that I had a prior loyalty to Ian, and also I liked his book very much. She felt it was "an untenable association," professionally anyway, so I discontinued the role of agent, but I continued to know her and heard all about her from a variety of friends. I was a friend and indeed an agent for Andrew Harvey, who played a part in her life.

Caroline was asked to appear on a television program, *The South Bank Show,* presented by Melvyn Bragg, in a segment devoted to Lowell. According to Hamilton, "she sent one of her daughters instead and had her read a condemnatory letter against the biography."

During Hamilton's research and writing of his Lowell biography, Caroline occasionally called up and asked him to come to her London house to see a letter or a document she had found. But sometimes when he arrived, she was too drunk to find it. She'd rummage through desk drawers or open a large trunk, but Hamilton often went away empty-handed. "Or she would give me spoken permission to quote, and then later deny having given it," Hamilton complained. Nonetheless, the accounts she gave about her life with Lowell are vivid and moving; without them, Lowell's life in London and at Milgate—and the travails and turmoil that went into the making of *The Dolphin*—would not have been so fully described.

Hamilton perceived that in the early stages of their marriage, the two almost "relished being manic together—there was a romantic, literary quality to it. They seemed well suited at first." His depiction of Caroline in the biography of Lowell is a model of objectivity and tact, but, in truth, Hamilton had the impression that Caroline, like many alcoholics, was "a manipulator who used people to get what she wanted." Furthermore, "she had an aristocratic sense of entitlement and was capable of great vindictiveness when she *didn't* get what she wanted." Hamilton also noticed that Caroline liked surrounding herself with men who could be of service to her. He felt that "Bob Silvers was a somewhat problematical third party in the Lowell marriage. He was always kept in the wings by Caroline as the family fixer, the caretaker, the enabler who saw to details. He was the one who arranged the memorial service for Lowell at the American Place Theater." Hamilton thought that Caroline may have wanted to turn him into one of her factotums, a role he absolutely resisted.

Hamilton also concluded that Caroline had initially begun writing, under Lowell's influence, as a way to justify belonging to the artistic, bohemian circles she inhabited, but he recognized that after Lowell's death she did indeed become a serious writer. The "romantic, literary" pose burned away, and the writer endured. It's entirely possible that Caroline's writing saved her, by giving her valuable tasks that would take her mind off of her tragedies, by giving her the means to "make and re-make" her soul, in Yeats's phrase, and to come to terms, often through black humor, with her bleak vision of the world. The decade following Natalya's death turned out to be Caroline's most prolific.

Between 1983 and 1987, Caroline published four more books: a

collection of short stories, a novel, and two works of nonfiction. Although they garnered mostly good reviews, none sold well enough to
earn the loyalty of her publishers. In 1983 William Heinemann Ltd.
brought out her collection of short stories, *Good Night Sweet Ladies*. The five tales—"Matron," "Taft's Wife," "Addy," "Olga," and
"Angelica"—present women coping with life-altering crises. They
appear to have been written over the course of six years. "Taft's
Wife," the only one with a male protagonist, was first published in
The Observer on August 13, 1978 (under the title "The Lunch"), and
"Olga" was published in 1983 (as "Olga's Cocktail Hour") in *The
New Edinburgh Review*. The reviews of the subtle and well-written
collection usually appeared within large, omnibus essays (under the
catchall title "Ogres" in *The New Statesman*, for example), but Caroline's characters, for a change, are not ogres. They are sometimes silly
and not particularly likable, but they inspire both recognition and
pity. That alone may have disappointed some reviewers and caused
the collection to be overlooked ("the writing, as always, is stylish and
close to the bone, but there is a sense in this collection that perhaps
this time she might have gone just a little further than she has. Her
vision is, one suspects, blacker than she is yet prepared to admit").[5] Or
the book may have been treated as slight because of its mere 136
pages. Caroline had always been something of a miniaturist. But these
five stories are admirably crafted, and if they lack some of the bizarre
and hilarious horror of *Great Granny Webster*, they are beautifully
controlled, psychologically discerning, and full of brilliant and witty
observations.

"Matron," the first in the collection, is an exercise in black
comedy, perhaps based on Caroline's stay at the Queen Victoria Burns
Unit with Ivana. She's another version of the bullying nurse from
Caroline's first collection ("The Baby Nurse" in *For All That I Have
Found There*), and the type would recur in Caroline's next novel.
(Miss Alley, Caroline's frightening nanny, was probably the model
for such creatures.) In "Matron," the protagonist is stern, martial,
self-sufficient, rule-abiding, and alone. Her crisis comes when she

inexplicably breaks one of her own rules by allowing Mrs. Appleseed, the aging wife of a dying, elderly patient, to receive hospital meals during her death watch. She's so upset by her sudden act of mercy that she decides it's time to retire. Caroline's characteristic black humor resides in the aborted attempt of two nurses to force a pair of ill-fitting dentures into the mouth of the deceased patient before rigor mortis sets in (a grisly detail Caroline may have learned about—and relished—during her familiarity with hospitals when she was married to Lowell). The two nurses become helpless with laughter as the dentures keep popping out of the dead man's mouth. Here is Caroline's response to death: laughing at the absurdity of it all—the frailty of the human form, the inadequacy of our rules and rituals in dealing with death and disaster, the cosmic joke that death makes of life. At the end of the story, Mrs. Appleseed timidly asks for the dentures she had removed and left in her husband's hospital room. The nurses had been trying to fit her dead husband with the wrong set. When the widow finally breaks down and weeps, Matron attempts to console her:

> "Even if you feel that you have nothing much to live for, you must try to carry on," Matron said. "You will find that life won't let you do anything else, Mrs. Appleseed. While you are still living—carrying on—that is all that life is about."[6]

This is Caroline's most optimistic statement in *Good Night Sweet Ladies*, yet the cumulative effect of the five stories is the brave hope that, by recognizing how we deceive ourselves and each other, we can begin to live life on truer terms, "white of the ancient lies," as Andrew Harvey wrote in the voice of Caroline.

In each story, the protagonist is tempted to give up on life yet finds a way to keep going, in small, antiheroic ways. "Olga" is perhaps the most autobiographical; it eerily predicts the struggle with cancer that would nearly destroy Caroline nine years later. Olga is a self-portrait with a bit of Maureen mixed in, Caroline's resentment toward her

Caroline fled Hollywood in 1958 and landed in New York City, where she met Walker Evans, who would take many photographs of her, including this haunting portrait. *Copyright Walker Evans Archive, The Metropolitan Museum of Art*

The gifted composer and pianist Israel Citkowitz became Caroline's second husband. *Courtesy of Elena Citkowitz*

Caroline with her first child, Natalya, in their West Fourth Street townhouse in Greenwich Village. *Copyright Walker Evans Archive, The Metropolitan Museum of Art*

Robert Lowell as a young man, then married to the novelist Jean Stafford. *By permission of the Houghton Library, Harvard University*

Lowell in 1974, dean of American poets and Caroline's third husband. *Thomas Victor*

Caroline bought this townhouse on a corner of Radcliffe Square in London. Lowell shared the top flat with Caroline, Citkowitz sometimes occupied the middle flat, and the children lived below with a succession of nannies.

Caroline's brother Sheridan, Lord Dufferin and Ava, and his wife Lindy, the marchioness and daughter of Loel Guinness, at Clandeboye. *Lady Dufferin and Lord Dufferin by kind permission of the Ulster Architectural Heritage Society*

LEFT: Caroline and Lowell with their son Sheridan, at Milgate, Blackwood's country house in Kent. Walker Evans visited them and took a series of photographs. *Copyright Walker Evans Archive, The Metropolitan Museum of Art*

BELOW: Caroline and Lowell with baby Sheridan and Caroline's daughter Ivana, taken at their temporary home in Brookline, Massachusetts, while Lowell taught at Harvard. *Thomas Victor*

RIGHT: An intensely
staring Caroline. *Thomas
Victor.*

BELOW: Caroline by Walker
Evans, taken at Milgate.
*Copyright Walker Evans Archive,
The Metropolitan Museum of Art*

LEFT: A Fellow of All Souls, Oxford, the poet and writer Andrew Harvey befriended Caroline after Lowell's death. *Courtesy of Andrew Harvey*

BELOW: Caroline with Steven M. L. Aronson, on the occasion of Aronson's birthday party, New York City. *Courtesy of Steven Aronson*

ABOVE: Caroline's last home, built by a whaling captain, in Sag Harbor, New York.

RIGHT: Caroline in her Sag Harbor garden, at the end of her life. *Maxine Hicks*

mother showing up in the emotions of Olga's only son, Oliver. Olga, seventy and dying of an unnamed disease, is, like Caroline, a fading beauty with huge, childlike eyes, a woman who loves her cocktail hour but has been ordered by her doctor to limit herself to one drink a day.[7]

Olga holds court during cocktail hour, enchanting Oliver's guests with her brilliant conversation and striking presence. But like any actress, Olga is not sure who the "real Olga" is. One evening she asks her son and the gathered guests: "Was the child, Olga, me? . . . Was the rebellious teenager the proper me? . . . Was it me when I stayed out all night dancing in night-clubs and spent the next day in bed? . . . Was the bride the me that really counted?"[8] Of course, no one can answer.

We then discover that Oliver resents his mother's vivacity, which, he believes, has drained him of all color and interest. He's convinced that after his mother dies, none of his friends will visit him again, because it was Olga they had always come to see.

Oliver also resents having to fill the house with guests so that his dying mother won't feel alone. He knows that his presence bores her. Feeling guilty when he goes out and leaves Olga, he consoles himself with the thought that "there are so many Olgas . . . All those different Olgas can keep her company."[9] But we know that her many selves will not keep her from dying alone; we've seen how mothers and children can prey upon one another, how mothers can drain the life out of their children (as Cressida did to Mary Rose), and how children can have their final revenge by leaving their mothers captive to the frailty and loneliness of old age.

Angelica, the subject of the final story in the collection, is a retired actress who gives up the stage when she suddenly finds that she no longer has the nerve to perform. "In the theatre they called it 'corpsing,' " Caroline wrote. "The very idea of facing any audience had now become enough to make her start shaking."[10] Like Olga, Angelica is also "Maureenish"—an aging beauty who dresses with great theatricality, whose makeup is applied with a heavy hand, and who dyes her hair ever brighter shades of blond. She relishes her great wealth, gained by marrying a rich husband whom she despises, and she's used to commanding attention from all around her. She has replaced the adoration of audiences with the social successes of her dinner parties. But when her much younger lover, the beautiful but weak Jason, abandons her, she is plunged into a mood so black that her self-pity spills over to inanimate objects—the raveled fringe of her bath mat, the tube of toothpaste that's lost its cap. Deep in depression, she is distracted by none of her former pleasures; at social gatherings she becomes obsessed with the peculiarities and grotesqueries of the human ear. Caroline is positively surreal—and mordantly brilliant—in her cataloging of this usually ignored aspect of human anatomy, which looks to her like fungi.

Angelica's regret and her luxurious, useless life have made her cruel; her greatest acts of cruelty are aimed at her daughter, Susan, a suburban wife, mother, and kindergarten teacher. She can't believe she spawned such a wholesome *Hausfrau* as Susan. "Angelica" is another of Caroline's explorations of mother-daughter relationships tinged with cruelty and guilt. Angelica bullies and insults her daughter, telling her that it was her birth that ended Angelica's stage career—a patent lie, which of course gives rise to guilt in her long-suffering daughter.

Nothing assuages Angelica's depression until she stumbles on the solution herself: taking long walks through Brompton Cemetery, off the Old Brompton Road. She finds that after spending time among the dead, she leaves the cemetery with a calmer mind and a renewed sense of vitality, as if their silence were capable of drowning out "the ugly and trivial noises of the living."[11] Ironically, the fear of "corpsing" began Angelica's long decline, but "corpsing" in a different sense will put it right.

During her perambulations among the gravestones, Angelica becomes fixated on the tombstone of one Major Arthur Coleman, killed at twenty-two during the First World War. She starts to fantasize, transforming him into a ghost lover—a dashing soldier whose courage and bearing show up Jason's essential weakness. She haunts his grave as though she were his grieving widow. The *memento mori*—the endless rows of graves and Major Coleman's tombstone in particular—allow her to see through her own pretenses. The gravestone of an unknown officer, killed in action, has more solidity to Angelica than does her life of lies and half-truths.

Caroline may well have had in mind the ghost of her father. Raised in a world of vain and childish women, Caroline experienced her father's absence as the hollow core within the apparent solidity of the world. The ghost of Major Coleman lifts Angelica's depression, if only temporarily, and restores to her a sense of wholeness and calm.

One of the advantages of living in London was Caroline's proximity to her brother, Sheridan, who in 1945 had become the fifth Marquess of Dufferin and Ava. Although brother and sister inhabited different social circles, Caroline occasionally saw Sheridan and his wife, Lindy (Selina Belinda Rosemary Guinness, daughter of Loel Guinness, of the banking line, and Sheridan's cousin). Caroline's circle was by now mostly literary; Sheridan and Lindy were fixtures of the glittering, aristocrat social life of London that centered on a roster of MPs, dukes, earls, viscounts, counts, countesses, lords and ladies as well as a cadre of London's most colorful and talented artists, such as David Hockney, R. B. Kitaj, and the Bloomsbury artist Duncan Grant. There had been eighteen hundred guests at Sheridan and Lindy's 1964 society wedding, including Princess Margaret—a far cry from Caroline's Registry Office wedding to Lucian Freud. Sheridan was part owner, with his partner John Kasmin, of London's Kasmin Gallery in Bond Street, which specialized in modern painting, and a trustee of the National Gallery and the Wallace Collection. Charming and puckish, with the characteristic Blackwood wit, Sheridan was sought after as a guest and admired as a discerning art dealer; he has been credited with launching the career of David Hockney, who painted a much-admired portrait of his friend. Sheridan also sat for

the notorious artist manqué and film producer-director Donald Cammell, whose 1953 portrait of Sheridan, dressed as a pageboy for the
coronation of Queen Elizabeth II, was considered "the society portrait
of the year."[12]

It may have been through Cammell, and through his association
with the art dealer and interior decorator Christopher Gibbs, that
Sheridan came into contact with the more *louche* side of London life,
embodied by denizens of Chelsea and disturbingly captured in Cammell's 1970 cult film, *Performance*. (Gibbs, a dandy, was present at
Redlands, Keith Richards's country estate, during the infamous 1967
drug bust of Mick Jagger, Marianne Faithfull, Richards, and others.)
Sheridan himself was described as "something of a cult figure in the
heady whirl of the so-called Swinging Sixties."[13] He once gave a
birthday party for himself and David Hockney at which his shirt
maker, Michael Fish, appeared in a gold miniskirt and a gold-and-
mauve lamé jacket.[14] Sheridan indulged his interests by backing a
number of films: one about Liberace; one about Hugh Hefner,
founder of *Playboy*; and Derek Jarman's avant-garde, homoerotic
film about St. Sebastian. Sheridan's respectability was shored up
through his directorship of the Arthur Guinness Trust. He also played
serious tennis at Queen's Club championships, and he was "an excellent game shot" on the three thousand acres of the Clandeboye estate,
which he had, of course, inherited along with his title.[15] He seemed
to be devoted to Lindy, yet his life was divided between the more traditional pursuits of aristocratic life, in London and at Clandeboye, and
his homosexual life among artists, decorators, art dealers, and rock
stars. And not just those in London. John Richardson recalled that
"[Sheridan] led a very gay life . . . he used to come over here [to the
United States] and have these big gay affairs. And he made no bones
about it—he was quite open."[16] The interior designer Nicholas
Haslam, who had been at Eton with Sheridan and who knew Caroline
through his romantic involvement with Michael Wishart,[17] recalled
that Sheridan "was adored at school. He was a generous sportsman
and a very good tennis player. He didn't seem to have a gay life while

a student, but it seemed to have emerged around the time of his marriage to Lindy. And he didn't have any one, enduring lover; they were more like one-night stands."[18]

Roy Strong, the former director of the National Portrait Gallery and of the Victoria and Albert Museum, described the Dufferins as bridging London's "old guard and its young" in the late 1960s.[19] He first met Sheridan and Lindy at a dinner party in 1968, and he described Sheridan as "droll and saturnine, with the face of a depressed if affectionate basset hound,"[20] though others have remarked on Sheridan's usual expression of faint amusement.[21] His sickliness as a youth probably contributed to his slight frame and perpetually boyish appearance. Lindy, with the delicate, long-nosed look of a whippet, has a distinctly aristocratic face. "With her superb bone structure, halo of curly hair and almost mad laugh," Roy Strong wrote in his diary, "Lindy seemed to exude energy, so much so that she often generated it in other people."[22] Their London house in Holland Villas Road, with its many canvases by Hockney, was the scene of brilliant parties:

> *Everyone who was brightest, most creative, or just plain beautiful frequently gathered. Sheridan's annual birthday party, which floated on an ocean of champagne with about two hundred guests scattered through the candlelit garden, became one of the great events of the year.*[23]

When London palled, there were shooting parties at Clandeboye, and, on at least one occasion, a trek to Morocco. Lindy, an inveterate traveler and a serious painter who had been mentored by Duncan Grant, gathered up select guests and whisked them away. Roy Strong recalled:

> *All of a sudden, we were off to Morocco. There were three of us: myself, Lindy, buoyant and pop-eyed as ever, as though in a permanent state of amazement at everything and everybody, and her*

"newly discovered" cousin, Bryan Moyne [a poet and playwright whose first wife, Diana Mitford, divorced him to become Lady Diana, wife of the Fascist Oswald Mosley] . . . We stayed a night in Rabat.[24]

In 1969 Sheridan created quite a splash by arranging for a Kasmin Gallery exhibition in Belfast, sponsored by Northern Ireland's Art Council. Several of the artists, flown in for the event, stayed with the Dufferins at Clandeboye. The gala opening was celebrated with a discothèque set up in Clandeboye's music room, along with "Nymphet and go-go girls" imported for the occasion.[25] Chris Gibbs was present and, again, Roy Strong, who described the event:

When it came to the artists and their hangers-on it was impossible to work out who was married or living with whom and whose children were whose. I gave up, but among them there was lovely David Hockney . . . The unsinkable and predatory Kasmin spent most of the weekend pursuing Catherine Pakenham . . . Lindy Dufferin summed up the whole event with characteristic panache while she was lolling behind me near the tennis court: "The trouble with all of them is they're common" . . . Just about everyone was on drugs except me, who declined even a puff.[26]

Ironically, the newsmaking art show, which contributed a touch of sophistication to Ulster's cultural life, took place on "the eve of Northern Ireland's new dark age."[27] After the Troubles began anew, Lindy and Sheridan took to barring the road to Clandeboye with heavy logs.

Though Caroline was not a fixture in the Dufferins' social scene, she did occasionally visit her brother and sister-in-law. Sheridan had long ago eschewed alcohol, recognizing his inability to handle it. John Richardson recalled that Sheridan, as a teenager, had once become violent while under the influence and from that point on had sworn off spirits.[28] As an adult, he drank nothing stronger than Coca-Cola.

Perhaps the sight of his sister in her cups was distressing to him; it was certainly distressing to Perdita. During one of Caroline's visits to Clandeboye, Perdita had asked her, "Do you really have to drink so much?" Caroline's response was a gruff, irritated "Now, don't *you* start!" To which Perdita replied, "I just wouldn't want it said that I didn't care enough to ask."[29]

Lindy Dufferin remembered Caroline's visiting Clandeboye while she was still involved with Andrew Harvey, probably in 1980 or 1981. Lindy, who knew the two were living together, felt that Caroline was "passionately in love" with Andrew.

> *Andrew was brilliant and extremely handsome . . . He was into mysticism, and had something to do with reprinting* The Tibetan Book of the Dead [The Tibetan Book of Living and Dying]. *Once they came to Clandeboye and she looked as if she had been in a car crash, she had become so slovenly. He wasn't, though. He didn't drink, like Caroline. And Caroline could be mean and a terrific bore when she drank.*[30]

If relations were a bit cool between the two sisters-in-law, Caroline adored her brother and was proud of his accomplishments as an art dealer and tastemaker.

By the end of the 1980s, Lindy would become the sole châtelaine of Clandeboye, which further removed Caroline from her childhood home. She made peace with having lost Clandeboye to Sheridan; she would next lose it to her sister-in-law, when, at some point in the mid-1980s, Sheridan began to manifest the symptoms of AIDS.

In 1984 Caroline was asked by an American magazine to write an article about the camp set up by the Women's Peace Movement on Greenham Common near the town of Newbury, outside an American nuclear base. Caroline visited the camp in March, her curiosity piqued by the virulent hatred aroused by these small, peaceful groups of women protesters, who had willingly given up their safety and comfort to protest the presence of nuclear armaments on British soil. By camping on the neutral ground outside the American cruise missile base, the women, of diverse ages and backgrounds, hoped to serve as "symbolic candles that represented the conscience of humanity."[31] As Caroline later told a journalist, "Perhaps women can only do things symbolically."[32] What they got in return was scorn, suspicion, sabotage, acts of violence, and obscenities hurled at them by townspeople and military personnel—even from the school-age children of American servicemen stationed at the nuclear site. Caroline wrote:

> *I was very curious to meet the Greenham women, for the press had decorated them with such loathsome and frightening adjectives, they had been made to sound almost mythical in their horror. They'd been described as "belligerent harpies," "a bunch of smelly lesbians," as "ragtag and bobtail," and "the screaming destructive witches of Greenham."[33]*

Auberon Waugh said the women smelled of "fish paste and bad oysters"[34]—a phrase with unpleasant sexual associations not lost on Caroline. How had these women—who had set up makeshift tents as dwellings around soggy campfires but who, under normal circumstances, were society's respected wives, daughters, mothers, sisters, and girlfriends—come to be vilified in sexual and graphic terms?

After having lampooned the radical Women's Theater in the 1970s (Lowell joked that they were going to be picketed by militant lesbians after Caroline's article was published), Caroline would not have been expected to be sympathetic to this plight and cause, yet she found herself drawn to their life on "the boundary of a fortified position"[35]— that fortified position being English society as well as the well-armed cruise missile base. Caroline decided that the journalistic piece she had intended to write should be expanded. *On the Perimeter,* a slim book on the women's peace encampment, was published in September 1984 by Heinemann. Partly because the subject itself was a long-entrenched controversy, and partly because the writer was Lady Caroline Blackwood, her book on the Greenham protest movement was well covered in the press, including a sarcastic lambasting from Bernard Levin in the London *Times*. Under the title "Baying at the Moon," Levin's article recounted that Lady Caroline Hamilton-Temple-Blackwood had been "mooned" by a busload of airmen. He then quoted her response, as recorded in *On the Perimeter*: "They were bending over like ostriches . . . I had a girl assistant with me and we were both shocked and appalled. I have never seen something so unpleasant."[36]

Levin took Caroline to task for her outrage, which he didn't believe in for a second. Lady Caroline, he wrote, "is a 51-year-old novelist . . . who has been married no fewer than three times . . . Not to put too fine a point on it, Lady Caroline has been around." After making fun of titled ladies who go slumming for a few days among the disenfranchised, Levin finally admonished Caroline for failing to respond in the only appropriate way: "Next time a platoon of airmen, or for that matter an entire regiment of soldiers, show their bottoms to you, try laughing."

Levin's article created such a stir that when *On the Perimeter* was published and Caroline was reviewed and interviewed on the subject, Levin's column was addressed head-on by at least one journalist, Laurie Taylor, in an interview with Caroline for the London *Times*.

The interview took place in Caroline's Redcliffe Square apartment. Despite her nervousness and her anger over Bernard Levin's jeering column, Caroline gave Taylor a thoughtful and revealing interview. She told the journalist something that had never before appeared in print: from an early age she had known she was a writer, though she wasn't the sort to "put things in drawers . . . I just started when I started."[37]

Caroline had always been offhand about her ambitions. The poet

Eleanor Ross Taylor recalled that Caroline never presented herself primarily as a writer:

She never talked about her writing as other people did. Jean Stafford [Lowell's first wife] always talked about her writing, and Elizabeth [Hardwick] quite a bit, too. Caroline did not. In a way she was a lot more sophisticated . . . and perhaps had more assurance.[18]

When Laurie Taylor, during the interview, asked whether Caroline considered herself an active feminist, Caroline replied, "No, I'm a sympathizer . . . all women have to be sympathizers." She then talked of the few nights she had spent with the protesters in their primitive encampments, where she came to admire their bravery and endurance. When asked why she didn't offer an argument for nuclear disarmament in *On the Perimeter*, which is clearly sympathetic to the women's peace vigil, Caroline replied that she decided not to, saying that books about megaton bombs were usually so technical, or strident, that they were unreadable. Her support of the Greenham women, as they came to be known, was shared by a lot of women, especially those with children. "[F]ear of an accident is what women deal with all day long . . . bringing up a small child is one long near-accident."

Caroline must have had Ivana's accident and Natalya's death in mind when she made that statement, and the great sense of vulnerability that comes with motherhood. In some sense *On the Perimeter* is the diamond created by the tremendous pressure of guilt over Ivana's scalding and Natalya's death: it's a clear-eyed, moving account of women on the edge that doesn't resort to cant or predicable sentiments; it's also a chilling revelation of the deep misogyny that underlies the civility of men and women alike, too easily set off by women who stop playing by the rules. At best, the Greenham protesters were described by their critics as "atrocious law-breaking trespassers," responsible for lowering local property values, and as "scum, contaminating the town's supermarkets, polluting its public baths and wash-

ing machines, dangerously contagious like lepers . . . they scare the
birds and (a charge brought against gypsies, Jews, tinkers, and pied
pipers of all sorts down the ages) steal the children of Newbury."[39]

The sight of dozens of ungroomed women living in the open,
flaunting the rules, keeping one another company without the presence of men, so unhinged a Master of Foxhounds traipsing through
the common with his hounds and his hunters, that he charged the
camp.

*He apparently felt that he hadn't sufficiently outraged the Green-
ham women and he'd come back to make a final demonstration of
his superiority and power. He turned into the lane that lay between
the women's benders. We had to jump out of the way of his horse
which he was riding as if he was engaged in a military charge.
When you are on foot, any horse that charges you seems enormous
and ferocious, and almost more deadly than a tank.*[40]

In the chaos that ensued, it was left to the women to round up his
abandoned hounds, which had been left "baying and yelping with terror as they went weaving blindly through the now fast-moving traffic
of the mainroad."[41]

Caroline was profoundly moved by this clash of worlds: the *haute*
society of tradition-bound Englishmen and -women riding to hounds,
versus the New Age, ragtag community of women protesters. The
seed for her next book was perhaps planted by the sight of the irate
MFH whipping his horse through the makeshift encampment of
unarmed women.

During the course of the *Times* interview, Laurie Taylor noticed Freud's "Girl in Bed" hanging over the mantelpiece in Caroline's "large and uncluttered room" and boldly asked whether she
was intimidated by it, "as you grow older and, well, less obviously
beautiful."

Caroline answered with a subversive statement. She didn't really
see the portrait as being *her.* "I think [one's] beauty . . . is fraudulent,"

she said. "Nothing to do with you." It was a theme she had sounded in *Good Night Sweet Ladies* and one she deeply believed.

A nd then came *Corrigan.* Caroline followed up *Good Night Sweet Ladies* and *On the Perimeter* with her fourth novel, which Heinemann brought out in Great Britain in 1984 and Viking Penguin published the following year in America. Something seemed to have happened to Caroline between her writing the bitter, ironic fictions of *Good Night Sweet Ladies* and the writing of *Corrigan,* a book that turned Caroline's entire ethos on its head. The novel's lonely grieving widow, Devina Blunt, not only carries on after the death of her husband; she absolutely flourishes. And she does so because she has come under the sway of a charming liar and con man: a wheelchair-bound, poetry-spouting Irishman named Corrigan. Far from being "washed clean of the ancient lies," Devina is transformed by illusion and lies—lies willfully and knowingly embraced. As one critic wrote in the *New York Times Book Review,* "Domesticity for Miss Blackwood has never been cozy; she listens for the ticking of the time bomb in the teapot." But the reviewer concluded that in *Corrigan* "the time bomb in the teapot is not only defused, it puts forth green shoots and blossoms into a rose."[42] The critic used the word "sunniness" in describing this novel. Could this really be Caroline Blackwood? If so, what had brought about this change of heart in what would turn out to be Caroline's last novel?

In some ways, *Corrigan* is the opposite of, or the antidote to, the short story "The Interview," published in 1973 and prophetic in its depiction of a bitter, whiskey-soaked, yet seductive widow of a famous artist. The novel and the story are opposite views of how a widow might live after a long and intense marriage. "The Interview" is a scathing, subversive little story about professional widowhood and the petty cruelties and shams inherent in the life of an artist.[43]

It opens with an imperious widow being interviewed by a journalist, with the hilarious name of Mr. Bunny, who seeks her response to a recent documentary film about the widow's husband, a well-known and highly regarded painter. The widow—unnamed in the story—is wickedly insulting about the film, which she describes as being filled with "awful mirage liveliness."[44] She alternately flirts with and insults the journalist, who has "eyes as cold as tiny frozen French peas."[45]

Caroline's depiction of the unnamed artist is devastating, leading one to wonder whether Lowell, still living when the story was written and published, or Lucian Freud saw any part of himself in the character. The widow dismisses her dead husband's *oevre* as second-rate (though acknowledging what an accomplishment it is that, "in the scale of things, the second-rate painter ranks really rather high").[46] She makes sure the journalist knows that her famous husband was incontinent at the end (not depicted, of course, in the deceitfully cheery documentary) and that she actually hated him. She confesses to toting bottles of whiskey into his hospital room and hiding them. She admits to having destroyed his canvases, and she characterizes the painter as a joyless companion, a morose lover ("as soft and green as asparagus!"),[47] a man burdened by self-doubt and feelings of fraudulence, dependent on alcohol, and involved with her in a sado-masochistic relationship ("I was like the punchballs that boxers use for practice").[48] She has mordant things to say about passivity and the role of the victim ("[it] can be quite solid you know").[49] She clearly relishes opening the eyes of the rapacious young journalist, who hadn't bargained for the truth. She tells him that she keeps pet monkeys and sometimes straps brushes to their wrists and lets them paint away. Occasionally the monkeys will "do something which is not entirely uninteresting."[50]

If Caroline had ever delighted in the romantic idea of being an artist together with Lowell, as Ian Hamilton suspected, it was an illusion she had ultimately seen through. Life with an artist, Caroline recognized, could be a special kind of hell.

In contrast, the newly widowed Devina Blunt, in *Corrigan*, is a somewhat vague, benign woman with a resentful daughter, Nadine, whose bad marriage to a monstrously selfish man makes her envy her mother's life. Devina had been so overly protected by her husband that she has no idea how to pay a bill or even how to collect the large insurance settlement her husband left her. Nadine fears that the death of her father, a former colonel who had served in India, has plunged her mother into a severe depression, because Devina neglects her "pretty little period house" and garden. She leaves all the household responsibilities to her loud and vulgar Irish housekeeper, Mrs. Murphy, another of the masculine, brash, but competent women who appear from time to time in Caroline's fiction.

Sabrina, Nadine's best friend, is a fashion model who detests her shallow life and recognizes that, in her twenties, she's about to become obsolescent. Here Caroline strikes her theme of the fraudulent nature of appearances:

> She had learnt that she was able to present the world with a façade that could sometimes be mistaken for physical perfection, but knowing she was creating an illusion, she despised her own ability to do so . . . she often felt that she was in competition with her own concocted and romanticised image.[51]

Sabrina complains that her career "will be about as lasting as an American domestic appliance,"[52] and she's at a loss as to what to do when she can no longer compete with the new crop of fifteen-year-olds. (Earlier, Caroline had presented a successful but insecure model-turned-journalist in the form of Gloria, Rowan's mistress, in *The Fate of Mary Rose*.) Caroline had reason to dismiss fashion modeling as an empty and unsatisfying career, one that lures with its surface glamour until "the camera goes click and it's all over."[53] She had briefly embarked on such a career until Walker Evans, and her own boredom, shamed her out of it. Sabrina is sent by Nadine to check up on the suspiciously charming Mr. Corrigan, a man in a wheelchair who has moved into Devina's house and is helping to spend Devina's money on what turn out to be phony charities. But if Sabrina leads us to believe that this is another novel revealing the ugly truth beneath the beautiful lies, Caroline completely surprises us. The con man does succeed in transforming Devina Blunt's—and Sabrina's—lives into far happier and useful ones than they had ever imagined. Devina learns to drive, overhauls her garden, plants fruit trees, takes up painting, and sells some of her work through a London art gallery. It's clear that she has fallen in love with the handsome scoundrel, and Nadine, suspicious of Corrigan, is outraged. She sets out to unveil Corrigan for the liar that he is, in part because of her outrage that her mother is being swindled and in part because of her envy of her mother's happiness.

Nadine discovers that her mother has known all along that Corrigan is a fraud. His wheelchair is just a prop; yet for her own reasons she has decided to go along with the game. It's as if Caroline has, for once in her life, decided that the illusion is sometimes worth believing in, may even be nurturing, if it brings about a kind of fulfillment. Or, to look at it another way, happiness is possible, but it is usually built on lies.

Caroline's usual point of view is expressed by Nadine, but we readers are heartened to see Devina flourishing. And we come to see Nadine for what she is: a nay-saying malcontent who has ruined her life with bad choices. We are on Devina's side, willingly fooled.

Did Caroline's involvement with the Women's Peace Camp at Greenham Common bring about a renewal of engagement with the world, as expressed in *Corrigan*? Or was her year-long affair with Andrew Harvey the alchemy that brought her from a bitter period of mourning for Lowell and Natalya into a place where she could once again imagine a future? Harvey thought that *On the Perimeter* "came out of her relationship with me. I tried to open her up to more social issues. She didn't want to be thought of as a rich old woman with no interests in the world but her own pleasure—Caroline's view of her mother—but I don't think Caroline would have been involved in those larger issues if it weren't for me."[54]

Whatever the catalyst, Caroline's extreme depression lifted, and she was able to get on with her life. She would complete one more book, a treatise on fox hunting, and then move her entire household to America—the place for new beginnings, the place one goes in order to escape the past.

Twelve

"SHE'S GOT A PROBLEM"

I thought her garden would work in the evening,
when moths came. I thought that
was perhaps what she wanted.[1]

aroline had been unexpectedly moved by the plight of the
Greenham women. They had been vilified as, among other
things, witches, and Caroline knew about witches. Witches were
women without power, relegated to the margins of society and made
scapegoats for others' misfortune; witches were women who were disheveled and uncared for, who smelled like "fish paste and bad oysters," who didn't bother to groom themselves or make themselves
attractive to men. Witches were eerily beautiful women, like Cressida
in the *The Fate of Mary Rose*, with pale hair and unearthly, light
blue eyes; witches were women like Maureen, women *with* power—
too much power, too much money, and an unquestioned sense of entitlement. Caroline knew witches.

In the Pink may have been inspired by Caroline's having witnessed an attempt by a Master of Foxhounds to trample the women protesters. It was a moment in which the symbolic nature of the ancient rivalry between the privileged and the disenfranchised shone through. *In the Pink* is Caroline's investigation into the current state of fox hunting, in which she pits the views embodied in the Duke of Beaufort, one of the last great Masters of Foxhounds, against Tim Morgan, a hunt saboteur and vegetarian who represents the extremes of the anti–fox hunting contingent. Both sides are made to look unsavory. The duke was addressed for most of his life as Master, Caroline notes, ever since his father gave him a pack of hounds on his ninth birthday. Caroline describes a photograph of the young Master in his jockey cap, "triumphantly waving in the air the head of a bleeding animal."[2]

Tim Morgan, on the other hand, is an aggressive pacifist who runs a sanctuary for wounded animals on a run-down farm in the north of England, surrounded by adoring, hippie-like girls reminiscent of a Charles Manson commune. Caroline describes Morgan's joyless and rigid sanctuary as a "haven for unlucky creatures. Even the turkeys and hens were depressed and depressing."[3] A fox that had been rescued from the hunt and raised as a pet languishes, alone, howling piteously and missing its human family, as a prologue to being set free in the countryside, where it will no doubt be quickly killed by predators.

Caroline explains to the uninitiated the ancient rituals that cling to fox hunting, with a witty and informative exegesis of hunting idioms: "Hounds do not smell the scent of a fox, they 'wind' it . . . Hounds never bark, they bay and 'speak' like humans. They also 'throw tongue' and 'make music.' "[4] When the fox retreats to its den, it "goes to ground in 'an earth.' " "Go in and tear him" is the cry of the kill.[5] Caroline defines the book's title by explaining that to be "in the pink" derives from Mr. Pink, a London tailor whose skills were so revered that the cognoscenti had their expensive coats cut only by him. Anyone who called the huntsman's coat "red" instead of "pink" was considered a bumpkin. She also points out that certain common phrases derive from the language of the hunt: "staying power," getting off to a "flying start," "toe the line"—even "have a good day."[6] Furthermore, "a fast woman" is originally a hunt term, referring to those brazen women who were first to ride astride their horses instead of sidesaddle.[7]

This would not be a Blackwood book, however, if it did not go into the violence of the sport, and especially its effect on children, with a great deal of detail and relish. She describes Francis Bacon's antipathy toward the blood sport and its traumatizing effect upon him as a child. She notices that whenever she questions him on the subject, the painter begins to wheeze. Caroline speculates that his remembered horror of the hunt is what lurks beneath the tortured images in his paintings.

She draws on Molly Keane—the last Anglo-Irish novelist to take as her main subject life in an ascendancy family—to illustrate the terror inflicted on young children forced to hunt from the age of five, lest they be considered cowards by their mothers. "You couldn't believe how my mother neglected her children," Molly Keane told Caroline.[8] Keane was expected to hunt but was never taught to ride; it was assumed that riding and hunting were in the genes. Keane's novel *The Rising Tide* (published under her pseudonym, M. J. Farrell) describes the traumatizing effect a hunt-mad mother has on her two children: "Susan and Simon were often borne along for miles with tears pouring down their faces, and everyone said how much they were enjoying themselves and how well they went for children of their age."[9] The two children dared not show their fear, even to each other:

Their mother has made them regard fear as a deeply shameful emotion. They often vomit before setting off for the meet. They know their mother will be livid if they don't "go well." She will be furious if they avoid jumps and cheat by using the gates, if they run over a hound, or let their ponies bolt. It will also enrage her if they

forget the names of any of the hounds. Most of all they fear her
anger if they are the last to be in at the kill.[10]

Cynthia, the children's mother in Keane's novel, is one of those upper-class women of leisure who possess "the semi-fanatic must-hunt attitude which is often stronger in women than in men."[11] She even postpones the date of her husband's funeral so that she can attend a meet.

Another hunt-mad mother, who goes unnamed in Caroline's book, can't be bothered to take her six-year-old daughter to the dentist, although the girl's mouth is throbbing in pain. Instead, she keeps an appointment with her blacksmith to have a mare shod; while there, she asks the blacksmith to extract her daughter's tooth. He does.

Finally, Caroline brings her subject up to date by reporting on a day spent "car hunting," a mid-twentieth-century development in which hunters and hounds are followed by bloodthirsty spectators in legions of cars, a trend so unsportsmanlike that it may be the very thing that finally kills off the sport. Even the Duke of Beaufort, too frail to sit on a horse, died at the age of eighty-three while riding to hounds in the backseat of a car.

In the Pink was published in 1987 in London but not in the States. Caroline's book touched a nerve, and was mainly criticized because the author didn't know enough, or wasn't accurate enough, about the arcane facts of the sport. Raymond Carr wrote in *The Spectator*, "It cannot be said that Lady Caroline knows much about the vast and boring literature on this touchy subject."[12] But *In the Pink* is chock-full of fascinating fact and lore surrounding the ancient blood sport; one wonders whether the cool reception was a response to Caroline's having *dared* to criticize, expose, and lampoon such a treasured pastime, one that has so often symbolized England's greatest qualities: courage, sportsmanship, tradition. Caroline's friend Peter Levi felt that *In the Pink* "is very funny," but that Caroline was *at her best when she was making things up. The funniest bit is about a print she describes—I'm sure she made it up—of a young man in the trenches, around 1915. As he's dying, he's looking up, and above his head is a fox hunting scene . . . there are the hounds, etc. It's screamingly funny the way she describes it, but I doubt if the print exists anywhere.*[13]

Even Perdita was not persuaded. An animal lover who nonetheless hunted, and who admired the courage it took to stay on a horse in full pursuit of a fox, Perdita felt that Caroline had gotten a number of things wrong. She had, for example, misstated the traditional number of hounds let loose in the hunt. And Perdita found Caroline's description of the mistreatment of the dogs particularly disturbing—and questionable. Caroline goes into graphic detail about how young terriers, bred for the job of digging into the earth wherever the quarry has gone to ground, are trained to their bloody task by rehearsing on a captured fox let loose among the pack. But that pales beside her description of the vicious fight that ensues when the fox goes to ground and the terriers go after it.

Just when you think that Caroline has exposed the sport to be mean, brutal, and cruel, she turns the tables by quoting James Teacher, a joint Master of the Quorn, on the rich, sensual pleasures of the hunt:

You get the smell of leather, all the saddles, and so on. You get the smells of the countryside in the early morning, fresh wet earth, cattle—all that. Then all the noises of hunting are beautiful, the sound of the horn, the music of the hounds, the clop of hooves on a road. The neighing, the snorting, it's all wonderful to the ear . . . When you see the hounds going up a frosty hill—they are such a beautiful sight. I think that most people only hunt because they love beauty—not because they love cruelty.[14]

By ending her book with this paean to the beauties of the hunt, Caroline reveals herself as a keen critic of the privileges and traditions of her kind, but one who could not entirely give them up.

In 1987 Caroline left England and moved to New York, where, except for the summer spent with Cornelia, she had not lived since her departure nearly twenty years earlier. Evgenia studied at Barnard College on the Upper West Side of Manhattan and preferred New York to London, finding it less "cliquey" and more diverse.[15] Caroline rented an apartment on the thirty-fourth floor of a modern, glass-and-steel high-rise at 265 East Sixty-sixth Street, which she shared with Ivana, twenty-one, while seventeen-year-old Sheridan attended Bedales in England. He, too, would eventually move to Manhattan and briefly attend Columbia University before gong to work for Stanley Moss at Sheep Meadow Press, a small publishing house that specialized in poetry. Caroline also bought a home in Sag Harbor, on the fashionable east end of Long Island.

Caroline's friends joked about the high-rise, calling it "tacky" and inhabited by "Euro-trash,"[16] but her home in Sag Harbor, two hours from New York, was more suited to Caroline's background and tastes. Some of the new friends she would make in New York and on Long Island felt that Caroline had moved to the island in order to escape her past. Robert Dash, a painter admired for his magnificent garden in Long Island's Sagaponack, befriended Caroline in her last years. He felt that she was "haunted by past events. When I knew her, I was knowing the ghost of Caroline Blackwood."[17]

In many ways, Sag Harbor was the ideal home for Caroline. First, her old friends Cornelia Foss and Stanley Moss owned summer houses nearby, in Bridgehampton. Jason Epstein, a senior editor at Random House and a close friend of Robert Silvers, was "just over the hedge." Though decidedly upscale, Sag Harbor still has the feel of a quaint fishing village and a reputation for being more literary than the trendier Hamptons, East and South. And because she could no longer drive, the village was small enough for Caroline to walk into the main part of town from her house on Union Street, to shop, go to the movies, or dine at the elegant American Hotel. Although she owned a burgundy Mercedes, presumably for her children to use when they visited her, she wasn't hampered by being unable to drive.

The white, Italianate Victorian house she bought for approximately $400,000 ("Victorian Venetian," like her Redcliffe Square house) sat impressively in the town's historic district. It had once been the "Summer White House" of Chester A. Arthur, attested to by a commemorative plaque. It had been built in 1796 by John Hulbert for a whaling captain, back when Sag Harbor boasted a whaling industry. When Caroline bought it, however, its most recent incarnation had been as a funeral home. According to Robert Dash, she kept the first floor of the house as it had been when it hosted funerals. "You walked in," he recalled, "and there was the banquette, where people sobbed and so on. She never changed the décor at all. It was a funeral parlor! You could just see it: the urns go here, the catafalque goes there . . . rather marvelous, really."[18] The three-story house has thirteen rooms (six bedrooms and four and a half baths), a "low-hipped roof," a swimming pool, and ample room for a garden on its nearly one-half acre. And, like Devina Blunt in *Corrigan*, Caroline discovered the pleasure of planting a pretty English garden: irises, parrot tulips, lilacs, wisteria, dahlias, and pansies.

"Caroline was a co-conspirator," her old friend Cornelia Foss said from her summer home in Bridgehampton. She could be tremendous fun, especially in the years she was married to Israel Citkowitz. But when Caroline moved back to New York in 1987, Cornelia saw less of her. "She called me at least once a day, if not five times a day," Foss recalled. "She was drinking heavily. I just couldn't see her; it was too painful, too hard."[19] Five years earlier they had written lyrics for Marianne Faithfull and her then companion, the musician Ben Brierly. Foss remembered that Brierly had called up Caroline one day, telling her that they were "desperate for lyrics!"

> *So Caroline called me and said, "Can you imagine! I mean, how*
> *hard can it be to write lyrics? Why don't we both try to write*
> *some?" So we both wrote some and sent them off to [Brierly]. A*
> *few days later, Caroline phoned screaming with laughter, and*
> *said, "Have you seen what's in the papers?" It was [Brierly],*
> *arrested for smuggling drugs. "Can you imagine, he's got our*
> *horrifying, personal lyrics in his pocket with our names on them!*
> *And we're going to be dragged through the courts now!" Of*
> *course it didn't happen, but she loved to dramatize.*[20]

Caroline's lyrics were recorded by Faithfull as "She's Got a Problem," released on the album *A Child's Adventure*. The words are Caroline at her most self-mocking:

> *Will I see whiskey as a Mother*
> *In the end. . .*
> *Will the world shake its sensible head*
> *And say the words that have to be said:*
> *She's got a problem.*
>
> *Every problem has a solution in the end*
> *And solutions must be final*
> *For help gets so unhelpful near the end.*[21]

In late May of 1988, the year after Caroline left London for America, she got word that her brother, Sheridan, was dying of AIDS. Caroline flew to Dublin and then took a train over the border between the Republic of Ireland and Northern Ireland so that she could be with him at Clandeboye. When she arrived, Caroline was shocked at her brother's deterioration. She posted herself at his bedside, agonizing with him over every physical indignity, to the point where it unnerved her sister-in-law, Lindy. Caroline recalled that the last thing Sheridan wanted to do was show her his garden, on which he had lavished much attention. Caroline believed his devoting himself to planting was his reaction to the "death sentence" of AIDS.

Sheridan, weakened by his illness, enlisted a servant to carry him out to the garden, which was quite a distance from the main house. In a cold Irish rain, Caroline stood in the garden with her brother and marveled at its beauty. She remembered that it was like *The Secret Garden*, full of dazzling and perfect blossoms. After painfully and slowly making his way back to the grand house, Sheridan became delirious. He did not recover.[22]

Sheridan died on May 29. The local *County Down Spectator* announced, "The Last Lord Dufferin Dies."[23] Hundreds of mourners— mostly titled—attended his memorial service on October 5, 1988, just as hundreds had attended his society wedding. Maureen was present, as were her two sisters, Aileen and Oonagh, and Evgenia and Ivana flew to London to attend the service at St. Margaret's, Westminster. Sheridan's father-in-law, Loel Guinness (a former MP from Bath), had outlived his son-in-law and was in attendance. Christopher Gibbs and the Earl of Arran "read the lessons."[24] The only person who mattered who was not listed as being in attendance was, curiously, Caroline Blackwood. She and her son, Sheridan, stayed away. Caroline, who had been eager to share her brother's dying moments, presumably could not bring herself to attend his memorial service. If she had moved to the States in part to escape being haunted by her past, as a number of her friends believed, then perhaps the sight of all those titled members of English and Anglo-Irish society would have stirred too many memories of the rarefied life she had spent years trying to escape.

The *Daily Telegraph* reported that, as Sheridan and Lindy had no children, with Sheridan's death the "Marquessate now becomes extinct, as do the Earldoms of Dufferin and of Ava and the Viscountcy and Barony of Clandeboye." However, the writer helpfully pointed out that "the Irish Barony of Dufferin and Clandeboye, of Ballyleidy and Killyleagh (not to be confused with the Barony of Killyleagh which was conferred on the Duke of York in 1986), together with a baronetcy, now passes to his kinsman, Sir Francis George Blackwood, 7th Bt., born 1916, who lives in New South Wales."[25]

In Sag Harbor Caroline derived much solace from her own garden, with the help of Donna Cohen, a young woman she had hired. She spent little time in Manhattan, preferring the peaceful pleasures of her life in "Sag," as she liked to call it, dragging the word out in her husky growl. "Donna loved Caroline," observed the former fiction editor and Sag Harbor resident Suzanne McNear. "Like me, she was not part of Caroline's past."[26] Robert Dash, whose vast garden is truly a work of genius, created over many years and ranging from grandeur to sublime whimsy, was a little dismissive of Caroline's much more modest creation. "It made no sense," he confided. "It was dribs of this and dribs of that and so forth. It was terribly incoherent. No substance or strength. But, then, I thought her garden would work in the evening, when moths came. I thought that was perhaps what she wanted."[27] Nonetheless, Caroline took much pride in her design and Donna Cohen's handiwork, and occupied the bedroom that faced the rear, overlooking the garden and swimming pool. The master bedroom, "the President's Room," she reserved for Ivana, the daughter she seemed to have been closest to, the one most like her in humor and temperament. "As you're going out of life, you put more into the soil," she later said when describing her brother Sheridan's secret garden. And so she did.[28]

Caroline had always been in some physical pain from the automobile accident she had had in her teens, practicing to get her driver's license with her cousin Doon at her side. The pain had never entirely vanished, to the point that she preferred to write longhand, because sitting at a typewriter hurt her back.[29] But further physical torments were to come. Not long after moving to Sag Harbor, Caroline was diagnosed, at the age of sixty-one, with cervical cancer. It called for surgery, and Caroline returned to London for the operation. It was not completely successful, and a second operation had to be performed. The cancer was removed, but because the surgeon cut too deep, Caroline was left in constant pain. Even worse, the operation had damaged her bladder, making it necessary for her to wear a urinary drain bag for the rest of her life. She now had to deal with the indignities of incontinence, like the lionized painter in her short story "The Interview." It was as if she had predicted her own fate.[30]

One wonders why Caroline chose to have the surgery in London rather than New York, where better medical treatment was available. Could it be that she was reluctant to spend the money necessary and wanted England's National Health to pay for the operation? If so, it was a gamble that did not pay off. She may not have known Britain's poor record on cancer treatment, which has been described as "nothing short of disgraceful, a stark example of the limitations of Britain's fraying system of socialized medicine,"[31] according to the journalist Sarah Lyall, who has reported on the chronic lack of funds, specialists, and cancer treatment centers in England. "The World Health Organization," Lyall wrote "says that 250,000 people die unnecessarily of cancer in Britain each year—people who would most likely have survived if they lived in countries with better standards of treatment, like France, Germany, or the United States." But Caroline *did* live in the United States. Could her choice have been a death wish? After all, she confided in one of her close friends when she first got the diagnosis of cancer that she "just wanted to die."[32]

The only silver lining to this terrible ordeal was that her friend Francis Bacon, though ill himself, threw a champagne party for Caroline at London's Halcyon Hotel almost as soon as she left the hospital. She was touched and grateful, particularly since the surgery had left her almost too weak to walk. It would, however, be the last time she saw Francis Bacon, who suffered a fatal heart attack in Madrid later that year.

Caroline had begun a short story before the operation, but when she returned to Sag Harbor, she was unable to resume writing. "Once you've accepted you're dead, why write?" she told Michael Kimmelman, an art critic for the *New York Times*, in a 1995 interview.[33] But she did return to writing, apparently abandoning the short story and working instead on a film script of her novel *The Fate of Mary Rose*.

Caroline found that writing for film "is the opposite of writing a book; no words are needed."[34] She may have been inspired to write the film adaptation by her two daughters: Evgenia's new boyfriend was the actor Julian Sands, best known for his role in the film based on E. M. Forster's *A Room With a View*. Ivana, after a brief stint as an actress in London (she performed in a two-woman stage play based on Sylvia Plath's poetry, titled *That Mad Miniature Poet*, after a line from a Lowell poem), began working for the literary department of Miramax. Nothing, however, would come of Caroline's film script.

During this fallow period, Caroline lived reclusively, seeing few people besides her children. When she did socialize, it was usually with a number of Ivana's new friends. For a while Ivana shared Caroline's two-bedroom apartment in the "rich and dumb"[35] high-rise in Manhattan. Ivana's social nature and aristocratic pedigree placed her firmly in New York's social scene; she was later taken up by such society doyennes as Jayne Wrightsman and Mercedes Bass. But it was her younger friends whom Caroline took to, and who very much took to her: the witty songwriter and journalist Christopher Mason, the interior designer Charles Krewson and his housemate, Mark Simpson, who had been a footman at Buckingham Palace.

Christopher Mason, a gregarious Londoner in New York who has written for a number of Condé Nast publications and now writes for the *New York Times*, said that he had "always heard about the legend of Caroline."[36] When he first met "Lady Lowell," as she was known to the shopkeepers of Sag Harbor, he was working as a pianist and songwriter, composing and performing witty songs at a number of venues. They met at a dinner party given by Mark Simpson and Charles Krewson. "Whenever they invited Caroline," Mason remembered, "someone had to pick her up in Sag Harbor and then take her home at night and make sure she didn't topple into the swimming pool. She would always go home drunk." But Mason was fascinated. Her drinking notwithstanding, he was struck by Caroline's "exquisite manners" and by how shy she seemed with strangers. When he began visiting her Sag Harbor home, he noticed—as Robert Dash did later—that none of the clocks worked. "It was as if time had stopped still," he recalled. He also noticed that the *New York Times* was delivered to Caroline's front door, but *Newsday* and "trashier papers" were delivered to the back door. "Caroline always devoured *Newsday* before reading the *New York Times*. She *loved* tabloid journalism."

Mason thought that "there was a special link between Caroline and Ivana," and that Ivana looked a lot like her mother as a young girl. By now, Ivana had legally adopted her stepfather Robert Lowell's last name, abandoning the name Citkowitz. Mason thought she did so "for professional reasons," but he also wondered whether Ivana knew that Citkowitz, who died when she was six, was not her father.

Sometimes the closeness between mother and daughter, Mason observed, created problems for Ivana. While working at Miramax, she became involved with Bob Weinstein, one of the two brothers from Queens who founded and ran the extraordinarily successful film company, but it was a match Caroline apparently disapproved of. Mason recalled that Caroline, in the way of upper-class Brits, loved to attach unflattering nicknames to people and use them behind their backs: she called Weinstein "Big Bob." (Caroline was fond of nicknames anyway, like "champ" for champagne and "Sag" for Sag Harbor. A friend of hers she thought rather stupid she referred to as "Bone.") Just as Maureen had disapproved of her choices, Caroline tended to disapprove of anyone Ivana was seriously dating. Ivana, who would marry her interior designer, Matthew Miller, in 1999, admitted there was "no one she would have approved of."[37] Meanwhile, Caroline adored Julian Sands for his handsomeness, making it clear that he had set the standard for sons-in-law.

The friendship between Caroline and Christopher Mason cast Caroline as a mentor. She recognized Mason's abilities and suggested that he try his hand at journalism, which he did, with increasing success. At one point she invited him to accompany her to an exhibition of Lucian Freud's early works, which opened at the Robert Miller Gallery in Manhattan in late November 1993 and ran through the first week of January. It was a treat for Mason, who had the pleasure of examining some of Freud's early paintings while the model—now aged and weathered by decades of vodka and cigarettes—stood beside him.

Caroline, as Freud's former wife and model, was in a unique position to write a review of the Freud exhibition for *The New York Review of Books*. Despite any misgivings or regrets she may have had about that marriage, her review, published in December 1993, was insightful and admiring. At one point early in the review, Caroline brought together Freud and Lowell in her statement, "He now tends to treat his human figures as 'poor passing facts,'" quoting a phrase from Lowell's poem "Epilogue."[38] She also obliquely addressed the disturbing image of herself in "Hotel Bedroom," in which she looks anguished and prematurely aged. "His portraits have always been prophecies rather than snapshots of the sitter," she wrote. She herself, as well as the many admirers of Freud's portraits of her, was baffled by Lucian's painting a young girl looking "so distressingly old."[39]

In the article, Caroline made a connection between the sense of despair that permeates much of Freud's work and his participation in the postwar bohemian life of London's Soho: "There was a darker side to all the flamboyant, reckless popping of their champagne corks." She called Freud "the supreme chronicler" of the despair felt by so many of the postwar artists in London. Her tremendous respect for Freud's paintings was summed up in her last words: "We will remember them."[40]

Caroline continued to write book reviews during her long silence following the surgery, and in 1993 she was able to devise plans for a new book, a nonfiction work about the life of a postoperative transsexual. She had long been fascinated by the subject—her first short story was about the passionate curiosity aroused by a woman who had become a man—and, Mason recalled, she was particularly fascinated by the strange case of Billy Tipton, the jazz musician who, though female, lived her life as a man. Tipton had only been found out after her death.

Andrew Harvey, who had known this about Caroline, believed that she was "obsessed" with the phenomenon of sex reassignment. When an acquaintance of his underwent such surgery, Andrew said Caroline spent "hours talking with him about the details of the operation. She found it totally incomprehensible that people would put themselves through that, but she had an unbridled masculine side and didn't know what to do with it."[41]

Caroline persuaded Mason to accompany her to a transvestite bar in downtown New York, where she could do research and indulge her intense curiosity. She was fascinated by the clientele and the sense of danger involved in the secretive bars on the Lower East Side. (John Richardson characterized one such bar as "very, very dangerous; people knifing each other, [patronized by] transsexual and transvestite whores, drugged and mean.")[42] Caroline also tried to enlist Steven Aronson, who refused to accompany her on her fact-finding missions. He recalled:

> *She was always after me to go to one of those bars with her. Now, I had been to those bars before, as a "tourist," with celebrity friends like Andy Warhol—the Anvil, the Toilet, the Gilded Grape . . . I was protected by Andy's fame. Plus, he was passive and voyeuristic. I wouldn't go with Caroline, because with her, anything could happen—she was bound to provoke something. I guess she was out to prove that writing could be a dangerous trade.*[43]

Pat Sweeney, a Sag Harbor native in her mid-forties whom Caroline employed as a secretary, entreated Caroline not to go to such dangerous places alone, but she did so anyway.[44] On one visit, Caroline later confided to Aronson, she met someone who asked to go to the ladies room with her. Not only did she go into the bathroom with him, but "they went into a stall together and he—or was it a she?—locked the door behind them. They were in there for a good twenty minutes. And do you know what Caroline said he did to her?" Aronson asked. "He did her hair."

Apparently Caroline's new friend was a hairdresser, and "instead of doing anything unseemly, he styled her hair." Caroline must have been satisfied with the job he'd done, because she told Aronson, "I wish I could go to him regularly!"

Another new friend of Caroline's whom she met through Ivana was Charles Krewson, a rising interior designer. When they met around 1992, Caroline had returned to the long-abandoned manuscript about the Duchess of Windsor. She had come to the attention of the aggressive literary agent Andrew Wylie (nicknamed "the Jackal"), who had once been Gillon Aitken's business partner. With Maître Blum now deceased, plans were being made at last to publish *The Last of the Duchess*, but the manuscript needed a great deal of work. Krewson recalled pleasant days spent in Caroline's big, lively kitchen, admiring the garden, while she read from her work-in-progress. "She liked me because I was half-German," Krewson believed. "She didn't really *get* Americans. She had tremendous compassion, although she used cruel nicknames for you behind your back. Still, she was a very good person to moan with—to tell your troubles to."[45]

Like Mason, Krewson found Caroline to be nurturing of other people's talent. "She knew there was something holding me back from my designing career," Krewson said. "Oddly, it all came together after I sold my house in Bridgehampton."

Krewson, who helped Caroline and Ivana decorate their New York apartment, found the Sag Harbor house "untidy, informal—you always felt comfortable there." He liked to accompany Caroline on raids of the many local antique shops on the east end of Long Island, looking for the unusual lamp or genuine piece of Americana, just as Walker Evans had once scoured the shops with her in search of hand-lettered signs and farmers' tools. "She loved beautiful, odd objects, and she would race me through antique shops for all the thirty-five-dollar 'finds.' "

Krewson sensed that Caroline was basically shy, but "she loved socializing. She loved going to dinner parties. She liked the kind of gay man who liked women." By the time Krewson knew her, Caroline had finally become a decent cook, the kind, however, whose refrigerator is either completely empty or full of lobster tails and champagne. "No one ever discussed her drinking," he observed. "Caroline drank, but she wasn't a drunk. I saw her raving very few times." However, she would drink too much if she showed up at Krewson and Simpson's home for an intimate dinner and found other guests present. "She drank to overcome her shyness. She drank to still her mind. The first thing Caroline did? She would open up a bottle of vodka and throw the cap away."

John Richardson was one of the few friends from Caroline's past whom she continued to see after moving to New York, in part because he could give her invaluable help with her *Duchess* manuscript. After all, Richardson seemed to know, and to have known, everyone. He judged the published book about the duchess to be "wonderful in lots of ways, but full of such howlers!"[46] One howler was Caroline's characterization of a supposed affair between the duchess and Jimmy Donohue, a notorious American playboy known mostly for his gay exploits and his truly rotten behavior, which allegedly included castrating a young sailor he had picked up for a night of fun and games.

There's this man, Jimmy Donohue, whom the duchess had an affair with . . . whether it's true or not, Jimmy said to me, "It was like having sex with a very old sailor." And Caroline put this in as "it was like having sex with the Ancient Mariner." Which elides the whole point!

Richardson was clear-eyed about how much Caroline drank, but he felt that it didn't interfere with her

extraordinary warmth and magnetism. Right up to the end she had this sort of little-girl side, which was clever, vulnerable, hyper, drunken, wise—impossible! If you weren't careful, you could find yourself co-opted into doing things she wanted you to do, like

drinking more than you wanted to or going to a transsexual bar!
What she had was this extraordinary gift of intimacy. She was a co-
conspirator. We had lots of jokes about the Windsors, because I've
written about the Windsors, too. I've known them a bit. And we
shared this loathing of Mâitre Blum and so on. So we were always
hatching how to find out more, *short of hiring a detective.*

There were those among Caroline's friends who accepted her alcoholism, those who denied it, and those who tried ever so gingerly to
suggest that she seek treatment. Cornelia Foss, though she saw little
of Caroline throughout the 1990s, was in the last category. She remembered walking with Caroline one day in Sag Harbor as Caroline
told her, "You know, I'm really sick. I'm really a very sick person."[47]

Foss assumed that Caroline meant her devastating bout with cancer, until she realized that Caroline was referring to her alcoholism, a
subject she rarely broached. "She knew it was out of control," Foss
came to believe. "But she was afraid to go into treatment. I even offered to go with her to the Betty Ford Clinic, but she was afraid to go."

Foss also observed that none of Caroline's children "had the ability
to cope with their mother's alcoholism. Genia was the best equipped,
but she did the only thing she could: she removed herself from the
situation." By now Evgenia and Julian Sands had moved to Los Angeles. Foss remembered pushing Caroline on the question of seeking
treatment and Caroline refusing, saying, "I just want to die."

"But what about your children!" Foss asked.

"They'd be better off without me."

That statement, Foss thought, was probably "just the alcohol talking. It's important to know how much she adored her children. She
was fanatic about them," although her alcoholism put her in the position of a child in need of her children's parenting. Foss also believed
that Lowell had left Caroline "because of her drinking. Given his own
precarious state, he just couldn't handle it. And she was devastated
when Cal left her. She never got over it."

Another close friend of Caroline's during the seven years she lived in Sag Harbor was an editor at a major New York publishing house, who, with Caroline's encouragement, began writing fiction. They had first met nearly twenty years earlier, toward the end of Caroline's relationship with Andrew Harvey. "Caroline was the first and only person to see me as a writer," recalled the editor, who chooses to remain anonymous. "I hadn't written before, but with her encouragement, I wrote two novels."[48] Caroline advised her friend to write for the pleasure of writing, because the rest is a big letdown. Books don't stay in print, bad reviews make you feel terrible, and good reviews miss the point.

The editor was one of those who didn't consider Caroline an alcoholic, because she was able to work so hard and so consistently. "A drunk can't get up every morning and write for three or four hours, like Caroline. I know. I was raised by a drunk." He also found absurd the idea of "Lady Caroline Lowell" joining some kind of twelve-step program like Alcoholics Anonymous. "She was too smart. She saw through it all. Can you imagine her standing up at an AA meeting and saying, 'I am Lady Caroline Lowell, and I am an alcoholic'!"

But Caroline knew she had a problem. She once confided in Foss that, in England, had somebody discovered her lying dead drunk in a ditch but knew that she was "*Lady* Caroline," she would still have been treated with deference and respect. And that was a powerful disincentive for seeking treatment.

In March 1993 Steven Aronson, who had known Caroline casually for many years, asked whether she would agree to be the subject of a lengthy interview for the "Legendary Lives" series he was writing for *Town & Country*. He was seeking men and women who not only lived extraordinary lives but were good talkers as well, and Caroline was certainly that. "It was one of those celebratory interviews where you bring out the best of the subjects instead of trying to ensnare them in their own shortcomings," Aronson explained.[49]

The two were already on friendly terms. They had met years earlier at a dinner party in New York, and Aronson saw Caroline socially three or four times a year. She and Evgenia had come with Cornelia

Foss to a party for Aronson when his book *Hype* was published in 1983. Aronson always found her "incandescently—no, blazingly—intelligent." With his gift for mimicry, Aronson used to delight Caroline by imitating Lowell reading "Epilogue." He was worried at first that the imitation might offend her, "but she loved it," he recalled. "She asked me more than once to read that poem to her over the telephone in his voice."

Caroline was thrilled by the prospect of being interviewed. "She called *me* to make the appointment and nail it down," Aronson said, and he soon packed up his tape recorder and went to Sag Harbor to spend the weekend with her, although he did so with some trepidation, knowing that he might be in for a bumpy ride. He had long been on close terms with several members of the extended Guinness family, including Caroline's second cousin Bryan Guinness (Lord Moyne), the elder statesman of the brewing branch of the family, looked on as the conscience of the Guinness tribe. Aronson and Moyne carried on a correspondence for several decades, and in the late seventies, when he mentioned having met Caroline, Lord Moyne wrote back: "She is a caution and has a worm's-eye view of the world." He warned Aronson to "give her a wide berth."[50] Now, sixteen years later, he decided not to heed that advice; like so many others, he found Caroline compelling. And so he went ahead with what would turn out to be a series of interviews that took place over roughly four months.

Aronson thought her house on Union Street handsome, even stately, simply furnished, and well cared for. Caroline pointed out that the Freud paintings on the wall—"Girl in Bed" and others—were "good replicas" the Tate Gallery had made for her and that the originals were in bank vaults or on loan to the museum. She told Aronson that she was in the habit of leaving her door unlocked when she walked the few blocks into the village, so she "could not afford to have anything that valuable in the house."

With Caroline's permission, Aronson had brought along his three-year-old American water spaniel, James. While Caroline and Aronson were sitting in her English garden with the tape recorder whirring, the dog lifted its leg and peed against the picket fence. Caroline was horrified. "Oh, God, look what he's done!" she exclaimed.

"He's a male dog, Caroline. That's what they do," Aronson said in James's defense. But Caroline was not happy.

Not long into the visit, Aronson accompanied Caroline on a walk to the liquor store down the block, where a dozen bottles of vodka had been set aside for Lady Lowell. "She had reserved a case of her preferred brand, Stoli, but when we got there, she asked me which brand I favored, and I told her Absolut. So she promptly exchanged six bottles of the Stoli for six of Absolut. I said, 'Really, I'm not going to go through six! I'll just be having one vodka tonic a night.' She assumed everyone drank like her."

Later, on another short walk, when Aronson's spaniel lifted his leg against a hydrant, Caroline cried, "God, he's doing it again!"

"Caroline, you're an upper-class Englishwoman," Aronson said. "You grew up in a grand country house. You must have had dogs there."

"Yes," Caroline growled, "but they were all bitches!"

It was late April, and the next day was beautiful and sunny, so they drove to a nearby beach. But Aronson found that Caroline was having trouble walking. "She was wobbling. I had to prop her up, and after five minutes on the sand, she was champing to go back to the house." Meals were also a problem. "She had said, 'I'll cook for you,' but when I saw that she was having trouble making toast, I booked us a table at the nearest restaurant." Finally, after two days of life with Caroline, Aronson fled to the house of his friend Babs Simpson in Amagansett. When he returned a couple of weeks later for another round of interviews with Caroline, he stayed with friends in East Hampton, "because it was too harrowing. I'd look at her and I'd get gooseflesh sometimes, because she was so haunted."

Still, the tales and reminiscences he elicited from Caroline were fascinating. "Her comments on people—she could penetrate right through to their reality. That was her gift. She could discern 'the truth of truth,' even though she often had a field day with the truth of fact."

Aronson probably interviewed Caroline twenty times over the course of many lunches, dinners, and telephone conversations. He went over everything with her, again and again, driving her to make things sharper. "I wanted it to be the ultimate of what she could sound like. She *was* a living legend, and I wanted to capture that," he said.

When it came time to select photographs for the article, Caroline supplied *Town & Country* with a number of exquisite fashion photographs taken of her in 1959 by Evelyn Hoffer for *Vogue*. The magazine also planned to take a contemporary photograph of Caroline, but Aronson urged them to take one that "wasn't cruel. It would be too easy to exploit the drama of her changed looks by publishing a ravaged picture of her right next to one of her as a young beauty. *Town & Country*'s photographer posed her facing away from the camera," Aronson said, "as if she were looking ahead to the sunset of her days, instead of embodying them, which is precisely what she was doing."

When the interview was published as "Sophisticated Lady" in the September 1993 issue ("we both had a good laugh over the corny title the magazine came up with," said Aronson), the response was overwhelming. People began calling Caroline, offering all kinds of proposals, from book contracts to movie interest. "Men were actually proposing to her," Aronson said. "The article did a lot for her—it brought her back from the living dead. In a way, it canonized her. I must have gotten forty letters about it myself, and she claimed she got two hundred. She thanked me over and over again."

One of Caroline's more imaginative flights of fancy, Aronson remembered, was her description of the riding lessons Perdita gave to Belfast children with cerebral palsy and children whose mothers had taken thalidomide during their pregnancies. Caroline told Aronson that her sister was quite modest about her good works and wouldn't talk about them unless asked. It was a subject that somehow obsessed Caroline, and she explained that Perdita had to find exceptionally tame ponies for "the thalidomides"—ponies that were "almost dead, like a kind of sofa," because some of the children had no arms or legs. She launched into a Joycean fugue inspired by the image of "thalidomides" let breathtakingly loose on the backs of their ponies, urging the "old sofas" to ride swiftly over the Irish countryside, guiding the ponies by their teeth. In the minds of "the thalidomides," the broken-down ponies had become thoroughbreds, as they outraced their helpers and assistants, loving the power and the speed and the danger.[51]

Her image of glorious pursuit and freedom calls to mind Caroline's early pleasure in riding, and the wild freedom she and Perdita and Sheridan had had as children on the three thousand acres of Clandeboye. The image of armless and legless boys and girls riding hell-for-leather was, for Caroline, quintessentially *Grand Guignol*. But Caroline also confided in Aronson that *she* had been prescribed thalidomide when she was pregnant with Evgenia, but had decided not to take it. Caroline and her daughter were spared that particular experience.

Thirteen

THE LAST OF
THE MUSES

There was about her an extraordinary quality
which I can only describe as a brilliant darkness.
—Anna Haycraft[1]

R obert Dash remembered the first time he met Caroline Blackwood, some time in the mid-1990s. "I had seen her at several
parties, and we both looked at each other across the room before we were even introduced. She was someone I'd heard about. This
went on for a few years." Finally, they were seated next to each other
at one of Jason Epstein's parties. "At one time," said Dash, "I thought
she was smoking three cigarettes at once; she was terribly nervous and
distraught."[2]

Caroline turned to her dinner companion, who, in his sixties, is
tall, patrician, and saturnine, and who manages to be both elegant and
whimsical. She shyly asked him, "Is there a place . . . ?"

"Caroline, if you're asking whether there's a bathroom, do use it."

Which she did, and she thanked Dash when she got back, and the
two of them "chummed in after that." The painter and master gardener found Caroline to be "spectacular—in the sense of a ruin able

to rise up and be so splendid." He recalled going to her house once and being chided for being too early. Dash noticed that she hadn't changed her clocks from daylight saving time. But he was impressed that Caroline, who at first looked ravaged, bounded upstairs and came down forty seconds later looking "absolutely marvelous, in purple velvet, though her shoelaces were untied and they stayed untied. That was the style in her debutante days; you always left something undone. In dishabille."

Caroline and Dash didn't see each other often; they mostly chatted on the telephone. He had tremendous compassion for her, considering her "an extraordinary survivor of brutality." Part of it, he felt, was that she had sprung from the Guinnesses:

There are the daft Guinnesses, and the eccentric Guinnesses, and the totally mad Guinnesses. She was sort of straddling all those. The interesting thing is that she was able to perch herself in the middle after having married all those difficult fellows. I don't think she could cope with kindness. She had to go back into the surf so that she could get the angry water again. When I met her, I wanted to put my arms around her and say, "It's all right, it's all right!" She had these pansy blue eyes, she smoked as much as I did, and drank almost as much as I did. No. She drank more.

Sometimes Dash would lean down and light Caroline's cigarette, and she would look up at him, her eyes ablaze. "Oh, yes," Dash remembered. "She knew she had it. It was a bending and accepting the cigarette, and then—the eyes . . . and she knew she had it and she smiled. It was very nice."

Caroline and Dash made several plans to see each other. They planned to spend an afternoon crabbing at South Bridge, with a case of beer at their side, but they never did. They planned to take a car together into the city (Caroline hated to take the Hampton jitney), but they didn't. Dash invited Caroline to his New Year's Eve party at the end of 1995, but she wasn't feeling well, so she stayed home. "The woman was extremely reticent. She was delighted to be invited out, but she had to be driven home and so forth. I never saw her in New York. She was mostly out here."

Dash felt that her reticence had to do with her alcoholism, a subject he knows quite a bit about. "It's very difficult when you're dealing with such an alcoholic," he said. "It's hard to know, for example, what Marguerite Duras was thinking of when she wrote her last novel. Alcoholics have a different sense of time. They awake at different times, and their memories work in different ways. It's like trying to catch a bead of mercury that's going all over the table. I thought that she could have been saved by a good friend or a good husband or a good *something*. Someone who'd just shake her and say, 'Now look! Here we are.' "

Dash also confided that he felt Caroline had been loved more for her title and her wealth than for herself. "She had married extraordinary human beings who were abusive to her. Why she put up with it, why she didn't fight back—there was some basic, monstrous insecurity that her parents had made in her. She had a damaged childhood and went on to live a damaged life, in bewilderment."

Steven Aronson tended to agree with Dash's assessment of Caroline's marriages, at least to Freud and to Lowell. "She was titled, and Lowell certainly enjoyed that. And Lucian Freud would probably not have been immune to it. As to her 'fortune,' I don't know how one could know how much money she had; I'm not sure *she* knew. I often thought she had to sell one thing to buy another."[3]

Shortly after the twelve-thousand-word interview hit the stands, Caroline called Aronson, who was spending the summer in Maine, in a house lent to him by old friends, the financier Daniel Zilkha and his wife, Franny. The house was arguably one of the grandest in Portland, designed by the celebrated architect John Calvin Stevens around 1910 for the president of the Maine Railroad. "It has a famous pergola and a ballroom or two. You'd walk out in the mornings, and sometimes there'd be a group of architecture students out front, studying it. The house took up something like an acre," Aronson said.

Caroline asked whether she could visit, and Aronson agreed, though reluctantly.

She arrived on a Tuesday for a stay of several days, a length of time Aronson considered "disproportionate—even in a huge house where she would have a whole wing to herself. I mean, the house was Clandeboye Revisited." When he spotted her at the terminal, where he'd gone to pick her up, he thought she looked "disheveled and distressed—she was a shambles. She walked unsteadily, and people were moving out of the way, giving her room. She looked as if she had a problem. And I'm thinking, 'Oh dear,' because it wasn't my own house I was taking her to; it belonged to friends, and they had some beautiful, breakable things."

The first problem was claiming Caroline's suitcase. Once the luggage had been unloaded, Aronson asked Caroline to point out which one was hers.

"I don't *know* which one is mine."

They waited, and when there were only about ten bags left, Aronson asked again, "Which do you think is yours?"

"That one!" she answered, pointing to a bag.

"Are you sure?"

"I'm *sure*."

But as soon as Aronson picked up the suitcase, a man screamed, "That's *my* bag!" They tried again, and this time Caroline, pointing to a faded paisley bag, said, "*That's* it—I'm positive!"

Just to make sure, Aronson discreetly unzipped the bag and showed her the contents. "No, that's not it," she said.

A few minutes later, when there were only five or six suitcases left, Caroline pointed to her final choice. "That's it. I *swear* to you it is!"

So Aronson went over and partially unzipped it. "I knew right away, without even having to ask," he said. "There was a crumpled old frock and a bottle of vodka inside. It was *her*, all right."

They drove back to the Zilkhas' house, and Aronson showed Caroline to her room. Since his guest was a heavy smoker, a friend had suggested that he fill three or four buckets with water and place them at strategic intervals along the hall of her wing, in case she set the place on fire. If Caroline noticed the buckets, she didn't say anything; perhaps she assumed they were for the plants.

The first morning of her stay, Caroline announced that she wanted to see the two places where Lowell had lived in Maine: the white clapboard house on three acres of land in small, picturesque Damariscotta Mills, where he and Jean Stafford had "simmer[ed] like wasps / in our tent of books"[4] during the first year of their tumultuous marriage, and Lowell's beloved summer home in Castine, which he had inherited from Aunt Harriet Winslow and later lost to Elizabeth Hardwick in the divorce settlement.

"Now," Aronson recalled, "we happened to be in the middle of the most intense heat wave that Maine has practically ever known. The mercury shot up to a hundred, in a place where you sometimes had to wear a sweater at night even in August, and no one had air-conditioning."

Caroline did not take the heat well, but it didn't stop her from wanting to be driven to Castine, and at least the car was air-conditioned. But Aronson, understandably, didn't want to "just spring Caroline on Elizabeth," whom he was planning to drop in on later that summer. "I didn't want to walk the streets of Castine with Caroline without knowing that she would be welcome. I didn't want to sponsor *that* particular visit."

But Damariscotta Mills seemed safe, relegated as it was to the mists of literary history. It was the setting of Jean Stafford's *New Yorker* short story "An Influx of Poets," about her and Cal's unhappy cohabitation in the house she'd bought with the money from *Boston Adventure*. So off they drove to Damariscotta, on a staggeringly hot day.

Most of the local population had lived there for decades, so Aronson and Caroline asked for directions to Lowell and Stafford's old house.

No one had even heard of them.

"Robert Lowell has to be the most famous person ever to have lived in Damariscotta Mills, and Jean Stafford has to be a close second," Aronson said. "You'd think their house would be on some literary map of Maine."

Caroline and Aronson tracked down the town historian and woke him up from his nap. He gave them directions to a house he thought might be the one they were looking for—and if it wasn't, maybe it was the one next to it, or the one up the hill, or around the corner . . . At one of the houses, Caroline asked sardonically, "Do you think *this* is where they were busy being geniuses together?"

She liked that idea, Aronson thought, because Cal and Caroline, not so long ago, had been geniuses together themselves, in Milgate and Redcliffe Square. Aronson commented,

I think that was the title of the autobiography by Robert McAl-mon, the Lost Generation writer and publisher. She was saying it in inverted quotes. Every house we passed looked like a house where two people could have been "geniuses together." And she and I were being literary pilgrims together. But the whole time, she was trying to get me to change my mind and drive her to Castine, which was of far more dramatic interest to her. That was where the putative action was—the possibility of collision. She was intent—and intense! The temperature of the conversation was going up, just like the mercury.

Caroline had soured on Damariscotta ("I think Sag Harbor is much nicer, don't you?" she asked Aronson), and she was petulant about not being taken to Castine, but when they passed a sign for Belfast, she said, "Let's go there!"

In a tourist shop Caroline bought a T-shirt with BELFAST in billboard-size letters. She put it on over her clothes—an artist's smock and cotton leggings—and asked Aronson to take a photograph of her that she could send to Perdita, in the other Belfast.

The vodka bottle, meanwhile, had traveled with her.

When they returned to Portland and the Zilkhas' house, Aronson switched on the television. It just so happened that it was tuned to a cable channel showing a grisly surgical operation in progress. Caroline was riveted. "We watched an entire operation together," Arsonson said. "I was surprised that she would want to see it, since she'd recently had major surgery. There were scenes when I wanted to turn away, but she made me look: 'No, no, it's fine now!' I think it was an operation on a colon." And then Caroline gleefully offered to take her host to dinner—"My treat!" Aronson, with a shudder, saw that she was beginning to feel very much at home.

By the end of the week, another guest was sprung on Aronson, an Italian-born friend from New York, the decorator Milly de Cabrol, then married to a French baron, and her five-year-old son, Charles. At first Aronson suggested that this might not be the best time to visit, because he had "a problematic houseguest," but then he thought that Milly and Charles might just turn out to be heaven sent. They could soften the impact of Caroline's impending visit to Prouts Neck, the exclusive seaside resort fifteen minutes away, where Winslow Homer had lived and painted for a time and which he made famous in such iconic masterpieces as "Canon Rock."

"It's snobbish," Aronson explained, "like Fishers Island and Hobe Sound, but even more so because it's smaller. The summer of Caroline, I had been proposed for the Prouts Neck Bathing Corporation, which was the only way anyone could get to use the heart-shaped beach, one of the few in Maine that actually had sand. I was on sufferance there, and somewhat apprehensive, because I knew that the folks at Prouts Neck were not so insular that they wouldn't notice that Caroline was out of it."

Milly de Cabrol, an attractive woman in her forties, and her young son wanted only to escape the extreme heat by resting on the beach. But the fair-skinned Caroline announced, "I'm not interested in *beach*." Since there was only Aronson's car, Caroline had the choice of accompanying them, staying by herself at the house and reading in the garden, or getting a cab into Portland. There was a caveat, however: if she stayed at the house, she'd have to master the alarm system. Aronson had promised the Zilkhas that he would always switch on the alarm when he left the house, even if it was just to mail a letter across the street. He asked Caroline to do the same. But when she proved incapable of working the device, she decided to go along with them to the beach.

Aronson recalled, "She couldn't take the sun, so here's what I set up for her: I rented a big umbrella and a bunch of beach chairs. And there was always the clubhouse. It may have been Spartan-simple, but it did have awnings. She wasn't the only one who couldn't handle summer sun."

Their day at the beach, however, turned out to be no day at the beach. In addition to the heat, there was an infernal wind. The umbrella was knocked over in no time, and the wind kept snatching Caroline's hat, so she left the beach and sought refuge under the awning. She'd borrowed from the Zilkhas' library a paperback of Jean Rhys's grim novel *After Leaving Mr. Mackenzie*. The beach club at this point was open for lunch. Aronson noticed that Caroline was

moving uncertainly, and she looked very strange as she went up to the kiosk and ordered a double vodka. But the thing is, this was a dry place. You could order iced tea or tomato juice or Clamato juice or V-8 or a Sprite or something—you know, your normal choices of beverage. They patiently explained that they didn't serve alcohol, so she sat back down on the boardwalk, and she was bored.

The next day the thermometer rose again into the high nineties. Out of necessity, plans were made to return to the beach, but this time Caroline put her foot down and refused to go. Aronson hoped she would be content to stay alone at the house, or venture into town if she chose, so he and Cabrol made another effort to teach her how to work the alarm system. Once again, she couldn't master it; she was even having trouble turning the key in the front door. This time, she agreed to being dropped off in Portland, where she said she would get her hair done, have lunch in a restaurant, see a movie, and return to the house around seven. Arsonson gave her "detailed directions back to the Zilkhas' and several numbers where I could be reached in Prouts. I gave her everything but an anklet and a beeper!"

When Aronson and the Cabrols returned from the beach, they made a quick scan as they turned onto their street. They were alarmed to see that Caroline wasn't in the garden or on the porch. She was nowhere to be seen. Then they spied her curled up by the front door. "She was just taking a little kitten nap," Aronson explained. "She'd indeed had her hair done, and she looked very pretty. And she *had* gone to a movie, and lunched in a nice restaurant, and gone into shops, and had herself a very nice day."

They woke her up, went in for a drink, and then went out to dinner.

The next night, Aronson arranged for a Prouts Neck friend to give a dinner party. Margo Wintersteen had volunteered to prepare a three-course meal for twenty or thirty people. She was a brilliant cook, but her gesture was pure heroism, given the appalling heat.

Wintersteen occupied the vast McIlhenny house, which had belonged to her late mother-in-law, the sister of the Philadelphia art collector, aesthete, and gas-meter heir Henry McIlhenny. (Caroline would have known the enormous estate and castle of Glenveagh in County Donegal, which Henry McIlhenny had owned.) "The McIlhenny house," Aronson pointed out, "used to have two ballrooms, but was now down to one. Again, I was providing ballrooms for Lady Caroline."

Caroline was excited about the dinner party; "she was like a little girl," Aronson noted. She wasn't invited out much anymore, except to the homes of Ivana's friends, who had become her friends. For this evening, Caroline dressed in a black tunic with black cotton leggings and a striking, ethnic necklace. "It was amazing," Aronson said, "how quickly she could go from looking seedy to looking soignée when she wanted to."

Aronson seated Caroline between Kenyon Bolton III, an architect from Boston, known as Tim, and a friend of Aronson's from Christ Church, Oxford, an amiable Englishman named Anthony Hawser, who was renting the big house next to the McIlhenny place that summer. "He was very amusing," Aronson said, "and Tim was amusing enough, so I thought that, of all these very proper and predictable Prouts Neckers, they were the best two for her."

Caroline seemed to truly enjoy herself, but at the end of the dinner party, she complained to Aronson, *sotto voce*, about Bolton: "He's *boring*."

"I don't find him boring, Caroline, and he's very popular here," Aronson said. "He's one of the most interesting people on the Neck."

"He's *boring*," Caroline insisted. "He's got a *flair* for it."

Caroline's reaction to Anthony Hawser, however, was even more troubling. She falsely told Aronson that his old friend had "talked dirty to her."

She told me—and everybody else within earshot—that he had told her that he liked women "with tiny orifices." Then he told her that since he'd put on a little weight, whenever he looked down at himself he couldn't even see his penis. It just seemed to me that it was the last *thing Anthony would ever have said. And he looked at me, when I later passed along her comments, and he said, "She's mad."*

" 'Mad, bad, and dangerous to know' is more like it," Aronson later said, quoting another Lady Caroline—Lady Caroline Lamb's description of Lord Byron. "She took great pleasure in her power to alarm."

After the dinner party, they drove back to Portland, and Aronson retired to the master bedroom, a long way from where he had installed Caroline. Then, at two-thirty in the morning, there was a pounding on his door. He woke up with a start.

"Let me in. It's Caroline. I've been burned. *You* burned me!"

Aronson warily opened the door.

"You've got to take me to hospital."

"What for?"

"I told you I couldn't take the sun! And now you've burned me. You burned me on purpose. You burned me with the sun!"

Aronson saw that Caroline was hysterical, and he did notice that she must have gotten some sun sitting under the awning, because her face was slightly red. "I told you I don't like beach!" she screamed. "I'm on fire! Don't you understand! I've got to be taken to hospital!"

So Aronson, dazed and baffled, got dressed and drove her to the emergency room of Maine Medical.

The emergency room was a mass of confusion. Caroline was given a preliminary interview within a few minutes of arrival. When she was asked what was wrong, she pointed to Aronson and said, "He burned me!"

"What's your name?" the clerk asked her, starting the paperwork.

"Lady Caroline." The clerk looked confused.

"What's your address?"

"I don't know." She looked at Aronson, who said, "She's staying with me on Vaughan Street."

"Do you have insurance?"

"National Health." Of course, no one knew what she was talking about, but she was told to take a seat and was assured that she'd be seen by a doctor.

She and Aronson waited for an hour, with the TV blaring and victims of street accidents streaming in. Around four o'clock, Caroline jumped up and told her suffering host, "Let's go. I'm feeling much better!" Aronson surmised that it may have dawned on her, at the moment when she was about to be seen by a doctor, that she could be in for a dose of trouble—real trouble she could not easily get out of. A doctor would see that there was more to treat than mild sunburn. "She was in a strange state," Aronson felt. "When she said, 'Let's go,' I asked, 'Are you absolutely sure?' and she said, 'I'm sure.' "

Out in the parking lot, Caroline acted like someone who had just pulled off a real escape. She embraced Aronson and then spun off and did a little jig. "Let's go somewhere amusing, darling."

"But, Caroline, it's four-fifteen in the morning—in Portland, Maine! Not only is there nowhere amusing to go; there's *nowhere* to go."

"Then let's go home and have a little toddy!"

They returned to the house, Caroline went up to her room to retrieve her bottle of vodka, and the two of them shared a companionable sip. "She was as changeable as a Constable sky," Aronson remarked about her quick recovery.

Six days had passed since her arrival, and Caroline was showing no signs of ending her stay. By now, word of her behavior had reached the Zilkhas. Though not unsympathetic, they were growing concerned about their house. Their eldest daughter, Leonora, a student at Princeton, volunteered to assist in getting Caroline on the earliest flight out of Portland. But it was the end of summer, and flights were hard to book on short notice. There was another problem: Caroline did not want to forfeit a penny on her prepaid ticket. After a couple of hours on the phone, Leonora Zilkha came up with a flight that entailed Caroline's changing planes in Boston and landing in Islip, smack in the middle of Long Island, for $190. But Caroline did not cotton to being dislodged before her time; she wanted to stay two more days and use her original ticket back to New York.

Aronson pointed out that, since Islip is roughly halfway between Manhattan and Sag Harbor, she'd be halfway home.

She fought me hard on this. I had about five minutes to think how to make her do it, because we had to confirm the new reservation. So I told her, "Caroline, if you fly into New York as planned, you'll have to take a cab from the airport, right? That's $30. And you'll have dinner in the city—that'll cost $50, right?" "Yah," she said, jotting all the numbers down. "And with drinks it might be another $30. That's already over $100 extra if you stick to your original *plan. And then there's the additional plane fare to East Hampton, which'll run you more than what you'd have to pay a driver to get you home from Islip."*

Aronson figured that Caroline might save all of $15 by taking the proposed flight. That did it. And so the visit, which had begun on Monday, August 23, ended on Sunday, August 29.

The next morning, the Zilkhas' maid arrived. When she went to the room Caroline had occupied, she backed right out and said, "Mr. Aronson, don't go in there." Something had already warned him not to enter Caroline's room. When he asked the maid what was wrong, she described the chaos—empty pill bottles and vodka bottles strewn all over the floor, and an acrid odor. Aronson learned later from a friend in the industry that Caroline "was on a list that hoteliers keep of undesirable guests."

Despite Caroline's difficult visit, when Aronson settled back in New York, the two continued to see each other. Caroline called one evening to ask if he would take a look at her manuscript about the Duchess of Windsor. Earlier, around 1982, Aronson had put her in touch with friends who had known and entertained the Windsors in New York and Palm Beach, particularly Joanne Cummings, former wife of Nathan Cummings, the founder of Consolidated Foods and Sara Lee. (Joanne later confided in Aronson that she had found Caroline "amazing" and her take on the duchess "a little wild but original.") Caroline had incorporated most of the finishing touches Aronson had suggested for her *New York Review* article on Freud's recent exhibition, so she was particularly interested in whether he thought *The Last of the Duchess* was good enough to publish.

"It was a real spellbinder," he thought after reading the manuscript, "but it did need a lot more work." So Caroline offered to pay Aronson handsomely for editing her book, but after mulling over the offer, in the end he declined. "I was afraid she'd feel that she owned me—and act accordingly."

He continued to see Caroline occasionally. They went to see Lucian Freud's retrospective at the Met, where they ran into Margo Wintersteen, who looked at Aronson and rolled her eyes. Aronson found it "fascinating to see Caroline look at Freud's pictures. She was very proprietary about all those early Lucians, including the ones that weren't of her." Caroline also invited Aronson to the opening of "Lucian Freud: Early Works" at the Robert Miller Gallery in November 1993. Afterward, she took him to dinner at the gallery owner's elegant maisonette on East End Avenue, where she spent most of the evening talking to Anne Dunn, her old friend from Downham School days, who was once married to Michael Wishart and was now the widow of the painter Rodrigo Moynihan. In some ways the two women had had parallel lives, beginning with their school days and advancing to each one's relationship with Lucian and their closeness to Michael Wishart (who had truly loved Caroline, Anne believed). Both women had been sought-after beauties who had worked to define themselves as artists. Now they sat amiably side by side, in an elegant setting at an exclusive dinner party, celebrating the work of a dark genius who had passed through both of their lives.

On November 11, Caroline attended a gala birthday party that Aronson threw for himself in New York. As she had for the Wintersteen party, Caroline made the effort to look stunning. Among the three hundred guests, she encountered several people whom she hadn't seen in years, such as Mary McCarthy's former husband Bowden Broadwater and Claus von Bülow (into whose arms she practically fell, Aronson recalled). She had brought along Ivana and Sheridan.

Sheridan, after having attended the University of London and, briefly, Columbia University, was now living in Manhattan, working for left-wing political causes. Caroline took evident pleasure in introducing her son to her old acquaintances. She was especially protective of Sheridan; she had confided her fear that he might one day exhibit the manic symptoms that had so blighted his father's life.

Caroline later told Aronson that she was proud of all the attention Ivana had garnered at the party, and she took the opportunity to rail once again against Bob Weinstein, whom she considered an extremely unsuitable match for Ivana. "She was obsessed with it," Aronson believed. "And her tone was the same as when she told me that Israel's family name had had to be changed at Ellis Island *to* Citkowitz, from 'something Polishly unpronounceable.' At the end of the day, she wasn't her mother's daughter for nothing."

A few weeks after the party, Aronson heard from Caroline's mother. Maureen Dufferin had her solicitors send a letter to *Town & Country* explaining that the marchioness was extremely upset by some of the things her daughter had said about her in the interview. She was particularly incensed that Caroline had characterized her as someone who had no idea who Sigmund Freud was. "The letter said something to the effect that 'the marchioness is a very intelligent woman and of course would have known who Freud was,'" Aronson recalled. Maureen also believed that she and Lowell had enjoyed a friendly relationship, and she chafed under Caroline's assertion that the lines in Lowell's poem about a certain socialite "licking the palate of her Peke" were based on her.

The letter also claimed in no uncertain terms that Maureen had by no means cut Caroline off from the family when she married Lucian Freud, as Caroline had long claimed. In fact, the year after Caroline's marriage, Maureen settled on her children half of Ernest Guinness's Canadian fortune, placing Caroline squarely in the same millionaire bracket as Sheridan, her brother. "What it was saying," Aronson explained, "is that if the newly married Caroline was able to have a nice house in London, a country place in Dorset, and a hunter to boot, it wasn't because she had sold a couple of stories to a newspaper or magazine, but because she had the most generous of mothers!"

An even sorer point with the marchioness was Caroline's statement that her mother had reported Lucian's father to the police as a German spy, which Maureen's lawyers categorically denied on her behalf, calling it an especially painful accusation against Lady Dufferin.

The lawyers' letter emphasized how much Caroline really loved Maureen, enclosing as proof an uncharacteristically affectionate letter that Caroline had written to her mother in April 1987, shortly after leaving England to live in America. Maureen's lawyers pointed out that it was hardly the letter of a disinherited daughter.

Caroline's letter began "Darling Mummy" and went on to thank Maureen for a most generous check, which Caroline refused because she thought that her mother had worries, too—apparently about finances. Caroline described herself as being "only English 'broke' " but managing all right in the States, hoping to buy a house on Long Island. She wrote to her mother that her move to the States was not final, and she promised to come back for "endless visits."

"Caroline's letter sounded to me a little like the Duke of Windsor's abdication speech," Aronson commented. "Only what Caroline was abdicating was her mother! It was obviously a letter written to keep a galling parent at more than arm's length."

Aronson, like so many others, believed that Caroline's basic emotion toward her mother was hatred. "There was never a time I was with her when she wasn't excoriating her mother, and with a really unnatural energy."

Aronson immediately phoned Caroline and said, "I've just received a copy of a letter from some lawyers of your mother's."

"This is trouble," Caroline answered, "but I'll defend you. I'll defend you anywhere and everywhere!"

"Is what they said about your mother giving you all that money true?"

Caroline replied, "I don't know what they're talking about."

"Well, can you prove what you said she did to Ernst Freud?"

"I'll *swear* to it! She *did* report Ernst Freud as a spy!"

"Will Lucian Freud corroborate this?"

"I don't know whether Lucian will say it," Caroline admitted, adding that anyone who knew her mother would believe that she had it in her to denounce Lucian's father to the authorities.

Caroline, Aronson recalled, became extremely upset, saying, "Oh,

God, how I hate her! She's such a bruiser!" Caroline was terrified that her mother would come after her and even try to take her money away. "She was afraid she was going to be punished. It was, 'Oh, I knew she'd get me in the end!' She felt infantilized by her."

That's when Caroline explained that her mother was notoriously litigious, specializing in lawsuits with present and former servants. "Maureen dismissed her butler [at Owl House] in Kent and accused him of pilfering crabapples from her tree, and it wound up before the industrial tribunal," Aronson would discover. In the end, Maureen did not bring suit. Instead, she asked *Town & Country* to republish a flattering article about her that had appeared in *Harpers & Queen*, and they did so.

"Will whiskey be my Mother in the end?" Caroline had written in "She's Got a Problem," making light of the two malign forces in her life that she could not conquer.

When *The Last of the Duchess* was published by Pantheon in February 1995, Caroline invited Aronson to the publication party and presented him with an inscribed copy of the book: "In memory of our summer. Love, Caroline." Aronson liked that "she had turned it into a *shared* nightmare, as if she hadn't been the cause of it." He added, "By then our relationship had just kind of diminuendoed. She was permanently annoyed that I'd declined to edit the *Duchess*, and I was permanently annoyed with her for making remarks that had provoked her mother, when she knew how much her mother loved to sue."

A guest who had met Caroline at the Wintersteen dinner party in Prouts Neck wrote to Aronson afterward, "I enjoyed her presence. It was disturbing but exciting." Aronson said that the guest had gotten it exactly right: "negative excitement" was just the sort of attraction that Caroline had to offer. Another guest commented that Caroline had acted as if she expected the world to fall at her feet. Aronson agreed. "Even though Caroline was a self-avowed bohemian, and in many ways a self-fulfilled one, she loved—and used—being 'Lady Caroline.' She was the most entitled titled person I've ever known."

Still, Aronson had to admit that glamour clung to Caroline. "She had, in the poet Jimmy Merrill's phrase, 'the glamour of pure identity,' as well as the reflected glamour of two of her husbands, with their resounding names." Added to that was the legendary aura of the Guinnesses—not to mention the putative curse. Aronson thought that Caroline didn't believe in the Guinness curse, although "at times she felt cursed in herself." In a large family like the Guinnesses, many will die young or recklessly. There was Caroline's cousin Tara Oranmore and Browne, smashing his expensive sports car into a wall. And her cousin Henrietta Guinness, who jumped off an aqueduct in Spoleto for love. And Dennis Key Guinness, dead at a young age from a drug overdose. And her brother, Sheridan, not young but not old, dying of AIDS. And Lord Moyne's son, Diarmuid, being groomed to take over as head of the brewery but dying of cancer in his thirties. And Lindy Dufferin's brother, Patrick, who also died young in a car crash. And then, of course, there was Natalya, whose useless death, Caroline confided in Christopher Mason, haunted her every day of her life.

Four years earlier, Maureen, then eighty-four years old and enjoying excellent health, had turned her attention to the dispensation of her share of her father's trust, now worth £15 million.

In 1948, as a young woman, she had already turned over the income from the estate to Caroline, Perdita, and Sheridan, in an effort to minimize taxes—that bane of the rich. For herself, she kept an annual income of £18,000, her house in Knightsbridge, and the country estate called Owl House in Lamberhurst, Kent. Five years later, Maureen gave her children a half-share in richly endowed Canadian trusts the Guinness family owned in Vancouver, and used the rest to restore Clandeboye and free it from debt. The lion's share of the Iveagh Will Trust, and Clandeboye itself, went of course to Sheridan. On his death, in 1988, Lindy received approximately £15 million, Sheridan having increased his share through shrewd business dealings. Perdita was able to buy her fifty acres in County Down and establish Cavallo Farms, where she breeds racehorses. In 1995 Caroline's wealth was estimated at $2 million, and her house in Sag Harbor was worth close to $1 million, in addition to paintings she owned by Lucian Freud and Francis Bacon.

No one knows why Maureen decided, in 1991, to turn over the income from and eventually the entire Iveagh Will Trust to her two granddaughters, Evgenia and Ivana. Some news reports of the firestorm and court case that followed chalked it up to a tax dodge. Others pointed out that the granddaughters had become especially close to their grandmother. Maureen told the press that she had already made her own children rich by turning over the trust's income to them in 1948; she felt "the time had come to give what was left within her power to appoint to the next generation."[5]

Caroline, Perdita, and Lindy did not agree. In February 1995 they took Maureen to court.

In essence, the plaintiffs—Caroline, Perdita, and Lindy—questioned whether Maureen had the right to act as trustee of her father's estate, having already given it to her three children in the 1948 deed of transference. That was the crux of their argument, but Maureen believed that she retained the power to name the trust's beneficiaries, and she hired Ludovic de Walden as her solicitor. The High Court would have to decide.

Much was made in the press of the feud that pitted Maureen against her daughters and daughter-in-law, with Caroline opposing *her* two daughters, who were joined as defendants with Maureen. Caroline told the *New York Times* reporter Michael Kimmelman that she decided to go to court, technically against her daughters' interests, in order to protect those of her son, Sheridan. Why was he left out of his grandmother's generous trust? Some thought it was because Maureen had never liked Robert Lowell (although she was pleased with his pedigree), and that she extended her dislike to Sheridan. Perhaps it was payback for "she loves to lick the palate of her Peke." Others thought it was because of a special bond she felt for Evgenia and

Ivana, although, according to one family member, the two young women were afraid of Maureen. It's entirely possible, however, that Maureen knew the dislike her daughters felt for her, and this was her last act of revenge. She would go to her grave insisting that Caroline's animosity toward her was an invention of the press, and she continued to deny any rumors of ill feelings between the generations, even in the midst of the much ballyhooed court battle. She had been publicly humiliated, she felt, in Caroline's *Town & Country* interview. Now Maureen was able to have the last word in the decades-old battle between mother and daughter. "I am deeply sad," she told the *Times* of London, "that [my] daughters and daughter-in-law caused the family distress by bringing the action."[6] Always aware of her public image, she managed to claim the high road for herself: "I am puzzled and heartbroken that my grandchildren's own mother and their two aunts are insisting on going to court. All three of them are sweet, charming people."[7] And, later: "I hope that my children, my daughter-in-law and my grandchildren and I can now put this all behind us and be a happy and united family as I have at all times wished and made known to them all."[8] Maureen *did* wish that she and her daughters could have constituted "a happy and united family," but the evidence was abundant that such had never been the case. She was genuinely hurt and baffled by her children's rejection of her, not realizing that her selfishness and incapacities had made it impossible for them to love her. But she was always conscious of her public image, and up until the end, she tried to put the best face on it. And, in fact, she won her case.

On Friday, February 17, 1995, after a three-day hearing at the Chancery Division in London, the High Court ruled in the marchioness's favor. She retained the right to appoint the beneficiaries of her father's trust, and her wishes were upheld. The interest on £15 million would go directly to Evgenia and Ivana, who would then inherit, upon her death, the entire capital, as well as Maureen's London house on Hans Crescent and Owl House in Kent. Young Sheridan, it was ruled, had no claim whatsoever on his great-grandfather's

326 · *Dangerous Muse*

legacy, because he had been born before Lowell and Caroline were married. His illegitimacy ruled him ineligible to inherit. (Lowell had thought it rather fine of Caroline that she was in no hurry to marry. They could not have predicted what Maureen was capable of doing and what the long-term consequences would be.) Sheridan, for much the same reason, was also cut out of Aunt Sara Cotting's will.

"Caroline had thousands of books," remembered Suzanne McNear, who got to know Caroline in 1995, a year and a half before Caroline's death. "They were in the kitchen as well as in the library, and in the hallways and the dining room. She was almost always in the kitchen, which had been made into a wonderful sitting room overlooking the garden. You could hardly get through the books to reach the kitchen."[9]

Their friendship blossomed after they met at one of Robert Dash's luncheons. Suzanne remembered driving Caroline home, since they both lived in Sag Harbor. For a while, the two women saw each other nearly every day, walking downtown in the mornings and meeting for coffee, or spending the lunch hour in Suzanne's cozy house or in Caroline's splendid one, talking and reading stories and exchanging things they'd written. "She was very funny," McNear recalled. "She had a black sense of humor. We talked about people we knew in Sag Harbor; she was a wonderful mimic. She also talked about all her husbands. I know she cared deeply about Lowell." But Caroline was more reticent when speaking about Lucian. "She was so young when she married him," McNear pointed out. "She didn't speak fondly of him." Natalya, on the other hand, was someone Caroline never mentioned. McNear sensed that the subject was taboo with Caroline, who chose not to discuss anything painful; she also noticed, as did other friends of Caroline's, that there were no photographs of Natalya in the house.

Caroline turned down a number of invitations to dine with younger writers and journalists who had sought her out in the wake of Aronson's glamorous interview. Many wanted her help and advice on books and articles they were writing, and they would inundate her with manuscripts. Others wanted to interview her. "She would have none of that," McNear observed. "But she could be very kind and generous. She loved it when her children came out to Sag Harbor, and she'd cook for them. Particularly Sheridan, who would bring along friends when he was at Columbia. It made her happier than anything to have him come and stay for a few days." Sheridan, McNear thought, looked a great deal like his father, and, like Cal, was quick and funny and loved to talk.

The two women spent much of their time discussing writers and writing. McNear thought that Caroline preferred her own fiction to her nonfiction, but she was particularly proud of *The Last of the Duchess*—proud enough to consent to giving a reading at Canio's, a Sag Harbor bookstore much treasured by the local residents. Caroline seldom gave readings—she was too shy—and she didn't like her friends to attend the few readings she did give. But McNear attended the one at Canio's, just a few blocks from her home. "She was quick and witty and she read well. She seemed to be having a marvelous time, and everyone responded with laughter."

Caroline, knowing that McNear admired Francis Bacon's paintings, called one day and told her, "You must come over and have drinks, because David is here." McNear dropped by and had a lively chat with "David," although, she recalled, he mostly went on "about being fat and overeating and how New Yorkers talk about money all the time." The next day, Caroline called McNear and said she'd been disappointed in the conversation. That's when her friend realized that Caroline's guest was David Sylvester, the art critic and friend of Bacon's who had published his interview with the artist in 1993, the year after Bacon's death. Both women laughed. McNear had missed her opportunity to discuss her favorite painter with an art critic who had explored the depths of Bacon's work.

McNear remembered that, before leaving, Sylvester had looked at a postcard of a Bacon painting resting on a mantelpiece in Caroline's living room. "Well, *he's* gone," were his only words about the great painter.

"I didn't know how soon Caroline would be gone," McNear said.

In September 1995 Caroline confided in her friend that she wasn't feeling well. It was hard for her to eat. Robert Dash had already noticed that it was difficult to get Caroline to eat—sometimes she would dine on a single oyster. She was probably in the stage of alcoholism in which drink replaces food, but there was another reason as well. "I don't think she went to a doctor until right after Christmas," McNear recalled. "She went out here [in Sag Harbor], but the doctors she consulted weren't very helpful. She felt she couldn't find sophisticated medicine on Long Island, so she went into the city and had some tests done, and that's when she found out. It must have been January by then. I remember telling her 'Hurry home,' but she didn't come back. It was too quick."

Caroline may have known much earlier than September that something was terribly wrong. One of the things she had mentioned to Aronson over the course of their many interviews was her bout with cervical cancer in 1992. "She told me that she was cured," Aronson remembered, "which I now find poignant, because in her heart the ice-cold truth was breaking, and I think she knew that her fate was on her."[10]

After Caroline went to New York, in January 1996, to undergo treatment for cancer, she never returned to Sag Harbor. The cancer she thought she had conquered four years earlier had returned, and this time it was pervasive and inoperable. Like one of those magnificent elms the character based on Oonagh described in "How You Love Our Lady," Caroline was dying from within: *"Have you ever seen the way an elm dies, Theresa? An elm doesn't die like other trees . . . An elm dies from the inside. An elm dies in secret."*[11]

Lacking the strength to make the long commute back to Sag Harbor, Caroline checked into the elegant Mayfair Hotel, at the corner of Park Avenue and East Sixty-fifth Street, which at the time housed the famous restaurant Le Cirque. A close friend of Caroline's thought that it was a snowstorm that had kept her from returning to Sag Harbor; she didn't know that Caroline's doctor had given her three weeks to live. After Caroline checked into a tenth-floor suite at the Mayfair, she became too ill to be moved. Caroline's friend also thought that the suite was "frightfully expensive," even for Caroline. Charles Krewson and others believe that Bob Weinstein paid for the suite. If Caroline was on a secret list of people banned from Manhattan hotels, then it may have taken someone with Miramax's clout to get her into the Mayfair.

"Her suite was beautiful," McNear recalled. "There was a fire in the fireplace, the sitting room was large and pretty, and she could see her friends in a wonderful setting. It was a good place to sit and talk over tea or coffee. I don't think Caroline at that point was drinking anything but little sips of water. She really wanted to be in Sag Harbor, but she wouldn't have had an easy time seeing anyone there." Ivana, however, admitted that they gave Caroline champagne in addition to the morphine administered by her doctor.

Caroline, whose life had been so filled with tragedy and chaos, was blessed with a good death. All the important people in her life who were still among the living called her or came by to see her and bid her farewell. Her children scheduled the visits, making sure she wouldn't become exhausted or wouldn't have to see anyone she didn't want to see. Lucian phoned her from London, and they had a long, long talk. Ivana, listening to her mother on the telephone, was struck by how youthful and girlish Caroline's voice became the longer she spoke to Freud. Marianne Faithfull, who had asked for lyrics and had recorded Caroline's "She's Got a Problem," showed up at Caroline's bedside to bid her good-bye. Maybe because the two women were so much alike—both celebrated beauties, with famous lovers, who had endured years of addiction—that Caroline just rolled her eyes when she heard that Marianne Faithfull wanted to sing to her on her deathbed. But she allowed it.

"I feel pervasively ill," Caroline told Suzanne McNear, "but not at the moment." Caroline's close friend Anna Haycraft arrived, bringing water from Lourdes. When some of it spilled on the bedsheets, Caroline managed to joke, "I might have caught my death!"[12]

Julian Sands accompanied Evgenia and did what he could to lessen Caroline's suffering. At one point Sands lifted Caroline from the bed to carry her into the sitting room, and was surprised by how light she had become, how like a child. He remembered thinking what an intimate moment that was.[13]

And then Maureen arrived. At the age of eighty-nine, the marchioness flew to New York on the Concorde to be by her daughter's side. McNear, in whom Caroline seemed to have confided much toward the end of her life, said that Caroline told her it had been "a good reunion." For the first time in her life, Caroline's fear and hatred of her mother had slipped away. Caroline was struck by how frail her mother was. "She's so old!" Caroline told McNear, who later commented, "She didn't say it in so many words, but it's how I felt about my own mother. Here's this frail woman—she's no longer the person you were doing battle with for all those years. You knew exactly that she's not that raging person you once had to cope with. Not anymore."

So the Marchioness of Dufferin and Ava, one of the former Fabulous Guinness Girls, sat frail but resplendent in Caroline's expensive hotel suite, and the two women tried to remember what they had quarreled about for so many years. Maureen was no longer the all-powerful matriarch, capable of cutting Caroline off without a cent, removing her from the list of beneficiaries from Ernest Guinness's sumptuous estate, because Caroline was beyond harm; she would outwit her mother by dying first. Estranged from Perdita and to some degree from Lindy, Maureen would be left alone, struggling each year to make the trip to her villa in Sardinia, the one that Sheridan had jokingly christened Villa Costalotta, because it was so expensive to maintain. Her closest relationship now was with a paid companion, a private secretary from Boston, younger than her daughters, who would fulfill those daughterly functions Perdita and Caroline were unwilling to perform.

One of the secrets that was finally resolved on Caroline's deathbed, according to a number of her friends, was Ivana's paternity. Caroline had reportedly taken her youngest daughter aside and told her that her father was not Israel Citkowitz, nor was it Bob Silvers, as many suspected. Her real father, Caroline said, was Ivan Moffat, who had unsuccessfully courted Caroline and had "waited with humor"[14] all those years for Caroline to come around. She never did, although her friend Anne Moynihan believed that Caroline had truly loved Ivan.

As befitting a woman known, in part, for her lovers and husbands, Caroline Blackwood died on St. Valentine's Day, 1996. Julian Sands opened the window of Caroline's suite to allow her soul to escape, an old Irish custom. Unlike Cyd Alton, the fictional character in "Please Baby Don't Cry," who could no longer close her eyes, Caroline ended her long, unflinching gaze at the world. The eulogizing began.

In his *New York Times* obituary, Michael Kimmelman summarized Caroline's life, reporting the family's view that Lowell was not returning to Elizabeth Hardwick when he died in a taxicab clutching "Girl in Bed." Hardwick just "happened to live in the same apartment house."[15] Anna Haycraft, under her pen name Alice Thomas Ellis, wrote: "The lights have started going out. One which I shall miss most until the end of my own days is Caroline Blackwood . . . There was about her an extraordinary quality which I can only describe as a brilliant darkness."[16]

In his obituary, Grey Gowrie described Caroline as "one of the most beautiful women of her generation . . . Even in the last years, when life and illness ravaged her, you could not look at anyone else when she was in the room."[17]

A month after their mother's death, Evgenia and Ivana organized a memorial for Caroline, held on March 22 at the Century Club, an exclusive, WASP, "old money" enclave on West Forty-third Street. When the afternoon arrived, a cold, fierce rain prevailed. A small group of family and friends gathered to listen to the tributes and to declare how lucky they had been to know such "an extraordinary woman."[18]

Cornelia Foss attended, and read her eulogy:

Elegance and aplomb were her forte. One unbearably hot summer . . . we shared a house in Watermill. We wanted desperately to swim in the pool that belonged to the next house. Sheridan, then age four, was enlisted to climb over the fence and open the gate for us. As we were paddling blissfully, I asked what we were going to do if they suddenly came home.

Her proud reply was "Oh, I'm dreadfully sorry. I thought this was my house!"[19]

Jonathan Raban, unable to fly in from his home in Seattle, faxed his eulogy:

It's her silences that I find myself remembering now—the sudden silence that would yawn between us across a restaurant table or over a long-distance phone line. They were voids*—depthless, black, abrupt . . . Her untamed intelligence and imagination, her ribald wit, made her seem like some great natural force, like a famous waterfall. Dinner with Niagara . . . But one never ceased to be aware of that silence, always encroaching, the words fending it off at every turn.*[20]

Ivan Moffat was one of those who did fly in from the coast, from his home in Los Angeles. In his eulogy he said that he felt Caroline had not known herself, and that her many books, stories, and articles were her attempt to forge an identity, to come to know herself as she truly was. If Moffat had wanted to acknowledge a special bond with Ivana, the memorial came and passed without his doing so. His wistful feelings about Caroline would be expressed later, when he said, "Sometimes I was capable of making her laugh."[21]

Perhaps a key to Caroline resides in her early memoir, "Piggy," published in her first collection in 1973, in which she recalled what it was like to be one of the few girls allowed to attend Rockport, the private school she called Stoneyport Preparatory School in her memoir.[22] She threw her lot in with McDougal, the school bully, to prevent him from terrorizing her. But when he turned his beady little pig's eyes on Caroline and demanded that she strip for him and his friends, she fatefully went along with the boys to some rhododendron bushes near the school.

As Caroline undressed for the gawky and sneaking boys, the occasion took on the solemn air of a funeral. She knew that in Presbyterian Ulster, nakedness is feared. McDougal seemed more troubled by his inbred prudery than any of the other boys. He admitted with trembling lips that he'd never seen a naked girl before.

The four prepubescent boys stood, shamed, before Caroline's white, girlish body, glowing among the rhododendron bushes like a detail from a painting by Hieronymus Bosch. When McDougal asked her if she'd had the "curse" yet, Caroline answered with one of her famous silences. She knew by the fear in his beady eyes that the curse was "anathema to him" and could be used "as a weapon to terrorize him."[23]

Caroline had stumbled upon a strange new power: she'd found a way, through "the curse" and the shocking nakedness of her body, to mystify and defeat her tormentor. From that moment on, McDougal feared Caroline, for Caroline had become dangerous.

· Epilogue ·

Shortly after Caroline discovered how ill she was and sought medical treatment in New York, a shattering event took place in the life of her secretary, Pat Sweeney. In late January 1996 Sweeney got word that her mother and stepfather had burned their house to the ground and committed suicide. Caroline had been deeply impressed. "Oh, Pat, you poor thing!" she consoled her secretary. "First your parents, and now *I'm* dying! It's the *worst* . . ."[1] Perhaps that tragedy was uppermost in her mind when she made out her will on February 12, two days before her death in the Mayfair Hotel. Although she left most of her estate to her children, as was expected, she left $50,000 to "my friend, Patricia Sweeney."[2] She also left $40,000 and "my Michael Wishart painting of a dog and cat getting married" to a longtime friend, the editor whom she had encouraged to become a novelist. To her sister, Perdita, who had always considered herself more a Blackwood than a Guinness, she gave the portrait of their father. To her beautiful doppelgänger cousin Countess Doon Granville ("Miss Icicle" to Caroline's "Miss Fireworks"[3]), still residing in the Hebrides ("where they own half the island"[4]), Caroline left her set of Persian mirrors from her Sag Harbor home. The Persian mirrors from her Manhattan apartment Caroline left to her friend Anna Haycraft, the Catholic writer who had attempted to revive her with the curative waters of Lourdes. Perhaps to express her gratitude, she left her Afghan rug "with tank design" to Bob Weinstein. To Julian Sands, already a serious collector of contemporary British art, Caroline left Michael Wishart's painting of a bird in roses.

Of her remaining three children, Ivana seems to have been most generously rewarded. Caroline left her a Lucian Freud painting, "Head of Boy," as well as her beloved Sag Harbor home and all its furniture. After her mother's death, Ivana would offer the furnished house for sale for $985,000, describing its contents as "the works of 20th century masters including Wright, Le Corbusier, Mackintosh and Hoffman."[5] She would later change her mind about selling the house, and she now divides her time between London and New York, spending summers in Sag Harbor in the Victorian house on Union Street. "It made sense for her to get the house," a friend of the family observed. "Evgenia was living her life in Hollywood, and Sheridan wasn't ready for such responsibility."

The painting that Lowell had clutched to his breast during his fatal heart attack, Freud's "Girl in Bed," Caroline left to Evgenia.

The rest of her estate, including a number of Lucian Freud paintings on loan to the Tate, she left in trust for Sheridan.

After Caroline's death, Ivana asked Charles Krewson to come in and redecorate the Sag Harbor house, now hers, "to remove the feeling of death from it."[6] As Krewson wandered among Caroline's artwork and furniture, he was haunted by her presence. "I felt her ghost in the house. Caroline always collected a lot of lamps. She loved beautiful objects. One day when I was removing some of the lamps to put away, one of them jumped off a shelf and hit me in the head." Krewson also gathered a number of Caroline's papers and put them together in a small, unused room on the top floor. One day, the papers mysteriously burst into flames. No one was in the house at the time, but someone on the street smelled smoke and called the fire department, which sent its men to break in and put out the flames.

Two years after Caroline's death, Maureen, the Marchioness of Dufferin and Ava, gave up the ghost at the age of ninety-one. She had endured, and she had prevailed. Three years after Caroline's death, Ivana married Matthew Miller and gave birth to a daughter, whom she named Daisy. Curious at last about her own paternity, Ivana asked Ivan Moffat and Bob Silvers to undergo DNA tests.[7]

The clue was always there, hidden in plain sight by Caroline Blackwood: Ivana was indeed named for her father, Ivan Moffat. For Caroline, the great embellisher and teller of tales, it was the truth, especially at the end, that mattered.

· *Notes* ·

1 Lord Dufferin, "Growing Up at Clandeboye," *Clandeboye* (Ulster Architectural Heritage Society, 1985, 1997), p. 5.

2 Author's interview with Lady Perdita Blackwood, November 24, 1997.

3 I'm indebted to Caroline's sister-in-law, Lady Dufferin, for this description. "Clandeboye in My Life," *Clandeboye,* p. 10.

4 Robert Lowell, "Fall Weekend at Milgate," *The Dolphin* (New York: Farrar, Straus and Giroux, 1973) p. 29.

5 Lowell, "Fall Weekend," p. 29.

6 Lowell, "Mermaid 5," *The Dolphin,* p. 37.

7 Author's interview with Andrew Harvey, August 24, 1999.

8 Arlene Croce, "Is the Muse Dead?" *New Yorker,* February 26, 1996, p. 164.

9 Lowell, *The Dolphin,* p. 35.

10 Croce, p. 164.

11 Croce, p. 166.

12 Croce, p. 166.

13 Letter from Lord Dufferin to his children, dated March 25, 1945.

14 Eulogy of Caroline Blackwood written by Jonathan Raban.

15 Quotation attributed to the Native American writer N. Scott Momaday.

CHAPTER ONE: THE HOUSE OF BLACKWOOD

1 Caroline Blackwood, "Please Baby Don't Cry," *For All That I Found There* (London: Gerald Duckworth and Co. Ltd., 1973), p. 21.

2 Definition given in Michael Powell's 1960 film *Peeping Tom.*

3 Victoria Glendinning, *Elizabeth Bowen* (New York: Knopf, 1978), p. xvii.

4 Glendinning, quoting Spencer Curtis Brown, p. xvi.

5 Molly Keane, *The Knight of the Cheerful Countenance* (London: Virago Press, 1993), p. 5.

6 Keane, p. 6.

7 Keane, pp. 8–9.

8 Desmond Guinness and William Ryan, *Irish Houses & Castles* (New York: The Viking Press, 1971), p. 7.

9 Keane, p. 10.

10 Caroline Blackwood, "A Big House in Ireland," review of David Thomson's *Woodbrook, Listener,* December 12, 1974, p. 783.

11 Blackwood, "A Big House in Ireland," p. 783.

12 Author's interview with Xandra Hardie, May 19, 1997.

13 Caroline Blackwood, *Great Granny Webster* (New York: Charles Scribner's Sons, 1977), pp. 83–84.

14 Harold Nicolson, *Helen's Tower* (New York: Harcourt Brace and Co., 1938), p. 34.

15 Nicolson, p. 34.

16 *Oxford Companion to English Literature* (Oxford University Press, 1985), p. 898.

17 Nicolson, p. 42.

18 Steven M. L. Aronson, "Sophisticated Lady," *Town & Country,* September 1993, p. 148.

19 Aronson, p. 145.

20 John Gray, "The Dufferins in Canada, 1872–1878," exhibition catalog, Queens University (Bangor: The Dufferin Foundation and The Linen Hall Library, 1997) p. 5.

21 Aronson, p. 111.

22 Nicolson, p. 35.

23 James Lees-Milne, *Harold Nicolson: A Biography,* vol. 2, 1930–68 (Herndon, Conn.: Archon Books, 1984), p. 82.

24 Nicolson, p. 82.

25 Nicolson, p. 84.

26 Nicolson, p. 140.

27 Author's interview with Lady Perdita Blackwood, November 24, 1997.

28 Aronson, p. 144.

29 Nicolson, p. 59.

30 Nicolson, p. 142.

31 Aronson, p. 144.

32 Katie Donovan, A. Norman Jeffares, and Brendan Kennelly, eds., *Ireland's Women, Writings Past and Present* (New York: Norton, 1995), pp. 497–98.

33 William Gladstone's First Land Act in 1870 attempted to correct the inequities caused by the system of absentee landownership throughout Ireland. Gladstone's support of home rule for Ireland ruined his third term as England's prime minister.

34 Nicolson, p. 53.

35 Author's interview with Lady Perdita Blackwood.

36 Author's interview with Lady Perdita Blackwood.

37 Candida Lycett Green, ed., *John Betjeman, Letters,* vol. 1, 1926–51 (London: Mandarin, 1995), p. 39n.

38 Blackwood, *Great Granny Webster,* p. 103.

39 Blackwood, *Great Granny Webster,* p. 103.

40 Author's interview with Michael Bloch, July 21, 1997.

41 William Maguire, "The Blackwoods of Ballyleidy," *Clandeboye,* p. 41.

42 Sir Roy Harrod, *The Life of John Maynard Keynes* (New York: Harcourt, Brace, 1951).

43 Bevis Hillier, *Young Betjeman* (London: John Murray, 1988), p. 174.

44 Hillier, p. 174.

45 Green, pp. 38–39.

46 Green, p. 39.

47 Hillier, p. 174.

48 Hillier, p. 181.

49 Blackwood, *Great Granny Webster,* p. 56.

50 Hillier, p. 206.

51 Hillier, p. 372.

52 Green, p. 296.

53 Lady Perdita Blackwood.

54 Author's interview with Anne Dunn Moynihan, May 5, 2000.

55 Aronson, p. 145.

56 Aronson.

57 Frederic Mullally, *Silver Salver: The Story of the Guinness Family* (London: Grenada Publishing Ltd., 1981), p. 141.

58 Author's interviews with John Richardson, July 15, 1997, and Stanley Moss, June 30, 1997.

59 Mullally, p. 141.

60 Letter from Lord Dufferin to Maureen, fourth Marchioness of Dufferin and Ava.

61 Letter from Lord Dufferin to his children, dated March 25, 1945.

62 Green, p. 387.

63 John Betjeman, *Collected Poems* (Boston: Houghton Mifflin, 1971), pp. 146–47.

CHAPTER TWO: THE PARISH OF RICH WOMEN

1 The phrase, of course, is from W. H. Auden's "In Memory of W. B. Yeats."

2 Michael O'Sullivan, *Brendan Behan: A Life* (Dublin: Blackwater Press, 1997), p. 196.

3 John Huston, *An Open Book* (New York: Ballantine Books, 1981), p. 245.

4 Steven M. L. Aronson, "Sophisticated Lady," *Town & Country,* September 1993, p. 110.

5 Frederic Mullally, *The Silver Salver: The Story of the Guinness Family* (London: Grenada Publishing Ltd., 1981), p. 2.

6 Quoted in Michael Kimmelman, "Titled Bohemian: Caroline Blackwood," *New York Times Magazine,* April 2, 1995, p. 33.

7 Mullally, p. 239n.

8 Mullally, Introduction.

9 Mullally, p. 12.

10 Mullally, p. 3.

11 Mullally, p. 3.

12 Letter from Maureen Dufferin to Caroline Blackwood; "Cal" was Robert Lowell's nickname.

13 Author's interview with Stanley Moss, June 30, 1997.

14 Author's interview with Perdita Blackwood, November 24, 1997.

15 Mullally, p. 163.

16 Mullally, pp. 163–64.

17 Author's interview with Perdita Blackwood.

18 Mullally, p. 156.

19 Author's interview with Perdita Blackwood.

20 Robert Lowell, "Artist's Model, 2," *The Dolphin* (New York: Farrar, Straus and Giroux, 1973), p. 52.

21 Quoted in Aronson, p. 149.

22 Author's interview with Jonathan Raban, February 22, 1997.

23 Mullally, p. 153.

24 This and following quotations from author's interview with John Richardson, July 15, 1997.

25 Mullally, p. 146.

26 Mullally, p. 146.

27 Huston, p. 245.

28 Mullally, p. 147.

29 Mullally, p. 148.

30 Author's interview with John Richardson.

31 O'Sullivan, p. 139.

32 O'Sullivan, p. 198.

33 O'Sullivan, p. 199.

34 Mullally, p. 150.

35 Caroline Blackwood, "How You Love Our Lady," *For All That I Found There* (London: Gerald Duckworth and Co., 1973), p. 69.

36 Blackwood, "How You Love Our Lady," p. 69.

37 O'Sullivan, p. 197.

38 Caroline Blackwood, *Great Granny Webster* (New York: Charles Scribner's Sons, 1977), p. 45.

39 Blackwood, *Great Granny Webster,* p. 59.

40 Author's interview with Alan Ross, May 19, 1997.

41 Lord Dufferin, "Growing Up at Clandeboye," *Clandeboye,* Ulster Architectural Heritage Society, 1985, p. 5.

42 Quoted in Terence de Vere White, *The Anglo-Irish* (London: Victor Gollancz Ltd., 1972), p. 17.

43 Captioned photograph, *Belfast Telegraph,* Monday, July 5, 1942.

44 This and further quotations from author's interview with Perdita Blackwood.

45 *Clandeboye*, Ulster Architectural Heritage Society, p. 5.

46 Caroline Blackwood, "Piggy," *For All That I Found There* (London: Gerald Duckworth and Co., 1973), pp. 130–31.

47 Blackwood, "Piggy," p. 131.

48 Blackwood, "Memories of Ulster," *For All That I Found There*, p. 141.

49 Blackwood, "Memories of Ulster," p. 139.

50 Blackwood, "Memories of Ulster," p. 141.

51 "A Talent to Be a Muse," *Daily Telegraph Magazine*, April 8, 1995, p. 37.

52 Author's conversation with Charis Ryder.

53 Author's interview with Anne Dunn Moynihan, May 5, 2000.

54 This and further quotes from Blackwood, *New York Review of Books*, September 24, 1992, p. 34.

CHAPTER THREE: WHEN CAROLINE MET LUCIAN

1 Christopher Bram, *Father of Frankenstein* (New York: Plume/Penguin, 1995), p. 20.

2 This and further quotations from *The Roy Strong Diaries* (London: Weidenfeld and Nicolson, 1997), p. 285.

3 Mark Armory, *The Letters of Ann Fleming* (London: Collins Harvill, 1985), p. 45.

4 Andrew Lycett, *Ian Fleming: The Man Behind James Bond* (Atlanta: Turner Publishing Inc., 1995), p. 172.

5 Jeremy Lewis, *Cyril Connolly: A Life* (London: Jonathan Cape, 1997), p. 239n.

6 Tom Hopkinson, ed., *Picture Post, 1938–1950* (London: Penguin Press, 1970), p. 11.

7 Author's interview with Jeremy Lewis, May 22, 1997.

8 "Classics from 60's Are Big Draw at Sotheby's," *New York Times,* May 20, 1999.

9 Lycett, p. 239.

10 Charlotte Mosley, ed., *The Letters of Nancy Mitford and Evelyn Waugh* (London: Hoddard and Stoughton, 1996), p. 243.

11 Mosley, p. 245.

12 Mosley, p. 249.

13 Selina Hastings, *Evelyn Waugh* (Boston: Houghton Mifflin, 1994), p. 570.

14 Martin Filler, "The Naked and the Id," *Vanity Fair,* November 1993, p. 198.

15 Filler, p. 198.

16 Filler, p. 198.

17 Filler, p. 198.

18 Daniel Farson, "A Freudian Lunch in Mayfair," *Sacred Monsters* (London: Bloomsbury Publishing Ltd., 1988), p. 174.

19 Catherine Lambert, *Lucian Freud: Recent Work,* catalog (London: Whitechapel Art Gallery, 1993), p. 14.

20 Filler, p. 198.

21 Filler, p. 198.

22 Filler, p. 195.

23 Author's interview with Cornelia Foss, June 3, 1997.

24 Author's interview with Anne Dunn Moynihan, May 5, 2000.

25 Ned Rorem, *Knowing When to Stop* (New York: Simon and Schuster, 1994), p. 521.

26 John Goldsmith, ed., *Stephen Spender, Journals 1939–1983* (New York: Random House, 1986), p. 108.

27 Farson, p. 135.

28 Marina Warner, "Lucian Freud, the Unblinking Eye," *New York Times Magazine,* December 4, 1993.

29 Farson, p. 176.

30 Farson, p. 146.

31 Bruce Bernard and Derek Birdsall, eds., *Lucian Freud* (London: Jonathan Cape, 1996), p. 9.

32 Bernard and Birdsall, p. 9.

33 Filler, p. 197.

34 Lambert, p. 14.

35 Bernard and Birdsall, p. 9.

36 Bernard and Birdsall, pp. 9–10.

37 Michael Wishart, *High Diver* (London: Blond and Briggs Ltd., 1977), p. 26.

38 Lewis, p. 333.

39 Wishart, p. 27.

40 Lambert, p. 15.

41 John Richardson, "Paint Becomes Flesh," *New Yorker,* December 13, 1993, p. 137.

42 Wishart, p. 24.

43 Filler, p. 197.

44 Wishart, p. 37.

45 Catalog copy for Lucian Freud's exhibition of early works, Robert Miller Gallery, New York, 1993.

46 John Richardson, Robert Miller Gallery catalog.

47 Joan Wyndham, *Anything Once* (London: Sinclair-Stevenson Ltd., 1992), p. 10.

48 Wyndham, p. 8.

49 Wyndham, p. 10.

50 Quoted in Richard Calvocoressi, *Early Works: Lucian Freud* (Scottish National Gallery of Modern Art, 1997), p. 14.

51 Catalog copy, Robert Miller Gallery.

52 Author's interview with Joan Wyndham, July 26, 1997.

53 Wyndham, p. 10.

54 Stephan Gardiner, *Epstein: Artist Against the Establishment* (New York: Viking, 1992), p. 411.

55 Gardiner, p. 451.

56 Mark Amory, ed., *The Letters of Ann Fleming* (London: Collins Harvill, 1985), p. 122.

57 Amory, p. 123.

58 This and further quotations from author's interview with Perdita Blackwood, November 24, 1997.

59 Quoted in Aronson, p. 146.

60 Aronson, p. 146.

61 Amory, p. 431.

62 Aronson, p. 146.

63 Aronson, p. 146.

64 Mosley, p. 335.

65 Filler, p. 198.

66 Aronson, p. 146.

67 Rorem, p. 521.

68 Author's interview with Ned Rorem, May 1, 1997.

69 Letter from Lady Dufferin to author.

70 Barbara Skelton, *Tears Before Bedtime* (London: Hamish Hamilton Ltd., 1987), p. 96.

71 Amory, p. 123.

72 Author's interview with Joan Wyndham.

73 Author's interview with Bruce Bernard, May 15, 1997.

74 Quoted in Michael O'Sullivan, *Brendan Behan: A Life* (Dublin: Black-water Press, 1997), p. 198.

CHAPTER FOUR: THE SOHO CIRCLE

1 Tambimutto, quoted in Daniel Farson, *Soho in the Fifties* (London: Michael Joseph Ltd., 1987), p. 81.

2 Steven M. L. Aronson, "Sophisticated Lady," *Town & Country*, September 1993, p. 147.

3 Author's interview with Anne Dunn Moynihan, May 5, 2000.

4 Michael Peppiatt, *Francis Bacon: Anatomy of an Enigma* (New York: Farrar, Straus and Giroux, 1996), p. 158.

5 Christophe Domino, *Francis Bacon: 'Taking Reality by Surprise'* (New Horizons; London: Thames and Hudson, 1997), p. 116.

6 Daniel Farson, *The Gilded Gutter Life of Francis Bacon* (New York: Pantheon, 1993), p. 65.

7 Farson, *Soho*, p. 40.

8 Farson, *Soho*, p. 40.

9 Farson, *Soho*, p. 49.

10 Farson, *Soho*, p. 44.

11 Martin Filler, "Lucian Freud," *Vanity Fair*, November 1993, p. 198.

12 Farson, *Soho*, p. 32.

13 Farson, *Soho*, p. 99.

14 Michael Kimmelman, "Titled Bohemian: Caroline Blackwood," *New York Times*, April 2, 1995.

15 Michael Luke, *David Tennant and the Gargoyle Years* (London: Weidenfeld and Nicolson, 1991), p. 176.

16 Farson, *Soho*, p. 85.

17 Farson, *Soho*, p. 84.

18 Farson, *The Gilded Gutter Life of Francis Bacon*, p. 18.

19 Caroline Blackwood, *In the Pink* (London: Bloomsbury, 1987), p. 90.

20 Farson, *The Gilded Gutter Life of Francis Bacon*, p. 19.

21 Farson, *The Gilded Gutter Life of Francis Bacon*, p. 18.

22 Farson, *The Gilded Gutter Life of Francis Bacon*, p. 26.

23 Peppiatt, p. 42.

24 Conversation with Pat Sweeney, Caroline's personal secretary.

25 Michael Wishart, *High Diver* (London: Bland and Briggs Ltd., 1977), p. 155.

26 Aronson, p. 147.

27 Robert Kraft, *Igor Stravinsky* (New York: Doubleday and Co., 1963), pp. 180–81. Stravinsky also observed that "other people's talk bores him and makes him restless . . . He tells us that many psychoanalysts now agree that 'women want to go much further back than the womb; in fact, all the way back to father's penis.' "

28 Richard Buckle, ed., *Cecil Beaton: Self-Portrait With Friends* (New York: Crown Publishing Group, 1979), p. 273.

29 Clive Fisher, *Cyril Connolly* (New York: St. Martin's Press, 1995), p. 317.

30 Jeremy Lewis, *Cyril Connolly* (London: Jonathan Cape, 1997), p. 106.

31 Fisher, p. 314.

32 Fisher, p. 314.

33 Mark Amory, ed., *The Letters of Ann Fleming* (London: Collins Harvill, 1985).

34 Barbara Skelton, *Tears Before Bedtime* (London: Hamish Hamilton Ltd., 1987), pp. 139–40.

35 Anthony Powell, *Journals 1982–1986* (London: Heinemann, 1995), p. 57.

36 Fisher, p. 324.

37 Fisher, p. 324.

38 Lewis, p. 469.

39 Skelton, *Tears Before Bedtime*, p. 5.

40 Daniel Farson, *Sacred Monsters* (London: Bloomsbury Publishing, 1988), p. 178.

41 Peppiatt, p. 105.

42 Author's interview with Anne Dunn Moynihan.

43 Farson, *Sacred Monsters*, p. 178.

44 Author's interview with Alan Ross, May 19, 1997.

45 Farson, *Sacred Monsters*, p. 179.

46 Author's interview with Alan Ross.

47 Author's interview with Anne Dunn Moynihan.

48 Letter from John Craxton to author, no date.

49 Fisher, p. 344.

50 Lewis, p. 548.

51 Aronson, p. 147.

52 Author's interview with Joan Wyndham, July 26, 1997.

53 Nancy Mitford, "The English Aristocracy," *Encounter*, September 1955.

54 Bruce Bernard, *Lucian Freud* (London: Jonathan Cape, 1996), pp. 14–15.

55 John Russell, Introduction, catalog copy for Lucian Freud exhibition at Hayward Gallery, 1974.

56 Notes provided to author by Lorraine Karafel.

57 Author's interview with Xandra Hardie, May 19, 1997.

58 Filler, p. 167.

59 Filler, p. 167.

60 Author's interview with Alan Ross.

61 Author's interview with Alan Ross.

62 Author's conversation with Nicholas Haslam, January 28, 2000.

63 Author's interview with Alan Ross.

64 Filler, p. 167.

CHAPTER FIVE: THE HORROR OF HOLLYWOOD

1 Caroline Blackwood, quoted in Steven M. L. Aronson, "Sophisticated Lady," *Town & Country*, September 1993, p. 147.

2 Aronson, p. 147.

3 Michael Luke, *David Tennant and the Gargoyle Years* (London: Weidenfeld and Nicolson, 1991), p. 125.

4 Luke, p. 146.

5 Christopher Isherwood, *Diaries, Volume One: 1939–1960* (New York: Michael di Capua Books/HarperCollins, 1997), p. 425.

6 Isherwood, p. 619.

7 Isherwood, p. 534.

8 Isherwood, p. 618.

9 This and further quotations from author's interview with Ivan Moffat, July 19, 1996.

10 Isherwood, p. 618.

11 Isherwood, p. 977.

12 Isherwood, p. 618.

13 Luke, p. 127.

14 Isherwood, p. 768.

15 Isherwood, p. 803.

16 Isherwood, p. 803.

17 Author's interview with Don Bachardy, November 1998.

18 Author's interview with Leonard Rosenman, December 15, 1998.

19 Isherwood, p. 688.

20 Ralph G. Martin, *Henry and Clare: An Intimate Portrait of the Luces* (New York: G. P. Putnam's Sons, 1991), p. 335.

21 Belinda Rathbone, *Walker Evans, A Biography* (New York and Boston: Houghton Mifflin Co., 1995), p. 232.

22 Author's conversation with Jane Mayhall, October 20, 1997.

23 Rathbone, p. 231.

24 Rathbone, p. 230.

25 Rathbone, p. 232.

26 Rathbone, p. 232.

27 Rathbone, p. 233.

28 Both manuscripts housed at the Walker Evans Archive, Metropolitan Museum of Art, New York.

29 This and further quotations from author's conversation with David Diamond.

30 Author's conversation with Karl Miller, May 16, 1997.

31 Author's interview with Leonard Rosenman.

32 Isherwood, p. 822.

33 They were, in fact, married in the Beverly Hills home of the producer and writer Dominick Dunne, according to the *Los Angeles Examiner*, September 23, 1961.

CHAPTER SIX: *SAUVE QUI PEUT:*
CAROLINE AND ISRAEL

1 Letter to Aaron Copland, September 1927, Copland Archive, Library of Congress, Washington, D.C.

2 Author's interview with Ellen Adler, June 5, 1997.

3 Jeremy Lewis, *Cyril Connolly: A Life* (London: Jonathan Cape, 1997), p. 341.

4 Ned Rorem, *Knowing When to Stop* (New York: Simon and Schuster, 1994), p. 463.

5 This and further quotations from author's interview with Leonard Rosenman, December 15, 1998.

6 Rorem, p. 266.

7 Author's interview with Ellen Adler.

8 Author's interview with Ellen Adler.

9 Howard Pollack, *Aaron Copland, The Life and Work of an Uncommon Man* (New York: Henry Holt, 1999), p. 179.

10 Copland Archives, Library of Congress.

11 Pollack, p. 180.

12 Pollack, p. 180.

13 Pollack, p. 179.

14 Author's interview with Ned Rorem, May 1, 1997.

15 Pollack, p. 180.

16 *New York Times*, September 16, 1935.

17 Author's interview with Leonard Rosenman.

18 Author's interview with Cornelia Foss, June 3, 1997.

19 Author's interview with Leonard Rosenman.

20 Author's interview with Ellen Adler.

21 Rorem, p. 521.

22 Stephen Spender, *Journals, 1939–1983,* ed. John Goldsmith (New York: Random House, 1986), p. 97.

23 Spender, p. 129.

24 Ian Hamilton, *Robert Lowell: A Biography* (New York: Random House, 1982), p. 397.

25 Caroline Blackwood, "Portrait of the Beatnik," *For All That I Found There* (New York: George Braziller, 1973), p. 35.

26 Blackwood, "Portrait of the Beatnik," p. 90.

27 Blackwood, "Portrait of the Beatnik," p. 94.

28 Blackwood, "Portrait of the Beatnik," p. 95.

29 This and further quotations from author's interview with Cornelia Foss.

30 Blackwood, "The Baby Nurse," *For All That I Found There*, p. 36.

31 Blackwood, "The Baby Nurse," p. 36.

32 Blackwood, "The Baby Nurse," p. 37.

33 Blackwood, "The Baby Nurse," p. 37.

34 Author's interview with John Richardson, July 15, 1997.

35 Author's interview with Leonard Rosenman.

36 This and further quotations from author's interview with Xandra Hardie, May 19, 1997.

37 Author's interview with Cornelia Foss.

38 Robert Lowell, "Mermaid," *The Dolphin* (New York: Farrar, Straus and Giroux, 1973), p. 37.

39 Barbara Skelton, *Tears Before Bedtime* (London: Hamish Hamilton Ltd., 1989), p. 83.

40 Barbara Skelton, *Born Losers* (London: Alan Ross Ltd., 1965), pp. 14–15.

41 Skelton, *Born Losers*, pp. 22–23.

42 Skelton, *Born Losers*, p. 22.

43 Barbara Skelton, *Weep No More* (London: Hamish Hamilton Ltd., 1989), p. 83.

44 Skelton, *Weep No More*, p. 94.

45 Skelton, p. 90.

46 Skelton, *Born Losers*, p. 22.

47 Skelton, *Weep No More*, p. 105.

48 Skelton, *Born Losers*, p. 22.

49 Skelton, *Weep No More*, p. 105.

50 Skelton, *Weep No More*, p. 107.

51 Author's interview with Cornelia Foss.

52 Author's interview with John Richardson.

CHAPTER SEVEN: "MERMAID EMERGING":

CAROLINE AND CAL

1 Robert Lowell, "Mermaid," *The Dolphin* (New York: Farrar, Straus and Giroux, 1973), p. 37.

2 Ian Hamilton, *Robert Lowell: A Biography* (New York: Random House, 1982), p. 398.

3 Hamilton, p. 398.

4 Quoted in Suzanne Lowry, "Doom and the Lady Under One Roof," *Observer*, February 22, 1981, p. 40.

5 Author's conversation with Stanley Moss, June 30, 1997.

6 Lowry, p. 40.

7 Author's interview with Jonathan Raban, February 22, 1997.

8 This and further quotations from author's interview with Ivan Moffat, July 19, 1996.

9 Author's interview with Cornelia Foss, June 3, 1997.

10 Hamilton, p. 374.

11 *Anthony Powell Journals, 1982–1986* (London: Heinemann Ltd., 1995), p. 57.

12 Oscar Levant, *The Unimportance of Being Oscar* (New York: G. P. Putnam's Sons, 1968), pp. 174–75.

13 Robert Lowell, "Anne Dick 1. 1936," *Selected Poems*, rev. ed. (New York: Noonday Press, 1993), p. 194.

14 Quoted in Hamilton, p. 393.

15 Hamilton, p. 393.

16 Hamilton, p. 396.

17 Author's interview with Derek Walcott for the PBS documentary on Robert Lowell, "A Mania for Phrases." Walcott comments on Lowell's slight Southern accent, curious for a Boston native, and speculates that it was probably Elizabeth Hardwick's influence.

18 Author's interview with Xandra Hardie (formerly Gowrie), May 19, 1997.

19 Stephen M. L. Aronson, "Sophisticated Lady," *Town & Country*, September 1993, p. 149.

20 Caroline quoted in Hamilton, p. 399.

21 Hamilton, p. 399.

22 Author's interview with Xandra Hardie.

23 Sarah Payne Stuart, *My First Cousin Once Removed* (New York: HarperCollins, 1998), p. 213.

24 Robert Lowell, "Mermaid 2," *The Dolphin* (New York: Farrar, Straus and Giroux, 1973), p. 35.

25 Lowell, "Mermaid 3," p. 36.

26 Lowell, "Mermaid 5," p. 37.

27 Lowell, *The Dolphin*, p. 18.

28 Author's interview with Jonathan Raban.

29 Undated letter from Caroline Blackwood, Lowell Collection, Harry R. Ransom Center for the Humanities archive (HRC).

30 Author's interview with Jonathan Raban.

31 Caroline Blackwood, "Women's Theatre," *Listener*, June 3, 1971, pp. 697–98.

32 Quoted in Paul Mariani, *Lost Puritan* (New York: W. W. Norton, 1994), p. 398.

33 Hamilton, p. 400.

34 Hamilton, p. 400.

35 Lowell, "Marriage?" *The Dolphin*, p. 26.

36 Lowell, "July–August," *The Dolphin*, p. 26.

37 Lowell, "Marriage?" p. 26.

38 Quoted in Hamilton, p. 401.

39 Michael Kimmelman, "Titled Bohemian, Caroline Blackwood," *New York Times Magazine*, April 2, 1995, p. 35.

40 Quoted in Hamilton, p. 404.

41 Hamilton, pp. 404–5.

42 Hamilton, p. 406.

43 Lowell, "With Caroline at the Air-Terminal," *The Dolphin*, p. 72.

44 Lowell's letter to Blair Clark quoted in Hamilton, p. 406.

45 Hamilton, p. 409.

46 Hamilton, p. 409.

47 Hamilton, p. 410.

48 Lowell's letter to William Alfred quoted in Hamilton, p. 411.

49 Lowell's letter to Blair Clark quoted in Hamilton, p. 412.

50 Lowell's letter to Peter Taylor quoted in Hamilton, pp. 411–12.

51 Author's interview with Jonathan Raban.

52 Jonathan Freyer's letter to author, September 29, 1997.

53 Letters and poems from Lowell Collection, HRC archive.

54 Lowell's letter to Harriet quoted in Hamilton, p. 413.

55 Lowell, "Mermaid Emerging," *The Dolphin*, p. 54.

56 Lowell, "Fishnet," *The Dolphin*, p. 15.

57 Hamilton, p. 413.

58 Hamilton, p. 415.

59 Author's interview with Xandra Hardie.

60 Lowell, "Fall Weekend at Milgate," *The Dolphin*, p. 30.

61 Mariani, p. 403.

62 Author's interview with Xandra Hardie.

63 Author's interview with Jonathan Raban.

64 Lowell, "Nine Months," *The Dolphin*, p. 60.

65 Letter to Harriet quoted in Mariani, p. 403.

66 Lowell, "Robert Sheridan Lowell," *The Dolphin*, p. 61.

67 Lowell, "Careless Night," *The Dolphin*, p. 62.

68 Mariani, p. 405.

69 Letter from Lorna Sage to author, October 4, 1997.

70 Mariani, p. 405.

71 Lowell, "Mermaid," *The Dolphin*, p. 35.

CHAPTER EIGHT: DISSOLUTION AND DESPAIR

1 Robert Lowell, "Summer Between Terms," *The Dolphin* (New York: Farrar, Straus and Giroux, 1973), p. 28.

2 Elizabeth Bishop, *One Art, Letters,* ed. Robert Giroux (New York: Farrar, Straus and Giroux, 1994), p. 562.

3 Sarah Payne Stuart, *My First Cousin Once Removed* (New York: Harper-Collins, 1998), p. 214.

4 Stuart, p. 214.

5 Stuart, p. 214.

6 Lowell, "Another Summer" ("4. Alimony"), *The Dolphin,* p. 64.

7 Paul Mariani, *Lost Puritan: A Life of Robert Lowell* (New York: W. W. Norton, 1994), p. 420.

8 Author's interview with Frank Bidart, April 9, 1997.

9 Lowell, *The Dolphin,* p. 28.

10 Author's interview with Frank Bidart.

11 Author's interview with Frank Bidart.

12 Mariani, p. 407.

13 Quoted in Ian Hamilton, *Robert Lowell: A Biography* (New York: Random House, 1982), p. 421.

14 Author's interview with Andrew Harvey, August 20, 1999.

15 Mariani, p. 410.

16 Bishop, pp. 561–62.

17 Mariani, p. 410.

18 Author's interview with Xandra Hardie, May 19, 1997.

19 Author's interview with Dr. Paul Brass, July 22, 1997.

20 Author's interview with Frank Bidart.

21 Blackwood, "Burns Unit," *For All That I Found There* (London: Gerald Duckworth and Co., 1973), p. 109.

22 Blackwood, "Burns Unit," p. 109.

23 Blackwood, "Burns Unit," p. 109.

24 Blackwood, "Burns Unit," p. 112.

25 Blackwood, "Burns Unit," p. 113.

26 *The Times Diary,* December 1, 1976.

27 Letter quoted in Mariani, p. 413.

28 Author's interview with Stanley Moss, June 30, 1997.

29 Lowell, *The Dolphin,* p. 49.

30 Lowell, *The Dolphin,* p. 63.

31 Lowell, "Christmas," *The Dolphin*, p. 77.

32 Lowell, "Morning Away from You," *The Dolphin*, p. 62.

33 Lowell, "Randall Jarrell," *History* (London: Faber and Faber Ltd., 1973), p. 135.

34 Ann Hulbert, *The Interior Castle* (New York: Knopf, 1992), pp. 87–88.

35 Stuart, p. 93.

36 Robert Lowell, *Selected Poems* (New York: Noonday Press, Farrar Straus and Giroux, 1993), p. 96.

37 Lowell, *Selected Poems*, p. 137.

38 Lowell, *Selected Poems*, p. 71.

39 Letter from Michael Wishart to Caroline Blackwood Lowell, August 20, 1972, Lowell Archive, Humanities Research Center (HRC), University of Texas, Austin.

40 Stuart, p. 84.

41 Hamilton, p. 430.

42 Mariani, p. 415.

43 Mariani, p. 418.

44 Author's interview with Frank Bidart.

45 Letter from Wishart to Blackwood, March 9, 1973, Lowell Archive, HRC.

46 Quoted in Mariani, p. 433.

47 Mariani, p. 434.

48 Mariani, p. 435.

49 Author's interview with Andrew Harvey, August 20, 1999.

50 Mariani, p. 419.

51 Jonathan Raban wrote that when Lowell called Caroline "panic . . . [he] never idly used a classical reference: he was talking about Pan the brilliant piper, also the god of the terrors of the night." Raban's eulogy for Caroline Blackwood.

52 Unpublished letter from Walker Evans to James and Tania Stern, August 29, 1973.

53 Stuart, p. 216.

54 Stuart, p. 216.

55 *The Listener*, December 12, 1974, p. 783.

56 *The Listener*, December 27, 1973, p. 891.

57 *Times*, December 13, 1973.

58 Quoted in *Contemporary Authors, New Revision Series*, vol. 32, p. 46.

59 Steven M. L. Aronson, "Sophisticated Lady," *Town & Country*, September 1993, p. 150.

60 Robert Lowell, *Day by Day* (New York: Farrar, Straus and Giroux, 1977), p. 39.

61 Lowell, *Day by Day,* p. 40.

62 "Great white hope" was Caroline's description (Aronson interview, unpublished transcript).

63 Bishop's letter, October 18, 1974, Lowell Archive, HRC.

64 Author's interview with Frank Bidart.

65 Lowell Archive, HRC.

66 Quoted in Hamilton, p. 443.

67 Letter dated October 18, 1974, Lowell Archive, HRC.

68 Letter dated March 19, 1975, Lowell Archive, HRC.

69 Lowell, "Caroline in Sickness," *Day by Day,* p. 104.

70 Blackwood, "Lovesome Things," *The Listener,* October 24, 1975.

71 Letter from Anne Williamson to *The New Review,* June 2, 1974, Lowell Archive, HRC.

72 Aronson, p. 149.

73 Author's interview with Andrew Harvey.

74 Author's interview with Dr. Brass.

75 Hamilton, p. 449.

76 Author's interview with Dr. Brass.

77 Author's interview with Eleanor Ross Taylor, January 12, 1997.

78 Lowell, "Mermaid," *The Dolphin,* p. 35.

79 Rafaella Barker, "Three Times a Muse," *Harper's & Queen,* September 1993, p. 159.

80 Author's interview with Frank Bidart.

81 Author's interview with Frank Bidart.

82 Author's interview with Frank Bidart.

83 Lowell, "Mermaid 4," *The Dolphin,* p. 36.

84 Lowell, "Mermaid 1," *The Dolphin,* p. 35.

85 *The Listener,* May 20, 1976.

86 *Times,* May 27, 1976.

87 Hamilton, p. 464.

88 Letter from Peter Taylor to Caroline Blackwood, August 7, 1976, Lowell Archive, HRC.

89 Undated letter from Gertrude Buckman, Lowell Archive, HRC.

90 *The Times Diary,* December 1, 1976.

91 Author's interview with Blair Clark, October 21, 1997.

92 Letter from Elizabeth Hardwick to Blair Clark, October 23, 1970.

93 Author's interview with Joanna Clark, October 21, 1997.

94 Author's interview with Blair Clark.

95 Hamilton, p. 457.

96 Mariani, p. 446.

97 Mariani, p. 446.

98 Author's interview with Frank Bidart.

99 The ideas and some of the prose of *Great Granny Webster* were first published in "A Big House in Ireland," Blackwood's review of David Thomson's *Woodbrook, The Listener,* December 12, 1974, p. 782–83.

100 Lowell, "Runaway," *Day by Day,* p. 103.

101 Mark Amory, ed. *The Letters of Ann Fleming* (London: Collins Harvill, 1985), 24 October [1976], p. 416.

102 Hamilton, p. 456.

103 Hamilton, p. 456.

104 Quoted in Hamilton, p. 457.

105 Mariani, p. 448.

106 Mariani, p. 448.

107 Mariani, p. 448.

108 Lowell, "Mermaid," *The Dolphin,* p. 37.

109 Author's interview with Frank Bidart.

110 Lowell, "Mermaid Emerging," *The Dolphin,* p. 54.

CHAPTER NINE: UNLEASHED

1 Robert Lowell, "Leaf-lace Dress," *The Dolphin,* p. 56.

2 Michael Wishart, *High Diver* (London: Bond and Briggs Ltd., 1977), p. 60.

3 Sarah Payne Stuart, *My First Cousin, Once Removed* (New York: HarperCollins, 1998), p. 219.

4 Stuart, p. 220.

5 "Dolphin" (New York: Farrar, Straus and Giroux, 1973), p. 78.

6 Author's interview with Blair Clark, October 21, 1997.

7 Desmond Guinness and William Ryan, *Irish Houses and Castles* (New York: The Viking Press, 1971), p. 8.

8 Author's interview with Andrew Harvey, August 24, 1999.

9 Sarah Payne Stuart wrote in *My First Cousin Once Removed*: "Everyone

in the family loved Elizabeth . . . Charlotte knew Elizabeth would take care of Bobby," p. 122.

10 *Soho Weekly News* quoted in Ian Hamilton, *Robert Lowell, A Biography* (New York: Random House, 1982), p. 459.

11 Lowell, *Day by Day* (New York: Farrar, Straus and Giroux, 1977), pp. 4–6.

12 Quoted in Hamilton, p. 461.

13 Hamilton, p. 462.

14 Hamilton, p. 463.

15 Author's interview with Ivan Moffatt.

16 Hamilton, p. 464.

17 Blair Clark's notes toward a memoir quoted in Hamilton, p. 464.

18 Hamilton, p. 465.

19 Robert Boyers, "The Visit," *Parnassus,* vol. 24, no. 1 (1999), p. 134.

20 Boyers, p. 135.

21 Boyers, p. 138.

22 Boyers, p. 139.

23 Boyers, p. 139.

24 Boyers, p. 139.

25 Boyers, p. 138.

26 Boyers, pp. 148–49.

27 Boyers, p. 150.

28 Boyers, p. 153.

29 Related in Author's interview with Robert Boyers, September 20, 1999.

30 Paul Mariani, *Lost Puritan* (New York: W. W. Norton, 1994) p. 456.

31 Mariani, p. 456.

32 Mariani, p. 456.

33 Letter from Mary McCarthy to Robert Lowell, November 8, 1970, Lowell Archive, Humanities Research Center (HRC), University of Texas, Austin.

34 Mariani, p. 458.

35 Mariani, p. 458.

36 Hamilton, p. 472.

37 Caroline Blackwood, *In the Pink* (London: Bloomsbury Publishing Inc., 1987), p. 157.

38 Lowell had bought the painting from its original owner, Colin Tennant (Lord Glenconner); he also bought "Girl Reading" from Cyril Connolly.

39 Author's interview with Cornelia Foss.

40 Hamilton, p. 473.

41 Letter from Lord Gowrie to Caroline Lowell, Lowell Archive, HRC.

42 Hamilton, p. 473.

43 Hamilton, p. 473.

44 Stuart, p. 221.

45 Stuart, p. 222.

46 Stuart, p. 222.

47 Stuart, p. 222.

48 Mariani, p. 461.

49 Stuart, p. 224.

50 Lowell, "Runaway," *Day by Day*, p. 103.

51 Anne Redmon, *Sunday Times*, September 25, 1977.

52 Redmon.

53 "Books of the Year," *Sunday Times*, December 4, 1977.

54 Jacky Gillott, London *Times*, September 8, 1977.

55 Caroline Blackwood, *Great Granny Webster* (New York: Charles Scribner's Sons, 1977), pp. 133–34.

56 Blackwood, *Great Granny Webster*, p. 135.

57 London *Times*, September 8, 1977.

58 Author's phone conversation with Karl Miller, May 16, 1997.

59 Quoted in Steven M. L. Aronson's "Sophisticated Lady," *Town & Country*, September 1993, p. 149.

60 Karl Miller, "Ladies in Distress," *New York Review of Books*, November 9, 1978, p. 24.

61 Author's interview with Jonathan Raban, February 22, 1997.

62 Blackwood, *Great Granny Webster*, pp. 130–31.

63 Author's interview with Andrew Harvey.

64 Rafaella Barker, "Once, Twice, Three Times a Muse," *Harpers & Queen*, September 1993, p. 159.

65 "Death After a Party," *Guardian*, August 8, 1978.

66 Author's interview with Xandra Hardie, May 19, 1997.

67 "How Guinness Girl, 17, Died in the Bath," *Evening Standard*, August 7, 1978.

68 Author's interview with Simon Blow, July 24, 1997.

69 *Guardian*.

70 Wishart, p. 60.

71 Author's interview with Jonathan Raban.

72 Gowrie, "Lady Caroline Blackwood," obituary, *Independent,* February 15, 1996.

73 Author's interview with Frank Bidart, April 9, 1997.

74 Author's interview with Xandra Hardie.

CHAPTER TEN: *THE FATE OF MARY ROSE*

1 Author's interview with Andrew Harvey, August 18, 1999.

2 Quoted by Andrew Harvey, author's interview.

3 Suzanne Lowry, "Doom and the Lady Under One Roof," *Observer,* February 22, 1981, p. 40.

4 Caroline Blackwood and Anna Haycraft, *Darling, You Shouldn't Have Gone to So Much Trouble* (London: Warner Books, reprint, 1994; first printing Jonathan Cape, 1980).

5 Blackwood and Haycraft, p. 10.

6 Blackwood and Haycraft, p. 12.

7 Anita Brookner, "Cuisine Menteur," *Times Literary Supplement,* November 14, 1980, p. 1282.

8 Brookner.

9 Caroline Blackwood, "Home Cooking," To the Editor, *TLS,* November 28, 1980, p. 1360.

10 Blackwood, "Home Cooking," to the editor, *TLS,* December 5, 1980, p. 1389.

11 Author's interview with Stanley Moss, June 30, 1997.

12 Caroline Blackwood, *The Fate of Mary Rose* (New York: Summit Books, 1981), p. 64.

13 Peter Kemp, "Wounded Children," *Listener,* February 26, 1982, p. 288.

14 Blackwood, *The Fate of Mary Rose,* p. 53.

15 Blackwood, *The Fate of Mary Rose,* pp. 202–3.

16 Blackwood, *The Fate of Mary Rose,* p. 208.

17 Blackwood, *The Fate of Mary Rose,* p. 208.

18 Blackwood, *The Fate of Mary Rose,* p. 38.

19 Author's interview with Steven M. L. Aronson.

20 Blackwood, *The Fate of Mary Rose,* p. 208.

21 Author's interview with Andrew Harvey, August 18, 1999.

22 Author's interview with Andrew Harvey, August 24, 1999.

23 Author's interview with Andrew Harvey, August 20, 1999.

24 Andrew Barrow, "The Sleeping Booty," *Spectator,* April 1, 1995, p. 32.

25 Barrow, p. 32.

26 Caroline Blackwood, *The Last of the Duchess* (New York: Picador, 1996), Reader's Note.

27 "Debunking a Dark Fairy Tale," *Evening Standard,* March 13, 1995, p. 27.

28 Author's interview with Andrew Harvey, August 24, 1999.

29 Author's interview with Michael Bloch, July 21, 1997.

30 Caroline Blackwood, *The Last of the Duchess* (New York: Pantheon Books, 1995), p. 86–87.

31 Blackwood, *The Last of the Duchess,* p. 253.

32 Blackwood, *The Last of the Duchess,* p. 241.

33 Blackwood, *The Last of the Duchess,* p. 241.

34 "My Goodness, a Literary Feud," *Evening Standard,* March 17, 1995.

35 Quoted in "Lady Blackwood Dies at 64," *Belfast Telegraph,* February 16, 1996.

36 All quotations from author's interview with Andrew Harvey, August 18, 20, and 24, 1999.

37 Andrew Harvey, *No Diamonds, No Hat, No Honey* (Boston: Houghton Mifflin, 1985), Poem II, p. 10.

38 Harvey, Poem IV, p. 12.

39 Harvey, p. 13.

40 Harvey, p. 69.

41 Harvey, Poem XXXVI, p. 66.

42 All further Harvey quotations from author's interview with Andrew Harvey, August 24, 1999.

43 Author's conversations with Peter Levi and Cornelia Foss.

CHAPTER ELEVEN: *ON THE PERIMETER*

1 Caroline Blackwood, "Angelica," *Good Night Sweet Ladies* (London: William Heinemann Ltd., 1983), p. 101.

2 All Ian Hamilton quotations from author's interview with Ian Hamilton, May 12, 1997.

3 Author's conversation with Steven Aronson.

4 Author's interview with Gillon Aitken.

5 Grace Ingoldby, "Ogres," *New Statesman,* vol. 106, September 16, 1983, p. 23.

6 Blackwood, "Matron," *Good Night Sweet Ladies,* pp. 37–38.

7 Blackwood, "Olga," *Good Night Sweet Ladies,* p. 80.

8 Blackwood, "Olga," p. 82.

9 Blackwood, "Olga," p. 88.

10 Blackwood, "Angelica," pp. 117–18.

11 Blackwood, "Angelica," p. 109.

12 Colin McCabe, *Performance* (London: BFI Film Classics, 1998), p. 12.

13 *Daily Telegraph,* May 30, 1988.

14 *Daily Telegraph,* May 30, 1988.

15 *Daily Telegraph,* May 30, 1988.

16 Author's interview with John Richardson, July 15, 1997.

17 "I'm the 'Nicky' in Michael Wishart's *High Diver,*" Wishart's adored lover for two years. Author's interview with Nicholas Haslam, January 28, 2000.

18 Author's interview with Nicholas Haslam.

19 Roy Strong, *The Roy Strong Diaries, 1967–1987* (London: Weidenfeld and Nicolson, 1997), p. 10.

20 Strong, p. 10.

21 *Times,* June 2, 1988.

22 Strong, p. 10.

23 Strong, p. 10.

24 Strong, p. 36.

25 Strong, p. 44.

26 Strong, p. 44.

27 *Daily Telegraph,* May 30, 1988.

28 Author's interview with John Richardson.

29 Author's interview with Perdita Blackwood, November 26, 1997.

30 Author's conversation with Lady Belinda, Marchioness of Dufferin and Ava, November 26, 1997.

31 Caroline Blackwood, *On the Perimeter* (Flamingo/Fontana, 1984), p. 112.

32 Quoted in interview by Laurie Taylor, "Symbolic Strength of the Women of Peace Without Power," *Times,* September 5, 1984, p. 11.

33 Laurie Taylor, p. 1.

34 Laurie Taylor, p. 2.

35 Blackwood's definition of "perimeter," quoted in the frontispiece of *On the Perimeter.*

36 Bernard Levin, "Baying at the Moon," *Times*, August 24, 1984.

37 Laurie Taylor, p. 2.

38 Author's interview with Eleanor Ross Taylor, January 12, 1997.

39 Hilary Sperling, "Cassandras of Greenham," *Observer*, September 9, 1984.

40 Laurie Taylor, p. 45.

41 Laurie Taylor, p. 46.

42 Carolyn Gaiser, "Victim or Victor?" *New York Times Book Review*, July 14, 1985.

43 Caroline Blackwood, "The Interview," *For All That I Found There* (London: Gerald Duckworth and Co. Ltd., 1973), p. 58.

44 Blackwood, "The Interview," p. 54.

45 Blackwood, "The Interview," p. 54.

46 Blackwood, "The Interview," p. 60.

47 Blackwood, "The Interview," p. 64.

48 Blackwood, "The Interview," p. 58.

49 Blackwood, "The Interview," p. 63.

50 Blackwood, "The Interview," p. 66.

51 Blackwood, *Corrigan* (New York: Viking Penguin, 1985), p. 48.

52 Blackwood, *Corrigan*, p. 51.

53 Blackwood, *Corrigan*, p. 51.

54 Author's interview with Andrew Harvey, August 20, 1999.

CHAPTER TWELVE: "SHE'S GOT A PROBLEM"

1 Author's interview with Robert Dash, September 11, 1999.

2 Caroline Blackwood, *In the Pink* (London: Bloomsbury, 1987), pp. 13–14.

3 Blackwood, *In the Pink*, p. 43.

4 Blackwood, *In the Pink*, p. 73.

5 Blackwood, *In the Pink*, p. 74.

6 Blackwood, *In the Pink*, p. 75.

7 Blackwood, *In the Pink*, pp. 75–76.

8 Blackwood, *In the Pink*, pp. 90–91.

9 Molly Keane, *The Rising Tide* (London: Virago Press, 1984), p. 132.

10 Blackwood, *In the Pink*, pp. 91–92.

11 Keane, p. 107.

12 Raymond Carr, quoted in *Contemporary Authors, New Revised Series,* vol. 32, p. 46.

13 Phone conversation with Peter Levi, May 22, 1997.

14 Blackwood, *In the Pink,* p. 163.

15 Hamish Bowles, "Shifting Sands," *Vogue,* February 1995, p. 285.

16 Author's interview with Steven Aronson, December 16, 1999.

17 Author's interview with Robert Dash, September 11, 1999.

18 Author's interview with Robert Dash.

19 Author's interview with Cornelia Foss, June 3, 1997.

20 All Foss quotations from author's interview.

21 ©1983 B. Brierley, C. Blackwood/Island Music Inc./BMI. Reprinted with permission.

22 Described in Steven M. L. Aronson's "Sophisticated Lady," *Town & Country,* September 1993, p. 148.

23 Thursday, June 2, 1988, p. 1.

24 "Memorial Services," *Times,* October 6, 1988.

25 "Marquess of Duffferin and Ava," *Daily Telegraph,* May 30, 1988.

26 Author's interview with Suzanne McNear, September 8, 1999.

27 Author's interview with Robert Dash.

28 Aronson, p. 148.

29 Michael Kimmelman, "Titled Bohemian: Caroline Blackwood," *New York Times Magazine,* April 2, 1995.

30 Caroline Blackwood, "The Interview," *For All That I Found There,* (London: Gerald Duckworth and Co. Ltd., 1973), p. 56.

31 Sarah Lyall, "In Britain's Health Service, Sick Itself, Cancer Care Is Dismal," *New York Times,* February 10, 2000.

32 Author's interview with Caroline's friend, who wishes to remain anonymous, September 7, 1999.

33 Michael Kimmelman, "Titled Bohemian," *New York Times,* April 2, 1995.

34 Quoted in Raffaella Barker, "Once, Twice, Three Times a Muse," *Harpers & Queen,* September 1993, p. 158.

35 "Rich and dumb": how Caroline characterized it, according to John Richardson.

36 These and following remarks from author's interview with Christopher Mason, August 4, 1997.

37 Quoted in Melissa Ceria, "Poetic License," *W,* October 1999, p. 100.

38 Caroline Blackwood, "Portraits by Freud," *New York Review of Books,* December 16, 1993, p. 18.

39 Blackwood, "Portraits by Freud," p. 19.

40 Blackwood, "Portraits by Freud."

41 Author's interview with Andrew Harvey, August 24, 1999.

42 Author's interview with John Richardson, July 15, 1997.

43 This and further quotations from author's interview with Steven Aronson, December 16, 1999.

44 Author's conversation with Pat Sweeney (undated).

45 This and further quotations from author's interview with Charles Krewson, October 17, 1997.

46 This and further quotations from author's interview with John Richardson, July 15, 1997.

47 Author's interview with Cornelia Foss, June 3, 1997.

48 Author's conversation with Caroline's friend, who wishes to remain anonymous, September 7, 1999.

49 This and further quotations from author's interview with Steven Aronson, December 16, 1999.

50 Letter from Lord Moyne (Bryan Guinness) to Steven Aronson, quoted in Aronson interview, March 6, 2000.

51 Further conversations with Steven Aronson.

CHAPTER THIRTEEN: THE LAST OF THE MUSES

1 "Humour and Fragility," Blackwood obituary, *Guardian*, February 16, 1996.

2 All Robert Dash quotations from author's interview, September 11, 1999.

3 This and further quotations from author's interview with Stephen Aronson.

4 Robert Lowell, "The Old Flame," *Selected Poems*, 15th ed. (New York: Noonday Press, Farrar, Straus and Giroux, 1993), p. 101.

5 Dan Conaghan, "£15m Legacy for the Dufferin Grandchildren," *Daily Telegraph*, February 18, 1995.

6 Emma Wilkins, "Judge Rules Granddaughters of Marchioness Can Inherit £15m" *Times*, February 18, 1995.

7 Emma Wilkins, "Daughters Fight £15m Trust Fund of Marchioness," *Times*, February 15, 1995.

8 Wilkins, "Judge Rules . . ."

9 This and further quotations from author's interview with Suzanne McNear, September 8, 1999.

10 Author's interview with Steven Aronson.

11 Caroline Blackwood, "How You Love Our Lady," *For All That I Found There* (London: Duckworth and Co. Ltd., 1973), p. 69.

12 Grey Gowrie, "Lady Caroline Blackwood," obituary, *Independent*, February 15, 1996.

13 Author's conversation with Julian Sands.

14 Christopher Isherwood's phrase.

15 Michael Kimmelman, "Lady Caroline Blackwood, Wry Novelist, Is Dead at 64," *New York Times*, February 15, 1996.

16 "Humour and Fragility," Blackwood obituary, *Guardian*, February 16, 1996.

17 Gowrie, "Lady Caroline Blackwood," *Independent*.

18 Anonymous attendant at Blackwood's memorial, "Caroline Blackwood," published on-line under "A Common Reader," *http://www.akadine.com/1/1619.html*.

19 Provided by Cornelia Foss, during author's interview, June 3, 1997.

20 Eulogy provided by Jonathan Raban.

21 Author's interview with Ivan Moffat, July 19, 1996.

22 Caroline Blackwood, "Piggy," *For All That I Found There*, p. 129.

23 Blackwood, "Piggy," p. 132.

EPILOGUE

1 Author's conversations with Pat Sweeney and with Christopher Mason, August 4, 1997.

2 All details of Caroline Blackwood's will from the Last Will and Testament of Lady Caroline Maureen Lowell, filed with the surrogate court of Suffolk County, New York, March 21, 1996.

3 From Robert Lowell's poem "Caroline in Sickness," *Day by Day* (New York: Farrar, Straus and Giroux, 1977), p. 104.

4 Author's conversation with Jonathan Raban, February 22, 1997.

5 President Chester A. Arthur "Summer White House" prospectus, offered by Roland and Joan Descombes.

6 Author's interview with Charles Krewson, October 17, 1997.

7 John Graham, "Kiss and Don't Tell," *Tatler*, March 2001, p. 148.

· *Index* ·

Michael, and, 79–80; womanizing, 107; Wyndham, Joan, 81–82, 83

WORKS: anxiety in, 75–76; "Birds of Olivier Laronde, The," 81; CB and Perdita, unfinished, 90; change after CB departure, 112; "Dead Bird," 80; "Dead Monkey," 80; "Double Portrait," 72; early portraits of Kitty Garman, 70, 77, 86; early style of, 2–3; education and mentors, 75, 77–80, 81; "Evacuee Boy," 76, 80; first exhibition, 80; "Girl in Bed," 2, 86, 109, 111, 197, 229, 277, 302, 331, 335, 357n.; "Girl in a Dark Jacket," 77; "Girl in a White Dress," 77; "Girl Reading," 2, 86, 89, 101, 109, 111, 357n.; "Girl's Head," 86; "Girl With a Kitten," 77; "Girl With Leaves," 77; "Girl With Roses," 77; "Girl With Starfish Necklace," 86, 111; grotesque in, 80; Haywood Gallery retrospective, 1974, 110; "Head of Boy," 335; "Hotel Bedroom," 109–11, 225, 296; Metropolitan retrospective, 319; Minton portrait, 97; models, 72; of mother, 74–75; "Naked Girl, The," 72; Paddington, London, and, 79, 81; "Painter's Mother Dead, The," 74–75; price of, 70; realism of, 77; "Refugees, The," 75–76, 78; Robert Miller Gallery exhibition, 295, 319; "Rotted Puffin," 80, 250; Wishart drawings, 79; "Woman in a Butterfly Jersey," 72; "Woman in a Fur Coat, 1967–8," 72

Freud, Lucie Brasch, 74–75
Freud, Sigmund, 76
Fryer, Jonathan, 172

Gargoyle Club, 74, 96–97, 115
Garman, Kathleen, 69, 83
Garman, Kitty, 69–70, 72–73, 82–83, 90
Garnett, Richard, 21
Gibbs, Christopher, 271, 273, 292
Giroux, Robert, 176
Glenconner, Lord, 2
Glendinning, Victoria, 10
Goldsmith, Lady Annabel, 72
Good Behavior (Keane), 100
Gowing, Lawrence, 111

Gowrie, Lady Adelaide, 235–36
Gowrie, Lord Greysteil "Grey," 145, 146, 162, 176, 229, 237–38, 331
Grant, Duncan, 269, 271
Green, Candida Lycett, 26
Greene, Graham, 96
Guinness, Arthur, 38, 39
Guinness, Arthur Ernest, 40, 41, 49
Guinness, Bryan, 302
Guinness, Dennis Key, 323
Guinness, Desmond, 12, 72, 219
Guinness, Edward Cecil, Earl of Iveagh, 39–40, 42
Guinness, Henrietta, 237, 323
Guinness, Loel, 45, 291
Guinness, Marie Clothilde "Chloe" Russell, 40
Guinness, Rupert Edward, 40
Guinness, Walter Edward, 40
Guinness family, 4, 307; Basil and, 33; curse, 4, 323; Farmleigh, family seat, 41; Golden, or Fabulous, Guinness Girls, 40, 47–48; history, 38–40; mansions, 40, 41; Mullally book on, 33, 38, 42; royalty and, 40; social climbing, 39; Trust, 42, 49, 88, 270; values of, 39; wealth, 4, 40, 42

Hamilton, Anne, 15
Hamilton, Henry, Lord Clanbrassil, 15
Hamilton, Ian, 167, 174, 214, 228, 262–64
Hansen, Waldemar, 82
Hardie, Xandra (Gowrie), 13, 111, 146–48, 162, 164, 174, 186–87, 215, 235, 238, 241
Hardwick, Elizabeth, 151, 154, 158–59, 161, 162, 167–68, 169–70, 171, 179–80, 182–83, 185–86, 192, 195–96, 207, 211–13, 218, 219, 220, 222, 227, 229, 230, 351n.
Harrod, Sir Roy, 28
Hartman, Mortimer, 122
Harvey, Andrew: books of, 257–58, 273; breach with CB, 257–59; CB as muse, 4, 5, 195–96, 259–60; characterization of CB, 4, 247–48, 250; characterization of Lowell, 248; homosexuality of, 5, 248; love affair with CB, 4, 248–50, 273

Haslam, Nicholas, 113, 270, 361n.
Haycraft, Anna (Alice Thomas Ellis),
240–43, 306, 330, 331, 335
Haycraft, Colin, 240
Heaney, Seamus, 221
Helen's Tower (Nicolson), 20, 21, 22
High Diver (Wishart), 79, 237, 361n.
Hillier, Bevis, 28
Hockney, David, 269, 272
Holmes, James, 136
Homosexuality: Betjeman and, 30; British
artists and, 78–79, 98–99; CB
fascination with, writing on, 99, 100,
128, 296–98; Connolly, Cyril, and,
102–3; Guinness sisters, husbands of,
42, 49; Isherwood and, 118–119;
London art circles, Gibbs, and
Sheridan, 269–72; Oxford and, 28–30,
102; Skelton, Barbara, and gay men,
100–1, 103; Soho's demimonde and,
78, 92–97, 98–99
Horizon, 78, 134, 135
Hulbert, Ann, 190
Humphries, Barry, 95
Huston, John, 38, 47–48
Huxley, Aldous, 69, 118

"Influx of Poets, An" (Stafford), 175, 310
"In Memory of Basil" (Betjeman), 36–37
In Search of Corvo (Symons), 251
"Irish Emigrant, The" (H. S. Blackwood),
17, 22
Isherwood, Christopher, 116, 118–19, 121,
132, 140

James, Edward, 28
Jarrell, Randall, 190
Jenkins, Roy, 68

Karafel, Lorraine, 110
Kasmin, John, 269
Kasmin Gallery, 269, 272
Keane, Molly (M. J. Farrell), 10, 11–12, 100,
285–86
Kemp, Peter, 244
Kimmelman, Michael, 293, 324, 331
Kindersley, Gay, 46, 47, 48
Kindersley, Philip, 46

Kindersley, Tessa, 46
Kitaj, R. B., 93, 269
Krewson, Charles, 294, 298–99, 329,
335
Kristol, Irving, 140

Lambert, Lady Catherine, 72, 77
Lampson, Jacquetta, 72
Lampton, Lady Belinda "Bindy," 72
Larkin, Philip, 25, 233
Larronde, Olivier, 81
Letters From High Latitudes
(F. Blackwood), 23
Lett-Haines, Arthur, 77, 78
Levi, Peter, 260, 286
Levin, Bernard, 275
Lewis, Jeremy, 70, 135
Lightfoot, Jessie, 105
Lindsay, Derek, 90
Lipton, Lawrence, 141–42
Lispings in Low Latitudes
(H. S. Blackwood), 23
Listener, The, 166–67, 198, 203, 209,
244
London Magazine, 53, 106, 112, 199
Longman, Janie, 72
Lorant, Stefan, 69
Lost Puritan (Mariani), 175, 184, 196
Loved One, The (Waugh), 118
Lowell, Charlotte Winslow, 160, 164–65, 191
Lowell, Harriet, 161, 163, 177, 192, 219
Lowell, Robert "Cal," 154–55; alcohol and,
160, 200–1; antiwar stance, 160;
appearance, 159; attraction to CB, 164,
173; auto accidents, 190–91, 193;
Boston and Cambridge residences
with CB, 196–197, 208; CB as muse,
3–4, 5, 154, 169, 170, 216, 226;
characterizations of CB, 3, 4, 164, 165;
childhood issues, 160–61; daughter,
Harriet (*see* Lowell, Harriet); death, 4,
229, 331; death, premonitions of,
189–90, 191, 218; divorce from
Elizabeth Hardwick, 182–83, 192–93,
310; ending of marriage to CB, 219–22,
226–29, 300; funeral, 230–31; Harvard
and, 145–46, 159, 161, 164, 179,
192–93, 197, 208, 218, 227; health,

Dangerous Muse
was typeset in Monotype Walbaum
with Torino Modern.
Composed by Creative Graphics,
Allentown, Pennsylvania.
Printed and bound by Berryville Graphics,
Berryville, Virginia.
Book design by Jennifer Ann Daddio.

Made in the USA
Lexington, KY
29 December 2010